Mastering the Nikon D800

Darrell Young (*Digital Darrell*) is an information technology engineer by trade. He's been an avid photographer since 1968 when his mother gave him a Brownie Hawkeye camera.

Darrell has used Nikon cameras and Nikkor lenses since 1980. He has an incurable case of Nikon Acquisition Syndrome (NAS) and delights in working with Nikon's newest digital cameras.

Living near Great Smoky Mountains National Park has given him a real concern for the natural environment and a deep interest in nature photography.

He loves to write, as you can see in the Resources area of the Nikonians Online community (www.Nikonians.org). He joined the community in the year 2000, and his literary contributions led to his invitation to become a Founding Member of the Nikonians Writers Guild.

Mastering the Nikon D800

Darrell Young

Darrell Young (aka Digital Darrell)

Editor (Rocky Nook): Gerhard Rossbach
Editor (Nikonians): Tom Boné
Production Editor: Jocelyn Howell
Layout and Type: Almute Kraus
Cover Design: Helmut Kraus, www.exclam.de
Printer: Sheridan Books, Inc.
Printed in USA

Cover photo: Nikon USA
Back cover photo: Darrell Young

1st Edition
© Darrell Young 2012
Rocky Nook Inc.
802 E. Cota Street, 3rd Floor
Santa Barbara, CA 93103

Library of Congress Cataloging-in-Publication Data

Young, Darrell, 1958-
 Mastering the Nikon D800 / by Darrell Young. -- 1st edition.
     p. cm
 ISBN 978-1-937538-05-7 (pbk.)
 1. Nikon digital cameras--Handbooks, manuals, etc. 2. Single-lens reflex cameras--Hand-
books, manuals, etc. 3. Photography--Digital techniques--Handbooks, manuals, etc. I. Title.
 TR263.N5Y6854 2012
 771.3'2--dc23
                     2012025947

Distributed by O'Reilly Media
1005 Gravenstein Highway North
Sebastopol, CA 95472

This book is dedicated to:

My wife of many years, Brenda; the love of my life and best friend…

*My children, Autumn, David, Emily, Hannah, and Ethan,
five priceless gifts …*

*My mother and father, Barbara and Vaughn, who brought me into this world and
guided my early life, teaching me sound principles to live by …*

*My Nikonians editor, Tom Boné,
without whose assistance I could not possibly write books …*

*My friends J. Ramon Palacios and Bo Stahlbrandt, who make it possible to belong to
Nikonians.org, the world's best Nikon Users' Community …*

*The wonderful staff of Rocky Nook, including
Gerhard Rossbach, Joan Dixon, Jocelyn Howell, and Matthias Rossmanith …*

And, finally, to Nikon, who makes the world's best cameras and lenses.

Special thanks to:

Brad Berger of **www.Berger-Bros.com** (800-542-8811) for helping me obtain a Nikon D800 early in its production cycle so that I could write this book. I personally buy from and recommend Berger-Bros.com for Nikon cameras, lenses, and accessories.

Michael Tapes of **mtapesdesign.com** (321-752-9700) for providing samples of the excellent WhiBal and LensAlign products. For white balance ambient light (PRE) readings and focus fine tuning, these products are very useful.

Table of Contents

Nikonians Gold Membership

*Nikonian Sue Kane (Sue A)
took this picture
suek.redbubble.com*

Enter the following voucher code to obtain a *50%* discount for a Nikonians Gold Membership: **G81753**

Foreword

Through the past seven "Mastering the Nikon® DSLR" books authored by Nikonian Darrell Young (known to us as Digital Darrell), we have been delighted to witness an amazing evolution in the author's steadfast devotion to perfecting his craft, ever since becoming Founding Member of the Nikonians Writers Guild almost 8 years ago.

As engineers add and perfect features, each new camera introduced in the Nikon digital single-lens reflex inventory has exponentially become harder to describe in an easygoing and simple-to-understand manner. Yet, Darrell has proven equal to the task, by adjusting not only his descriptive writing style, but also innovating new layout and typeface adjustments. All of his improvements to the final product result in an easier learning experience for his readers.

This joint venture between nikonians.org and Rocky Nook has developed a strong following in the "camera instruction" genre, and Darrell's fastidious attention to detail has been the key ingredient in that trend.

His progression in writing and layout talent has been just as amazing as Nikon's progression in introducing a host of new and extremely complex features in each new camera.

His first book, *Mastering the Nikon D300*, was about 250 pages long. This book, *Mastering the Nikon D800*, is more than double in size at over 500 pages.

The Nikon D800 and D800E cameras introduced a seemingly insurmountable host of complexities for any author trying to provide easy-to-follow directions.

The Nikon D800 is the first 35mm form factor medium format HD-DSLR camera ever made. Its image quality rivals medium-format cameras costing up to ten times the price of the D800. Plus, there is more to it than just added resolution.

The Nikon D800, with its Movie live view video mode, is the world's first 35mm HD-DSLR to offer uncompressed, overlay-free, broadcast quality Full HD video output, which makes it a truly affordable commercial solution for serious videographers. Additionally, there are no time constraints on video output through the HDMI port.

We at nikonians.org are the largest organized group of Nikon enthusiasts, and this camera is arguably the perfect enthusiast's camera. It is not too heavy to carry, has the world's best lens selection, and is built to take years of heavy use. It boasts the world's best imaging sensor (according to DXO labs, not just us) with the widest dynamic range ever seen in any production camera (14.4 EV). DXO gives the D800 the highest rating ever awarded a camera by their labs, with a rating of 95.

Squeezing all these new features into a camera that many are calling the ultimate for Nikon enthusiasts has resulted in a steep learning curve. Darrell approached this book with the knowledge that the Nikon D800 sets a new world standard and that he would need to thoroughly explain every part of the camera's functionality.

Working with the camera, Darrell's first step is also the same step he recommends to all new Nikon users. He reads the User's Manual, not just once but as many times as it takes to understand important concepts. Once he grasps the concepts and the basic directions readily available through the manual, he takes those same concepts and directions into the field. He makes sure he understands how each feature works in basic photography and how it can be applied to specialty applications such as landscapes, weddings, events, and portraits. Once satisfied that he has mastered each new feature, he then translates his experience in a simple-to-understand sequence of profusely illustrated steps and then goes on to recommend the best initial settings and shooting techniques to match.

As you read the pages that follow, you will be the beneficiary of his diligence and painstaking attention to detail.

We are proud to include his impressive credentials and body of work in our ever-growing and never-ending resources for our community, such as the forums, The Nikonian eZine, Nikonians Academy Workshops, Nikonians News Blog, Nikonians podcasts, our Wiki, and eBooks. Our community now has three language versions (English, German, and French) and we continue to grow as we now surpass 400,000 members.

Nikonians, now in its 12th year, has earned a reputation as a friendly, reliable, informative, and passionate Nikon® users' community, thanks in great measure to members like Digital Darrell who have taken the time to share the results of their experiences with Nikon imaging equipment.

Enjoy this book, the Nikonians community, and your Nikons.

J. Ramón Palacios (*jrp*) and Bo Stahlbrandt (*bgs*)
Nikonians Founders
www.nikonians.org

Camera Setup and Control Reference

You Are Funny Dad! – Courtesy of Daniel Diggelmann (*Aerobat*)

Congratulations! You've purchased, or are about to purchase, Nikon's professional-level, smaller-bodied, full-frame (FX) format camera: the Nikon D800 or D800E.

While no digital camera is inexpensive, the D800/D800E provides passionate photographers with a professional-level camera with medium-format resolution at an attractive price. It is weather and dust sealed with a magnesium-alloy body and frame and a rubberized coating that makes it strong and reliable for years of faithful service.

The 36.3-megapixel imaging sensor and supporting Nikon Scene Recognition System (SRS) allow you to take complete creative control of the scene in front of your lens.

The camera has advanced firmware that does things like automatic chromatic aberration reduction and full color optimization via selectable Picture Controls, which allow you to create the best pictures you've ever made.

This book will explore your incredibly feature-rich camera in great detail, using everyday language. We'll cover virtually every button, dial, switch, and setting, giving you how, when, and why information so that you can become a master of your new, powerful imaging instrument. Your passion for excellent photography can be fully expressed with your Nikon D800 or D800E. Let's take control of it!

Figure 1.0A – Nikon D800 with AF-S Nikkor 24-70mm F2.8G ED VR lens

Medium-Format Resolution Sensor

In the olden days, pre-2002, I loved medium-format cameras. You would often find me in Great Smoky Mountains National Park lugging around a heavy Mamiya RB-67 medium-format camera, which gave me a large 6×7 cm Provia F transparency. As film started fading away and digital photography rose supreme in most people's eyes, true medium format went away for the everyday photographer. Sure, one could buy a nice Hasselblad digital medium format for $20,000, but few could afford that level of camera.

Now, with the exciting Nikon D800 and D800E cameras, Nikon has returned medium-format resolution to the everyday photographer who wants it. No more will we have to find a lab to process our 120 film, be forced to lug around huge medium-format film bodies, and have to settle for standard-size digital images.

At 36.3-megapixel resolution, the D800 moves soundly into medium-format territory. What's the difference between the D800 and a much more expensive true medium-format camera back? Although the D800 provides similar resolution, the imaging sensor on some medium-format cameras can be twice the size of the D800's, at 36.7×46.1 mm compared to the D800's 35.9×24.0 mm CMOS (FX) sensor (at red arrow in figure 1.1A).

Figure 1.1A – Nikon D800's 36.3-Megapixel Imaging Sensor (FX) 35.9×24.0 mm

Obviously, the larger medium-format camera backs will have larger pixels, providing better light-gathering capability and less noise. However, the cost entry point for most medium-format digital camera backs is around $10,000 and goes up very quickly with the number of megapixels. For about one-third of the lowest medium-format back price for a new D800, I'm inclined to tolerate a little more noise in higher ISO shots. However, the Nikon D800 has excellent noise control, even better than its predecessor, the Nikon D700, and that camera is well known for its excellent, low-noise images.

With the new D800, you can make an image with 36 megapixels (7360×4912 pixels). Do you realize the camera creates a 16×24-inch (40×60 cm) native print at 300 dpi (using FX format)? With careful post-processing and enlargement, the images can be made, as *National Geographic* photographer Jim Brandenburg says, "as large as a house!"

Imagine the expansive landscape shots with the massive detail that comes with the resolution of the D800. Imagine being able to make large portraits to hang on your wall. Think of how your clients will enjoy the various crops you'll be able to make from the huge image file. Consider the extra income from stock photography you'll gain from the larger pictures.

Medium-format resolution has distinct advantages, with only the disadvantage of having to store the much larger images. Of course, you could use the DX mode in the D800 for smaller image size and still have images of comparable size to the 16 megapixel Nikon D7000. Such flexibility!

Figure 1.1B – Back of Nikon D800

The Nikon D800/D800E is indeed a camera that sets new standards other manufacturers will have to scramble to approach. Nikon can at times seem slow about bringing out new technology, but when it does, nothing else on the market even comes close.

Both versions of the camera are very mature high-definition (HD) imaging devices designed to provide years of usage; you can put your money into better lenses instead of a new camera. Few photographers will need more power than the Nikon D800/D800E can deliver. With this camera, you are well equipped for years to come.

Now, let's start learning about this powerful, medium-format, high-definition, single-lens reflex (HD-SLR) camera!

How to Use This Book

This book is equally effective for users of the Nikon D800 and the Nikon D800E cameras. Both cameras are virtually identical, with the exception of a disabled optical low-pass filter (blur or AA filter) in the D800E model. There is information on the Internet that seems to apply primarily to the D800E, such as how to avoid moiré; however, in reality, this same information could easily apply to both cameras. The D800 has a relatively weak optical low-pass filter, so information about avoiding moiré may be valuable to owners of both the D800 and D800E under special circumstances. It is still possible to get false color and moiré on the D800 with extremely fine patterns, although it's much less likely than with the D800E. To save space and needless repetition, this book simply uses the term *Nikon D800* to refer to both cameras.

The upcoming sections and chapters are best read with your camera in hand, ready for configuration. There are literally hundreds of things to configure on this advanced HD-SLR. In this chapter, I'll give new D800 users a place to start. Later, as you progress through this book, we'll look at all the buttons, switches, dials, and menu settings in detail. That will allow you to fully master the operation of your Nikon D800.

There is a chapter or section for each menu in the camera. Plus, there is additional information on how to put it all together in chapters like **Metering, Exposure Modes, and Histogram**; **White Balance**; **Autofocus, AF-Area, and Release Modes**; and **Movie Live View**.

Because the Nikon D800 and D800E are cameras for advanced users, this book assumes you have knowledge of basic things like depth of field, lens focal length, and angle of view and how the aperture, shutter speed, and ISO sensitivity control exposure. If you need brushing up on those subjects, may I please refer you to one of my other books, *Beyond Point-and-Shoot*. It assumes absolutely no previous knowledge of photography and covers the basics for new users of DSLR cameras. You can find out more about *Beyond Point-and-Shoot* at my website:

http://www.PictureAndPen.com/BeyondPS

If you would like to contact me directly to comment on the book, ask questions, or report errata, please use the contact link at my website, **www.PictureAndPen.com**. You will find a series of downloadable resources for this book, along with a list of any errata corrections, at the two following websites:

http://www.Nikonians.org/NikonD800
http://rockynook.com/NikonD800

For excellent support of your new Nikon D800 and other Nikon equipment, be sure to stop by and visit with the fine members of **www.Nikonians.org**, the best Nikon users community on the web, full of friendly and knowledgeable world-class photographers. There is a voucher with a 50% discount on a Nikonians Gold Membership in the front of this book. Use the code to start or renew your Nikonians membership.

Nikon User's Manual Page References

Since many people appreciate additional reference points for research, I've included appropriate Nikon User's Manual page references under the subheadings throughout the book. Using these references is *entirely optional* and not necessary for complete understanding of your camera. However, many people, myself included,

---

Colors and Wording Legend

Throughout the book, you'll notice that in the numbered, step-by-step instructions there are colored terms as well as terms that are displayed in italic font.

1. Blue is used to refer to the camera's physical features.
2. Green is for functions and settings displayed on the camera's LCD screens.
3. *Italic* is for textual prompts seen on the camera's LCD screens.
4. *Italic* or ***bold italic*** is also used on select occasions for special emphasis.

Here is a sample paragraph with the colors and italic font in use:

Press the MENU button to reach the Setup Menu and then scroll to the Format memory card option by pressing the down arrow on the Multi selector. You will see the following message: *All images on Memory card will be deleted. OK?* Select Yes and then press the OK button. Please make sure you've transferred all your images first!

enjoy having a different perspective on things they are studying, especially when the subject is as complex as an HD-SLR.

What's in the Box?

The golden box containing the highly desirable Nikon D800 and accessories contains a total of 16 items in the American version. There may be slight differences in versions from other countries, but this will give you a good idea of what should be in your camera box.

Following is a list of each item shown in figure 1.2:

1. English User's Manual and Quick Guide
2. Spanish User's Manual and Quick Guide
3. MH-25 battery charger
4. 120v AC wire for battery charger
5. USB cable clip for tethering
6. AC wall adapter, used in place of 120v wire (4)
7. EN-EL15 li-ion battery with terminal cover
8. AN-DC6(E) neck strap labeled Nikon D800(E)
9. The Golden Box from Nikon
10. Nikon D800(E) camera body
11. BM-12 monitor cover (not shown)
12. BF-1B body cap

Figure 1.2 – Nikon D800 box contents

13. UC-E14 USB cable (USB 3.0)
14. BS-1 accessory shoe cover
15. View NX 2 installer CD
16. Warranty registration card

Initial Hardware Considerations for New Users

Although the D800 is a camera for enthusiasts and professionals, some new DSLR users have purchased a D800 as their first digital single lens reflex (DSLR) or HD-SLR camera. New users may not know how to attach and remove a lens, insert or charge the battery, and format and insert memory cards.

The majority of this book's readers, however, already know how to perform these tasks. I do not want to ask a more experienced DSLR user to read over the basics of DSLR use in this advanced book, so I've created a PDF document called **Initial Hardware Considerations**, which you can download from either of these websites:

http://www.Nikonians.org/NikonD800
http://rockynook.com/NikonD800

The document explains the basic information you will need to get started using your new camera. There are also other articles of interest to new Nikon D800 users on these web pages. To use these documents, you'll need Adobe Reader, which you can download for free at **www.adobe.com**.

Initial Camera Setup

This section is devoted to the first-time use and configuration of the camera. There are five specific settings you should configure when you first turn on the camera, before you shoot any pictures. I'll walk you through the settings. Later chapters will cover virtually all camera settings in detail.

When you first insert the battery into a factory-fresh Nikon D800, you will notice the word CLOCK flashing on the camera's upper Control panel and rear Monitor, if you press the info button. If you don't see CLOCK flashing, then your camera may have already been set up for initial use.

You may want to go through these steps even if the camera has been in use previously. That way you can make sure the initial settings are best for you.

Setting the Camera's Language – Step 1

The D800 is multilingual, or multinational. As partially shown in figure 1.3A, the menus can be displayed in 24 languages. Most likely the camera will already be configured to the language spoken in your area because various world distributors ship their cameras somewhat preconfigured. However, you may want to check and make sure.

Figure 1.3A – Language screen

Here are the steps to select your language:

1. Select Language from the Setup Menu and scroll to the right (figure 1.3A, screen 1).
2. Use the Multi selector to scroll up or down until your language is highlighted (figure 1.3A, screen 2). It may already be selected if your camera was set up by your distributor.
3. Press the OK button to select your language.

Next, let's move to the second screen in the setup series, the *Setup Menu > Time zone and date* screen.

Setting the Camera's Time Zone – Step 2

This is an easy screen to use as long as you can recognize the area of the world in which you live. Use the map shown in figure 1.3B to find your area, then select it.

Figure 1.3B – Time zone screen

Here are the steps to select the correct Time zone setting for your location:

1. Select Time zone and date from the Setup Menu and scroll to the right (figure 1.3B, screen 1).
2. Select Time zone from the Time zone and date screen and scroll to the right (figure 1.3B, screen 2).
3. You'll now see the Time zone screen with yellow arrows pointing to the left and right on either side of the small black and gray world map. With the Multi selector, scroll to the left or right until your world location is highlighted in yellow. You will see either a vertical yellow strip or a tiny yellow outline with a red dot. At the bottom of the screen, you will see the currently selected time zone. Mine is set to New York, Toronto, Lima (UTC-5), as shown in figure 1.3B, screen 3.
4. Press the OK button, and your Time zone setting will be locked in place.

Ok, let's examine the third screen in the series, the Date and time screen.

Setting the Camera's Date and Time – Step 3

This screen allows you to put in the current date and time. It is in year, month, day (Y, M, D) and hour, minute, second (H, M, S) format. Once you've configured this function, check to see if the blinking CLOCK notice has gone away from the top Control panel and Info screen.

Figure 1.3C – Date and time screen

Here are the steps to configure the Date and time setting:

1. Select Time zone and date from the Setup Menu and scroll to the right (figure 1.3C, screen 1).
2. Select Date and time from the Time zone and date screen and scroll to the right (figure 1.3C, screen 2).
3. Using the Multi selector, scroll to the left or right to select the date and time sections. Scroll up or down to set the values for each one (figure 1.3C, screen 3). A 24-hour clock is used for the time values.
4. Press the OK button when you've finished inputting the Date and time.

Setting the Camera's Date Format – Step 4

The English-speaking world uses various date formats. The Nikon D800 allows you to choose from the most common ones. There are three date formats you can select (figure 1.3D):

- Y/M/D – Year/Month/Day (2010/12/31)
- M/D/Y – Month/Day/Year (12/31/2010)
- D/M/Y – Day/Month/Year (31/12/2010)

Figure 1.3D – Selecting a Date format setting

American residents usually select the M/D/Y (Month/Day/Year) format. However, you may prefer a different format. Here are the steps to select the date format you like best:

1. Select Time zone and date from the Setup Menu and scroll to the right (figure 1.3D, screen 1).
2. Select Date format from the Time zone and date screen and scroll to the right (figure 1.3D, screen 2).
3. Using the Multi selector, scroll up or down to the position of the date format you prefer. I chose M/D/Y.
4. Press the OK button to select the format.

Now, let's configure the last screen in our series, and your camera will be ready to use.

Setting the Camera's Daylight Saving Time – Step 5

Many areas of the United States observe daylight saving time. In the springtime, many American residents set their clocks forward by one hour on a specified day each year. Then in the fall they set it back, leading to the clever saying, "spring forward and fall back."

Figure 1.3E – Selecting a Daylight saving time setting

To enable automatic daylight saving time, follow these steps:

1. Select Time zone and date from the Setup Menu and scroll to the right (figure 1.3E, screen 1).
2. Select Daylight saving time from the Time zone and date screen and scroll to the right (figure 1.3E, screen 2).
3. There are only two selections: On or Off. Choose the one you prefer by scrolling with the Multi selector until it is highlighted.
4. Press the OK button to select your choice.

If you set Daylight saving time to On, your D800 will automatically spring forward and fall back, adjusting your time forward by one hour in the spring and back by one hour in the fall.

Now that you've made the daylight saving time decision, the camera will move on to the last screen in the series of five, the Date and time screen.

Settings Recommendation: If you live in an area that observes daylight saving time, it's a good idea to set your camera to make this adjustment automatically. I always leave Daylight saving time set to On. Why not let the camera remember to change the time twice per year?

Control Location Reference

Following are the locations of all the controls mentioned in this book. You may want to place a bookmark here so you can refer back to this control location reference list when an unfamiliar control name is mentioned in the book. This list covers 60 separate external camera controls, showing their locations and Nikon-supplied names.

Following this section is a control function reference list with deeper explanations of what each control in this list does. Use the graphics in this section to learn the number of a control and then look up that number in the **Control Function Reference** section for more detailed information on the functions provided by the control.

Figure 1.4A – Back of camera

Back of Camera (figure 1.4A)

1. Accessory shoe (hot shoe)
2. Eyepiece shutter lever
3. Delete/Format button
4. Playback button
5. Viewfinder and Viewfinder eyepiece
6. MENU button
7. Protect/Picture Control/Help button
8. Playback zoom in button
9. Thumbnail/Playback zoom out button
10. OK button
11. Monitor
12. Ambient brightness sensor (for Monitor)
13. info button
14. Diopter adjustment control
15. Metering selector
16. AE/AF Lock button
17. AF-ON button
18. Main command dial
19. Multi selector
20. Multi selector center button
21. Focus selector lock
22. Speaker
23. Memory card slot cover
24. Live view selector
25. Live view button
26. Memory card access lamp

Figure 1.4B – Top of camera

Top of Camera (figure 1.4B)

27. Release mode dial lock release
28. QUAL button (image quality and size)
29. WB button (white balance)
30. ISO button (ISO sensitivity)
31. Release mode dial
32. BKT button (bracketing)
33. Power and backlight switch
34. Shutter-release button
35. Exposure compensation button
36. Movie-record button
37. MODE/Format button (exposure modes)
38. Control panel

Figure 1.4C – Front of camera

Front of Camera (figure 1.4C)

39. Built-in flash (closed)
40. AF-assist illuminator
41. Sub-command dial
42. Depth-of-field preview button
43. Fn (function) button
44. Lens mount (F-mount with cap)
45. Flash pop-up button
46. Flash mode/compensation button

47. Built-in microphone
48. Flash sync terminal cover
49. 10-pin remote terminal cover
50. Lens release button
51. AF-mode button
52. Focus-mode selector switch
53. Mounting index (lens)
54. Meter coupling lever

External Connectors (figure 1.4D; rubber Connector cover removed)

55. Connector cover (removed)
56. Connector for external microphone
57. USB connector (USB 3.0)
58. USB cable clamp mount hole
59. HDMI mini-pin connector (Type C)
60. Headphone connector

Figure 1.4D – Camera connectors under the Connector cover

Figure 1.4E – Bottom of camera

Bottom of Camera (figure 1.4E)

61. Battery-chamber cover latch
62. Battery-chamber cover
63. Contact cover for optional MB-D12 battery pack
64. Camera ID, battery info, and serial number plate
65. Tripod socket

Control Function Reference

Now, let's consider what each camera control does in a little more detail. This will, of course, be expanded upon in following chapters, but this section, along with the **Control Location Reference** in the previous section, are good reference points for where each control is located and what it accomplishes. For the descriptions, you'll need to match the number of each control in figures 1.4A–1.4D to the following list entries.

All control names are marked in blue to help delineate them as Nikon-created control names. Green items are words you will see on the camera LCD display. Each of these functions have a page number reference for this book following the control name—making this a handy guide to individual control configuration.

Back of Camera (figure 1.4A)

1. **Accessory shoe** – This hot shoe is where you will insert various accessory units that provide services for the camera. The primary use is for Speedlight flash units. However, you can also insert the SU-800 Speedlight commander in the Accessory shoe, or even the Nikon GP-1 GPS unit or an external stereo microphone. There are all sorts of items that you'll want to attach to the camera, and the Accessory shoe provides a place for attachment. Before inserting anything into the Accessory shoe, you'll need to remove the Nikon BS-1 Accessory Shoe Cover included from the factory.

2. **Eyepiece shutter lever** – This lever closes the eyepiece shutter, which prevents light from entering the Viewfinder (#5). The Eyepiece shutter lever is available only on cameras Nikon considers professional level. Use it when strong backlighting may influence the exposure due to light entering the Viewfinder.

3. **Delete/Format button** – Used to delete pictures when they are displayed on the Monitor (#11). Also used to delete characters when inserting comments in various functions such as *Setup Menu > Image comment*. In addition, this is one of the buttons you hold down to format memory cards, as signified by the FORMAT symbol below it. You use it with the MODE/Format button (#37) by holding both of them down at the same time until *For* starts flashing on the Control panel (#38), releasing them, and immediately reapplying both. You can hold the two format buttons down while turning the rear Main command dial (#18) to select which memory card to format. The memory card will then be formatted. More detailed information on card formatting, such as how to choose which of the two to format, is available in the chapter titled **Setup Menu** under the subheading **Format Memory Card**.

4. **Playback button** – Used to preview images you have just taken on the Monitor (#11). You'll press this button and the image(s) will appear. Then you can scroll through images with the Multi selector (#19).

5. **Viewfinder and Viewfinder eyepiece** – Place your eye here to see your subject through the lens using the reflex viewing system. Make sure the lens cap is off!

6. **MENU button** – Used to open the camera's menu system on the Monitor (#11). You'll use this button often when making changes to your camera configuration.

7. **Protect/Picture Control/Help button** – This is a context-sensitive, multifunction button. First, it allows you to protect images you are currently viewing on the Monitor (#11) by marking them with a key (locked) symbol as a picture that can't be deleted. Second, if you press the button when the Monitor is blank, it allows you to use the Multi selector (#19) to choose a Picture Control. Third, if you press the button when you have a menu open, it will display a help screen on the Monitor, showing what a particular function does.

8. **Playback zoom in button** – This button allows you to zoom into pictures you see on the Monitor (#11). It is used in partnership with the Thumbnail/Playback zoom out button (#9) to examine or display images from deep into a picture (up to 46x) to a list of tiny image thumbnails on the Monitor.

9. **Thumbnail/Playback zoom out button** – When you have zoomed in on an image on the Monitor (#11) using the Playback zoom in button (#8), the Thumbnail/Playback zoom out button allows you to zoom back out, or even display a list of multiple tiny thumbnail images. It is also used by some menu functions to open the Playback slot and folder menu, allowing you to select images from a particular memory card and folder.

10. **OK button** – The OK button is used to select all sorts of items and approve of various changes in menu system functions. Learn this control's location well. You'll use it often.

11. **Monitor** – This is the primary LCD display screen for the camera. This 3.2-inch thin film transistor TFT display will show you your pictures after you take them and let you select and modify functions under the menu system when you press the MENU button (#6).

12. **Ambient brightness sensor** – If you have *Setup Menu > Monitor Brightness > Auto* selected, the camera will use this sensor to detect the brightness of the ambient light surrounding the camera and adjust the brightness of the Monitor (#11) accordingly.

13. **info button** – This button has several uses. First, it opens the Information display screen and, with another press, the Information display edit screen. Both of these are displayed on the Monitor (#11). Second, it is used in Live view and Movie modes to scroll through various useful screen overlays.

14. **Diopter adjustment control** – Used to adjust the optical strength of the Viewfinder eyepiece (#5) lens so that the subject looks sharper for your eyes. It is like adding a pair of glasses to the Viewfinder, except that it does not correct for astigmatism. Adjust this dial (+/-) until the image is clear and sharp in the Viewfinder. This has nothing to do with autofocus; it is merely a special lens to help you with any eye weaknesses you may have. If looking through the viewfinder gives you a headache or makes you dizzy, you need to adjust this dial.

15. **Metering selector** – You will use this tiny dial to select, from left to right, the spot meter, matrix meter, or center weighted meter.

16. **AE/AF Lock button** – Used to lock autoexposure and/or autofocus when it is held in. This is an assignable button. Its function can be changed to something else by modifying Custom setting f5.

17. **AF-ON button** – Used to initiate autofocus when you would rather not use the Shutter-release button (#34) for autofocus. Some photographers use Custom setting a4 to disable autofocus for the Shutter-release button, leaving AF on the AF-ON button only.

18. **Main command dial** – This is a very important multifunction dial. First, it is used to control the shutter speed for shooting modes that require manual adjustment. Second, it is used while configuring all sorts of functions in the camera's menu system. This is one of the camera's most important controls along with the front Sub-command dial (#41) and Multi selector (#19). Learn and remember this control's name and location well since it will be referred to often in this book.

19. **Multi selector** – This, too, is a primary control for the camera and very important to your everyday use. Any time you have to move between items in the menus, or scroll through pictures on the Monitor (#11), you'll use the Multi selector to do it. Embed this control in your memory. The OK button (#10), along with the rear Main command dial (#18) and front Sub-command dial (#41), will be your constant friends as you use this powerful camera.

20. **Multi selector center button** – While unnamed in the control reference section of the Nikon User's Manual (page 5), this button is in the center of the Multi selector (#19). It is referenced throughout the User's Manual as the Multi selector center button. It is usually used to select items within menu system functions and can often perform the same duties as the OK button (#10).

21. **Focus selector lock** – This is a toggle switch that locks or unlocks the ability to move the selected autofocus (AF) point around the Viewfinder (#5). When you unlock the AF point and use an appropriate AF-area mode, you can select and control which AF point(s) detects focus on your subject. If this switch is set to the dot position, it is unlocked. It is locked if pointing to the L position.

22. **Speaker** – If you have recorded a movie, this is where the sound will come out, unless you are listening through a set of headphones plugged into the Headphone connector (#60). If you have Beep enabled in Custom setting d1, you'll hear various camera sounds through this speaker.

23. **Memory card slot cover** – This is the cover (door) on the right side of the camera (when you are holding it in picture-taking position). Underneath this cover are the SD and CF card slots. You will slide the cover toward you to open it.

24. **Live view selector** – This little lever allows you to switch between Live view photography and Movie live view modes. In previous Nikon cameras, Live view photography mode was called Hand-held mode and Movie live view was called Tripod mode. Both modes work similarly in that they use contrast-detection autofocus (instead of phase-detection autofocus). When you use Live view photography mode, the camera is prepared to take still shots. When you use Movie live view, the camera prepares itself for recording movies, including initializing the sound system, which is not used in Live view photography (still) mode.

25. **Live view button** – This button acts like a toggle switch that places the camera in and out of one of the Live view (Lv) modes. The modes are controlled by the Live view selector (#24) switch. You'll use this to enter Lv mode when you want to either take pictures by looking at the Monitor (#11)—instead of peering through the Viewfinder eyepiece (#5)—or just before you start recording a movie with the Movie-record button (#36). Place the Live view selector switch into Movie live view if you are about to record a movie, otherwise the Movie-record button will have no effect.

26. **Memory card access lamp** – This lamp lights up anytime the camera accesses one of its memory cards in the CF card slot or SD card slot. You will see this light up in green while taking both pictures and movies, as it writes them to the memory cards.

1

Top of Camera (figure 1.4B)

27. **Release mode dial lock release** – Hold this button down and turn the Release mode dial (#31) to change Release modes.

28. **QUAL button** – You can set the image quality (RAW, TIFF, FINE, NORM, BASIC) and size (L, M, S) by holding down the QUAL button and turning the rear Main command dial (#18) for Image quality and the front Sub-command dial (#41) for Image size. The Control panel (#38) will reflect the various modes being selected.

29. **WB button** – The WB button is held down to change the camera's White balance in conjunction with the rear Main command dial (#18) and the Control panel (#38) on top, which will display a series of automatic and manual white balance choices. If the WB button is held down and the front Sub-command dial (#41) turned, you can fine-tune the white balance along the amber (A) and blue (B) axis in up to 12 steps (6+/6-), with each step being 5 mired. The Control panel will show the fine-tuning settings (e.g., A1, b1).

30. **ISO button** – You can set the camera's ISO sensitivity by holding down the ISO button and turning the rear Main command dial (#18) while watching the ISO numbers change on the Control panel (#38). Holding down the ISO button and turning the front Sub-command dial (#41) toggles the ISO-AUTO system. You can configure the ISO-AUTO system under *Shooting Menu > ISO sensitivity settings > Auto ISO sensitivity control*.

31. **Release mode dial** – The Release modes (S, CL, CH, Q, Self-timer, and MUP) are selected by holding down the Release mode dial lock release (#27) and turning this dial.

32. **BKT (bracketing) button** – Used to initiate bracketing of images for exposure and flash (AE & flash), Active D-Lighting (ADL), and White balance (WB). The button can also be assigned to other functions instead, by configuring Custom setting f8. When used with bracketing, holding down the BKT button and turning the rear Main command dial (#18) controls the number of exposures in the bracket. Holding the BKT button and turning the front Sub-command dial (#41) controls the degree of change in exposure, ADL level, or WB color temperature.

33. **Power and backlight switch** – Used to turn the camera on and off and also to turn on the backlight for the Control panel (#38).

34. **Shutter-release button** – This is the most used control on the camera and has multiple purposes. First, the Shutter-release button is used to release the shutter and take a picture. Second, it is used to activate the exposure meter. Third, it activates autofocus. The exposure meter is activated and autofocus happens anytime you hold the button halfway down.

35. **Exposure compensation button** – This button allows you to override the camera's exposure meter and choose up to 5 EV steps of exposure compensation, either toward under- or overexposure (+/-). You'll hold down the Exposure compensation button and turn the rear Main command dial (#18) while watching compensation settings change on the Control panel (#38). You'll learn more about exposure compensation in the chapter titled **Metering, Exposure Modes, and Histogram**.

36. **Movie-record button** – Once you have set the Live view selector (#24) to Movie live view and pressed the Live view button (#25), you can press the Movie-record button to start and stop recording movies.

37. **MODE/Format button** – This button is provided to allow rapid switching of shooting modes (P, S, A, and M). The Mode button works in conjunction with the rear Main command dial (#18) for choosing modes. It can also be used as a Format button along with the Delete/Format button (#3) to format the memory cards (see #3 for details).

38. **Control panel** – This is the secondary LCD (upper) screen for the camera. It provides a constant readout of the most important camera settings, such as the flash mode, image quality, image size, AF-area mode, autofocus mode, white balance, meter type, shutter speed and aperture, memory card in use, GPS, and number of images remaining (plus more). You'll be referring to this frequently while using the camera, so it's a good idea to become familiar with each of the symbols shown on the Control panel.

Front of Camera (figure 1.4C)

39. Built-in flash – This little pop-up Speedlight flash is opened by pressing the Flash pop-up button (#45). It can help light a dim scene or be used as a Commander (CMD) to control other Nikon Speedlight flash units under the Nikon Creative Lighting System. You must configure Custom Setting e3 to have it control other Speedlights.

40. AF-assist illuminator – First, this small but powerful light is used to assist with autofocus when the light is low—only if you are using the center AF point. Second, it shines brightly to make your subject's pupils contract in the flash's red-eye reduction mode. Third, it blinks while the self-timer is counting down, doubling the blink speed a couple of seconds before the shutter fires.

41. Sub-command dial – This is a very important multifunction dial. First, it is used to control the aperture when using shooting modes that require manual adjustment. Second, it is used while configuring various functions in the camera's menu system. This is one of the camera's more important controls, along with the rear Main command dial (#18) and Multi selector (#19). Learn its name and location since it will be referred to often in this book.

42. Depth-of-field preview button – This button allows you to view the actual depth of field in a particular image. It "stops down" the aperture, darkening the Viewfinder (#5) since you are looking through the actual aperture opening.

43. Fn (function) button – This is one of several assignable buttons that can be used to control various functions in the camera. There are 20 functions you can choose from by modifying Custom Setting f4. Once you assign one of these functions to the Fn button, it will execute that function when you press the button. We will discuss button assignment in detail in the chapter titled **Custom Setting Menu**.

44. Lens mount – This is where the lens mounts to the front of your camera. The silver-colored ring behind the body cap is called the F-Mount and has been in use by Nikon cameras since the late 1950s. Nikon has never changed this bayonet mount, so virtually any lens made by Nikon for their SLR and DSLR cameras can be mounted to your camera. Most aftermarket lens manufacturers make lenses for the Nikon F-Mount. **Note:** Do not mount old non-AI lenses on your camera. They can damage the Meter coupling lever (#54). If you are unsure what a non-AI lens looks like, please find out before you try to use one and damage your camera. (See #54 for more details.)

45. Flash pop-up button – Press the Flash pop-up button to open or pop up the camera's Built-in flash (#39).

46. **Flash mode/compensation button** – The Flash mode/compensation button is used to select flash modes (e.g., Fill flash, Slow sync, Red-eye reduction) by holding it down while turning the rear Main command dial (#18) and viewing the changes on the upper Control panel (#38). If you hold the button down while turning the front Sub-command dial (#41), you can add or subtract exposure when using the flash by up to -3 EV or +1EV.

47. **Built-in microphone** – The three holes below the D800 logo are connected to the camera's mono Built-in microphone. They allow sound into the camera. Be careful that you don't cover these holes when you are recording a video or you will have very muted sound. Also, the wind tends to make a loud rushing sound on the recording when allowed to hit this microphone. Plug a Nikon Accessory-shoe (#1) mounted external microphone into the Connector for external microphone (#56) to overcome many of the problems with this basic microphone.

48. **Flash sync terminal cover** – When you open this cover you are greeted by the flash sync terminal, which allows you to plug a flash sync cable or other device into your camera for remote flash firing. An alternative is to use the Commander mode built into your camera to control multiple banks of Nikon Speedlight flash units with Nikon CLS.

49. **10-pin remote terminal cover** – Opening this cover reveals the camera's ten-pin remote terminal. You can use this terminal to plug in various devices that need to interface with the camera, such as a Nikon GP-1 GPS unit, a wireless transmitter, or a remote radio flash triggering system.

50. **Lens release button** – The big D-shaped Lens release button allows you to remove a lens from the camera. Once latched to the body, the lens is attached semi-permanently. You press this button and turn the lens clockwise to remove it from the camera.

51. **AF-mode button** – The AF-mode button allows you to change the camera's Autofocus and AF-area modes. You hold in the AF-mode button while turning the rear Main command dial (#18) to change the Autofocus mode (e.g., AF-S and AF-C) or the front Sub-command dial (#41) to change the AF-area mode (e.g., Single point AF, Dynamic-area AF, 3D-Tracking, and Auto-area AF). The AF-mode button is in the middle of the Focus-mode selector switch (#52).

52. **Focus-mode selector switch** – This toggle switch is a fast way to disable autofocus and disengage the Built-in autofocus motor actuator. It physically pulls the actuator's tip back into the camera body so that you can safely turn the autofocus ring on older AF lenses that could otherwise be damaged by that action.

53. **Mounting index** – This raised white dot is an alignment mark for attaching a lens to the camera's Lens mount (#44). There is a similar, smaller white dot on each Nikkor lens. You must align the two dots, insert the lens into the camera's Lens mount, and turn the lens counterclockwise until it audibly latches. See the downloadable resource **Initial Hardware Considerations for New Users** at: **http://www.Nikonians.org/NikonD800** or **http://rockynook.com/NikonD800**

54. **Meter coupling lever** – This small lever couples with non-G-style lenses. It is also known as an Ai lever in older Nikon literature. Many older AF Nikkors, plus the AI and AI-S-style manual-focus lenses require this lever for transmitting aperture ring position information to the camera. An old non-AI lens has no place for this lever to connect and could conceivably break it off if you mount the lens. Do not mount non-AI lenses on your camera! Do a Google search with the specific sentence "What is the difference between an AI lens, an AI-S lens, and Non-AI lens?" to learn about how to identify the ones that might harm your camera. Look for the link to Nikon's support website (**http://support. nikonusa.com**) for an article that explains (with pictures) how to tell which older lenses are safe and which aren't.

External Connectors (figure 1.4D)

55. **Connector cover** – When you are holding the camera in picture-taking position, the rubber Connector cover is on the left side of the camera. Underneath it are five connectors that allow you to interface your camera with various devices (see #56–60).

56. **Connector for external microphone** – Plug a Nikon Accessory-shoe (#1) mounted external microphone into the Connector for external microphone (#56) to override the Built-in microphone (#47) and provide a much higher level of sound quality for your HD movies.

57. **USB connector** – The Nikon D800 image files are so gigantic due to the 36.3 MP resolution that Nikon wisely included a USB 3.0 transfer system that is 10 times faster than other cameras' USB 2.0 systems. USB 3.0 theoretically allows for transfer of up to 5 GB per second, whereas the older USB 2.0 allows only 60 megapixel per second. A huge difference in speed! The USB 3.0 subsystem in the D800 is backward compatible with USB 2.0.

58. **USB cable clamp mount hole** – If you decide to tether the camera to your computer, it is wise to use the USB cable clip provided by Nikon for its pro-level cameras. This allows you to securely attach the USB 3.0 cable to your camera and prevents wear or damage to the USB port while moving around with the camera. The USB cable clip drops a plastic prong into the USB cable clamp hole for stability.

59. **HDMI mini-pin connector (Type C)** – The D800 uses this port to interface with HDMI devices such as HDTVs, external displays, and video recording devices. One of the strong points of the camera is its ability to provide an endless stream of clean broadcast-quality video through the High-Definition Multi-media Interface (HDMI) port. The HDMI port can be used for Live view photography and Movie live view outputs. The camera interface requires a mini-pin type C cable or adapter.

60. **Headphone connector** – The Nikon D800 provides broadcast-quality, clean-output video for high-end video capture. Using an external mic and a set of headphones is a good idea so that you can control the sound quality for the video. You can plug a set of headphones into the Headphone connector under the Connector cover (#55).

Bottom of Camera (figure 1.4E)

61. **Battery-chamber cover latch** – Use this latch to open the battery chamber when you need to change batteries.

62. **Battery-chamber cover** – This cover opens to reveal the battery. Use the Battery-chamber cover latch (#61) to open this cover.

63. **Contact cover for optional MB-D12 battery pack** – Before attaching the optional Nikon MB-D12 battery pack, you will need to remove and store this rubber cover. Underneath it is a connector that interfaces the camera with the MB-D12 battery pack.

64. **Camera ID, battery info, and serial number plate** – This plate lists the camera identification (type and maker), battery voltage and amperage information, and the camera's serial number.

65. **Tripod socket** – Use this socket to attach a tripod head or removable tripod plate to your camera.

Using the Nikon D800 Menu System

(User's Manual – Page 15)

The next several chapters will consider the camera menu subsystems. The D800's menu system consists of six menus, as shown in figure 1.5.

Figure 1.5 – Six primary menu systems in the Nikon D800

There are literally hundreds of configuration options in these six menus. Additionally, there is a seventh menu (not shown in figure 1.5) called Recent Settings. My Menu is the default final menu in the camera, and it can be toggled in and out with the Recent Settings menu by selecting it under *My Menu > Choose tab* or *Recent Settings > Choose tab*. We'll discuss these two final menus and why they work this way in the chapter titled **My Menu and Recent Settings**. The Recent Settings menu always contains the last 20 functions you've adjusted on your camera, while My Menu lets you place your favorite, most-configured menu selections under your own custom menu.

In case you've never used a Nikon DSLR before, you enter the menu system by pressing the MENU button next to the top left of the camera's Monitor. As you scroll up and down on the toolbar at the left of each menu you will scroll through the six available menus.

Author's Conclusions

This first chapter helped you get your camera ready for initial use. It also provided camera control descriptions, locations, and references like few other books on the market. With this book you have a complete reference for your Nikon D800 or D800E camera.

We'll examine each setting on each menu, starting now. Do you have your camera near you? You'll need it to test the numerous ways each function can be configured. You'll learn and remember the functions much better if you take the time to adjust your camera while you are reading.

Congratulations on purchasing one of the most powerful Nikons this author has ever seen. Let's get down to examining its details!

Playback Menu

Delighted Emily – Courtesy of Nigel Danson (*ndanson1*)

The Nikon D800 has a big 3.2-inch high-resolution TFT Monitor, which you can use to examine in great detail the images you have taken. You can zoom in past the 100 percent pixel-peeping level to make sure an image is sharp enough. You can view, copy, delete, and hide images and examine detailed shooting information on each picture. You can even use the Monitor to view a slide show or output the show to a much larger HDMI device, such as a television (HDTV).

The Playback Menu has everything you need to control your camera's image playback and copying and printing functions. You'll be taking thousands of pictures and will view most of them on the Monitor; therefore, it is a good idea to learn to use the Playback Menu well.

By now you may have quite a few pictures on your camera's memory card. Let's consider how you can best view, move, and print those images using the Playback Menu. The Playback functions are as follows:

- **Delete** – Allows you to delete all or selected images from your camera's memory card(s).
- **Playback folder** – Allows you to set which image folders your camera will display if you have multiple folders on the camera's memory card(s).
- **Hide image** – Lets you conceal images so they won't be displayed on the camera's Monitor.
- **Playback display options** – Controls how many informational screens the camera will display for each image.
- **Copy image(s)** – Gives you functions to copy images between the two memory cards.
- **Image review** – Turns the camera's post-shot automatic image review on or off.
- **After delete** – Determines which image is displayed next when you delete an image from a memory card.
- **Rotate tall** – Allows you to choose whether portrait-orientation images (vertical) are displayed in an upright position or lying on their side on the horizontal Monitor.
- **Slide show** – Allows you to display all the images on your camera's memory card(s) in a sequential display, like the slide shows of olden days (pre-2002). No projector required.
- **DPOF print order** – Lets you print your images directly from a PictBridge-compatible printer without using a computer—either by using digital print order format (DPOF) directly from a memory card or by connecting a USB cable to the camera.

Now, let's examine each of these settings in detail, with full explanations on how, why, and when to configure each item.

> ### Technical LCD Monitor Information
>
> As mentioned previously, the D800 has a 3.2-inch Monitor with enough res-
> olution, size, and viewing angle to allow you to really enjoy using it for pre-
> viewing images. It has VGA resolution (640×480), based on a 921,000-dot, or
> 921K-dot, liquid crystal display (LCD). If anything you read says the LCD Monitor
> has 921,000 *pixels* of resolution—or is significantly higher than VGA—the writer
> is uninformed. Nikon lists the resolution as 921,000 *dots*, not pixels.
>
> The bottom line is that this 3.2-inch screen has amazing clarity for your image
> previewing needs. You can zoom for review up to 46x for Large (L) images, 34x
> for Medium (M) images, and 22x for Small (S) images. That's zooming in to pix-
> el-peeping levels.
>
> Now, if you want to get technical—here's the extra geek stuff.
>
> A pixel on your camera's Monitor is a combination of three color dots—red,
> green, and blue (RGB). The three dots are blended together to provide shades of
> color and are equal to one pixel. This means the Monitor is limited to one-third
> of 921,000 dots, or 307,000 pixels of real image resolution. The VGA standard
> has 307,200 pixels (640×480), so the D800's Monitor has VGA resolution with a
> 170-degree viewing angle and 100 percent frame coverage.

Which Memory Card and Folder?

Before we get into the individual functions on the Playback Menu, there is something you need to understand that will help you avoid confusion as you use your
camera's menu functions. Because the D800 has multiple memory cards (playback
slots) and image folders (playback folders), you will need a good way to know which
memory card and folder contain a particular image. The information in this section
explains how the camera informs you of where a highlighted image is stored.

The D800 has multiple card slots, so many functions can affect multiple memory
cards when *Playback Menu > Playback folder > All* is selected (see the upcoming section, **Playback Folder**).

How can you tell which memory card and folder is being affected by the current function? As an example, I am using the first setting on the Playback Menu,
the Delete image function. However, this concept of card slots (i.e., CF and SD) and
folders (e.g., 100ND800 and 101ND800) applies to many functions in this camera.
You can use this knowledge as you work your way through the entire book.

Figure 2.0A – Active memory card slot

Notice in figure 2.0A that there are two tiny memory card symbols above the image thumbnails (see arrows). Each card slot is labeled. One is CF and the other is SD. If your camera has only one card inserted, the other card will be grayed out.

As you use various functions that affect displayed images, the memory card symbol will be underlined for the card containing the image you are modifying, and the playback folder name will be displayed to the right of the card slot name (red arrows in figure 2.0A). In figure 2.0A, it is apparent that there are two memory cards in use because neither card is grayed out. The selected card is highlighted in yellow and the other card is white.

The three screens in figure 2.0A represent what appears on the Monitor while scrolling through images. Moving from left to right in the three screens, you will notice the playback folder number is different in screens 1 and 2 (red arrows). Screen 1 shows that the CF card has a folder named 100ND800, while screen 2 shows that the CF card has a second folder, named 101ND800. If you look at the highlighted pictures in screens 1 and 2, you will see that folder 100ND800 has 179 pictures and picture 100-179 is selected, and in the folder named 101ND800 picture 101-1 is selected. It is apparent there are no more pictures after 101-1 because you don't see a continuance of the 101 picture count; it stops with 101-1. Now, in figure 2.0A, screen 3, you can see that I have switched to the SD card. There is only one playback folder showing and it is named 100ND800.

The camera automatically switches between these cards and folders as you scroll through images if *Playback Menu > Playback folder > All* is selected. However, if *Playback Menu > Playback folder > ND800* or *Current* is selected, the choice of folders and images may be more limited. See the section called **Playback Folder** later in this chapter for information on the Playback folder option.

Had there been only one card in the camera, the other card would have been grayed out and unselectable. The memory card containing the currently selected image will always be underlined and highlighted in yellow. As you scroll through the images, notice that the yellow underline and highlighting will jump to whatever card and folder contain the image that is highlighted at that moment.

What if you don't want to take the time to scroll through hundreds of images trying to determine which playback folder they are in? Fortunately, there is a shortcut for selecting images on only one card or in one playback folder. Again, I am using the Delete function as an example, but this method applies to multiple functions in this book (figure 2.0B).

Figure 2.0B – Choosing a Playback slot and folder

Figure 2.0B shows the steps to choose a playback slot (memory card) and folder.

1. Select the Delete function from the Playback Menu and scroll to the right (figure 2.0B, screen 1).
2. Choose Selected and scroll to the right (figure 2.0B, screen 2).
3. While the screen shown in figure 2.0B, screen 3, is on the Monitor, press the Thumbnail/Playback zoom out button.
4. The menu shown in figure 2.0B, screen 4, will now appear. This Playback slot and folder menu gives you a choice of the active playback slots (memory cards) the camera is currently using. Choose one of the two (SD card slot or CF card slot) and scroll to the right.
5. Now choose which playback folder you want to use and press the OK button (figure 2.0B, screen 5). Playback folder 101ND800 is selected in figure 2.0B.
6. You will now note in figure 2.0B, screen 6, that the yellow rectangle is surrounding the first image in the folder 101ND800 on the CF card. There is only one image in this folder currently (101-1).

You can use this method anytime you want to drill down into a specific card and folder to use or modify a certain image or images. This method of moving between cards and folders will apply to many functions throughout this book, so always be on the lookout for which memory card and playback folder contain the picture you are working with.

Why am I talking about these two functions at the beginning of the chapter instead of adding them to each individual section? Simply because many functions use this same methodology and there is no point in wasting book space to repeat the same instructions over and over. Just remember, please, that anytime you see a Monitor screen full of images, you can likely press the Thumbnail/Playback zoom out button and open the Playback slot and folder menu to select a particular memory card and folder.

Also, I am putting this information at the beginning of the Playback Menu chapter because it is so closely controlled by the settings of the *Playback Menu > Playback folder* function. You need to learn this well so that you can use this information as you study this book and when you are using your camera in the field.

Now, let's examine each of the settings on the Playback Menu in detail.

Delete

(User's Manual – Page 236)
The Delete function allows you to selectively delete individual images from a group of images in a single folder or multiple folders on your camera's memory card(s). It also allows you to clear all images in the folders without deleting the folders. This is sort of like a card format that affects only images. However, if you have protected or hidden images, this function will not delete them.

Note: I wish Nikon had chosen to put Playback folder first on the Playback Menu instead of the Delete function. Delete, which is first, does different things according to how you have Playback folder configured. It is really best to understand and configure Playback folder before using the Delete function.

There are two selections on the **Delete** screen:

- Selected
- All

Selected
Figure 2.1A shows the menu screens you'll use to control the Delete function for selected images.

Notice in screen 3 of figure 2.1A that there is a list of images, each with a number in its lower-right corner. These numbers run in sequence from 1 to however many images you have in your current image folder, or on the entire memory card. The number of images shown on the Monitor will vary according to how you have the Playback folder settings configured. (See the next section of this chapter, **Playback Folder**.)

Figure 2.1A – Delete menu screens for the Selected option

If you have Playback folder set to Current, the camera will show you only the images found in your current playback folder. If you have Playback folder set to ND800, the camera will display all the images created by the D800 in any folder on your camera's memory cards. If Playback folder is set to All, the camera will display all images on both cards, whether they were created by the D800 or another Nikon camera. The safest setting when deleting images is to use *Playback Menu > Playback folder > All*.

Here are the steps to delete one or more images. These steps will work however you have *Playback Menu > Playback folder* configured; however, you will be limited in the number of images you can see to delete when you are using the *Playback Menu > Playback folder > Current* setting.

1. Select the Delete function from the Playback Menu and scroll to the right (figure 2.1A, screen 1).
2. Choose Selected and scroll to the right (figure 2.1A, screen 2).
3. Locate the images for deletion with the Multi selector and then press the Multi selector center button. This button will mark or unmark images for deletion. It toggles a small trash can symbol on and off on the top right of the selected image (red arrow in figure 2.1A, screen 3). Only one image is selected, number 100-1. However, you can select as many images as you want by highlighting them with the yellow box and pressing the Multi selector center button.
4. Select the images you want to throw away and then press the OK button. A screen will appear asking you to confirm the deletion of the images you have selected (figure 2.1A, screen 4).
5. To finish deleting the images, select Yes and press the OK button. To cancel, select No and press the OK button (figure 2.1A, screen 5).

6. A final screen will appear briefly with the word *Done* over a grayed-out Playback Menu and then the camera will return to the normal Playback Menu.

While you are selecting or deselecting images to delete, you can press the Playback zoom in button to see a larger version of the currently selected image. This lets you examine the image in more detail to see if you really want to delete it. You can also use the Thumbnail/Playback zoom out button to open the Playback slot and folder menu, allowing you to select a particular memory card and folder (as discussed at the beginning of this chapter).

Now, how can you delete all images from a memory card without removing the folders on it?

All

This option is like a formatting a card, except that it will not delete folders, only images (figure 2.1B). As mentioned previously, it will not delete protected or hidden images, either. Using this option is a quick way to format your card while maintaining your favorite folder structure.

Figure 2.1B – Delete menu screens for the All option

Here are the steps to delete all images on the card (or in the current folder):

1. Select the Delete function from the Playback Menu and scroll to the right (figure 2.1B, screen 1).
2. Choose All and scroll to the right (figure 2.1B, screen 2).
3. Select the slot from which to delete images. You can select either SD card slot or CF card slot (figure 2.1B, screen 3). If there is a memory card missing from one of the slots, it will be grayed out and unavailable. Press the OK button to choose the slot.

4. A screen will appear asking you to confirm the deletion of all images. All means what it says, as step five more deeply discusses. Read it carefully! You must understand that how you have the Playback folder option (the next function in the Playback Menu) configured affects how many images will be deleted. See the next section of this chapter, **Playback Folder**, for information on the Playback folder option.

5. Choose Yes from the next screen with the big red exclamation point and dire warning of imminent deletion (figure 2.1B, image 5). ***Be very careful from this point forward!*** If you have Playback folder set to ND800, the camera will delete all images in *every* folder that was created by the D800, and the warning will say, *All images will be deleted. OK?*, followed by ND800. If you have Playback folder set to Current, the camera will delete only the images in the folder that is currently in use, and the warning will say, *All images will be deleted. OK?*, followed by Current. If you have Playback folder set to All, the camera will delete all images in all folders, and the warning will say, *All images in all folders will be deleted. OK?* The camera is prepared to delete every image in every folder (created by any camera) on the selected memory card if *Playback Menu > Playback folder > All* is selected.

6. When you select Yes and press the OK button, a final screen with the word *Done* will pop up briefly, informing you that the deed has been accomplished (figure 2.1B, screen 6).

Being the paranoid type, I tested this thoroughly and found that the D800 really will not delete protected and hidden images. Plus, it will keep any folders you have created. However, if you are a worrier, maybe you should transfer the images off the card before deleting any of them.

Settings Recommendation: I don't use the *Delete > All* function often because I usually don't create special folders for each type of image. If you maintain a series of folders on your memory card(s), you may enjoy using the All function. Most of the time, I just use the Selected option and remove particular images. Any other time I want to clear the card, I use the Format memory card function in the Setup Menu or hold down the two buttons with the red Format label next to them. We'll discuss formatting the memory card in the chapter titled **Setup Menu**, under the heading **Format Memory Card**.

Another way I rid myself of images I don't want is to view them on the Monitor by pressing the Playback button, and then press the Delete button on the top left of the camera back (labeled with a trash can symbol). You have several convenient ways to rid yourself of unwanted images with the D800; choose your favorite.

Recovering Deleted Images

If you accidentally delete an image or a group of images, or even if you format the entire memory card and then realize with great pain that you didn't really mean to, all is not lost. Simply remove the card from your camera immediately and do not use it until you can run image recovery software on the card. Deleting or formatting doesn't permanently remove the images from the card. It merely marks them as deleted and removes the references to the images from the memory card's file allocation table (FAT). The images are still there and can usually be recovered as long as you don't write any new data to the card before trying to recover them.

It's wise to have a good image recovery program on your computer at all times. Sooner or later you'll have a problem with a card and will need to recover images. Many of the better brands of memory cards include recovery software either on the card itself or on a separate CD that comes with the card. Make sure you install the software on your computer before formatting the brand-new memory card!

My favorite image recovery software is File Recover by PC Tools, found at the following web address:

http://www.pctools.com/file-recover/trial/d/2/

I have used it several times to recover lost files from damaged memory cards, and it works very well. It will also recover other standard file types, such as MP3 files, on any computer hard drive or memory card.

Playback Folder

(User's Manual – Page 260)

The Playback folder setting allows your camera to display images during preview and slide shows. You can have the D800 show you images created by the D800 *only*, in all folders; images that were created by the D800 and any other Nikon cameras, in all folders; or only the images in the current folder.

If you regularly use your memory card in multiple cameras, as I do, and sometimes forget to transfer images, adjusting the Playback folder setting is a good idea. I use a D800, D300S, and D7000 on a fairly regular basis. Often, I'll grab an 8 GB card out of one of the cameras and stick it in another one for a few shots. If I'm not careful, I'll later transfer the images from one camera and forget that I have folders created by the other camera on the memory card. It's usually only after I have pressed the format buttons that I remember the other camera's images on my memory card. The D800 comes to my rescue with its *Playback folder > All* function.

With All set, I can see all the images in all folders on both memory cards from all Nikon cameras.

Let's look at how the Playback folder function works by first looking at what each selection does and the steps needed to select the best function for you (figure 2.2).

The three selections (ND800, All, and Current) are described as follows:

- **ND800** – The camera will display images created by the D800 from all folders on both the SD and CF memory cards. This is good to use if you are interested in seeing only D800-created images, wherever they may reside.
- **All** – The D800 will obligingly show you every image—created by any Nikon camera—it can find in all the folders on both memory cards. During playback, or before deletion, the D800 will display images from other Nikon cameras you've used with the current memory card. Each camera usually creates its own unique folders, and normally the other folders are not visible. When you select All, the D800 intelligently displays its own images and any other Nikon-created images in any folder on the two cards.
- **Current** – This is the most limited playback mode. Images in the image folder the camera is currently using will be displayed during playback, whether the images were created by the D800 or another Nikon camera. No other images or folders will be displayed.

Figure 2.2 – Selecting a Playback folder source

Use the following steps to select the folder(s) from which your camera will display images:

1. Select Playback folder from the Playback Menu and scroll to the right (figure 2.2, screen 1).
2. Choose ND800, All, or Current and press the OK button (figure 2.2, screen 2).

Settings Recommendation: Using anything except All makes it possible for you to accidentally lose images. If you don't have any other Nikon cameras, this may not be a critical issue. However, if you have a series of older Nikon cameras around, you may switch memory cards between them. If there's an image on any of my memory cards, I want to see it and know it's there. Until I started using the All setting, I was sometimes formatting cards with forgotten images on them. From my pain comes a strong recommendation: Use All!

Playback Folder and Hidden Images

The display of images to select for hiding (see the next section) obeys the *Playback Menu > Playback folder* selection that we considered in this section. You can hide only the images you can see in the Hide image selection screen. If you don't have All selected for *Playback Menu > Playback folder*, you may not see all of the images on the card. If you regularly hide images, you may want to leave your Playback folder set to All. That way, all the images on the card will appear on the Hide image screen and you can select any of them to hide.

Hide Image

(User's Manual – Page 260)

The Hide image function lets you mark images so they won't show up on the camera's Monitor. If you sometimes take images that would not be appropriate for others to view until you have a chance to transfer them to your computer, this setting is for you. You can hide one or many images, and when they are hidden, they cannot be viewed on the camera's Monitor in the normal way. After they are hidden, the only way the images can be viewed again in-camera is by opening the *Playback Menu > Hide image > Select/set* function again, which displays the hidden images (figure 2.3A, screen 2).

There are two selections in this menu:

- Select/set
- Deselect all?

Figure 2.3A – Hide images with Select/set

Select/set

This selection allows you to hide one or several images (figure 2.3A, screen 3), or you can use this function to unhide images that have already been hidden. Here's how to hide or unhide an image:

1. Select Hide image from the Playback Menu and scroll to the right (figure 2.3A, screen 1).
2. Choose Select/set from the list and scroll to the right (figure 2.3A, screen 2).
3. Scroll to the image you want to hide and press the Multi selector center button to select the image. You'll see a little dotted rectangle with a slash symbol appear in the top-right corner of the image you've selected (red arrow in figure 2.3A, screen 3). You can do this multiple times to select several images. Both picture numbers, 100-8 and 100-9, are set for hiding in screen 3. (**Note**: To unhide a single image or several images, simply press the Multi selector center button while highlighting an image with the hide mark showing.)
4. Press the OK button to hide or unhide the image(s). *Done* will appear on the Monitor when the process is complete (figure 2.3A, screen 4).

The number of images reported does not change when you hide images. If you have 50 images on the card and you hide 10, the camera still displays 50 as the number of images on the card. A clever person could figure out that there are hidden images by watching the number of images as they scroll through the viewable ones. If you hide all the images on the card and then try to view images, the D800 will tersely inform you, *All images are hidden*.

You can also use these steps to unhide one or many images by reversing the process described earlier. As you scroll through the images, as shown in figure 2.3A, screen 3, you can deselect them with the Multi selector center button and then press the OK button to unhide them.

While you are selecting or deselecting images to hide, you can use the Playback zoom in button to see a larger version of the image you currently have selected. You can also use the Thumbnail/Playback zoom out button to open the Playback slot and folder menu, allowing you to select a particular memory card and folder (as discussed at the beginning of this chapter). This lets you examine the image in more detail to see if you really want to hide it.

Deselect all?

This is a much simpler way to unhide the previously hidden images on the card all at once. Here are the steps to unhide (deselect) all images marked as hidden:

1. Select Hide image from the Playback Menu and scroll to the right (figure 2.3B, screen 1).
2. Choose Deselect all? from the list and scroll to the right (figure 2.3B, screen 2).

Losing Protection When You Deselect All Images (Unhide)

If you have images that are both hidden and protected from deletion and you unhide them, the deletion protection is removed at the same time.

---

3. When prompted with, *Reveal all hidden images?*, select Yes and press the OK button. All hidden images on the card will then be viewable (figure 2.3B, screen 3).
4. After the images are unhidden, the Monitor will display the message, *Marking removed from all images* (figure 2.3B, screen 4).

Figure 2.3B – Unhide images with Deselect all?

Note: As mentioned previously, you can also use the steps connected to figure 2.3A to unhide a single image or a few images instead of unhiding all hidden images at once with the steps shown for figure 2.3B.

Playback Display Options

(User's Manual – Pages 261, 222)

The *Playback display options* selection allows you to customize how the D800 displays several histogram and data screens for each image. You get to those screens by displaying an image on the camera's Monitor and scrolling up or down with the Multi selector.

When you want to see a lot of detailed information about each image, you can select it here. Or, if you would rather take a minimalist approach to image information, simply turn off some of the screens.

If you turn off certain screens, the camera still records the information—such as lens used, shutter speed, and aperture—for each image. However, with no data screens selected, you'll see only two screens when you scroll up or down. One is the main image view, and the other is a summary screen with a luminance histogram and basic shooting information. I have not found a way to turn this summary screen off. You get to the screens by using the Multi selector to scroll vertically. I leave my camera set so I can scroll through my images by pressing left or right on the Multi selector. Then I can scroll through the data screens by pressing up or down on the Multi selector.

Here are the selections in this menu:

Basic photo info
- Focus point

Additional photo info
- None (image only)
- Highlights
- RGB histogram
- Shooting data
- Overview

When you modify these selections, be sure to scroll up to Done and press the OK button to save your setting (figure 2.4A, screen 3).

Figure 2.4A – Playback display options menu screens

Use the following steps to enable or disable any of the six playback display screens:

1. Select Playback display options from the Playback Menu and scroll to the right (figure 2.4A, screen 1).
2. Choose any of the six available screens by highlighting a line in yellow with the Multi selector and scrolling to the right to put a check mark in the box for that item (red arrow in figure 2.4A, screen 2). You must scroll down to see the final selection, Overview, which does not show on the main screen. In figure 2.4A, only Highlights and RGB histogram are selected.

3. After you have put check marks in the boxes for all the screens you want to use, scroll up to Done and press the OK button (figure 2.4A, screen 3).

Now, let's look at what each of these selections accomplishes (figures 2.4B to 2.4K).

Focus point

If you are curious about which autofocus (AF) sensor was focused on your subject during an exposure, use this mode to easily find out. If you are using Single-point AF or Dynamic-area AF, you'll see a single red AF indicator where the camera was focused when you took the picture (figure 2.4B, screen 2). If you are using Auto-area AF, you'll see all the AF points that were providing autofocus in your image. This is a useful function for reviewing how the camera's AF system performs in different imaging situations. In figure 2.4B, screen 2 you can see the red AF indicator over the baby's eye, which is the focus point of this image.

Figure 2.4B – Enabling the Focus point display

None (image only)

This setting is designed to give you a somewhat larger view of the current image, using all of the available screen space to show the image (figure 2.4C, screen 2). There are no text overlays, just the image by itself. This is a good selection for when you want to zoom in to the image to look at details. Since only the image itself is displayed, it is easier to scroll around within it for deep looks when using the camera's two zoom buttons (zoom in and out). You can zoom all the way in to 46x the normal image view. There is a tremendous level of detail buried inside each 36.3-megapixel image. You have an easy way to view it with None (image only).

Figure 2.4C – Enabling the None (image only) display

Highlights

If you decide to use the Highlights selection, as shown in figure 2.4D, you will turn on what I call the "blink mode" of the camera. You'll see the words RGB Highlights at the bottom left of the image. When any area of the image is overexposed, that area will blink white and black. A rectangle surrounding the word RGB will blink from black to yellow at the same time.

This is a warning that the areas of the image that blink black and white are overexposed and have lost detail. You will need to use exposure compensation or manually control the camera to contain the exposure within the dynamic range of the camera's sensor.

Figure 2.4D – Enabling the Highlights display

Look above the cute baby's head in figure 2.4D, screens 2 and 3. In screen 2 there are white areas above the baby's head, while in screen 3 those areas are black. If you were looking at this image on your camera's Monitor, you would see the area above the baby's head repeatedly blinking white to black.

When you have Highlights enabled and you see an area blinking white and black in an image on the Monitor, it means that area of the image has turned completely white and lost all detail, or has blown out.

If you examine the histogram for an overexposed (blown-out) image, you'll see that it's cut off, or clipped, on the right side. Current software cannot usually recover any image data from the blown-out sections. The exposure has exceeded the range of the sensor and the image has become completely overexposed in the blinking area. We'll discuss how to deal with images that have light ranges exceeding the sensor's recording capacity in the chapter called **Metering, Exposure Modes, and Histogram**.

Highlights mode conveniently warns you when you have surpassed what the sensor can capture and lets you know that portions of the image will be overexposed.

RGB histogram

A histogram is a digital readout that shows the range of light and color in an image. If there is too much contrast, the histogram display will be cut off. We'll examine the histogram in great detail later. For now, let's see how to turn the display on and off.

I like this feature since it allows me to view not just a basic luminance (brightness) histogram as some cameras do, but all three color (chrominance) histograms—red, green, and blue—and a luminance histogram on one screen (figure 2.4E, screen 2). The D800 stacks the four histograms on the right side of the screen, with luminance on top (white histogram) and the RGB color histograms underneath.

It is quite useful to see each color channel in its own histogram because it is possible to overexpose, or blow out, only one color channel. The luminance (white) histogram usually looks similar to the green channel histogram because green is the most common color. We'll discuss more about the luminance histogram, and the three RGB channel histograms, in the chapter called **Metering, Exposure Modes, and Histogram**.

Figure 2.4E – Enabling the RGB histogram display

Shooting data

This setting gives you four additional image shooting data screens to scroll through (figure 2.4F). Normally these shooting data screens overlay a pale version of the image they represent, so you will see a faint image beneath the screens. However, to make the information on the screens more legible, I took pictures of a gray background. The data on these screens includes the following information.

Figure 2.4F – Enabling the Shooting data display

Shooting data, screen 1 (figure 2.4G)
- Light meter in use (Matrix, Spot, or Averaging), Shutter speed, and Aperture
- Exposure mode (P, S, A, M) and ISO sensitivity
- Exposure compensation value and optimal exposure tuning
- Lens focal length

- Lens overview data (e.g., 50 mm f/1.4)
- Focus mode and VR (vibration reduction)
- Flash type and commander mode (CMD)
- Flash sync mode
- Flash control and compensation
- Commander mode info (if used)

Figure 2.4G – Shooting data, screen 1

Shooting data, screen 2 (figure 2.4H)
- White balance (WB), color temperature, WB fine tuning, and Preset manual
- Color space (sRGB, AdobeRGB)
- Picture control detail (i.e., Standard, Neutral, Vivid, Monochrome, Portrait, Land-scape) and adjustments: Quick adjust and Original Picture Control, Sharpening, Contrast, Brightness, Saturation and filter effects, and Hue and toning.

Figure 2.4H – Shooting data, screen 2

Shooting data, screen 3 (figure 2.4I)
- High ISO noise reduction, Long exposure noise reduction
- Active D-Lighting (Off, Low, Normal, High)
- HDR exposure differential and smoothing
- Vignette control
- Retouch history
- Image comment

Shooting data, screen 4 (figure 2.4J)
- Artist
- Copyright

Figure 2.4I – Shooting data, screen 3   **Figure 2.4J** – Shooting data, screen 4

Overview

This screen provides an overview of the image detail for each picture (figure 2.4K). It is packed with 28 items of information on each image, all in one convenient place. With this screen and the always-available File information screen (figure 2.4L), you will have enough information to determine the most important details about a particular image. Whether you select any other screens is entirely up to you and is determined by how much information you want for each image you have taken.

Figure 2.4K – Enabling the Overview screen

File information

This screen is not selectable under the Playback display options for the simple reason that it is always turned on and available for each image (figure 2.4L). You cannot turn it off; although, if you have *Playback display options > Focus point* enabled, the Focus point and File information screens will combine into just one screen. File information includes a large, clear view of the picture with only basic image details.

Figure 2.4L – File information screen

GPS screen

If you take a picture with a GPS unit attached and active on your D800, you'll have an additional screen available (figure 2.4M)—even if you don't have Shooting data selected. It will not show up unless a GPS unit is attached to the camera when the picture is taken. We will consider the details of the GPS function and screen in the chapter named **Shooting Menu** under the **GPS** heading.

Figure 2.4M – GPS screen

That's a lot of screens to scroll through, but they provide a great deal of information about the image. Look how far we've come from the days when cameras wrote date information on the lower-right portion of an image (permanently marking it) or between the frames on pro-level cameras.

Settings Recommendation: The screens I use all the time on my D800 are as follows: None (image only) as seen in figure 2.4C, Highlights (figure 2.4D), RGB histogram (figure 2.4E), and Overview (figure 2.4K).

I like None (image only) because I love to drill down deep into these enormous 36-megapixel images to see what detail I've been able to capture. I've never before had a Nikon give me such deep, overwhelmingly detailed images. I love this setting because it lets me examine the image with no text overlay distractions.

The Highlights screen is very useful because at a glance I can see where I have overexposed an image and can take immediate corrective action. The black and white blinking action grabs my attention and I can change my settings for the better immediately.

The RGB histogram is also important to me because it allows me to see all the color channels, just in case one of them is being clipped off on the light or dark sides (no detail). It also allows me to see how well I am keeping my exposure balanced for light and dark.

The Overview screen gives me, at a glance, most of the important information I need to know about the image, along with a larger luminance histogram. If I only had one screen, I'd want it to be the Overview screen.

The Shooting data and Focus point screens are not very important to me personally. Also, if I have the Shooting data screens enabled, I'll have to scroll through four more screens to get to the screens I like to use.

However, those are my preferences. If you want to examine a large amount of extra image data, then you should enable the other screens, too. Nikon gives us very thorough picture detail screens. Use what you like best.

Copy Image(s)

(User's Manual – Page 262)

The D800 provides a means to copy images between the camera's two card slots. If you've been shooting and decide you want a backup on the card in the other slot or want to give images on one of your cards to someone else, you can use this function to copy images between the two cards. You must have memory cards in both slots to use Copy image(s), otherwise the menu selection will be grayed out.

This convenient function has several steps to copy images. First, select a source card—if both cards have images—and the source folder, then select the images to copy, and then select the folder on the destination card in which you want to place the images. Figure 2.5A shows the screens used to copy images.

If Select source is grayed out, there are two potential reasons; see them following the step-by-step instructions shown next.

Figure 2.5A – Selecting a source for images to copy

Refer to figure 2.5A and follow these steps to select a source card:

1. Select Copy image(s) from the Playback Menu and scroll to the right (figure 2.5A, screen 1).
2. Choose Select source from the list and scroll to the right (figure 2.5A, screen 2).
3. Choose one of the card slots. I use CF card slot as my primary card slot, so figure 2.5A, screen 3, shows that I selected it as the source. **Note:** You can use *Shooting Menu > Primary slot selection* to choose which card slot is primary for your camera.
4. Press the OK button to lock in your choice.

Why is Select source grayed out? – When I first opened the menu shown in figure 2.5A, screen 2, I found only one item available: the Select image(s) choice. The rest

---

Accidentally Inserting a Write-Locked Card

The camera cannot write to an SD card with the write lock set to On. If the locked SD card is the only one inserted into the camera, you will see the word *CArd* blinking on the top Control panel (yes, for some reason it has an uppercase *A*). Also, if you press the Shutter-release button, a message will appear on the Monitor, saying, *Memory card is locked. Slide lock to "write" position.*

If there are two memory cards in the camera and one of them is locked, a blinking card slot icon will appear on the Control panel and Information display screen (press the info button once for the Information display screen). The blinking card symbol on the Information display screen will have a key icon in the middle, symbolizing that the card needs to be unlocked (it is protected). If you don't notice the blinking card icons, it may take a while to realize that you've accidentally moved the write-lock switch to the locked position on one of the cards.

The camera is smart enough to write to the other available card slot when it can't access one of the two memory cards, so you may be happily snapping images thinking they are being saved to the primary card when they are actually being sent to the secondary card, or vice versa.

The camera will continue displaying images found on the locked card if it contains images and Playback folder is set to All in the Playback Menu. The D800 can still read the card and display images from a write-locked card.

There are only a few CF cards on the market with a write-lock switch available. On the other hand, virtually all SD cards have a write-lock switch. In most cases, problems with a locked card are caused by an SD card, which is relatively easy to write-lock accidentally upon insertion.

---

of the choices were grayed out. I was quite puzzled at first, but then I figured out that there are two reasons Select image(s) may be the only option available.

First, there might be images on only one of the cards. Think about this for a moment. If only one card has images on it, it has to be the source. This is the most likely scenario.

Second, an SD card's (or in rare cases a CF card's) write-lock switch might be in the On position. This usually happens when the SD card is inserted into a card reader or a camera at a slight angle. The switch is on the side, and sometimes it accidentally gets moved from the Off to the On position. See the sidebar **Accidentally Inserting a Write-Locked Card** for more information about what happens when a write-locked card is inserted into one of the camera's memory card slots.

The following instructions assume that you have a card in each slot and there are images on both cards. If you have images on only one card, you can skip this process. Refer to figure 2.5A and follow the steps to select a source card.

Figure 2.5B – Selecting a source folder for images to copy

When you have chosen a source, it's time to select images to copy. First, follow these steps to choose a folder:

1. Choose Select image(s) from the list and scroll to the right (figure 2.5B, screen 1).
2. Choose the folder that contains the images you want to copy (figure 2.5B, screen 2). My cards currently have two folders available and I chose the folder named 100ND800. Your cards may have several existing folders or only one. After you have chosen a folder, scroll to the right.
3. There are three options for copying images: Deselect all, Select all images, and Select protected images (figure 2.5C). Each option has a slightly different way of doing things (the description for each option is listed between steps 3 and 4). Choose one option for your copy operation, follow the directions for your chosen option, and continue with step 4.

Figure 2.5C – Deselecting all images to copy

- **Deselect all** (figure 2.5C) – Choose Deselect all from the Images selected by default menu and scroll to the right. Deselect all opens a list of images, none of which have been selected. It sounds a little weird to select images for copying while using a function named Deselect all, but this means that the camera automatically deselects all the images so you can choose which images to copy. You'll need to scroll around with the yellow rectangle and select images one at a time. Mark an image for copying by pressing the Multi selector center button, and you'll see a small white check mark appear in the top-right corner of the image thumbnail. Figure 2.5C, screen 2, shows only one picture selected, number 100-178. It is the only one with a check mark. Now move on to step 4.

Figure 2.5D – Selecting all images to copy

- **Select all images** (figure 2.5D) – Choose Select all images from the Images selected by default menu and scroll to the right. The Select all images screen will appear, with all images selected. If you want to copy all of the images, move on to step 4 now. If you want to deselect a few of them before copying, scroll to an image and press the Multi selector center button. This action will remove the check mark from the image thumbnail. After you've unchecked the images you don't want to copy, move on to step 4.

Figure 2.5E – Selecting protected images to copy

- **Select protected images** (figure 2.5E) – Choose Select protected images from the Images selected by default menu and scroll to the right. If you have used the Help/protect button to mark images as protected, they will appear with a little key symbol and a check mark in the list of images, indicating that they are already checked for copying (figure 2.5E, screen 2, pictures 100-153 to 100-155). If you have a lot of images on the card and only a few are protected, it may be hard to find the protected images. Rest assured that the camera knows which ones to copy. It will display all the images but only copy the protected ones. You can see the number of protected images that will be copied in the upper-right corner of the display (red arrow in figure 2.5E, screen 2). This figure shows that I will copy 5 protected images out of 179 images on the CF card from folder 100ND800. Now move on to step 4.

Figure 2.5F – Selecting a destination folder

4. After you have selected all the images you want to copy, press the OK button and the Monitor will display the Copy images(s) menu. Now it's time to select a destination folder into which you'll copy the images (figure 2.5F).

5. Choose Select destination folder from the Copy image(s) menu and scroll to the right (figure 2.5F). You will have two options: Select folder by number or Select folder from list (figures 2.5G and 2.5H). Before we move on to step 6, let's investigate these options. Pick an option, follow the instructions for your option, and then move on to step 6.

Figure 2.5G – Selecting a destination folder by number

- **Select folder by number** (figure 2.5G) – Choose Select folder by number from the Select destination folder menu and scroll to the right. The next screen will display a folder number that can be changed to any number between 100 and 999 (figure 2.5G, screen 2). If you select a number for a folder that already exists on the destination card, the images will be copied into that folder. If you select a folder number for which a corresponding folder does not exist on the destination card, the folder will be created and the source images will be copied into the new folder on the destination card. Notice the little folder symbol the red arrow points to in screen 2. The folder symbol appears only when you are copying into an existing folder. My cards already contained existing folders 100ND800 and 101ND800, as seen in figures 2.5B and 2.5H. In figure 2.5G, screen 2, if I had scrolled up where the yellow highlighted 1 is, changing it to a 2 instead, the camera would have created a folder on the destination card named 102ND800 in preparation for copying the files. Now move on to step 6.

Figure 2.5H – Selecting a destination folder from a list of folders

- **Select folder from list** (figure 2.5H) – If there are no existing folders on the destination card, this option will be grayed out. Obviously, you can't copy images to a folder that doesn't exist, so use the Select folder by number option to create a new folder. If this option is not grayed out, choose Select folder from list and scroll to the right. The next screen will show you a list of folders. My list in figure 2.5H, screen 2, has two folders in it. I chose to use the folder named 101ND800. After you have selected the destination folder, move on to step 6.

Figure 2.5I – Copying images

6. Now it's finally time to copy some images. We've selected a source card and folder, some images, and a destination folder. Notice that you don't have to select a destination memory card. Since we've already selected a source card, the other card automatically becomes the destination. The D800 does not support copying images to the same memory card; you can copy only to the other card. All that's left is to select Copy image(s)? and press the OK button.

7. Figure 2.5I shows the screens for this step and step 8. After you have selected Copy image(s)?, you'll see a screen asking for verification. Mine says, *Copy? 5 images* (figure 2.5I, screen 2). Select Yes and press the OK button. Figure 2.5I, screen 3, shows that the camera is copying 5 pictures from the source card to the destination card. Notice how the *Copying* screen shows the progress of the copy action with a green progress bar. This will take several minutes to complete if you are copying a large number of images.

8. When the copying is finished, you will see a small white box that says, *Copy complete* and the number of images successfully copied, in this case five of five (5/5). You must press the OK button to return to the Copy image(s) screen. That completes the copying process.

There's one more screen to be aware of, in case you try to copy images into a folder where they already exist. If an identical file name already exists in the destination folder, you may or may not want to overwrite it.

The camera will warn you with the screen shown in figure 2.5J, helpfully showing you thumbnails of both images. You can view the two thumbnails and choose Replace existing image, Replace all, Skip, or Cancel.

Figure 2.5J – Image overwrite warning

Image Review

(User's Manual – Page 265)
Image review does exactly what it says; it displays an image you've just taken on your camera's Monitor. With this function set to On, you'll see each picture you take just after you take it. You can review the image for quality and usefulness.

With Image review set to Off, you won't see each picture unless you press the Playback button afterward. This saves battery life. However, the camera's battery is long lived because the D800 does not use a lot of power. If you prefer to review each image after you take it, then you'll need to set this feature to On.

You can control how long each image is displayed on the Monitor before it shuts off by adjusting *Custom Setting Menu > c Timers/AElock > c4 Monitor off delay > Image review*. This custom image review time can be adjusted to display pictures from 2 seconds to 10 minutes. We'll discuss this in more detail in the chapter titled **Custom Setting Menu**.

There are two Image review settings, as shown in figure 2.6:

* **On** – Shows a picture on the Monitor after each shutter release.
* **Off** – Causes the Monitor to stay off when you take pictures.

Figure 2.6 – Enabling Image review

Here are the steps to choose an Image review setting:

1. Choose Image review from the Playback Menu and scroll to the right.
2. Select On or Off from the Image review screen.
3. Press the OK button.

Most of us will turn this feature on right away. Otherwise, the only way to view an image after taking it is to press the Playback button.

Settings Recommendation: Because the camera's battery lasts a long time, I leave Image review set to On. I am an unashamed image chimper (see sidebar **Are You a Chimper Too?**) and always examine each image, if there's time. Photography is enjoyable, and one of the good things is the satisfaction you feel when you capture a really nice image. However, if you are shooting a sports event and blasting through hundreds of shots per hour, there's not much time to view each image. It all boils down to how you shoot. If you aren't inclined to view your images as you take them, then it may be a good idea to set Image review to Off—merely to save battery life.

After Delete

(User's Manual – Page 266)

If you delete an image during playback, one of your other images will be displayed on the camera's Monitor. The After delete function lets you select which image is displayed after you delete an image. The camera can display the next image or the previous image, or it can detect which direction you were scrolling—forward or backward—and let that determine which image appears after you delete another.

Are You a Chimper Too?

Chimping means reviewing images on the Monitor after each shot. I guess people think you look like a monkey if you review each image. Well, I do it anyway! Sometimes I even make monkey noises when I'm chimping my images. Try saying, "Oo, Oo, Oo, Ah, Ah, Ah" really fast when you're looking at an image and are happy with it. That's chimping with style, and it's why the word was invented.

The three selections on the After delete menu are Show next, Show previous, and Continue as before (figure 2.7).

- **Show next** – If you delete an image and it wasn't the last image on the memory card, the camera will display the next image on the Monitor. If you delete the last image on the card, the previous image will be displayed. Show next is the factory default behavior of the D800.
- **Show previous** – If you delete the first image on the memory card, the camera will display the next image. If you delete an image somewhere in the middle or at the end of the memory card, the previous image will be displayed.
- **Continue as before** – This weird little setting shows the flexibility of computerized camera technology in all its glory. If you are scrolling to the right (the order in which the images were taken) and decide to delete an image, the camera uses the Show next method to display the next image. If you happen to be scrolling to the left (opposite from the order in which the images were taken) when you decide to delete a picture, the camera will use the Show previous method instead.

Figure 2.7 – Playback Menu – After delete

Use the following steps to choose an After delete setting (figure 2.7):

1. Choose After delete from the Playback Menu and scroll to the right (figure 2.7, screen 1).
2. Select one of the settings from the After delete screen (figure 2.7, screen 2).
3. Press the OK button to lock in the setting.

Settings Recommendation: When I delete an image, I'm not overly concerned about which image shows next—most of the time. However, this functionality is handy in certain styles of shooting and when I am deleting rejects.

For instance, some sports or wildlife shooters might like to move backward through a long sequence of images, starting with the last image taken. They can then delete the images that are not usable in the sequence, and the camera will immediately show the previous image for review. When they reach the first image in the sequence, the entire series is clean and ready to use.

I leave my camera set to Continue as before, as shown in figure 2.7, because it will use the direction I was scrolling to decide which image to display after deleting one.

Rotate Tall

(User's Manual – Page 266)

When you shoot a portrait-oriented (vertical) image with the camera turned sideways, the image can later be viewed as a horizontal image lying on its side or as a smaller, upright (tall) image on the camera's horizontal (wide) Monitor.

If you view the image immediately after taking it, the camera's software assumes that you are still holding the camera in the rotated position and the image will be displayed correctly for that angle. Later, if you are reviewing the image with the camera's playback functionality and have Rotate tall set to On, the image will be displayed as an upright, vertical image that is smaller so it will fit on the horizontal Monitor. You can zoom in to see sharpness detail, if needed.

If you would rather have the camera leave the image lying on its side in a horizontal view, forcing you to turn the camera 90 degrees to view it, you'll need to choose Off.

The following two settings are available on the Rotate tall menu (figure 2.8):

- **On** – When you take a vertical image, the camera will rotate it so you don't have to turn your camera to view it naturally during playback. This resizes the view of the image so that a vertical image fits in the horizontal frame of the Monitor. The image will be a bit smaller than normal. When you first view the image after taking it, the camera does not rotate it because it assumes you are still holding the camera in a vertical orientation. It also senses which end of the camera is up—if the Shutter-release button is up or down—and displays the image accordingly.
- **Off** – Vertical images are left in a horizontal direction, lying on their side; you'll need to turn the camera to view the images in the same orientation as when they were taken. This provides a slightly larger view of a portrait-oriented image.

Figure 2.8 – Playback Menu – Rotate tall

Here are the three steps to choose a Rotate tall setting:

1. Choose Rotate tall from the Playback Menu and scroll to the right (figure 2.8, screen 1).
2. Select On or Off from the Rotate tall screen (figure 2.8, screen 2).
3. Press the OK button to finish.

There is another camera function that affects how this works. It's called Auto image rotation, under the Setup Menu. We'll discuss this function more deeply in the chapter titled **Setup Menu**. Auto image rotation causes the camera to record the angle at which you are holding it as part of the image's metadata. Auto image rotation should be set to On so that an image will report how it should be displayed on the camera's Monitor and on your computer.

In other words, Rotate tall and Auto image rotation work together to display your image in the correct orientation. Rotate tall gives you the choice of how the image is viewed based on the orientation information it finds in the image's metadata. *Setup Menu > Auto image rotation* causes the camera to store how the image was taken so it will know whether the image has a vertical or horizontal composition. It can then report this information to the Rotate tall function.

Settings Recommendation: I leave Rotate tall set to On. That way I can view a portrait-oriented image in its natural, vertical orientation without turning my camera. Be sure you understand the relationship between this function and Auto image rotation, which stores orientation data with the picture. I always set *Rotate tall* and *Setup Menu > Auto image rotation* to On.

Slide Show

(User's Manual – Page 267)

A slide show is a convenient way to view a large number of images instead of having to scroll through them one by one. The camera can also be connected to an HDMI display device to show a slide show on a larger device. With the size of some of today's flat-screen televisions, we've come full circle to the old days of family slide shows. With the D800's big 3.2-inch Monitor for viewing immediately or its HDMI output for viewing later, slide shows are back! But instead of a portable screen and slide projector, we have the D800 and an HDTV.

Note: Connecting to an HDTV requires the separate purchase of an HDMI (Type A) to mini-HDMI (Type C) cable (not included with camera). The D800 uses the Type C, mini-HDMI connector, while the HDTV uses the larger Type A connector.

Figure 2.9A – Playback Menu – Slide show

As shown in figure 2.9A, the easy way to start a slide show is to simply select the *Playback Menu > Slide show* setting, scroll right, select Start, and press the OK button. The slide show will commence immediately with a default display time of 2 seconds (2s) per image.

You can control how long each image is displayed with the Frame interval setting. If you want to allow a little more time for each image to show, you'll need to change the Frame interval (display time).

Figure 2.9B shows the menus where you can make the Frame interval changes. Your choices are as follows:

- 2s – 2 seconds
- 3s – 3 seconds
- 5s – 5 seconds
- 10s – 10 seconds

Figure 2.9B – Playback Menu – Slide show Frame interval

To start the slide show after you change the Frame interval setting, repeat the steps shown in figure 2.9A. The slide show will now run at the speed you chose.

Settings Recommendation: I usually set the Frame interval to 3s. If the images are especially beautiful, I might set it to 5s. I've found that 2s is not quite enough, and 5s or 10s may be too long. I wish there were a 4s setting, but 3s seems to work well most of the time.

Changing the Slide Show Image Flow

There are several options that affect how the images are displayed during the slide show. None of these options are in the camera menus; they are available through the camera's controls only. Your options are as follows:

- *Skip back/Skip ahead* – During the slide show, you can go back to the previous image for another viewing by simply pressing left on the Multi selector. You can also see the next image with no delay by pressing right on the Multi selector. This is a quick way to skip images or review previous images without stopping the slide show.
- *View additional photo information* – While the slide show is running, you can press up or down on the Multi selector to view the additional data screens. The screens you will see depends on how you have configured your camera's *Playback Menu > Playback display options* settings, such as Focus point, None (image only), Highlights, RGB Histogram, and so on. See the section called **Playback Display Options** earlier in this chapter. If any of these screens are enabled, they can be used during the slide show.
- *Pause slide show* – During the slide show you may want to pause, change the frame interval, or even exit the show. If you press the OK button, the slide show will be suspended and you will see the Pause screen (figure 2.9C).

Figure 2.9C – Playback Menu – Slide show Pause and Restart

Using the screens shown in figure 2.9C, you can select any of the following:

- **Restart** – Selecting OK or scrolling to the right with the Multi selector continues the slide show, starting with the image following the last one that was viewed.
- **Frame interval** – Scrolling to the right with the Multi selector takes you to the screen that allows you to change the display time to one of four values. You can choose 2s, 3s, 5s, or 10s. After choosing the new Frame interval, you'll have to select Restart to continue the slide show where you left off.
- **Exit** – Selecting this option exits the slide show.

Exiting the Slide Show

There are several ways you can exit a slide show while it is running:

- **Press OK to pause** – Then select Exit from the Pause menu (figure 2.9C). The camera jumps back to the Playback Menu with Slide show highlighted so you can start again quickly.
- **Exit to the Playback Menu** – If you want to quickly exit the slide show, simply press the MENU button and the camera will jump directly back to the Playback Menu, with no items selected.
- **Exit to playback mode** – You can press the Playback button to stop the slide show and switch to a normal full-frame or thumbnail view of the last image seen in the slide show. This exits the show on the last image viewed.
- **Exit to shooting mode** – If you press the Shutter-release button halfway down, the slide show will stop. The camera is now in shooting mode, meaning that it is ready to take some pictures.

These days, instead of hauling out a slide projector and boxes of slides, you can simply plug your D800 into the closest high-definition (HD) device, such as an HDTV, because the camera has a high-definition multimedia interface (HDMI) port. We'll talk more about HDMI in a later chapter.

DPOF Print Order

(User's Manual – Page 254)

At first I thought it was odd that Nikon chose to put image printing functions in the Playback Menu. Then I realized that printing is a permanent form of image playback. You play (print) the images to your printer and then view them without a camera or a computer. What a concept!

There are two ways to print images from your camera without using a computer. One way is to use DPOF to create a print order on a memory card. This function is called Print set (DPOF). The second way is to plug in a USB cable and print directly to a PictBridge-compatible printer. Both of these methods are generally used by nonprofessional camera users to print pictures from Joint Photographic Experts Group (JPEG) files at home or at the local lab, with no post-processing.

Most advanced amateur and professional users of the D800 will want to post-process their images in computer software such as Nikon Capture NX 2, Lightroom, Photoshop, or Aperture before printing, so this functionality is not used as often as other functions. However, it can be useful for someone who would rather simply take pictures and print them at home or at a store than manipulate images on their computer.

Since these seldom-used functions require multiple pages to describe and many people do not use them, I have relegated this information to a detailed document called **DPOF Print Order** and included it in the downloadable resources at **http://rockynook.com/NikonD800**.

Note: DPOF print order can be used only with JPEG images. It does not apply to NEF (RAW) files.

Author's Conclusions

Wow! The D800 sure does have a lot of playback screens and menus. I remember the old days when if you wanted to see your images, you'd have to find the old shoebox full of pictures or open an album and flip pages. Sometimes I miss photo albums. I have a bookcase full of old prints from the film days, but no digital prints. Hmmm.

You know what? I'm going down to the superstore right now to buy several albums. Then I'll have some images printed and put them into the albums. Better yet, I think I'll go buy a PictBridge-compatible printer so I can print my own images for the albums. Do you have new albums full of digital prints? If not, why not? They're awfully convenient and fun to view.

Anyway, let's move on to the next menu system in the camera, the Shooting Menu. This is one of the most important menus because it affects how the camera is configured to shoot pictures. Learn these upcoming settings well!

Shooting Menu

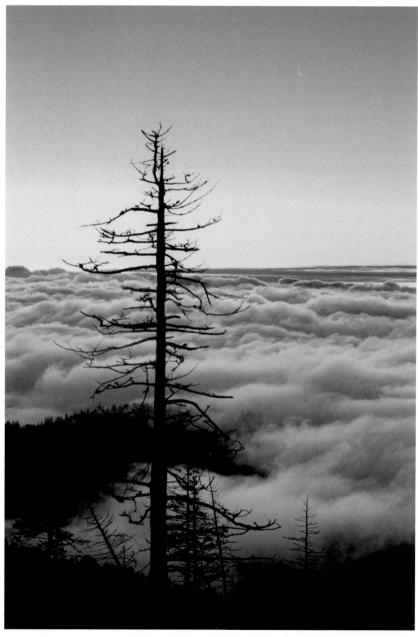

Sunrise on Clingman's Dome – Courtesy of David Jolley (*DAJolley*)

The Shooting Menu settings are some of the most used functions in the camera. Spend time carefully learning about each of these selections because you will use them often. They affect how your camera takes pictures in all sorts of ways.

Here is a list and overview of the 26 items found on the D800 Shooting Menu. Each of these items can be configured in different ways by using the four available Shooting menu banks.

- **Shooting menu bank** – Allows configuration of the camera in four separate ways so that it can act like four different cameras as you change banks.
- **Extended menu banks** – You can save not only the internal camera Shooting Menu function configurations but also the exposure mode and shutter speed (when you use S and M exposure modes) and the exposure mode and aperture (when you use A and M exposure modes). Later, when you select a Shooting menu bank, the exposure mode and the aperture or shutter speed setting will be recalled along with that bank's previous configuration.
- **Storage folder** – Selects the folder into which subsequent images will be stored on the camera's memory card(s).
- **File naming** – Lets you change three characters of the image's file name so that it is personalized.
- **Primary slot selection** – You can select either the SD or CF memory card slot to be the primary slot that receives images.
- **Secondary slot function** – Allows you to select either the SD or CF memory card slot to be the secondary slot that receives image overflow or copies.
- **Image quality** – You can select from eight image quality types, such as JPEG fine or NEF (RAW).
- **Image size** – You can choose to shoot **Large** (7360×4912, 36.2 MP), **Medium** (5520×3680, 20.3 MP), or **Small** (3680×2456, 9.0 MP) images when using FX mode. This image size will vary according to whether you have FX (3:2), 1.2x, DX (1.5x), or 5:4 Image area modes selected.
- **Image area** – You have the choice of letting the camera automatically select DX mode when a DX lens is mounted, or you can select that it stay in FX mode (On or Off). Also, you have four different image sizes available for your pictures. They are FX (36×24), 1.2x (30×20), DX (24×16), and 5:4 (30×24).
- **JPEG compression** – You can select Size priority or Optimal quality for your best JPEG images.
- **NEF (RAW) recording** – Sets the compression type and bit depth for NEF (RAW) files.
- **White balance** – You can choose from nine different White balance types, including the ability to measure the ambient light's color balance (PRE).
- **Set Picture Control** – You can choose from several Picture Controls that modify how the pictures look.

- **Manage Picture Control** – Lets you save, load, rename, or delete custom Picture Controls from your camera's internal memory or card slots.
- **Color space** – You can choose either the industry printing standard Adobe RGB or the Internet and home use standard sRGB color space for your camera.
- **Active D-Lighting** – Allows you to select from several levels of automatic contrast correction for your images. The camera itself will protect your images from a degree of under- or overexposure.
- **HDR (high dynamic range)** – You can create a two-exposure HDR image. The camera will automatically combine them. Use for JPEG or TIFF images only.
- **Vignette control** – Provides for three levels of vignette control when using an FX lens of the G or D type. Excludes DX and PC lenses. This function allows you to automatically remove various amounts of the corner darkness resulting from using certain lenses at maximum aperture with a full-frame sensor.
- **Auto distortion control** – With a G or D type lens (PC, fisheye, and certain other lenses excluded), the camera can automatically reduce barrel distortion when using a wide-angle lens and pincushion distortion when using a telephoto lens. May cause image edge cropping as the distortion is automatically removed. Can reduce distortion in DX lenses when the camera is in DX mode.
- **Long exposure NR** – Uses the "dark-frame subtraction" method to significantly reduce noise in long exposures. A very powerful and useful function if you make long exposures because it is not as damaging to the image as blurring noise reduction. Slows camera frame rate and reduces memory buffer size when turned on.
- **High ISO NR** – Uses a blurring and resharpening method to remove noise from images shot with high ISO sensitivity values.
- **ISO sensitivity settings** – Allows you to manually set the ISO sensitivity between ISO 50 and 25,600 or let the camera decide for you automatically with Auto ISO sensitivity control.
- **Multiple exposure** – Allows you to take more than one exposure in a single frame and then combine the exposures in interesting ways.
- **Interval timer shooting** – You can put your camera on a tripod and set it to make one to several exposures at customizable time intervals.
- **Time-lapse photography** – Similar to Interval timer shooting, except more movie oriented. You can make a time-lapse movie with this function, obeying the options selected in *Shooting Menu > Movie settings*. Shooting things like a time exposure of a flower opening becomes easy with the D800.
- **Movie settings** – You can use this to set the movie quality, frame size, and frame rate of the video stream in Movie mode. You may also select how the Microphone works and the Destination card slot for the movies.

Now, let's consider each of these 26 Shooting Menu functions in deeper detail.

Shooting Menu Bank

(User's Manual – Pages 269, 170)

The Shooting menu banks are unique to professional-level cameras. Most Nikons have a Shooting Menu, but only the best have multiple Shooting menu banks. Using the four banks, your D800 can change from a pro camera to a point-and-shoot, and anything in between, with just a few button presses. Let me give you a couple of examples of what I mean.

It can shoot RAW files using ISO 100 in Adobe RGB Color space with the Fn button assigned to Spot metering for serious professional shooting, and very quickly change to Normal quality JPEGs at ISO 400 in sRGB Color space with high image sharpening for that party where you don't want to think about anything but having a good time. These are only two variations of the many available combinations of bank settings you can design.

The D800 has not only four Shooting menu banks, but also four Custom settings banks (covered in the next chapter). There are no direct relationships between the Shooting menu banks and the Custom settings banks, although you could create one by naming them in a similar way and configuring them for similar purposes. You can easily configure the functionality of each bank with different settings, name them accordingly, and use them to quickly change the way your camera behaves. Multiple cameras in one!

There are four default bank names: A, B, C, and D. You can add your own labels to any of these. In this chapter, we'll assume that your camera banks have not yet been adjusted and that you are not entirely familiar with the process. Let's learn how to label bank A with a more useful name and set its individual features. When you've done this once, you'll be ready to set up your camera for special uses and switch between banks quickly.

We will only fully configure a single bank in this book (bank A). Just repeat the same process for each bank, with different settings.

Following are the steps and screens used to modify the label for bank A of the Shooting menu banks (figure 3.1).

Figure 3.1A – Selecting and changing a Shooting menu bank

Following are the steps to label Shooting menu bank A. Repeat the steps to label the other three banks (B–D):

1. Notice in figure 3.1A, screen 1, there's a selection called Shooting menu bank with an A after it. This means the camera is using Shooting menu bank A. If any letter other than A is showing, you are using a different Shooting menu bank. Let's give Shooting menu bank A a new label so you'll be able to see at a glance what this particular bank is set up to accomplish. Select Shooting menu bank from the Shooting Menu and scroll to the right.

2. Assuming you haven't yet renamed any of your Shooting menu banks, you'll see the four banks called A, B, C, D, with a blank line following each letter (figure 3.1A, screen 2). The factory default for an unnamed bank is simply a blank field following the letter. Using the Multi selector, scroll to the right on the bank you want to rename (figure 3.1A, screen 2). If you press the OK button instead of scrolling to the right, you will simply select the bank. You must scroll right when the bank is highlighted in order to modify its name.

3. As shown in figure 3.1A, screen 3, you'll see a series of numbers and letters at the top of the screen. There is a space character at the end of the lowercase letters, after the small z. You can find various symbols by scrolling down below the numbers and letters. Notice the line of dashes in the gray text field at the bottom of the screen. This field is where you will enter the text that renames the bank. I added the words *General Purpose* there (figure 3.1A, screen 3). To add the new name for your camera's bank A, scroll around with the Multi selector and use the Multi selector center button to select letters, numbers, and symbols with the yellow cursor. You should see each character appear in the gray text field when you select it with the Multi selector center button. You can hold

down the checkered Thumbnail/playback zoom out button and use the Multi selector to move back and forth in the gray text field. If you want to delete a character from the gray text field, move the darker gray cursor over the top of the letter and press the Delete button (garbage can). You are limited to 20 characters in the new bank name.

4. Press the OK button to save the new name. When you check the bank's name under the Shooting menu bank A setting, you'll see the bank's new label (figure 3.1A, screen 4). If you were renaming bank A, it is now selected also.

Settings Recommendation: I generally name my banks as shown in the following list. Each of the label names describes at a glance how I intend to use a bank when shooting. You may want to use different names and settings for each bank, but this list may give you some ideas:

- ***Bank A – General Purpose:*** Bank A is my general purpose bank. I use it when I'm just walking around with my camera doing general photography. I will often modify the camera's settings when using bank A. I know to check before shooting when using this bank. I generally shoot in RAW mode but might switch to JPEG as needed. This is a completely variable bank and the only one I modify regularly.

- ***Bank B – Best Quality RAW:*** Bank B is for when I am shooting commercially, with the best quality my camera can muster. I use this on any type of shoot that requires me to post-process the images in-computer. My critical settings for bank B are Image quality at NEF (RAW), with *NEF (RAW) recording > Type* set to Lossless compressed and NEF (RAW) bit depth at 14-bit, Image size set to Large, Image area set to FX, White balance to AUTO, Neutral (NL) Picture Control, Color space to Adobe RGB, Active D-Lighting to Off (or Low), ISO sensitivity to ISO 100, and Aperture-priority mode with the aperture set to f/8. (If *Shooting Menu > Extended menu banks* is set to On, the camera will remember the last exposure mode and aperture or shutter speed, saving it under the current bank with the rest of your settings for that bank. See the section **Extended Menu Banks** for more information.) Once it's set, I rarely modify this bank. If I'm shooting landscapes from a tripod, I may lower the ISO sensitivity to ISO 50 (L 1.0) by holding down the ISO button and turning the rear Main command dial.

- ***Bank C – Best Quality JPEG:*** Bank C is for when I have no time to post-process the images. I need them as soon as I shoot them but must have maximum quality. My critical settings for bank C are Image quality set to JPEG fine, Image size set to Large, Image area set to FX, JPEG compression to Optimal quality, White balance to AUTO, Standard (SD) Picture Control, Color space to Adobe RGB, Active D-Lighting to Low, and ISO sensitivity to ISO 200. Once it's set, I rarely change this bank. I also use Extended menu banks set to On with Aperture-priority mode selected and aperture set to f/8.

- ***Bank D – Party JPEG:*** When I am going to a party with friends, I'll simply switch to this bank and fire away. I could use bank A, but then I'd have to reset it to higher quality later. Instead, I use this bank to have some fun with my camera and friends. The images must be high enough quality to get good prints, at least 11×14 inches (27×35 cm) in size. The critical settings for bank D are Image quality set to JPEG fine, Image size set to Medium (20.3 MP), JPEG compression set to Size priority, White balance to AUTO, Standard (SD) Picture Control, Color space to sRGB, Active D-Lighting to Normal, and Auto ISO sensitivity control set to On, with a Maximum sensitivity of ISO 1600 and Minimum shutter speed of 1/60s. Even though I turned on Auto ISO, I also set ISO sensitivity to ISO 400. I'll explain why in the upcoming note. Finally, I set Extended menu banks to On with Programmed auto exposure mode selected for thought-free shooting. My camera is like a heavy Coolpix point-and-shoot for party time while still giving me 20-megapixel JPEG images.

Note: Why did I set a manual ISO sensitivity in Shooting menu bank D – Party JPEG? I also turned on the Auto ISO sensitivity control. Shouldn't that automatically handle all my ISO sensitivity needs? Good questions!

I set a manual ISO sensitivity because of an undocumented feature in most Nikons. If you set ISO sensitivity to a certain number when you have the Auto ISO sensitivity control enabled, the ISO you set manually becomes a minimum ISO, while the Auto ISO sensitivity control sets the maximum ISO.

So, in my case, by setting an ISO of 400, I set a minimum ISO that my camera will not go below. The Auto ISO sensitivity control is set to never exceed ISO 1600 in my bank D setting. I have now created a range of ISO 400 to 1600 that my camera can shoot within, adjusting ISO sensitivity automatically, as needed, in my set range.

Alternate Shooting Menu Bank Access

If you would prefer, you can access the Shooting menu banks without pressing the MENU button. Instead, you can access the Shooting menu banks from the Information display edit screen (figure 3.1B).

Figure 3.1B – Accessing the Shooting menu banks with the info button

Combining Shooting Menu Banks and Custom Settings Banks

Can you see how flexible having these four Shooting menu banks will make your D800? You can create your own bank names and apply the underlying settings however you wish. If you want, you can match these Shooting menu banks to similarly named Custom settings banks, which allow you to set things like the Autofocus and Metering/exposure types. When the Shooting menu banks and Custom settings banks are combined in this manner, the D800 becomes a very powerful camera with strong flexibility to match different photographic needs and styles. There are *no* direct connections between the Shooting menu banks and Custom settings banks. I make my own mental connection by giving both similar names and then changing to them at the same time.

Use these steps to change Shooting menu banks quickly (figure 3.1B):

1. Press the info button twice (figure 3.1B, screen 1). This will cause the Information display edit screen to appear.
2. Scroll to the Shooting menu bank position and press the OK button (figure 3.1B, screen 2).
3. The Shooting menu bank screen will now appear, allowing you to change quickly to a different bank (figure 3.1B, screen 3). Notice the names of my fully configured Shooting menu banks.

Working with Shooting Menu Settings

Each of the settings mentioned in my list of banks are Shooting Menu settings. We will discuss each of them in this chapter. If you don't know where to find them, do not attempt to set up your own banks until you have read over this chapter. You may have a completely different idea on how to configure your banks. Think about the way you shoot, and then name and configure the banks accordingly.

To select a particular bank, simply go to *Shooting Menu > Shooting menu bank*, highlight a particular bank, and press the OK button. The letter for the bank should appear to the right of the Shooting menu bank, as seen in figure 3.1A, screen 1.

We're using Shooting menu bank A as our example and must now set up the camera functionality for this bank; there are 25 functions left to set. Let's scroll down in the Shooting Menu and configure each individual line item available there. They will each be saved as part of bank A, which we renamed and selected. Changes in one bank do not affect changes in another bank. Each bank is a standalone bank with separately stored function settings, with a few exceptions that affect all four Shooting menu banks at once, as follows:

- Multiple exposure settings
- Interval timer shooting settings
- Time-lapse photography settings
- Changes to White balance preset settings

If you change any of these settings, they will affect all four banks (A–D) simultaneously. Changing other settings affects only the bank your camera is currently using. Since each bank can be configured with most items having different settings, your D800 can act like four different cameras.

Extended Menu Banks

(User's Manual – Page 270)

Extended menu banks is a simple function that sounds complex. All it does is ask your camera to remember the last exposure mode you used in a particular bank (P, S, A, or M) and the aperture if you are using A or M or the shutter speed if you are using S or M. Here is how it works:

- **Scenario 1**: Let's say you are using bank A and the exposure mode is set to Aperture-priority (A) mode with an aperture setting of f/8. You now switch to bank B where you use Shutter-priority (S) mode for a while. Even if your camera is set to Shutter-priority in bank B, when you switch back to bank A, the camera remembers that you were previously using Aperture-priority mode and an aperture setting of f/8 and sets the camera back to those settings automatically.
- **Scenario 2**: You are using bank C and the exposure mode is set to Manual (M) with an aperture of f/11 and a shutter speed of 1/125s. Now you switch to bank D, which is using Programmed auto (P) mode. You shoot with bank D for a while, then switch back to bank C. The camera, upon entering bank C, remembers that you were using Manual mode with an aperture of f/11 and shutter speed of 1/125s previously and sets the camera back to those settings.
- **Scenario 3**: You are using bank B with the exposure mode set to Shutter-priority (S) and a shutter speed of 1/2000s because you are shooting an air show with flying airplanes. You decide to take a picture showing the crowd, so you switch quickly to bank A, which is using Aperture-priority mode. When you are done shooting the crowd, you switch back to bank B and the camera remembers that you were using Shutter-priority and a shutter speed of 1/2000s previously and sets the camera back to those settings. You continue shooting the air show.

With Extended menu banks enabled, your camera will remember the last exposure mode and related settings used for each bank. The following list shows which settings it remembers for each exposure mode selected:

- *Programmed auto (P) mode* – The camera will remember that you were using P or P* (flexible program) modes. Since P mode asks the camera to automatically adjust the aperture and shutter speed, it will *not* remember your previous aperture and shutter speed settings when you switch banks. However, if you have overridden P mode by placing the camera into flexible-program P* mode, the camera will remember that you were in P* mode and the aperture you were using when you switched away from the bank.
- *Shutter-priority (S) mode* – The camera will remember that you were using Shutter-priority mode and the shutter speed you last used before switching away from the bank.
- *Aperture-priority (A) mode* – The camera will remember that you were using Aperture-priority mode and the aperture you last used before switching away from the bank.
- *Manual (M) mode* – The camera will remember that you were using Manual mode and the shutter speed and aperture you last used before switching away from the bank.

The camera remembers the information about the mode and settings without you manually saving anything. When you switch away from a bank and then return to the bank, it will remember your previous settings without you doing anything more than having Extended menu banks set to On. If you turn Extended menu banks off, the camera will not remember any of your exposure mode, shutter speed, and aperture settings for each bank.

Use these steps to configure the Extended menu banks setting:

1. Select Extended menu banks from the Shooting Menu and scroll to the right (figure 3.2, screen 1).
2. Choose either On or Off from the menu (figure 3.2, screen 2).
3. Press the OK button to save the setting.

Figure 3.2 – Enabling or disabling Extended menu banks

Settings Recommendation: I leave this turned on because I find it to be quite convenient. Having the camera remember my last exposure mode setting lets me enter a familiar shooting environment when I return to a particular bank. If I used a certain exposure mode previously with that bank, the odds are very high that I will want to use similar settings in the future. If you do not want the camera to remember your previous exposure mode settings, leave this set to Off. It will not affect how the camera remembers any of the other Shooting Menu settings.

Storage Folder

(User's Manual – Page 271)

The D800 automatically creates a folder on its primary memory card called 100ND800. This folder can contain up to 999 images. If you want to store images in separate folders on the memory card, you might want to create a new folder, such as 101ND800 or 200ND800. Each folder you create can hold 999 images, and using *Storage folder*, you can select any folder as the default folder.

This is a good way to isolate certain types of images on a photographic outing. Maybe you'll put landscapes in folder 100ND800, and people shots in 101ND800. Whenever the camera senses that the current folder contains 999 images or when an image reaches a file number of 9999, a new folder is created, with the value of the first three digits of the folder name increased by one. If you are using a folder named 100ND800, the camera will automatically create a new folder called 101ND800 when you exceed 999 images or reach image number 9999 in folder 100ND800.

When manually creating folder names, you may want to leave room for the camera's automatic folder creation and naming. If you try to create a folder name that already exists, the camera doesn't give you a warning; it simply switches to the already existing folder. Let's look at how to create a new folder with a number of your choice, from 101 to 999 (101ND800 or 999ND800).

Figure 3.3A – Creating and numbering a new folder

Use these steps to create or select a folder with a number of your choice (figure 3.3A):

1. Select Storage folder from the Shooting Menu and scroll to the right (figure 3.3A, screen 1).
2. Choose Select folder by number and scroll to the right (figure 3.3A, screen 2).
3. You will now see a screen that allows you to enter a folder number between 100 and 999 (figure 3.3A, screen 3). Create your new number by scrolling up or down in any of the three available number positions. This number will have ND800 appended to it when you are done, and a new folder by that name will appear on the camera's current primary memory card. Notice the little folder at the point of the red arrow in screen 3. This little folder appears only when you have an existing folder with the number shown on the screen. Were I to change the number to 105, the little folder would disappear because my camera does not have a folder named 105ND800. If I actually tried to save the settings from screen 3, the camera would not create a new folder named 101ND800 because it clearly already exists. Instead the camera would simply switch to that folder.
4. Press the OK button to create the new folder or switch to an existing folder.

When you see a folder next to a folder number, as shown in figure 3.3A, screen 3, you should take note of how full the folder is. In screen 3, the camera indicates that there are existing files in the folder by showing it with a white filler. There are only three settings: empty (no white fill), partially full (partial white fill as in screen 3), and full (all white fill). If the folder contains fewer than 999 images, it is considered partially full. If it has 999 files, or a file numbered 9999, the folder will show as full.

You cannot create a folder with any number less than 100. Remember that the three-digit number you select will have ND800 appended to it, and the actual folder name will look something like 101ND800 when you have finished.

Once you have created a new folder, the camera will automatically switch to it. What if you want to simply start using an existing folder, choosing it from a list of folders instead of making a new one? The D800 makes that easy with the following screens and steps (figure 3.3B).

Figure 3.3B – Selecting an existing folder from the list of available folders

Use the following steps to choose an existing folder from a list of folders (figure 3.3B):

1. Select Storage folder from the Shooting Menu and scroll to the right (figure 3.3B, screen 1).
2. Choose Select folder from list and scroll to the right (figure 3.3B, screen 2).
3. Choose a folder from the list of current folders (figure 3.3B, screen 3). My camera happens to have three folders on it. If yours only has one, that is all you will see in screen 3 (most likely 100ND800).
4. Press the OK button and the camera will switch back to the Shooting Menu main screen, with the first three numbers of the selected folder showing next to Storage folder.

All images will now be saved to this folder until you exceed 999 images in the folder or manually change to another.

One note of caution: If you are using a folder named 999ND800 and the camera records the 999th image or if it records image number 9999, the Shutter-release button will be disabled until you change to a different folder. Normally, when those conditions occur, the camera increments the folder number by one and creates a new folder with the incremented number, and the next image simply goes into the new folder. However, if you are using folder number 999 (999ND800), the camera cannot create a new folder because it cannot increment larger than 999 on a folder number. Therefore, it locks the Shutter-release button until you remove the memory card containing folder 999ND800 or create a new folder manually. In my opinion, it is not wise to create a folder numbered 999, especially if you shoot a lot of images and may exceed 999 pictures in the folder.

Settings Recommendation: As memory cards get bigger and bigger, I can see a time when this functionality will become very important. Last year I shot around 125 GB of image files. With the newest memory cards now hitting 256 GB, I can foresee a time when the card(s) in my camera will become a year-long backup source. Of course, the image files are so much larger on this D800, with its medium-format resolution, that large-capacity memory cards are very welcome.

At the present time, I do not use the Storage folder functionality all that much, but I guarantee you I will in the near future. This is a good function to learn how to use!

File Naming

(User's Manual – Page 273)

File naming allows you to control the first three letters of the file name for each of your images. The default is DSC, but you can change it to any three alphanumeric characters provided by the camera.

The camera defaults to using the following file naming convention for your images:

- sRGB color space: **DSC_1234**
- Adobe RGB color space: **_DSC1234**

According to the color space you are using, the camera adds an underscore character to the end of the three DSC characters in sRGB or to the beginning in Adobe RGB.

I use this feature on my camera in a special way. Because the camera can count images in a sequence (see Custom setting d5) from 0001 to 9999, I use File naming to help me personalize my images. The camera cannot count images higher than 9999. Instead, it rolls back over to 0001 for the 10,000th image.

When I first got my D800, I changed the three default characters from DSC to 1DY. The 1 tells me how many times my camera has passed 9999 images, and DY are my initials, thereby helping me protect the copyright of my images in case they are ever stolen and misused.

Because the camera's image File number sequence counter rolls back over to 0001 when you exceed 9999 images, you need a way to keep from accidentally overwriting images from the first set of 9999 images you took. I use this method:

- First 9999 images: 1DY_0001 through 1DY_9999
- Second 9999 images: 2DY_0001 through 2DY_9999
- Third 9999 images: 3DY_0001 through 3DY_9999
- Fourth 9999 images: 4DY_0001 through 4DY_9999

See how simple that is. The listed numbers show a range of just under 40,000 images. Since the D800 is tested to the pro level of 200,000 images, you will surely need to use a counting system like this one.

My system works up to only 89991 images (9999 × 9). If you wanted to start your camera at 0 instead (0DY9999), you could count up to 99990 images.

If Nikon would ever give us just one extra digit in our image counter, we could count in sequences of just under 100,000 images instead of 10,000 images. I suppose that many of us will have traded on up to the next Nikon DSLR before we reach enough images so that this really becomes a constraint.

This is merely the way I'm using this useful feature in my D800. If my method doesn't work for you, you could use the three characters to classify your image names in all sorts of creative ways.

To rename your three custom characters, please refer to figure 3.4. This works similarly to the method for naming the Shooting menu banks discussed in the section **Shooting Menu Bank** at the beginning of this chapter (figure 3.1A), except that you have only uppercase characters and numbers from which to select.

Here are the steps to set up your custom file naming characters (figure 3.4):

1. Select File naming from the Shooting Menu and scroll to the right (figure 3.4, screen 1).

2. Figure 3.4, screen 2 shows the sample screen that lets you view the current formatting for file names. If you have changed the characters to something other than DSC, those characters will be shown in the sample file names below the File naming selection in screen 2.

3. Use the Multi selector to scroll through the numbers and letters to find the characters you want to use (figure 3.4, screen 3). Press the Multi selector center button to select and insert a character. You can move around within the three characters by holding down the checkered Thumbnail/Playback zoom out button and moving left or right with the Multi selector. Highlight a character to delete and the press the Delete button (garbage can) to remove it, or simply overwrite it with a new character.

4. Press the OK button to save your three new custom characters. They will now appear at the beginning of each new image file name as shown at the red arrow in figure 3.4, screen 4.

Figure 3.4 – File naming

File Number Sequence

Custom Setting Menu > d Shooting/display > d5 File number sequence controls the File number sequence. That function works along with File naming to let you control how your image files are named. If File number sequence is set to Off, the D800 will reset the four-digit number—after the first three custom characters in File naming—to 0001 each time you format your camera's memory card. I made sure File number sequence was set to On as soon as I got my camera so it would remember the sequence all the way up to 9999 images. The factory default is On for File number sequence, but I would check it just in case. I want to know exactly how many pictures I've taken over time. We'll talk more about File number sequence in the chapter titled **Custom Setting Menu**.

Settings Recommendation: We discussed how I use these three custom characters in the beginning of this section. You may want to use all three of your initials or some other numbers or letters. Some will even leave these three letters at their default of DSC. I recommend at least using your initials so that you can easily identify the images as yours. With my family of four Nikon shooters, it sure makes it easier for me! If you use my method, just be sure to watch for the images to roll over to 9999 so that you can rename the first character for the next sequence of 9999 images.

Primary Slot Selection

(User's Manual – Page 89)

Primary slot selection allows you to select which memory card (SD or CF) you want to use as the primary card for writing images and recording movies.

This function and the next, Secondary slot function, are concerned with where your camera stores its image files. If you're using two memory cards, an SD and CF, you'll need to set these two functions to control where files go and what happens when a card fills up.

You'll need to decide which card type you want to shoot with most often. If you have more of one type than the other, or simply like one card style better, this function will let you choose your favorite.

Figure 3.5 – Choosing the primary card slot

Here are the steps to select the primary card slot (figure 3.5):

1. Select Primary slot selection from the Shooting Menu and scroll to the right (figure 3.5, screen 1).
2. Choose your favorite card slot from the Primary slot selection screen. Your choices are SD card slot and CF card slot (figure 3.5, screen 2).
3. Press the OK button to lock in your choice.

Settings Recommendation: I happen to prefer the CF cards for my D800, merely because they seem more robust. Therefore, I set my primary slot to CF card slot. If you upgraded from a less costly DX Nikon DSLR, you may want to use the SD card slot as the primary slot because you'll probably have several SD cards from previous cameras. However, you may prefer the CF card type, especially if you previously used a D700 or will use the D800 as a backup to a D4/D3/D3s/D3x. You don't have to use both cards slots if you don't have one of the two types; the camera will work fine with just one card. If you have Primary slot selection set to the SD slot—with a CF card in the CF card slot—and then accidentally leave the SD card out of the camera, the camera is smart enough to use whatever card type it can find—in this case the CF card.

Secondary Slot Function

(User's Manual – Page 89)
The *Secondary slot function* is designed to let you do image flow control. You decide where and when images get written to the memory card combo. You can make the camera fill up one card and overflow onto the other when the first is full, write to both cards at the same time, or write a separate NEF (RAW) and JPEG image to each card.

Here is a deeper description of the three different ways you can set the Secondary slot function (figure 3.6):

- *Overflow* – Have you ever gotten the dreaded "Card full" message? Well, if you select Overflow, it will take a lot longer to get this message. Overflow writes all images to the card you have selected under Primary slot selection. Then when the primary card is full, the rest of the images are sent to the secondary card. The image number shown on the Control panel will go down as you take pictures and they are written to the primary card. When the image count hits zero, the camera will switch to the secondary card and the available image count number on the Control panel will increase to however many images will fit on the secondary card. It is a good idea, although not absolutely necessary, to use cards with a similar capacity when using this function. The camera will gradually fill up all available space on both cards as you take pictures.

- *Backup* – This function is a backup method for those shooting critical images. Every image you take is written to both the primary and secondary memory cards at the same time. You have an automatic backup system when you use the Backup function. If you are a computer geek (like me), you'll recognize this as RAID 1, or card mirroring. Because your camera is very much a computer, a function like this is great to have. Be sure that both cards are of equal capacity or that the secondary card is larger than the primary card when you use this function. Otherwise, you'll have reduced capacity shown for the primary card. The camera is required to write a duplicate image to each card, so the smallest card in the two slots sets the maximum capacity of the camera's storage.

- *RAW primary, JPEG secondary* – For those who like to shoot NEF (RAW) files, this function can save some time. You'll have a JPEG for immediate use and a RAW file for later post-processing. When you take a picture, the camera will write the RAW file to the primary card and a JPEG file to the secondary card. There is no choice in this arrangement—RAW always goes to primary and JPEG to secondary. Also, this function works as described only when you have *Shooting Menu > Image quality* set to some form of NEF (RAW) + JPEG. If you set Image quality to just NEF (RAW) or JPEG fine alone—instead of NEF (RAW) + JPEG fine—the camera will simply write a duplicate file to both cards instead of a RAW on one and a JPEG on the other. In other words, if Image quality is set to NEF (RAW), the camera will write two NEF files; if set to JPEG, two JPG files; and if set to TIFF (RGB), two TIFF files—one on each card. Basically, unless you set *Shooting Menu > Image quality* to some form of NEF (RAW) + JPEG, this function acts like the Backup function mentioned previously.

Figure 3.6 – Choosing the Secondary slot function

Here are the steps to select a Secondary slot function (figure 3.6):

1. Select Secondary slot function from the Shooting Menu and scroll to the right (figure 3.6, screen 1).
2. Choose one of the three selections from the Secondary slot function screen (figure 3.6, screen 2).
3. Press the OK button to lock it in for use.

Settings Recommendation: When I'm out shooting commerically or for any type of photography where maximum image capacity is of primary importance, I select Overflow. This causes the camera to fill up the primary card and then automatically switch to the secondary card for increased image storage. If I'm shooting images that I cannot afford to lose, such as at a unique event like a wedding or graduation, I'll often use the Backup function for automatic backup of every image.

If I want both a RAW and JPEG file, I'll use the RAW primary, JPEG secondary function. This lets me have the best of both worlds when card capacity is not worrisome. This too allows a measure of redundancy, like the Backup method. In a sense, you are still backing up the same image, they are just in different formats—one RAW and one JPEG. RAW primary, JPEG secondary also benefits you by providing a JPEG for immediate use and a RAW file for later post-processing. I use each of these three selections from time to time, but my favorite is Overflow.

Image Quality

(User's Manual – Pages 56, 68)

Image quality is simply the type of image your camera can create. You can shoot several distinct image formats with your D800 (NEF/RAW, JPEG, and TIFF). We'll examine each format in detail and discuss the pros and cons of each. When we are done, you will have a better understanding of the formats and can choose an appropriate one for each of your styles of shooting. Following are the screens and steps to select an Image quality setting.

Figure 3.7A – Choosing an Image quality setting

Use these steps to select an image quality via the Shooting Menu (figure 3.7A):

1. Select Image quality from the Shooting Menu and scroll to the right (figure 3.1, screen 1).
2. Choose one of the eight Image quality types listed. Figure 3.7B, screen 2 shows JPEG fine as the selected format.
3. Press the OK button to select the format.

You can also use the QUAL button above the Release mode dial to set the image quality. This can be much faster than using the menus.

Figure 3.7B – Setting the Image quality with external controls

Use these steps to select an image quality with external camera controls (figure 3.7B):

1. Hold down the QUAL button (figure 3.7B, number 1).
2. Look at the Control panel to see the Image quality values (figure 3.7B, number 2).
3. Rotate the rear Main command dial to change the Image quality setting (i.e., RAW, TIFF, FINE, NORM, or BASIC). The FINE, NORM, and BASIC settings all refer to JPEG formats, with each having a stronger compression ratio. Again, I had FINE selected, as shown at the red number 2 on the Control panel.
4. Release the QUAL button to lock in the modified Image quality settings.

The camera supports the following eight Image quality types (figure 3.7A, screen 2):

- NEF (RAW) + JPEG fine
- NEF (RAW) + JPEG normal
- NEF (RAW) + JPEG basic
- NEF (RAW)
- TIFF (RGB)
- JPEG fine
- JPEG normal
- JPEG basic

New DSLR users may feel unsure about which format is best to use. In fact, it is a good idea to use all three formats at different times. We will briefly discuss the basics of the formats, as a nice review for all shooters:

- **NEF (RAW)** – The 12- or 14-bit NEF (RAW) format is designed for those photographers who have the time and inclination to work on, or post-process, each image. The camera merely captures light information when shooting in RAW but does not process the data into a usable image. It is up to you to develop a workflow that allows finalizing the image within the computer. The reward for this extra work is the highest possible image quality that can be achieved with the camera. **Note:** The D800 also has a NEF (RAW) processing function on the Retouch Menu that allows you to convert to JPEG from a RAW file on the memory card. A D800 NEF (RAW) is in the 40 to 50 MB range when Lossless compressed NEF files are used. Uncompressed, a NEF file is around 70 MB in size.
- **JPEG** – The 8-bit JPEG format is for those times when you must have a finished image right now! The image comes out of the camera in ready-to-use form. JPEG is a lossy format, however, and it throws away a considerable amount of image data when the camera converts the 12- or 14-bit RAW file down to 8 bits. The image data that is left is of the highest quality and is ready to use. However, a JPEG cannot be modified and resaved more than a time or two without JPEG compression losses damaging the image. Use JPEG when you have to use the

image right away or when you do not have the time or inclination to work with RAW images. JPEG files are smaller than NEF files by far, with an average size for a JPEG file being from 4 to 25 MB, according to the complexity of the scene and compression ratio used. The camera uses the following compression ratios for a JPEG file: JPEG fine = 1:4, JPEG normal = 1:8, and JPEG basic = 1:16. The smallest Large (L) JPEG file I've seen out of my own D800 is about 4 MB (bland subject) and the largest is about 24 MB (very complex subject).

- **TIFF (RGB)** – The 8-bit TIFF file type, as created by the camera, is basically like a JPEG with no compression routines applied. The image file can be used immediately without conversion. The 12- to 14-bit RAW file is converted into an 8-bit file, throwing away considerable data, so TIFF is initially a lossy format, losing from 4 to 6 bits of image data. However, once the file is created, you can modify and resave it without compressing the data or losing any more image detail. If you are in a situation that requires an immediate-use file and a JPEG won't do because image modification is required, and you have no interest in or experience with NEF (RAW) files, the TIFF format is a good candidate. The biggest drawback to a TIFF file is its large file size. An average TIFF file is a little over 100 MB in size. It won't take many of those to fill up a memory card or two.

Combined NEF and JPEG Shooting (Two Images at Once)

Some shooters use the three storage modes at the top of the list in figure 3.7A, screen 2, whereby the D800 takes two images at the same time—NEF (RAW) + JPEG fine, normal, or basic. This gives you the best of both worlds in that the camera captures a NEF file and creates an additional JPEG file each time you press the Shutter-release button.

Here are the first three modes found at the top of the *Shooting Menu > Image quality* setting list:

- NEF (RAW) + JPEG fine
- NEF (RAW) + JPEG normal
- NEF (RAW) + JPEG basic

You can set the *Shooting Menu > Secondary slot function* to write the NEF (RAW) file to one card and the JPEG to the other.

You can use the NEF (RAW) file to store all the image data and later process it into a masterpiece, or you can use the JPEG file immediately with no adjustment.

There is no need to go into any amount of detail about these modes since the NEF (RAW) + JPEG modes have the same features as each individual mode. In other words, the RAW file in NEF (RAW) + JPEG mode is just like a normal RAW file if you were using the standalone NEF (RAW) mode. The JPEG in the NEF (RAW) + JPEG mode is just like a standalone JPEG fine, normal, or basic image without the NEF (RAW) file.

Settings Recommendation: Which format do I prefer? Why, NEF (RAW), of course! However, it does require a bit of a commitment to shoot in this format. The camera is simply an image-capturing device, and you are the image manipulator. You decide the final format, compression ratios, sizes, color balances, and so on instead of letting Nikon's software engineers decide. You create the final image when you post-process it with your computer and save it in a final format, such as JPEG. Your RAW file stays untouched and ready for reuse.

By shooting in NEF (RAW) mode, you have the absolute best image your camera can produce. It is not modified by the camera's software and is ready for your personal touch. No camera processing allowed!

If you get nothing else from this section of the chapter, remember this: When your camera is processing the images in *any* way, it is modifying or throwing away image data. There is only a finite amount of data for each image that can be stored on your camera, and later on the computer. With JPEG or TIFF mode, your camera optimizes the image according to the assumptions recorded in its memory. Data is being thrown away permanently, in varying amounts.

If you want to keep *all* of the image data that was recorded with your images, you must store your originals in RAW format. Otherwise, you'll never again be able to access that original data to change how the image looks. A RAW file is the closest thing to a film negative or a transparency that your digital camera can make.

That's important if you would like to modify the image later. If you are concerned with maximum quality, you should shoot and store your images in RAW format. Later, when you have the urge to make another masterpiece out of the original RAW image file, you'll have all of the original picture data intact for the highest-quality image.

I shoot in NEF (RAW) format for my most important work and JPEG fine for the rest. Some people find that JPEG fine is sufficient for everything they shoot. Those individuals generally do not like working with files in-computer or do not have time. NEF (RAW) files are not yet usable images and must be converted to another format. You'll use both RAW and JPEG, I'm sure. The format you use most often will be controlled by your time constraints and digital workflow. Most of us use TIFF only when we convert a RAW file in-computer into that format. I rarely, if ever, shoot images in TIFF. There are just not enough benefits in TIFF files to deal with the larger files and slower transfer speeds, in my opinion. Shoot RAW for the best and JPEG for the rest!

Image Size

(User's Manual – Page 87)

Image size lets you shoot with your camera set to various megapixel (M) ratings. The default Image size setting for the D800 is Large FX, or 36.2 M (36.2 megapixels). You can change this rating in quite a few ways, based on the Image area settings discussed in the next section.

Image size applies only to images captured in TIFF (RGB) or JPEG fine/normal/basic modes. If you're shooting with your camera in any of the NEF (RAW) + JPEG modes, it applies only to the JPEG image in the pair. Image size does not apply to a NEF (RAW) image.

This setting is relatively simple because it just affects the megapixel size of the image. Following are the screens and steps to select the Image size.

Figure 3.8A – Choosing an Image size setting

Use these steps to choose an Image size setting (figure 3.8A):

1. Select Image size from the Shooting Menu and scroll to the right (figure 3.8A, screen 1).
2. Choose one of the three Image size settings listed. Large is selected in figure 3.8A, screen 2.
3. Press the OK button to choose the size.

You can also choose the Image size by using external camera controls, as shown in figure 3.8B. Use the following steps:

1. Hold down the QUAL button (figure 3.8B, number 1).
2. Look at the Control panel to see the Image size values (figure 3.8B, number 2).
3. Rotate the front Sub-command dial (figure 3.8, number 3) to change the Image size setting (L, M, or S). Large (L) is selected at number 2.
4. Release the QUAL button to lock in the modified Image size settings.

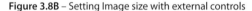

Figure 3.8B – Setting Image size with external controls

I normally shoot at the largest possible size and crop the image if needed. However, there are reasons to shoot at the lower megapixel levels, such as when a smaller resolution image is all that will ever be needed or if card space is at an absolute premium. Even medium and small size D800 images are plenty big!

Setting Image quality to JPEG basic, Image size to Small, and JPEG compression to Size priority allows the camera to capture 19,000 images on a 32-gigabyte card. The pictures are 9.0 MP in resolution and are compressed to the maximum, but there are a large number of them. If I were to set off today to walk completely around the earth and I had only one 32-gigabyte memory card to take with me, well, my camera would give me 19K images on one card—so I could at least document my trip well.

Taking Still Images in Movie Live View

If you want to take still images that closely match the format of an HDTV or modern flat-screen computer monitor, you can do it by taking still images in Movie live view mode's 16:9 aspect ratio. FX and DX mode still images created in Movie live view have the following Image sizes:

FX format in Movie live view mode (16:9)
- Large – 6270×3776 – 23.7 M
- Medium – 5040×2832 – 14.3 M
- Small – 3360×1888 – 6.3 M

DX format in Movie live view mode (16:9)
- Large – 4800×2704 – 12.9 M
- Medium – 3600×2024 – 7.3 M
- Small – 2400×1352 – 3.2 M

Settings Recommendation: You'll get the best images at 36.2 M (FX), of course. Using the smaller sizes won't affect the quality of a smaller print, but it will limit your ability to enlarge your images. I recommend leaving your camera set to Large unless you have a specific reason to shoot smaller images or you have low-capacity memory cards, which is anything under 16 GB with the D800.

The D800 gives you several image formats that match various industry standards. I recommend trying the different formats by adjusting the Image area (next section). The maximum image size is provided by the FX Image area setting. However, the FX image size from the D800 is so large (Native FX = 16x24 inches, or 40x60 centimeters, at 300 dpi) that you will have room to use various image crops. If you don't like any of the provided Image area formats, you can crop to your own specifications in your computer. Having such a large image size gives us maximum flexibility. Cropping is back!

Image Area

(User's Manual – Page 79)

Image area is a convenient built-in crop of the FX image to a smaller size. Where the FX (3:2) "area" is 36×24 mm, the camera can provide three additional image areas: 1.2x–30×20 mm, DX (1.5x)–24×16 mm, and 5:4–30×24 mm. If you need these particular image areas, you will be familiar with the industry-standard formats they provide.

The camera can automatically switch to DX mode when it detects that you have mounted a DX lens. Or, you can set it so that it stays in the FX format (or the other three formats) unless you select DX. You will use Auto DX crop to make that decision. If Auto DX crop is set to On, the camera will automatically switch formats when you mount a DX lens. Setting Auto DX crop to Off means the camera will ignore the lens you have mounted and stay in its current format. Following are the screens and steps for changing Auto DX crop (factory default is On; figure 3.9A).

Figure 3.9A – Choosing Auto DX crop

Use the following steps to select Auto DX crop (figure 3.9A):

1. Select Image area from the Shooting Menu and scroll to the right (figure 3.9A, screen 1).
2. Choose Auto DX crop and scroll to the right (figure 3.9A, screen 2).
3. Select On or Off.
4. Press the OK button to save the setting.

Now, let's take a look at the various Image area formats by examining a series of pictures I took in all four formats. These images are of a Kodak Brownie Hawkeye like the one my mother gave me in 1968, getting me started on a lifetime of photography. I did not vary the camera position so you can see how the change in image areas affects the size (crop) of the subject.

Figure 3.9B – The four Image area formats

Following is a detailed list of specifications for the four available image areas, including sensor format crop (mm), Image size, pixel count, and megapixel (M) rating:

FX (1.0x at 3:2) Image area (36×24 mm):
- Large – 7360×4912 – 36.2 M
- Medium – 5520×3680 – 20.3 M
- Small – 3680×2456 – 9.0 M

1.2x Image area (30×20 mm):
- Large – 6144×4080 – 25.1 M
- Medium – 4608×3056 – 14.1 M
- Small – 3072×2040 – 6.3 M

DX (1.5x at 3:2) Image area (24×16 mm):

- Large – 4800×3200 – 15.4 M
- Medium – 3600×2400 – 8.6 M
- Small – 2400×1600 – 3.8 M

5:4 Image area (30×24 mm):

- Large – 6144×4912 – 30.2 M
- Medium – 4608×3680 – 17.0 M
- Small – 3072×2456 – 7.5 M

Now, let's see how to select one of these Image area formats for those times you need to vary the Image area crop.

Figure 3.9C – Choosing an Image area format

Use the following steps to select one of the Image area formats (figure 3.9C):

1. Choose Image area from the Shooting Menu and scroll to the right (figure 3.9C, screen 1).
2. Select Choose image area and scroll to the right (figure 3.9C, screen 2).
3. Select one of the four image area crops. FX is selected in figure 3.9C, screen 3.
4. Press the OK button to save the Image area setting.

Note: You can also assign Image area to a camera button, such as the Fn, Preview, or AE-L/AF-L button. Then you can adjust the area on the fly without using the Shooting Menu. We will consider how to make the assignment in the next chapter, **Custom Setting Menu**, in the sections for Custom settings f4, f5, and f6.

Settings Recommendation: Being a nature shooter, I normally leave my camera set to FX, its largest image area. If I need a little extra reach, I may switch the camera to DX mode for convenience, although I could also simply crop the image later in the computer. These Image area formats are merely for convenience, to prevent you from having to manually crop the image later. Each Image area format is designed to match a standard someone needs to use. If you need any of these standards, you have them available. I choose the largest (FX). I can always crop later if I need something special.

JPEG Compression

(User's Manual – Page 86)

JPEG compression allows you to fine-tune the level of compression in your JPEG images. The JPEG format is always a compressed format. The Image quality settings for JPEG images include fine, normal, and basic. Each of these settings provides a certain level of compression of the picture's file size, as we've discussed briefly in a previous section. In review, here are the compression specifications:

- **JPEG fine** – 1:4 compression ratio (25 percent of original size)
- **JPEG normal** – 1:8 compression ratio (12.5 percent of original size)
- **JPEG basic** – 1:16 compression ratio (6.25 percent of original size)

The compression ratios listed are best-case scenarios. JPEG files will normally vary in size when the subject of one image is more complex than that of another. For instance, if you take a picture of a tree with lots of leaves and bark against a cloudy blue sky, JPEG's compression formatting has a lot more work to do than if you take a picture of a red balloon on a plain white background. All those little details in the leaves of the tree cause lots of color contrast changes, so the JPEG file size will naturally be bigger for the complex image. In the balloon image, there is little detail in the balloon or the background, so the JPEG file size will normally be much smaller. The less detail in an image, the more efficient JPEG compression is.

What if you want all of your JPEG images to be the same relative size? Or, what if file size doesn't matter as much to you, while quality is very important? That's what the JPEG compression menu allows you to control, the final quality of your JPEG images, by varying the amount of compression. Let's examine the two settings:

- *Size priority* – This compression setting is designed to keep all your JPEG files at a certain uniform size. The size will vary according to whether you selected JPEG fine, normal, or basic in the Image quality menu. Image quality controls the regular, everyday compression level of the JPEG file, while Size priority tweaks it even more. How does it work?

  With Size priority enabled, the camera's software tries to minimize file sizes, keeping them as uniform as possible while still maintaining good quality. If a JPEG file has lots of fine detail, it will require more compression than a file with less detail in order to maintain the same file size. By enabling this function, you are telling the camera that it has permission to throw away however much image data it must to get each file to a somewhat uniform size. How uniform? I did a test where I shot a relatively bland subject and the file size was 8.5 MB. Then I shot a medium-complexity subject and got a file size of 10.0 MB. Finally, I shot a very complex subject and the file size was 13.0 MB. So, the camera maintained a range from 8.5 to 13.0 MB on subjects with varying complexity. This type of compression could lower the quality of a complex landscape shot much more than a shot of a person standing by a blank wall. Size priority instructs the camera to sacrifice image quality—if necessary—to keep the file size fairly consistent. Use this function only for images that will not be used for fine art purposes. Otherwise, your image may not look as good as it could.

- *Optimal quality* – This setting really doesn't do much extra to your images; the camera simply uses less compression on complex subjects. In effect, you are telling the camera to go ahead and vary the file size so that image quality will be good for any subject, complex or plain. Instead of increasing compression to make an image of a complex nature scene fit a certain file size—as Size priority does—the camera compresses the image only to the standard compression level based on the Image quality setting you selected (JPEG fine, normal, or basic). Less image data is thrown away, so the image quality is higher. However, file size will vary significantly, depending on the complexity of the subject. How much variation? I shot the same subjects as before with Optimal quality enabled this time. On the plain subject, the file size was 9.7 MB. On the medium-complexity subject, the file size was 11.4 MB. Finally, on the complex subject, the file size jumped up to 24.2 MB. Whoa! As you know, 9.7 MB to 24.2 MB is quite a variation in file size. Clearly, the camera is not compressing the images with complex subjects nearly as much as when Size priority is enabled. Image quality will be higher on complex subjects, and on low-detail subjects, the quality will be similar to what it would be with Size priority enabled. Nikon states that the camera's internal memory buffer capacity is reduced when you use Optimal quality, as would be expected with the larger file sizes.

Why not test this for yourself and see what file sizes you get between the two modes? Now, let's examine how to select one of the JPEG compression types.

Figure 3.10 – Choosing a JPEG compression type

Here are the steps to choose a JPEG compression type (figure 3.10):

1. Select JPEG compression from the Shooting Menu and scroll to the right (figure 3.10, screen 1).
2. Choose Size priority or Optimal quality (figure 3.10, screen 2).
3. Press the OK button to choose the compression type.

Settings Recommendation: I normally use Optimal quality when I shoot JPEGs since the whole JPEG concept is one of lossy image compression and I don't want the potentially heavier compression of Size priority to lower the image quality. Size priority just adds more potential image quality loss, so I tend to avoid it. The only time I use Size priority is when I'm shooting snapshots. When I'm at a party taking pictures of friends having a good time, I'm not creating fine art and won't make an enlargement greater than an 8×10-inch (20×25 cm) size. In that case, I don't worry about extra compression. In fact, I might just welcome it to avoid storing larger-than-needed images on my computer's hard drive. Using Size priority lets the camera use fairly consistent files sizes. When consistent file size is not critical but maximum JPEG quality is, I use Optimal quality.

NEF (RAW) Recording

(User's Manual – Page 86)
NEF (RAW) recording is composed of two menu choices—Type and NEF (RAW) bit depth. Type is concerned with RAW image compression, while bit depth deals with color quality. We will look into both of these choices and see how our photography can benefit from them.

Type
In previous sections, we discussed how JPEG files have different levels of compression that vary the size of a finished image file. NEF (RAW) also has compression choices, though not as many. The nice thing about the RAW compression methods is that they don't throw away massive amounts of image data like JPEG compression does. NEF (RAW) is not considered a lossy format because the file stays complete, with virtually all the image data your camera captured.

One of the compression methods, called Compressed, is very slightly lossy. The other, Lossless compressed, keeps all the image data intact. Let's discuss how each of the available compression methods works.

There are three NEF (RAW) formats available, although you only see a single NEF (RAW) selection on the Image quality menu. Once you've selected NEF (RAW), you'll need to use *Shooting Menu > NEF (RAW) recording > Type* to select one of the three NEF (RAW) compression types, as follows:

- NEF (RAW) Lossless compressed (20–40% size reduction)
- NEF (RAW) Compressed (40–55% size reduction)
- NEF (RAW) Uncompressed (No compression – full file size)

Here are some details on each of these choices:

- **NEF (RAW) Lossless compressed** – The factory default for the NEF (RAW) format is NEF (RAW) Lossless compressed. According to Nikon, this compression will not affect image quality because it is a reversible compression algorithm. Because Lossless compressed shrinks the stored file size by 20 to 40 percent—with no image data loss—it's my favorite compression method to use. It works somewhat like a ZIP file on your computer—it compresses the file but allows you to use it later with all the data still available.

- **NEF (RAW) Compressed** – Before the newest generation of cameras, including the D800, this mode was known as "visually lossless." The image is compressed and the size is reduced by 35 to 55 percent, depending on the amount of detail in the image. There is a small amount of data loss involved in this compression method. Most people won't be able to see the loss because it doesn't affect the image visually. I've never really seen any loss in my images using this method. However, I've read that some have noticed slightly less highlight detail. Nikon says that this is a nonreversible compression, so once you've taken an image using this mode, any small amount of data loss is permanent. If this concerns you, then use the Lossless compressed method discussed previously. It won't compress the image quite as much (20–40 percent) but is guaranteed by Nikon to be a reversible compression that in no way affects the image.

- **NEF (RAW) Uncompressed** – No compression is applied to the image. The main drawback to this mode is that your images will be quite large. Each will be in the 70-megabyte range, so it will take larger storage media to contain your images. With Lossless compressed available, I feel that this method is semi-obsolete.

Figure 3.11A – RAW (NEF) recording – Type

Here are the steps to select one of the NEF (RAW) compression types (figure 3.11A):

1. Select NEF (RAW) recording from the Shooting Menu and scroll to the right (figure 3.11A, screen 1).
2. Select Type and scroll to the right (figure 3.11A, screen 2).
3. Select one of the three compression methods. I chose Lossless compressed (figure 3.11A, screen 3).
4. Press the OK button to save your selection.

3

> ## Card Capacity Reporting
>
> Why does your memory card's remaining image capacity seem to stay the same in NEF Lossless compressed and Compressed modes as in Uncompressed mode? Shouldn't it show lots more capacity in the compressed modes since they make the image smaller by 20 to 55 percent? The reason your camera does not show any increased image capacity on the Control panel in the compressed modes is because the D800 has no idea how well it will be able to compress a particular image.
>
> An image with a large amount of blank space, such as an expanse of sky, will compress a lot more efficiently than an image of a forest with lots of detail. The camera shows a certain amount of image storage capacity in NEF (RAW) modes—a little over 400 images with a 32-gigabyte card. You'll find that in the compressed modes, the D800 does not decrease the image capacity by one for each picture taken, as it does in Uncompressed mode.
>
> This means that the camera will decrease the number of available images only every two or three shots, according to how well it was able to compress each image. When the card is full, it might have more than twice as many images stored as it initially reported it could hold. Basically, your D800 deliberately underreports storage capacity when you are shooting in either of the NEF (RAW) compressed modes.

Settings Recommendation: I shoot in Lossless compressed RAW most of the time because I'm concerned with maximum quality along with good storage capacity. The Lossless compressed method makes the most sense to me. It gives me a file size significantly smaller (45–50 MB) than the Uncompressed setting's results (70+ MB). I do not use Compressed simply because Lossless compressed is available. Even though I might not be able to see any image quality loss, it bothers me that it is there, if only slightly. The 10 or 15 percent extra compression is not worth the potential small data loss to me. If I were running out of card space but wanted to keep shooting RAW, I might consider changing to Compressed temporarily. Otherwise, it's Lossless compressed for me!

NEF (RAW) Bit Depth

NEF (RAW) bit depth is a special feature for those of us concerned with capturing the best color in our images. The D800 has three color channels: one for red, another for green, and the final one for blue. It combines those color channels to form all the colors you see in your images. You may have seen the acronym RGB in your camera study. RGB stands for red, green, blue—the three color channels. Let's talk about how bit depth, or the number of colors per channel, can make your pictures even better.

With the D800, you can select the bit depth stored in an image. More bit depth equals potentially better color gradations. The default for the D800 is 14-bit (16,384 colors for each RGB channel). Or you can switch it to 12-bit (4,096 colors per RGB channel). The more color bit depth in your images, the better they can look, if there is a lot of color in your subject in the first place.

Why would anyone set their camera to a lower bit depth and reduce its color capacity and smoothness? Older DSLRs used to suffer with a slower frame rate when shooting bursts of images in continuous high-speed (CH) shooting mode. The D800 does not have a serious problem with significantly slower frame rates from 14-bit shooting.

However, a 14-bit image file is bigger and will make the internal buffer space in the camera hold less. Also, the additional file size from the greater color capacity in a 14-bit image can lead to a little slower image writing to the memory cards and transfer to the computer later.

Therefore, people who are concerned about maximum camera speed will often shoot in 12-bit mode. A photographer shooting a football game will not have as great a concern for maximum color depth; he wants shooting speed to capture *the* shot. On the other hand, a landscape artist wants as much color depth as her pictures can contain. She wants beautiful color gradations and maximum color fidelity.

Most serious sports shooters will opt for a camera like the Nikon D3 or D4 with extremely high frame rates. I would think that the majority of D800 owners are more concerned with the biggest and best image they can make or they would have purchased a different camera.

At the time this book was being written, DxO Labs rated the sensor in the D800 with a new highest score ever of 95. This score exeeded digital medium-format cameras costing many thousands of dollars more than the D800. Speaking of the sensor, DxO reported, "…the D800's Overall score is the best that has ever been achieved…" Additionally, when discussing the massive dynamic light range the D800 can record (14.4 EV), DxO said, "Here again, the D800 achieves the best score ever measured."

That's pretty impressive! Who wants to waste a sensor with that much quality by lowering its color capacity? Not me! If you do not fully understand the reasoning behind NEF (RAW) bit depth, please take a look at the next section, **Channel and Bit Depth Discussion**.

As mentioned earlier, the D800 has the following two bit depths available:

- **12-bit** – 4,096 colors per channel
- **14-bit** – 16,384 colors per channel

Figure 3.11B – NEF (RAW) bit depth

Here are the steps to choose a bit depth (figure 3.11B):

1. Select NEF (RAW) recording from the Shooting Menu and scroll to the right (figure 3.11B, screen 1).
2. Select NEF (RAW) bit depth and scroll to the right (figure 3.11B, screen 2).
3. Select 12-bit or 14-bit from the NEF (RAW) bit depth menu. I left my D800 at the 14-bit factory default (figure 3.11B, screen 3).
4. Press the OK button to save your selection.

Settings Recommendation: Which bit depth setting is best? Well, I always use 14-bit because I want all the color my camera can capture for the best pictures later. If you read my tutorial on bit depth in the next section, you'll understand why I feel that way. However, my style of shooting is nature oriented, so I am concerned with capturing every last drop of color I can.

There are some disadvantages to using the 14-bit mode. If you choose 14-bit, be aware that your file sizes will be 10 to 20 percent larger than they would be in 12-bit. There is a lot more color information being stored, after all. There's another drawback to the 14-bit mode that some may find objectionable. The internal camera buffer that stores images taken and being written to the memory card is about 21 frames with 12-bit Lossless compressed NEF (RAW) files. However, that drops to 17 frames if you shoot in 14-bit mode.

If you're a sports or action shooter, you might not want to use the 14-bit mode. If you're a nature shooter and don't need the highest frame rates and biggest internal buffer storage, 14-bit is best for the image.

Channel and Bit Depth Discussion

Many experienced D800 users may already have a handle on this bit-depth information. However, I decided to include this short tutorial in the book because it is very important information to a digital photographer. This information is a good review for most of us.

An image from your camera is an RGB image. As mentioned previously, RGB stands for red, green, blue. Each of the colors has its own "channel." If you are shooting in 12-bit mode, your camera will record up to 4,096 colors for each channel. Therefore, there will be up to 4,096 different reds, 4,096 different greens, and 4,096 different blues. Lots of color! In fact, almost 69,000,000,000 (69 billion) colors (4,096 × 4,096 × 4,096).

However, if you set your camera to 14-bit mode, instead of just 4,096 different colors per channel, the camera can now store 16,384 different colors in each channel. Wow! That's quite a lot more color—almost 4,400,000,000,000 (4.4 trillion) shades (16,384 × 16,384 × 16,384).

Is that important? Well, it can be, because the more color information you have available, the better the image. I always use the 14-bit mode now that it's available. That allows for smoother color changes when a large range of color is actually in the image. I like that!

Of course, once you save your image as a JPEG or TIFF, most of those colors are compressed, or thrown away. Shooting a TIFF or JPEG image in-camera (as opposed to a RAW image) means that the D800 converts from a 12- or 14-bit RGB file down to an 8-bit file. An 8-bit file can hold only 256 different colors per RGB channel, or a little over 16,700,000 colors. That sounds like quite a lot of color, and it is. However, when you compare the 16.7 million colors in a camera-created 8-bit JPEG or TIFF image to the potential 4.4 trillion colors in a 14-bit NEF (RAW) file, the 8-bit color potential is relatively small in comparison.

That's why I always shoot in RAW, so that later I can make full use of all those potential extra colors to create a different look for the same image if I'd like.

If you shoot RAW and in 14-bit, you can later save the file as a 16-bit TIFF and not lose any color information. The D800 will not create a 16-bit TIFF; it is limited to an 8-bit TIFF. Remember, 16-bit files can contain 65,536 different colors in each of the RGB channels. Lots of people save their files as 16-bit TIFFs when post-processing RAW files. TIFF is a known and safe industry-standard format that will fully contain all image color information from a RAW file. However, a 16-bit TIFF file from a D800 image is well over 200 MB in size. That's about four or five images per gigabyte of storage space. I will often post-process my images and save the intermediate results as a 16-bit TIFF file. However, once I have saved the post-processed TIFF file as the final JPEG file for image use, I delete the TIFF. The RAW file remains untouched and ready for reuse.

Lossless compressed NEF (RAW) is the best way to store your D800 images long term, at only about 45 to 50 MB each, with all potential color information included in the file.

White Balance

(User's Manual – Page 145)

White balance is designed to let you capture accurate colors in each of your camera's RGB color channels. Your images can reflect realistic colors if you understand how to use the White balance settings.

This may be one of the most important things to learn about digital photography. If you don't understand how white balance works, you'll have a hard time when you want consistent color across a number of images.

In this chapter we will look at white balance briefly and learn only how to select the various White balance settings. This is such an important concept to understand that an entire chapter—titled **White Balance**—is devoted to this subject. Please read that chapter very carefully. It is important that you thoroughly learn to control the White balance settings. A lot of what you'll do in computer post-processing requires a good understanding of white balance control.

Many people leave their cameras set to Auto White balance (figure 3.12A). This works fine most of the time because the camera is quite capable of rendering accurate color. However, it's hard to get exactly the same white balance in each consecutive picture when you are using Auto mode. The camera has to make a new white balance decision for each picture in Auto. This can cause the white balance to vary from picture to picture.

For many of us this isn't a problem. However, if you are shooting in a studio for a product shot, I'm sure your client will want the pictures to be the same color as the product. White balance lets you control that carefully when needed.

Figure 3.12A – Choosing a White balance setting

The steps to select a White balance setting are as follows:

1. Select White balance from the Shooting Menu and scroll to the right (figure 3.12A, screen 1).
2. Choose a White balance type, such as Auto or Flash, from the menu and scroll to the right (figure 3.12A, screen 2).
3. If you choose Auto, Fluorescent, Choose color temp., or Preset manual you will need to select from an intermediate screen, shown in figure 3.12A, screen 3. The other settings will skip screen 3 and go directly to screen 4. Auto presents two settings: Auto1 – Normal and Auto2 – Keep warm lighting colors. Fluorescent presents seven different types of fluorescent lighting. Choose color temp. lets you select a color temperature manually from a range of 2500 K (cool) to 10000 K (warm). Preset manual (PRE) shows the stored white balance memory locations d-0 through d-4 and allows you to use one of them. If you are unsure which is best, choose Auto1 – Normal for now. The chapter titled **White Balance** will explain how to use all these settings; therefore, consider this section an introduction to how to choose a white balance.
4. If you scroll to the right instead of pressing the OK button, as shown in figure 3.12A, screen 4, you'll arrive at the White balance fine-tuning screen. With this screen you can adjust how this particular White balance setting records color by introducing a color bias toward green, yellow, blue, or magenta. You do this by moving the little black square in the middle of the color box toward the edges of the box in any direction. If you make a mistake, simply move the black square to the middle of the color box. Most people do not change this setting.
5. After you have finished adjusting (or not) the colors, press the OK button to save your setting. Most people press the OK button as soon as they see the fine-tuning screen so they do not change the default settings for this particular White balance setting.

Figure 3.12B – Setting White balance with external camera controls

You'll also find it convenient and even faster to change the White balance settings by using external camera controls. Here are the steps to do so (figure 3.12B):

1. Hold down the WB button above the Release mode dial (figure 3.12B, number 1).
2. Turn the rear Main command dial (figure 3.12B, number 2) as you watch the WB icons change on the Control panel (figure 3.12B, number 3).
3. Release the WB button to lock in your choice.

Settings Recommendation: Until you've read the chapter on white balance, I suggest that you leave the camera set to Auto White balance. However, please do take the time to understand this setting by reading the dedicated chapter carefully. Understanding white balance is especially important if you plan on shooting JPEGs regularly.

Set Picture Control

(User's Manual – Page 163)

Set Picture Control allows you to choose a Picture Control for a shooting session. Nikon's Picture Control system lets you control how your image appears in several ways. Each control has a specific effect on the image's appearance. If you shot film a few years ago, you will remember that each film type has a distinct look. No two films produce color that looks the same.

In today's digital photography world, Picture Controls give you the ability to impart a specific look to your images. You can use Picture Controls as they are provided from the factory, or you can fine-tune Sharpening, Contrast, Brightness, Saturation, and Hue.

We'll discuss how to fine-tune a Nikon Picture Control later in this section. In the next section, **Manage Picture Control**, we'll discuss how to save a modified Picture Control under your own Custom Picture Control name. You can create up to nine Custom Picture Controls.

I'll refer to Picture Controls included in the camera as Nikon Picture Controls because that's how Nikon refers to them. You may also hear them called Original Picture Controls in some Nikon literature. If you modify and save a Nikon Picture Control under a new name, it becomes a Custom Picture Control. I'll also use the generic name of Picture Control when referring to any of them.

The cool thing about Picture Controls is that they are shareable. If you tweak a Nikon Picture Control and save it under a name of your choice, you can then share your control with others. Compatible cameras, software, and other devices can use these controls to maintain the look you want from the time you press the Shutter-release button until you print the picture.

Now, let's look closer at the Picture Control system. As shown in figure 3.13A, screen 2, there is a series of Picture Control selections that modify how your D800 captures an image. They are as follows:

- SD – Standard
- NL – Neutral
- VI – Vivid
- MC – Monochrome
- PT – Portrait
- LS – Landscape

Each of these settings has a different and variable combination of the following settings:

- Sharpening
- Contrast
- Brightness
- Saturation
- Hue
- Filter Effects   (applies only to MC – Monochrome)
- Toning   (applies only to MC – Monochrome)

You can select one of the controls (SD, NL, VI, MC, PT, or LS) and leave the settings at the factory default, or you can modify the settings (figure 3.13A, screen 3) and completely change how the D800 captures the image.

Note: If you are shooting in NEF (RAW) mode, the D800 does not apply these settings directly to the image as it does with a JPEG or TIFF, but it stores the settings with the image, allowing you to change to a different Picture Control later, in-computer using Nikon Capture NX 2 or Nikon View NX 2, if you so desire.

Figure 3.13A – Choosing a Nikon Picture Control from the menus

Here are the steps to choose a Picture Control from the Shooting Menu (figure 3.13A).

1. Select Set Picture Control from the Shooting Menu and scroll to the right (figure 3.13A, screen 1).
2. Choose one of the Nikon Picture Controls from the Set Picture Control screen (figure 3.13A, screen 2). At this point, you can simply press the OK button and the control you've chosen will be available for immediate use. It will show up as a two-letter name in the Shooting Menu next to Set Picture Control. You'll see this in figure 3.13A, screen 1, where SD shows next to Set Picture Control. You can also modify the currently highlighted control by scrolling to the right instead of pressing the OK button.
3. Scroll to the right when using the Set Picture Control menu shown in figure 3.13A, screen 2, and your camera will present the Picture Control fine-tuning screen, as shown in figure 3.13A, screen 3. You can adjust the Sharpening, Contrast, Brightness, Saturation, or Hue by scrolling up or down to select a line and then right or left (+/-) to change the value of that line item. Please notice the Quick adjust selection at the top of figure 3.13A, screen 3. By highlighting Quick adjust and scrolling left or right, you can emphasize or de-emphasize the current control settings by +2/-2 steps. By using Quick adjust instead of adjusting the individual settings, such as Sharpening or Brightness, you may tend to keep the control more in balance while making the effect of the control stronger or weaker.

If you do choose to modify the control using Quick adjust or with the individual line item settings (Sharpness, etc.), it is *not* yet a Custom Picture Control because you have not saved it under a new name. Instead, it is merely a modified Nikon Picture Control. We'll discuss how to name and save your own Custom Picture Controls in the upcoming section **Manage Picture Control**.

Figure 3.13B shows an asterisk after the Vivid control (VI* - Vivid*) in both Shooting Menu screens (see red arrows). This asterisk appears after you have made a modification to any of the Picture Control's inner settings (Contrast, etc.). The asterisk will go away if you set the control back to its factory settings.

Figure 3.13B – An adjusted Nikon Picture Control (see asterisks)

Because many of us change Picture Controls often, Nikon has given us a handy external button to quickly open the Picture Control menu (figure 3.13C).

Figure 3.13C – Using the Picture Control button to open Set Picture Control

Use the following steps to set a Picture Control by using an external camera control button:

1. As shown in figure 3.13C, you can press the Picture Control button, which is a combo button that has the rather long full name of Protect/Picture Control/ Help button (as evidenced by the other symbols above it). If there is nothing showing on the camera's Monitor and you press the Picture Control button, the menu shown in figure 3.13C, screen 2, will open, giving you immediate access to the Picture Controls.
2. Choose one of the Picture Controls and press the OK button.

Protect/Picture Control/ Help button details: If you press the button shown in figure 3.13C, screen 1, when a picture is showing on the Monitor, the camera will protect that picture from deletion (Protect button). When you press the button with nothing on the Monitor, as mentioned in step 1 of the preceding steps, the Set Picture Control screen opens (Picture Control Button). Finally, if you press the button when a menu item is showing, it will open a Help screen describing the functionality of that setting (Help button).

Let's examine the basic functionality of each of the Picture Controls.

Examining Picture Controls

Now it's time to break out my red, green, and blue (RGB) Lego blocks as sample subjects for Picture Control Sharpening, Contrast, Brightness, Saturation, and Hue variation comparisons.

Figure 3.13D provides a look at the differences in color saturation and shadow with the various controls. Due to limitations in printing, it may be hard to see the variations, but they are clearly visible in a picture. Saturation and Contrast depth increase within these Picture Control choices, in this order: NL (low) > SD (medium) > VI (high). PT appears to be a modified form of the NL control, and LS seems to be a modified form of the VI control.

Figure 3.13D – Sample color variations among Nikon Picture Controls

The following is an overview of what Nikon says about Picture Controls and what I see in my sample images taken with the various controls (figure 3.13D).

- **SD**, or **Standard**, is Nikon's recommendation for getting "balanced" results. Nikon recommends SD for most general situations. Use this if you want a balanced image and do not want to post-process it. It has what Nikon calls "standard image processing." The SD control provides what I would call medium saturation, with darker shadows to add contrast. If I were shooting JPEG images in a studio or during an event, I would seriously consider using the SD control. I would compare this setting to Fuji Provia or Kodak Kodachrome 64 slide films.
- **NL**, or **Neutral**, is best for an image that will be extensively post-processed in a computer. It has the widest available dynamic range of any of the Picture Controls. It too is a balanced image setting, but it applies minimal camera processing, so you'll have room to do more with the image during post-processing. NL has less saturation and weaker shadows, so the image will be less contrasty (wider dynamic range). The effects of the NL and SD controls are harder to see in figure 3.13D because there's not a marked difference. However, the NL control will give you extra dynamic range in each image due to more open shadows and slightly less saturated colors. If you've ever shot with Fuji NPS film or Kodak Portra negative films and liked them, you'll like this control.
- **VI**, or **Vivid**, is for those of us who love Fuji Velvia slide film! This setting places emphasis on saturating primary colors for intense imagery. The contrast is higher for striking shadow contrast, and the sharpness is higher too. If you are shooting JPEGs and want to imitate a saturated transparency film like Velvia, this mode is for you! If you look at the red block in the VI example in figure 3.13D, you'll see that it's pushed into deep saturation, almost to the point of oversaturation. Plus, the greens and blues are extra strong. That means your nature shots will look saturated and contrasty. Be careful when you are shooting on a high-contrast

day, such as in direct sunshine in the summer. If you use the VI control under these conditions, you may find that your images are too high in contrast. It may be better to back off to the SD or NL control when shooting in bright sunshine. Of course, with the higher inherent dynamic range in the D800, this is not as much of an issue as with previous Nikons. You will need to experiment with this to see what I mean. On a cloudy or foggy low-contrast day, when the shadows are weak, you may find that the VI control adds pleasing saturation and contrast to the image.

- **MC**, or **Monochrome**, allows the black-and-white lovers among us to shoot in toned black-and-white. The MC control basically removes the color by desaturation. It's still an RGB color image, but the colors have become levels of gray. It does not look the same as black-and-white film, in my opinion. The blacks are not as deep, and the whites are not as bright. To me, it seems that the MC control is fairly low contrast, and that's where the problem lies. Good black-and-white images should have bright whites and deep blacks. To get images like that from a digital camera, you'll have to manually work with the image in a graphics program like Photoshop, using the Channel Mixer (see the upcoming sidebar **Note on Photoshop for D800 Black-and-White Images**). However, if you want to experiment with black-and-white photography, this gives you a good starting point. Additionally, there are two extra settings in the MC control that allow you to experiment with Filter effects and Toning. We'll look at these settings in the upcoming section called **MC Picture Control Filter Effects and Toning**. The MC control creates a look that is somewhat like Kodak Plus-X Pan negative film, with blacks that are not as deep.

- **PT**, or **Portrait**, is a control that "lends a natural texture and rounded feel to the skin of portrait subjects" (Nikon's description). I've taken numerous images with the PT control and shot the same images with the NL control. The results are very similar. I'm sure that Nikon has included some software enhancements specifically for skin tones in this control, so I would defintely use this control for portraits of people. The results from the PT control look a bit like smooth Kodak Portra or Fuji NPS negative film.

- **LS**, or **Landscape**, is a control that "produces vibrant landscape and cityscapes," according to Nikon. That sounds like the VI control to me. I shot a series of images using both the LS and VI controls and got similar results. Compared to the VI control, the LS control seemed to have slightly less saturation in the reds and a tiny bit more saturation in the greens. The blues stayed about the same. It seems that Nikon has created the LS control to be similar to, but not quite as drastic as, the VI control. In my test images, the LS control created smoother transitions in color. However, there was so little difference between the two controls that you'd have to compare the images side by side to notice. Maybe this control is meant to be more natural than the super-saturated VI control. It will certainly improve the look of your landscape images. The look of this control is somewhere between Fuji Provia and Velvia. You get great saturation and contrast, with emphasis on the greens and blues in natural settings.

MC Picture Control Filter Effects and Toning

The Monochrome, or MC, Picture Control has some added features that are enjoyable for those who love black-and-white photography. As shown in figure 3.13E, there are Filter effects that simulate the effect of yellow (Y), orange (O), red (R), and green (G) filters on a monochrome image. Yellow, orange, and red (Y, O, R) change the contrast of the sky in black-and-white images. Green (G) is often used in black-and-white portrait work to change the appearance of skin tones. You do not have to go buy filters for your lenses; they are included in your D800.

Figure 3.13E – Monochrome Filter effects screen

Figure 3.13F – Monochrome Filter effects samples

In figure 3.13F, you'll see an unretouched sample of a color SD Picture Control (for comparison) alongside the five flavors of Monochrome (MC) Filter effects. It is rather interesting how the yellow, orange, red, and green filters affect the RGB Lego blocks.

The Filter effects settings are more pronounced than those you would achieve using a glass filter attached to your lens. Now, let's examine the MC Toning effects.

Figure 3.13G – Monochrome Toning screen and samples

As displayed in figure 3.13G, there are 10 variable Toning effects available—B&W (standard black-and-white), Sepia, Cyanotype, Red, Yellow, Green, Blue Green, Blue, Purple Blue, and Red Purple. Each of the Toning effects is variable within itself, and you can adjust the saturation of the individual tones. In figure 3.13G, I cranked them all the way up to the maximum setting, which tends to oversaturate the toning color. I wanted you to clearly see the maximum potential of the Toning settings. Compare how the RGB blocks look under the various toning settings. The red block is on top, green in the middle, and blue on the bottom. Clearly the toned blocks all look similar in brightness (with only minor variation) to the B&W blocks, showing that the underlying image for each of the color tones is simply black-and-white.

You can shoot a basic black-and-white image, use filters to change how colors appear, or tone the image in experimental ways. Can you see the potential for a lot of fun with these tones?

In the Monochrome menu screen at the top left of figure 3.13G, notice that to the right of the word *Toning* there is a row of 10 tiny rectangles with arrowhead pointers on each end. The first rectangle is half black and half white. That is the normal black-and-white (B&W) selection, and it has no extra toning. Next to that you'll see a golden-brown rectangle. That is the Sepia toning effect (selected). To the right of that is the bluish Cyanotype effect. The smaller rectangles that follow the first three selections are the other available colors for toning. Each color has seven saturation settings available in the little green bar below (next to Sepia, 4 in figure 3.13G). This bar allows you to select the depth of saturation for each of the colors. Sepia is set to the fourth saturation position in figure 3.13G.

Use the Multi selector to move around in the Filter effects and Toning settings. Press the OK button to select one of them.

Picture Control Grid Screen

Each Picture Control has a *Picture Control Grid* that allows you to compare the selected control to the other Nikon Picture Controls. By using the screens shown in figure 3.13H and then holding down the Thumbnail/Playback zoom out button (red arrow in figure 3.13H, screen 2), you can access the Picture Control Grid for each Picture Control (figure 3.13I).

Figure 3.13H – Accessing the Picture Control Grid

Figure 3.13I – Picture Control Grid

When you make a modification to the Saturation or Contrast setting of a particular control, you'll see the position of that control change on the Picture Control Grid. Figure 3.13I, screen 1, shows a Picture Control Grid in its unchanged condition, with all controls set to factory default.

In figure 3.13I, screen 2, the saturation is different. You can see how the S*—representing the modified Standard Picture Control Saturation setting—has moved from its starting location (figure 3.13I, screen 1) to its new location (red arrow in screen 2). Its original location is shown as a grayed-out S.

In figure 3.13I, screen 3, you can see that I've changed the Contrast setting. The S* moved from the location at the grayed-out S to its new location at the red arrow.

The Picture Control Grid allows you to see how each control compares to the others, before and after you've made a change. Once a change has been made, you'll see a gray square that marks the original location of the control and a yellow square that marks its new location. The new location will have the same name as the previous location, except you'll see an asterisk after it.

You scroll up or down with the Multi selector to move among the Picture Controls. You can see the little letters and what they represent in the list on the right side of each screen in figure 3.13I. This is a useful tool for comparing the relative Saturation and Contrast settings of each of the Picture Controls to the others.

Resetting a Nikon Picture Control

If you modify the Nikon Picture Controls, you may do what I did and forget what the original settings were when you want to change them back.

Worry not! Anytime you've modified a control, you can reset it by pressing the garbage can Delete button while you have the Picture Control adjustment screen open. The adjustment screen is the one with the settings for things like Sharpening and Contrast (figure 3.13J, screen 1). You'll notice the red arrow in screen 1 pointing to the asterisk. If you will remember, an asterisk next to the name of a Picture Control means one or more of its settings have been modified.

Figure 3.13J – Resetting a Nikon Picture Control

Instead of trying to remember which setting was modified, it may be easier to simply reset the control. Here are the steps:

1. Open to the screen for adjusting the Picture Control you want to reset (figure 3.13J, screen 1).
2. Press the Delete button (garbage can) and a message will appear saying, *Selected Picture Control will be reset to the default settings. OK?* Select Yes and press the OK button (figure 3.13J, screen 2).
3. The Picture Control will now display in its factory default setup (figure 3.13J, screen 3).
4. Press the OK Button to save and select the newly reset control.

> **Note on Photoshop for D800 Black-and-White Images**
>
> Since the RGB color channels are still intact in the camera's black-and-white image, you can use Photoshop's Channel Mixer *Image Menu > Adjustments > Channel Mixer…* to manipulate the color channels and improve the blacks and whites. If you use Photoshop to play with the channels, be sure to check the Monochrome box on the Channel Mixer window. If you don't, you'll simply add color back into your black-and-white image. The fact that you must check the Monochrome box proves that a D800 black-and-white image is really just a color image with the colors desaturated to levels of gray. The good thing about this is that you now have room to play with the three color channels, similar to how you use filters when shooting black-and-white film. You can add or subtract contrast by moving the channel sliders until you are happy with the results. There is a lot of discussion of these techniques on the Internet. Why not join the Nikonians.org forum to discuss how to best achieve beautiful black-and-white images? Look for the Nikonians Gold Membership 50% off coupon in the front of this book.

I'm sure you will agree that Nikon's Picture Control system is very powerful and flexible, especially for those who like to shoot mostly JPEG images. Now, let's see how to go about managing your own Custom Picture Controls in our next section, **Manage Picture Control**.

Manage Picture Control

(User's Manual – Page 169)

The *Manage Picture Control* function is designed to allow you to create and store Custom Picture Control settings for future use. You can take an existing Nikon Picture Control (SD, NL, VI, MC, PT, or LS), included with the camera, make modifications to it, and then rename it. If you modify a Picture Control using the Set Picture Control function discussed in the previous section, you simply create a one-off setting. If you'd like to go further and create your own named Custom Picture Controls, the D800 is happy to oblige.

There are four choices on the Manage Picture Control screen:

* Save/edit
* Rename
* Delete
* Load/save

Let's look at each of these settings and see how we can manage our Picture Controls effectively.

Save/Edit a Custom Picture Control

Figure 3.14A – Save/edit a Custom Picture Control

There are six screens used to save/edit a Nikon Picture Control (figure 3.14A)—storing the results for later use as a Custom Picture Control. Here are the steps to edit and save a Picture Control with a modified setting:

1. Select Manage Picture Control from the Shooting Menu and scroll to the right (figure 3.14A, screen 1).
2. Highlight Save/edit and scroll to the right (figure 3.14A, screen 2).
3. Choose a Picture Control that you want to use as a base for your new settings and then scroll to the right (figure 3.14A, screen 3). I am modifying the SD – Standard Picture Control and will save it under a different name.
4. Make your adjustments to Sharpening, Contrast, and so forth. I simply used the Quick adjust setting and added +1 to it, increasing the overall effect of Standard by 1 (out of 2). When you have modified the control in a way that makes it yours, press the OK button (figure 3.14A, screen 4). If you want to abandon your changes and start over, you can simply press the Delete button (garbage can) and it will reset the control to factory specs.
5. Select one of nine storage areas named C-1 to C-9 and scroll to the right (figure 3.14A, screen 5). In figure 3.14A, screen 5, they are all currently marked as Unused. I can save as many as nine different Custom Picture Controls here for later selection with Set Picture Control.

6. You will now see the Rename screen, which works just like the other screens you have used to rename things. Type in a new name by selecting characters from the list at the top of the screen and pressing the Multi selector center button to choose the highlighted character (figure 3.14A, screen 6). To correct an error, hold down the Thumbnail/Playback zoom out button and use the Multi selector to move back and forth along the field that contains the new name. The camera will create a default name for you by appending a dash and two numbers at the end of the current control name. I left it at the default of Standard–02.

7. Press the OK button when you have entered the name of your Custom Picture Control.

Figure 3.14B – Identifying the base of a Custom Picture Control

Once you have created and saved a Custom Picture Control, you can still tell which control was used as its base, just in case you name it in a way that does not suggest its origins. Notice the red arrow in the upper-right corner of the screen in figure 3.14B. This is the control we just created in the previous steps (Standard–02) and it is derived from an SD Nikon Picture Control, as shown by the SD label at which the arrow is pointing.

   Your camera is now set to your Custom Picture Control. You switch between your Custom Picture Controls and the basic Nikon Picture Controls by using Set Picture Control (see previous section titled **Set Picture Control**). In other words, each of your newly named Custom Picture Controls will appear in the Set Picture Control menu for later selection.

   Now, let's look at how to rename an existing Custom Picture Control.

Rename a Custom Picture Control

If you decide to rename an existing Custom Picture Control, you can do so with the following steps (figure 3.14C):

1. Select Manage Picture Control from the Shooting Menu and scroll to the right (figure 3.14C, screen 1).
2. Select Rename and scroll to the right (figure 3.14C, screen 2).

3. Select one of your Custom Picture Controls from the list (C-1 to C-9) and scroll to the right (figure 3.14C, screen 3). I selected to rename STANDARD-02. This is the Custom Picture Control we created in the preceding section.

4. You will now be presented with the Rename screen. To create a different name, hold down the Thumbnail/Playback zoom out button and use the Multi selector to scroll back and forth within the old name. When you have the small gray cursor positioned over a character, you can delete that character with the garbage can Delete button. To insert a new character, position the yellow cursor in the character list above and press the Multi selector center button. The character that is under the yellow cursor will appear on the name line below, at the position of the gray cursor. If there is already a character under the gray cursor, it will be pushed to the right. Please limit the name to a maximum of 19 characters (figure 3.14C, screen 4). I renamed the STANDARD-02 Custom Picture Control STANDARD-EX2.

5. Press the OK button when you have completed the new name.

Figure 3.14C – Rename a Custom Picture Control

Note: You can have more than one control with exactly the same name in your list of Custom Picture Controls. The camera does not get confused because each control has a different location (C-1 to C-9) to keep it separate from the rest. However, I don't suggest that you give several custom controls the same name. How would you tell them apart?

When a Custom Picture Control is no longer needed, you can easily delete it.

Delete a Custom Picture Control

You cannot delete a Nikon Picture Control (SD, NL, VI, MC, PT, or LS). In fact, they don't even appear in any of the Manage Picture Control menu screens.

However, you can delete one or more of your Custom Picture Controls with the following screens and steps:

Figure 3.14D – Delete a Custom Picture Control

1. Select Manage Picture Control from the Shooting Menu and scroll to the right (figure 3.14D, screen 1).
2. Select Delete from the Manage Picture Control screen and scroll to the right (figure 3.14D, screen 2).
3. Select one of your nine available Custom Picture Controls and scroll to the right (figure 3.14D, screen 3). I selected VIVID-WOW for deletion.
4. Choose Yes at the Delete Picture Control? prompt (figure 3.14D, screen 4).
5. Press the OK button and the Custom Picture Control will be deleted from your camera.

Now, let's move to our last menu selection from the Manage Picture Control screen, Load/save.

Load/Save a Custom Picture Control

There are three parts to the Load/save function. They allow you to copy Custom Picture Controls to and from the memory card or delete them from the card.

If you have two memory cards in the camera, the D800 will automatically choose the one assigned as Primary card slot when you save a custom control. You cannot choose to write to the Secondary card slot. However, you could write to the Secondary slot by removing the Primary card, leaving the camera no choice but to write to the only card it can find. (Use *Shooting Menu > Primary slot selection* to set one of the memory card slots to primary).

Figure 3.14E – Load/save a Custom Picture Control

Here are the three selections on the Load/save menu, as shown in figure 3.14E, screen 3:

- **Copy to camera** – Loads Custom Picture Controls from the memory card into your camera. You can store up to nine controls in your camera's nine available memory locations (C1–C9).
- **Delete from card** – Displays a list of any Custom Picture Controls found on the memory card. You can selectively delete them.
- **Copy to card** – Allows you to copy your carefully crafted Custom Picture Controls (C1–C9) from your camera to a memory card. You can then share them with others. The camera will display up to 99 control locations (01–99) on any single memory card.

Let's examine each of these selections and see how best to use them.

Copy to Camera

Figure 3.14F – Manage Picture Control – Copy to camera

You can use the *Copy to camera* function to copy Custom Picture Controls from your camera's memory card to the camera's Set Picture Control menu. Once you have transferred a Custom Picture Control from your memory card to your camera, it will show up in the *Shooting Menu > Set Picture Control* menu.

Here are the steps to copy a Custom Picture Control from the memory card to the camera itself (figure 3.14F):

1. Figure 3.14F continues from the last screen shown in figure 3.14E (Load/save on the Manage Picture Control menu). Choose Copy to camera and scroll to the right (figure 3.14F, screen 1).

2. You will be presented with the list of Custom Picture Controls that are currently on the memory card (figure 3.14F, screen 2). If there are no controls on the memory card, the camera will display a screen that says, *No Picture Control file found on memory card.* Figure 3.14F, screen 2, shows two controls—STANDARD-EX2 and STANDARD-EX3. Select a control from the list and press the OK button. (If you scroll to the right instead, you will be able to examine and adjust the control's settings before saving it to your camera [figure 3.14F, screen 3]. If you don't want to modify it, simply press the OK button.)

3. You will now see the Manage Picture Control Save as menu, which lists any Custom Picture Controls already in your camera (figure 3.14F, screen 4). Select one of the Unused memory locations and press the OK button.

Figure 3.14G – Manage Picture Control – Choose a new name (or Rename)

4. You'll now be presented with the Rename screen, just in case you want to change the name of the Custom Picture Control. If you don't want to change the name, simply press the OK button and the custom control will be added to your camera's Set Picture Control menu. It is okay to have multiple controls with exactly the same name. The camera keeps each control separate in its list of controls (C-1 to C-9). However, I always rename them to prevent future confusion. To create a different name, hold down the Thumbnail/Playback zoom out button and use the Multi selector to scroll back and forth within the old name. Once you have the small gray cursor positioned over a character, you can delete it with the garbage can Delete button. To insert a new character, position the yellow cursor in the character list above and press the Multi selector center button.

The character that is under the yellow cursor will appear on the name line below, at the position of the gray cursor. If there is already a character under the gray cursor, it will be pushed to the right. Please limit the name to a maximum of 19 characters. Press the OK button when you have completed the new name.

You can also create Custom Picture Controls in programs like Nikon Capture NX 2, which uses its Picture Control Utility, and load them into your camera using the preceding four steps.

Delete from Card

Once you've finished loading Custom Picture Controls or optional Nikon Picture Controls to your camera, you may be ready to delete a control or two from the memory card. You could format the memory card, but that will blow away all images and Picture Controls on the card. A less drastic method that allows you to be more selective in removing Picture Controls is the *Delete from card* function.

Figure 3.14H – Manage Picture Control – Delete from card

Here are the steps used to remove Custom Picture Controls from your camera's memory card (figure 3.14H):

1. Figure 3.14H continues where figure 3.14E left off. Choose Delete from card from the Load/save menu and scroll to the right (figure 3.14H, screen 1).
2. Choose one of the Custom Picture Controls that you want to delete (figure 3.14H, screen 2). I chose STANDARD-EX2. You can confirm that you are deleting the correct control by scrolling to the right, which gives you the fine-tuning screen with current adjustments for that control (figure 3.14H, screen 3). If you are sure that this is the control you want to delete, move on to the next step by pressing the OK button.

3. You will be shown a screen that asks, *Delete Picture Control?* Choose either Yes or No (figure 3.14H, screen 4). If you choose Yes, the Picture Control will be deleted from the memory card. If you choose No, you will return to the previous screen.

4. Press the OK button to execute your choice.

Copy to Card

After you create up to nine Custom Picture Controls using the instructions in the last few sections, you can use the *Copy to card* function to save them to a memory card. Once they are on a memory card, you can share your custom controls with friends who have compatible Nikon cameras.

Figure 3.14I – Manage Picture Control – Copy to card

When your Custom Picture Controls are ready to go, use the following steps to copy them to a memory card (figure 3.14I):

1. Figure 3.14I continues where figure 3.14E left off. Choose Copy to card from the Load/save menu and scroll to the right (figure 3.14I, screen 1).

2. Select one of your current Custom Picture Controls from the Copy to card menu and scroll to the right (figure 3.14I, screen 2).

3. Now you'll use the Choose destination menu to select the location in which you want to save the custom control (figure 3.14I, screen 3). You have 99 choices; select any Unused location. We previously deleted STANDARD-EX2 from the memory card, leaving card destination number 01 marked as Unused. Just to show that you can save to any of the 99 destination locations, I chose 03 instead of 01.

4. Press the OK button and you'll briefly see a screen that says, *Data saved to memory card*. Your Custom Picture Control is now ready to distribute to the world or load onto another of your compatible Nikon cameras.

Settings Recommendation: To help you understand Nikon Picture Controls even better, please download the **Nikon Picture Control Reference** PDF file from one of our downloadable resources web pages:

http://www.nikonians.org/NikonD800
http://rockynook.com/NikonD800

This document describes Picture Controls—with lots of pictures—to help you see the range of control you can achieve. It's a 24-page, 4.9 MB file named PicCon.pdf. I really enjoyed reading it because it explains Nikon Picture Controls well and even mentions software that will work with them. You'll need Adobe Reader, which you can download for free from **www.Adobe.com**, to read PDF files.

Where Is the Custom Control Stored on the Memory Card?

If you take the time to look at the contents of your camera's memory card with your computer once you've saved a Custom Picture Control, you'll find a new folder called NIKON with a subfolder called CUSTOMPC. This folder contains any Custom Picture Controls you might have saved, each with a filename ending in ".NCP." For instance, the STANDARD-EX4 Custom Picture Control we saved to the memory card in destination 03 is saved to the memory card as PICCON03.NCP in the CUSTOMPC subfolder. If I had used the first destination location (01), the filename would have been PICCON01.NCP. Therefore, you should realize that the memory card destination locations 01–99 are actually individual files in the CUSTOMPC folder, with a range of file names from PICCON01.NCP to PICCON99.NCP. Now you can access the saved custom controls for sharing or for backup to your computer.

Color Space

(User's Manual – Page 274)

Color spaces are an interesting and important part of digital photography. They help your images fit into a much broader range of imaging devices. Software, printers, monitors, and other devices recognize which Color space is attached to your image and use it, along with other color profiles, to help balance the image to the correct output colors for the device in use. The two Color spaces available on the Nikon D800—sRGB and Adobe RGB—each have a different gamut, or range of color. We'll discuss which might be better after we look into how to select one of the Color spaces.

Figure 3.15A – Choosing a Color space

Here's how to select your favorite Color space (figure 3.15A):

1. Choose Color space from the Shooting Menu and scroll to the right (figure 3.15A, screen 1).
2. Select the Color space setting that you want to use, keeping in mind that Adobe RGB has a larger color gamut (figure 3.15A, screen 2).
3. Press the OK button to lock in your choice.

You can also use the info button to open the Information display edit screen and select the Color space without drilling down in menus.

Figure 3.15B – Choosing a Color space

Use these steps to change Color space quickly (figure 3.15B):

1. Press the info button twice (figure 3.15B, screen 1).
2. This will cause the Information display edit screen to appear. Scroll to the Color space position and press the OK button (figure 3.15B, screen 2).
3. The Color space screen will appear, allowing you to change quickly to a different Color space setting (figure 3.15B, screen 3).

Now, let's look a little more deeply into how Color space works.

Which Color Space Is Best Technically?

There is a large color space used by the graphics industry called CIELAB (figure 3.15C). This particular color space approximates human vision. Adobe RGB covers about 50 percent of the CIELAB color space, while sRGB uses only 35 percent. In other words, Adobe RGB has a wider gamut. That means Adobe RGB gives your images access to significantly higher levels of color, especially cyans and greens.

Figure 3.15C – Color space graphs

Another important consideration for those who will be sending their work to companies that use offset printing—such as book and magazine publishers—is that Adobe RGB maps very well to the CMYK offset printing process. If you are shooting commercial work, you may want to seriously consider Adobe RGB. Stock photo shooters are nearly always required to shoot in Adobe RGB.

Once a JPEG file is created, in-camera or in-computer, the color gamut for both Adobe RGB and sRGB is compressed into the same number of color levels. A JPEG has only 256 levels for each of its red, green, and blue (RGB) channels. However, since Adobe RGB takes its colors from a wider spectrum, you will have a better representation of reality when there are lots of colors in your image.

If you shoot in RAW format a lot, you may want to consider using Adobe RGB to store the maximum number of colors in your image files for later reuse. Remember that a NEF (RAW) image file can contain 4,096 levels of color per RGB channel in 12-bit mode and 16,384 levels in 14-bit mode—instead of the 8-bit JPEG's 256 levels. Using Adobe RGB makes a lot of sense in NEF (RAW) mode because of its capacity to contain more colors as a base storage medium.

There are some drawbacks to using Adobe RGB, though. The sRGB color space is widely used in printing and display devices. Even many local labs print using sRGB because so many point-and-shoot digital camera users bring their pictures to them in that format. If you try to print directly to some ink-jet printers using the Adobe RGB color space, the colors may not be as brilliant as with sRGB. If you aren't going to modify your images in-computer and plan on printing them directly from your camera, you may want to use sRGB. If you shoot JPEGs for computer display only or for Internet usage, it might be better to stay with sRGB for everyday shooting.

If you are a RAW shooter and regularly post-process your images, you should consider using Adobe RGB. You will have a wider gamut of colors to work with and can make your images the best they can be. Later, you can convert your carefully crafted images to print with a good color profile and get great results from ink-jet printers and other printing devices.

So, here's a rough way to look at it:

- Many JPEG shooters use sRGB.
- Many RAW shooters use Adobe RGB.

These are not hard-and-fast rules but many people follow them, according to their style of shooting. I shoot RAW a lot, so I often use Adobe RGB. If you are shooting for money, such as for stock images, most places expect that you'll be using Adobe RGB. It has more colors, so it's the quality standard for commercial printing.

Technical Note: If you print to devices that do not support color management, use ExifPrint, or print directly on some household printers or at superstore kiosk printers, the print's colors may not be as vivid when using Adobe RGB. JPEG pictures taken in Adobe RGB color space are DCF compliant. Applications and devices that support the DCF protocol will select the correct color space automatically. If you shoot in TIFF, the camera will imbed an ICC color profile when you shoot in Adobe RGB. Applications and devices that support color management will automatically select the correct color space setting when using the TIFF file. It is a good idea to familiarize yourself with the capabilities of the device you are about to use so you can determine its color space capabilities. Nikon View NX 2 (included with camera) and Capture NX 2 automatically select the correct color space when opening your pictures. Make sure you are running version 2.3.0 or later for each of the programs.

Settings Recommendation: I use Adobe RGB most of the time because I shoot a lot of nature with a wide range of color. I want color that's as accurate as my camera will give me. Adobe RGB has a wider range of colors, so it can be more accurate when a wide range of colors is present in my subject. If you are shooting Optimal quality JPEGs for commercial purposes, I would still carefully consider using Adobe RGB. Even with a JPEG's limited color capacity, the colors in the JPEG represent a broader range of color when you use Adobe RGB. However, if you are just shooting JPEG snapshots, there's no need to worry about this. Leave the camera set to sRGB and have fun.

Active D-Lighting

(User's Manual – Page 174)

Active D-Lighting is used to help control contrast in your images. Often, the range of light around the subject is broader than your camera's sensor can capture fully. Although the D800 has 14.4 EVs (stops) of dynamic range, it is still possible for the range of light in some situations to exceed the range of the sensor's light capturing capability. Or, you may just want to have less image contrast.

The D800 allows you to "D-Light" the image and bring out additional shadow detail, or in other words, lower the image contrast. This extends the dynamic range by opening up the shadows and protecting the highlights. One of the penalties of using Active D-Lighting could be additional noise in shadow details; however, the D800 has excellent noise control, so this is less of a problem than with other cameras.

Active D-Lighting has these six settings:

- Auto
- Extra High
- High
- Normal
- Low
- Off (no Active D-Lighting)

Figure 3.16A – Choosing an Active D-Lighting level

Here are the steps to choose an Active D-Lighting level (figure 3.16A):

1. Choose Active D-Lighting from the Shooting Menu and scroll to the right (figure 3.16A, screen 1).
2. Select one of the Active D-Lighting levels (figure 3.16A, screen 2). Refer to figure 3.16C to see how each level affects the image.
3. Press the OK button to save your setting.

Additionally, you can open the Active D-Lighting menu without using the Shooting Menu directly. Instead, you can press the info button twice and select it from the Information display edit screen.

Figure 3.16B – Opening Active D-Lighting from the Information display edit screen

Use these steps to change Active D-Lighting quickly (figure 3.16B):

1. Press the info button twice (figure 3.16B, screen 1).
2. This will cause the Information edit screen to appear. Scroll to the Active D-Lighting position and press the OK button (figure 3.16B, screen 2).
3. The Active D-Lighting screen will now appear, allowing you to change quickly to a different level (figure 3.16B, screen 3).

Figure 3.16C – Active D-Lighting samples

Basically, Active D-Lighting will help bring out detail in areas of your image that are hidden in shadow due to excessive image contrast. It also tends to protect the highlights from blowing out, or becoming pure white with no detail. Figure 3.16C shows a series of six images with Active D-Lighting set to its various levels. I chose a backlit scene with heavy shadow to see how these six levels performed.

Settings Recommendation: You'll need to experiment with the Active D-Lighting settings to see which you like best. Active D-Lighting has the effect of lowering contrast, and some people do not like low-contrast images. Also, anytime you recover lost detail from shadows, there may be extra noise in the recovered areas.

This function can be useful for JPEG shooters in particular. Since you really shouldn't modify a JPEG file after shooting it, it's important that the image is created exactly right in the first place. When you are shooting in a contrasty setting, such as in direct sunlight, some degree of Active D-Lighting may help rein in the contrast.

Honestly, before the Nikon D800, I didn't use Active D-Lighting very often because it added noise in the darker areas it opened up. However, things have changed with this D800. I am still experimenting, but I have determined that Active D-Lighting doesn't seem to make as much noise as with previous Nikons. I am quite impressed with the intelligence of the camera, and when I must get a good shot, such as at a wedding ceremony, I am now more open to setting Active D-Lighting to Auto. It has the added benefit of reining in the highlights too, so I keep more detail in a bride's dress, which can be hard to do when shooting with flash in a low-light room.

Experiment with this by shooting images in a high-contrast and a low-contrast setting at all the various levels of Active D-Lighting. You'll see how the camera reacts and can better decide how you'll use this functionality.

HDR (High Dynamic Range)

(User's Manual – Page 176)

HDR (high dynamic range) asks the camera to combine two JPEG or TIFF exposures into a single image. It is not available in NEF (RAW) modes.

HDR combines details from an underexposed shot and an overexposed shot into one good, normally exposed picture with much greater dynamic range than normal. In figure 3.17A, you can see a sample, with the two images on the left combined, in-camera, to create the third image.

Figure 3.17A – HDR combination sample

HDR (high dynamic range) in the D800 is a form of simple bracketing that allows you to create an HDR image without setting up a bracketing series using the BKT button. There are three settings under HDR (high dynamic range):

- **HDR mode** – This setting has three options: On (series), On (single photo), and Off. When On (series) is selected, the camera will keep shooting its two-image HDR brackets until you set HDR mode to Off. When On (single photo) is chosen, the camera will take a single HDR bracket for one image. Off means the camera does not create an HDR image.

- **Exposure differential** – You can choose how much difference in stops (EV) there will be between the two images that are later combined. The choices are 1 EV, 2 EV, 3 EV, and Auto. Use 1, 2, or 3 EV when you want to make the decision; choose Auto when you want to let the camera decide. If you control the amount of Exposure differential, be careful to choose only what is needed or you may experience under- or overexposure in the final combined image. If a two-image exposure bracket is insufficient, you may want to investigate the exposure bracketing system connected to the BKT button. We will discuss how to use the camera's primary bracketing system in the chapter titled **Custom Setting Menu**. With it you can do up to a nine-shot bracket.

- **Smoothing** – This allows you to choose smoothing for the boundaries between the two images. There are three choices available: Low, Normal, and High. Each subject's boundaries are different, so you may have to experiment with these settings. Higher values make a smoother combined image. Watch out for uneven shading with some subjects.

Figure 3.17B – Choosing an HDR mode

First, let's examine how to configure the three settings and prepare for HDR shooting.

Use these steps to enable HDR mode for a single picture or a series (figure 3.17B):

1. Choose HDR (high dynamic range) from the Shooting Menu and scroll to the right (figure 3.17B, screen 1).
2. Select HDR mode and scroll to the right (figure 3.17B, screen 2).
3. Decide whether you want to make one or a series of HDR images and choose accordingly: On (single photo) for a single image or On (series) for a series of images (figure 3.17B, screen 3).
4. Press the OK button to prepare the camera for shooting in HDR mode.

When the D800 is set to HDR mode, you will see an HDR symbol displayed on the camera's Control panel and on the Information display (Monitor). It will go away when HDR mode is set to Off. Now, let's look into configuring the Exposure differential setting.

Figure 3.17C – Choosing an Exposure differential setting

Use the following steps to choose an Exposure differential setting (figure 3.17C):

1. Choose HDR (high dynamic range) from the Shooting Menu and scroll to the right (figure 3.17C, screen 1).
2. Select Exposure differential and scroll to the right (figure 3.17C, screen 2).
3. Choose one of the four settings, according to how much exposure variance you want between the two images that will be combined into one. Use Auto to let the camera decide, or choose from 1 EV to 3 EV (figure 3.17C, screen 3). If you have a high-contrast subject, you may want to try the 3 EV level first to see if it works best. For low- to medium-contrast subjects, choose 1 EV or 2 EV.
4. Press the OK Button to lock in your choice.

Finally, let's see how to configure the Smoothing selection for the best image edge boundary control.

Figure 3.17D – Choosing a Smoothing setting

Use these steps to configure Smoothing for the HDR image combination (figure 3.17D):

1. Choose HDR (high dynamic range) from the Shooting Menu and scroll to the right (figure 3.17D, screen 1).
2. Select Smoothing and scroll to the right (figure 3.17D, screen 2).
3. Select High, Normal, or Low. You will need to experiment and observe the differences in image boundaries when you vary this setting.
4. Press the OK button to choose your Smoothing level.

Now it's time to take an HDR picture or three. Here are some things you will need to know during and after the HDR process:

- The camera will take two exposures when you press the Shutter-release button all the way down once. It is a good idea to have the camera on a tripod during low-light HDR operations or you may have some nasty, blurry images as a result. If you do choose to handhold in low light, please brace yourself and do not allow camera movement. When light is very bright, the HDR process can be quite fast. It is much slower when light is low, taking several seconds to deliver a combined image.
- **HDR** will be displayed in the Control panel, on the Information display, and in Live view (Monitor) as soon as you enable HDR (high dynamic range).
- **HDR** will start blinking on the Control panel during the initial exposures.
- **HDR** will display in the lower-right side of the Monitor during Live view HDR shooting. During HDR exposure and image combination, the Live view screen will not display anything.
- **Job HDR** will flash in the viewfinder during image combination.
- **Job HDR** (blinking) will be displayed in the Control panel while the images are being combined.
- The edges of the image may be cropped out, so do not allow important parts of the subject to touch the edges if possible.
- If you detect shadows around bright objects or halos around dark objects, you can reduce this effect by adjusting the amount of smoothing. Try setting Smoothing to a lower level.
- You cannot select any form of NEF (RAW) shooting when you're already using HDR (high dynamic range), only JPEG or TIFF. HDR (high dynamic range) is grayed out on the Shooting Menu when you're using NEF (RAW).

Note: You can assign the BKT button to allow you to select HDR settings with external camera controls (instead of bracketing). See the chapter **Custom Setting Menu,** under the subheading **Custom Setting f8 – Assign BKT button.**

Settings Recommendation: I am a big fan of bracketing and HDR. You'll often find me on top of some Appalachian mountain shooting a five-bracket HDR shot of the valley below. Beautiful things can be done with HDR. I do not like the shadowless HDR that some photographers shoot. To me it looks fake and seems faddish. However, HDR, when used correctly, can help create images that the camera could not normally take due to excessive light range. If you are really into HDR or would like to be, check out the excellent second edition of *Practical HDRI*, by Jack Howard, published by Rocky Nook.

Photoshop has built-in software for HDR, or you can buy a less-costly dedicated package, such as Photomatix Pro by HDRsoft. I've been using Photomatix Pro for several years to combine my bracketed images into carefully tone-mapped HDR images.

There are some limitations to in-camera HDR, which is why people really serious about it use the main bracketing system and combine their images using professional HDR software. However, HDR (high dynamic range) in the D800 is an easy way to knock off a few quick HDRs for those times when only an HDR will do. Give it a try!

Vignette Control

(User's Manual – Page 275)

Vignette control allows you to reduce the amount of vignetting (slight darkening) that many lenses have in the corners at wide-open apertures. The angle at which light strikes a sensor on its edges is greater than the angle at which rays go straight through the lens to the center areas of the sensor. Because of the increased angle, some light falloff occurs at the extreme edges of the frame, especially at wide apertures, because more of the lens element is in use. Full-frame (FX) sensors have microlenses over the pixels that help reduce vignetting, but it is still there in varying degrees with different lenses.

In recognition of this fact, Nikon has provided the Vignette control setting. It can reduce the vignetting effect to a large degree. If more vignette control is required, you can use Photoshop or Nikon Capture NX 2 (or other software) to remove it.

Figure 3.18A shows a sample of what the Nikon D800 can accomplish on its own. I shot four pictures of the sky with an AF-S Nikkor 50mm f/1.4G lens at f/1.4 (wide open aperture). Each picture has more Vignette control applied, from Off to High.

Figure 3.18A – Vignette control range

Let's see how to configure the Vignette control for edge light falloff reduction with your lenses.

Figure 3.18B – Vignette control choices

Here are the steps to choose a Vignette control level for your D800 (figure 3.18B):

1. Choose Vignette control from the Shooting Menu and scroll to the right (figure 3.18B, screen 1).
2. Select a level from the list. I chose Normal in figure 3.18B, screen 2.
3. Press the OK button to lock in the level.

Note: Vignette control does not apply to DX lenses mounted on your D800. It will work only with FX lenses of the G and D types, except for PC lenses. Nikon warns that you may see noise, fog, or variations in brightness "…depending on the scene, shooting conditions, and type of lens." It may be a good idea to test each of your lenses and pixel peep the edges to see if you notice any problems. Vignette control does not work while shooting video or multiple exposures.

Settings Recommendation: The camera defaulted to Normal from the factory, so I have been shooting most of my images with it set to Normal. I like this control. It does help remove vignetting in the corners when I shoot with the aperture wide open. I have not noticed any additional noise or image degredation in the corrected areas. I suggest leaving your camera set to Normal at all times unless you are shooting with a lens that has a greater tendencey to vignette, in which case you can increase it to High. Even High does not seem to fully remove the vignetting when a lens is wide open, so this is not an aggressive algorithm that will leave white spots in the corners of your images. Why not shoot a few shots with your lenses at wide aperture and see how Vignette control works with your lens and camera combinations? Remember, you can remove vignetting in the computer with post-processing software if the camera's Vignette control setting does not entirely remove the problem.

Auto Distortion Control

(User's Manual – Page 276)
Auto distortion control is designed to automatically reduce barrel and pincushion distortion in your images. It will try to keep lines straight but may crop the edges of your image in the process. This function may be best used by architectural photographers who are very concerned about keeping lines and edges straight, for obvious reasons.

Figure 3.19A shows a greatly exaggerated sample of barrel and pincushion distortion. If you have a lens that does this, you might want to dispose of it, unless it is a fisheye or extreme wide angle, of course.

To prevent even mild cases of these two distortion types from ruining images that contain straight lines, you can use this control. Of course, if you are out shooting nature shots or portraits, it is unlikely that you will gain much benefit from this function. If you need automatic barrel and pincushion distortion, you will already know it from previous work. Most of us will leave this turned off.

Figure 3.19A – Extreme examples of barrel (left) and pincushion (right) distortion

Figure 3.19B – Auto distortion control

Use these steps to enable or disable Auto distortion control (figure 3.19B):

1. Choose Auto distortion control from the Shooting Menu and scroll to the right (figure 3.19B, screen 1).
2. Select On or Off (figure 3.19B, screen 2).
3. Press the OK button to save the setting.

Settings Recommendation: If you are a photographer who really needs this function, you will already know it. If you question whether it will benefit you, it probably won't. I prefer to remove distortion in software on my computer because I am working with a much larger image and can more easily see what needs to be done. This is an automatic function in the D800 and, like most automatic functions, does great sometimes and not so great other times. However, this may be a handy function for times when you are out in the field shooting and you need some distortion correction immediately. Just watch out and allow for edge cropping as the camera removes the distortion it detects.

Long Exposure NR

(User's Manual – Page 277)

Long exposure NR (noise reduction) is designed to combat visual noise in long exposures. Long-exposure noise is a little different from grainy-looking high-ISO sensitivity noise due to its cause. Nikon says long-exposure noise appears as: "*bright spots, randomly-spaced bright pixels, or fog.*" Why does this happen? During longer exposures, the imaging sensor can start to warm up a little, especially in warm ambient temperatures. This causes a condition called amp noise, in which warmer sections of the imaging sensor start to display more foggy noise than other sections. Additionally, when pixels are left turned on for a longer period of time, a few of them may become brighter than normal and record an improper color, often bright red. Those off-color, bright pixels should be removed by the camera. Long exposure NR does just that.

Long-exposure noise is best handled by this Long exposure NR function, while high-ISO noise is well handled by High ISO NR (next section). Sometimes, when you are shooting long exposures at higher ISO settings, both may be needed!

Nikon knows its imaging sensors well. It feels that images taken at shutter speeds longer than 1 second may exhibit more long-exposure noise than is acceptable for normal images. There are two settings for Long exposure NR, as shown in figure 3.20A.

Figure 3.20A – Choosing a Long exposure NR setting

- **On** – When you select On and the exposure goes over 1 second, the camera will take two exposures with the exact same time for each. The first exposure is the normal picture-taking exposure. The second is a dark-frame subtraction exposure, in which a second exposure is made for the same length of time as the first one, but with the shutter closed. The noise in the dark frame image is examined and then subtracted from the original image. It is really quite effective and beats having to blur the image to get rid of noise. I've taken exposures of around 30 seconds and had perfectly usable results. The only drawback is that the exposure time is doubled because two exposures are made. The dark frame exposure is not written to the memory card, so you'll have only one image, with much less noise, in the end. While the dark frame image is being processed, the words *Job nr* will blink on the Control panel and in the Viewfinder. During this second exposure, while *Job nr* is flashing, you cannot use the camera. If you turn it off while *Job nr* is flashing, the camera still keeps the first image; it just doesn't do any noise reduction on it. If Long exposure NR is set to On, the frame advance rate may slow down a little in Continuous release mode, and the capacity of the in-camera memory buffer will drop while the image is being processed.

- **Off** – If you select Off, then, of course, you will have no long exposure noise reduction with exposures longer than 1 second.

Here are the steps to choose a Long exposure NR setting (figure 3.20A):

1. Choose Long exposure NR from the Shooting Menu and scroll to the right (figure 3.20A, screen 1).
2. Select either On or Off (figure 3.20A, screen 2).
3. Press the OK button to save your setting.

You can also open the Long exposure NR menu without using the Shooting Menu directly. Instead, you can select it from the Information display edit screen.

Figure 3.20B – Opening Long exposure NR from the Information display edit screen

Use these steps to change Long exposure NR quickly (figure 3.20B):

1. Press the info button twice (figure 3.20B, screen 1).
2. This will cause the Information display edit screen to appear. Scroll to the Long exposure NR position and press the OK button (figure 3.20B, screen 2).
3. The Long exposure NR screen will now appear, allowing you to quickly turn it On or Off (figure 3.20B, screen 3).

Settings Recommendation: I personally like the benefits of Long exposure NR. I shoot a lot of waterfall and stream shots where I often need exposures of several seconds to really blur the water. Also, I like to take midnight shots of the sky and even shots of city scenes at night. Even though it may slow down the frame rate slightly and allow me fewer images in the in-camera memory buffer, I still use it most of the time.

If I were a sports or action shooter using Continuous release mode, I might leave Long exposure NR turned Off. It's unlikely I would be using exposures longer than 1 second, and I would want maximum frames per second as well as the ability to cram as many images into the camera buffer as possible. I wouldn't want my camera to slow down while writing images to the memory card.

Your style of shooting will govern whether this function is useful to you. Ask yourself one simple question: "Do I often shoot exposures longer than one second?" If so, you may want Long exposure NR set to On. Compare how the images look with and without it. I think you'll like Long exposure NR.

High ISO NR

(User's Manual – Page 277)

High ISO NR (noise reduction) lessens the effects of visual digital noise in your images when you use higher ISO sensitivity (exposure gain) settings. Nikon does not publish the point at which High ISO NR starts working (when enabled) except to say that even when set to Off, "…noise reduction is performed only at sensitivities of 1600 and higher."

With such a large pixel density, the camera probably does some minor noise reduction—if High ISO NR is enabled—at relatively low ISO settings (ISO 800–1600). If so, it is particularly effective.

You can choose the level of High ISO NR you would like to use from one of three active levels: Low, Normal, and High. If you have it set to Off, High ISO NR does nothing to images below ISO 1600, while above ISO 1600 the amount of noise reduction is less than the Low setting would provide when enabled.

When High ISO NR is enabled, the higher the setting you use (Low–High), the greater the blurring effect on the image to remove noise. However, the camera compensates after blurring by resharpening to a degree and seems to do a good job at creating very usable high-ISO images. If well exposed, even up to ISO 3200 the camera does a beautiful job, with relatively clean images. You should plan to experiment with the camera to determine your tolerance for noise and the camera's ability to reduce it.

Let's see how to enable or disable High ISO NR.

Figure 3.21A – High ISO NR choices

Use these steps to choose a High ISO NR setting (figure 3.21A):

1. Choose High ISO NR from the Shooting Menu and scroll to the right (figure 3.21A, screen 1).
2. Select one of the noise reduction levels: High, Normal, Low, or Off (figure 3.21A, screen 2).
3. Press the OK button to save your setting.

Additionally, you can open the High ISO NR menu without using the Shooting Menu directly. Instead, you can press the info button twice and select it from the Information display edit screen.

Figure 3.21B – Opening High ISO NR from the Information display edit screen

Use these steps to change High ISO NR quickly (figure 3.21B):

1. Press the info button twice (figure 3.21B, screen 1).
2. This will cause the Information edit screen to appear. Scroll to the High ISO NR position and press the OK button (figure 3.21B, screen 2).
3. The High ISO NR screen will now appear, allowing you to choose a level quickly (figure 3.21B, screen 3).

Note: If you are using High ISO NR and the Auto ISO sensitivity control at the same time, or if the ISO is set to 1600 or higher, the memory buffer capacity will be reduced while processing images.

Settings Recommendation: I leave High ISO NR set to Normal at all times. I appreciate a little noise reduction as long as it is not damaging to the sharpness of the images. If you haven't changed your D800, the factory default is Normal (medium). I think Nikon is trying to tell us that we ought to use a little High ISO NR with such a huge camera resolution and so many pixels packed into a 35 mm imaging sensor. While having medium-format resolution, the FX sensor is smaller than other medium-format cameras, so it will need a little noise reduction assistance at higher ISO sensitivity settings. Again, why not shoot a series of high-ISO images with the camera set to all four High ISO NR choices and see which you like best?

ISO Sensitivity Settings

(User's Manual – Page 109)

ISO sensitivity settings give you control over the light sensitivity of the imaging sensor, including whether you manually control it or the camera sets it automatically.

An ISO sensitivity number, such as 200 or 3200, is an agreed-upon sensitivity level for the image-capturing sensor. Virtually everywhere one goes in the world, all camera ISO numbers will mean the same thing. With that fact established, camera bodies and lenses can be designed to take advantage of the ISO sensitivity ranges they will have to deal with.

In figure 3.22A we see the external camera controls used to change the ISO sensitivity on the D800. This is a good way to adjust ISO sensitivity quickly. This is also the easiest method to change the camera's ISO sensitivity setting, although it doesn't involve the Shooting Menu, which we are now examining.

Figure 3.22A – External controls to set ISO manually

Here are the steps you'll use to manually adjust the camera's ISO sensitivity (figure 3.22A):

1. Hold down the ISO button above the Release mode dial (figure 3.22A, screen 1).
2. Rotate the rear Main command dial counterclockwise to increase the ISO sensitivity or clockwise to decrease sensitivity (figure 3.22A, screen 2).
3. The ISO sensitivity number will show on the Control panel, in the Viewfinder, and at the bottom right of the Live view screen. Figure 3.22A, screen 3, shows the Control panel, which is most often used.

ISO Sensitivity

You can also use ISO sensitivity settings directly from the Shooting Menu to change the camera's ISO sensitivity. Figure 3.22B shows the three screens used. Select your favorite ISO sensitivity for the circumstances in which you find yourself.

Notice in screen 3 of figure 3.22B that you have a scrollable list of ISO sensitivity settings, from Lo 1 (ISO 50) to Hi 1 (ISO 25,600). The "normal" ISO range for the D800 is ISO 100 to 6400. Lo 1 to Lo 0.3 represents ISO 50–80, and Hi 0.3 to Hi 2 represents ISO 8000–25,600 .

Figure 3.22B – Setting ISO sensitivity from the Shooting Menu

Here are the steps to select an ISO sensitivity setting (figure 3.22B):

1. Choose ISO sensitivity settings from the Shooting Menu and scroll to the right (figure 3.22B, screen 1).
2. Select ISO sensitivity from the menu and scroll to the right (figure 3.22B, screen 2).
3. Scroll up or down in the ISO sensitivity menu until you highlight the ISO value you want to use (figure 3.22B, screen 3).
4. Press the OK button to save the ISO sensitivity setting.

The standard minimum ISO sensitivity for the D800 is ISO 100. You may adjust the camera in a range from ISO 50 to 25,600, in 1/3 steps. You can set Custom setting b1 to 1/3, 1/2, or 1 step. We'll look at this more carefully in the upcoming chapter titled **Custom Setting Menu**.

Select your favorite ISO sensitivity setting, using either the external camera controls or the Shooting Menu's ISO sensitivity settings function. If you'd like, you can simply let your camera decide which ISO it would like to use. Let's consider this often-misunderstood feature in detail.

Auto ISO Sensitivity Control (ISO-AUTO)

You may have noticed in figure 3.22B, screen 2, that there is another setting available, *Auto ISO sensitivity control*, which defaults to Off. This setting allows the camera to control the ISO sensitivity and shutter speed according to the light levels sensed by the camera. Figure 3.22C shows the Shooting Menu screens used to enable Auto ISO sensitivity control.

Once you've set Auto ISO sensitivity control to On, you should immediately set two values, according to how you shoot: Maximum sensitivity and Minimum shutter speed. Let's discuss each of them.

Figure 3.22C – Enabling Auto ISO sensitivity control

Maximum Sensitivity

The *Maximum sensitivity* setting is a safeguard for you (figure 3.22D). It allows the camera to adjust its own ISO sensitivity from the minimum value you have set in ISO sensitivity (figure 3.22B) to the value set in Maximum sensitivity (figure 3.22D), according to light conditions. The camera will try to maintain the lowest ISO sensitivity it can to get the picture. However, if needed, it can rapidly rise to the Maximum sensitivity level to "get the picture" no matter what.

Figure 3.22D – Auto ISO sensitivity control – Maximum sensitivity

If you would prefer that the Maximum sensitivity setting not exceed a certain ISO value, simply select from the list shown in figure 3.22D, screen 3. The Maximum sensitivity default is ISO 6400. This setting will let the camera take the ISO sensitivity all the way up to ISO 6400 in a low-light situation. It is the maximum ISO value the camera will use to get a good exposure when the light drops.

What happens when the camera reaches the Maximum sensitivity setting and there still isn't enough light for a good exposure? Let's find out by examing the second part of the Auto ISO sensitivity control, Minimum shutter speed.

Minimum Shutter Speed

Because shutter speed helps control how sharp an image can be, depending on camera shake and subject movement, you will need some control over the minimum shutter speed allowed while the ISO sensitivity auto control is turned On (figure 3.22E).

Figure 3.22E – Auto ISO sensitivity control – Minimum shutter speed

The *Minimum shutter speed* setting allows you to select the minimum shutter speed that the camera will allow when the light diminishes. In exposure modes Programmed auto (P mode – camera controls shutter and aperture) and Aperture-priority (A mode – camera controls shutter and you control aperture), the camera will not go below the Minimum shutter speed unless the Maximum sensitivity setting still won't give you a good exposure.

This is the answer to our question in the last section about what happens when there is not enough light and the camera has reached the Maximum sensitivity level. Even though you've selected a Minimum shutter speed, the camera will go below the Minimum shutter speed when the Maximum sensitivity ISO number has been reached and the light is still too low for a good exposure.

In other words, in Programmed auto (P) or Aperture-priority (A) exposure modes, if you get into low light and try to take pictures, the camera will try to keep the ISO sensitivity as low as possible until the shutter speed drops to your selected Minimum shutter speed. Once it hits the selected Minimum shutter speed value—like the 1/30s shown in figure 3.22E, screen 3—the ISO sensitivity will begin to rise up to your selected Maximum sensitivity value, like the ISO 6400 shown in figure 3.22D, screen 3.

Once the camera hits the Maximum sensitivity value, if there still isn't enough light for a good exposure, it won't keep raising the ISO sensitivity. Instead, the camera will now go below your selected Minimum shutter speed, dropping below the 1/30s shown in figure 3.22E, screen 3. Be careful, because if the light gets that low, your camera can go all the way down to a shutter speed of 30 seconds to get a good exposure. You had better have your camera on a tripod and have a static subject with shutter speeds that low.

Look at the Minimum shutter speed value as the lowest "safe" speed, after which you'll put your camera on a tripod. Most people can handhold a camera down to about 1/60s if they are careful, and maybe 1/30s if they're extra careful and brace themselves. Below that, it's blur city for your images. It's even worse with telephoto lenses. Camera movement is greatly magnified with a long lens, and a Minimum shutter speed of 1/250s to 1/500s or more may be required.

The next section discusses an excellent solution the Nikon D800 gives us for those times when we are using a longer lens requiring a faster shutter speed to maintain sharp images—the Auto Minimum shutter speed setting.

Auto Minimum Shutter Speed

There is an important principle in photography called the *reciprocal of focal length shutter speed rule*. You may know the rule; however, a short review won't hurt. This impressive-sounding rule simply means that you should use a tripod (no hand-holding) whenever the shutter speed in use is below the reciprocal of the lens's focal length. For example, if you are using a 50mm zoom position on your lens, you should not use a shutter speed below 1/50s without having the camera on a tripod. With a 105mm focal length, the minimum handheld shutter speed is 1/100s or 1/125s. There is no 1/105s available, so you can use the closest one. If you are using a 300mm lens, you should not use a shutter speed below 1/300s.

The reason this rule exists is because a longer focal length tends to magnify the subject and any vibrations you introduce when you press the shutter-release button. With a shutter speed below the reciprocal of the lens focal length, you can introduce movement just from your heartbeat, the reflex mirror slap, or natural hand shakiness. If you are going to handhold the camera at slower shutter speeds, you need to learn how to brace yourself properly. The best thing is to use a tripod any time you have to shoot below the reciprocal of the lens's length. Otherwise, you will be known for your well exposed, yet blurry images (from camera shake).

When using the Auto ISO sensitivity control you have an opportunity to implement the *reciprocal of focal length shutter speed rule* in an automatic fashion. The Nikon D800 has added an Auto setting for Minimum shutter speed, which allows the camera to sense what focal length is currently in use and prohibits the camera from using a minimum shutter speed that would cause camera shake. Let's examine how to use it.

Figure 3.22F – Auto ISO sensitivity control – Auto Minimum shutter speed

Use these steps to enable Auto Minimum shutter speed (figure 3.22F):

1. Choose ISO sensitivity settings from the Shooting Menu and scroll to the right (figure 3.22F, screen 1).
2. Select Minimum shutter speed and scroll to the right (figure 3.22F, screen 2).
3. Select Auto from the top of the Minimum shutter speed list and scroll to the right (figure 3.22F, screen 3).

ISO Sensitivity Auto Control from the Camera's Perspective

For fun, let's listen to the camera talk to itself while you take pictures in low light with Auto ISO sensitivity control enabled. As we listen in on the D800 thinking, we need to know that the current Maximum sensitivity setting is ISO 1600 and the Minimum shutter speed setting is 1/50 s:

Nikon D800 thinking: "Okay, Auto ISO is on! The light is dropping and my current 1/60 s shutter speed and 100 ISO sensitivity won't let me make a good exposure. I'll slow the shutter speed to the minimum of 1/50 s, as my owner specified in my Minimum shutter speed setting. More pictures are incoming, and the light is still dropping! I can't go any lower on the shutter speed for now because my owner has instructed me to keep the Minimum shutter speed at 1/50 s unless I can't get a good picture. I'll have to start raising the ISO sensitivity. Here comes more pictures, and whew, it's getting dark! I've now raised the ISO sensitivity to my Maximum sensitivity level of ISO 1600, which is as high as I am allowed to go. I have no choice now but to go below the 1/50 s Minimum shutter speed my owner has specified. I hope I'm on a tripod!"

4. Adjust the Auto Minimum shutter speed fine-tuning scale (figure 3.22F, screen 4). Each position on the scale is the equivalent of one stop (1 EV). The camera will use the reciprocal of the focal length of the mounted lens if the yellow pointer is left in the center as seen in figure 3.22F, screen 4. If you move it one notch to the right of center the camera will switch to the reciprocal of the focal length plus one stop. If you are using a 50mm lens, the reciprocal of 50mm plus one stop is 1/100s (1/50s plus 1 EV) for the camera's minimum shutter speed. If you move the scale one notch to the left of center, the camera will use 1/25s instead (1/50s less 1 EV). Here is a list matching what each position on the scale represents if you are using a 50mm lens: 1/13s, 1/25s, 1/50s, 1/100s, 1/200s. Of course, these numbers will vary with the focal length of the lens mounted on the camera.

5. Press the OK button to lock in the fine-tuned Auto Minimum shutter speed.

Settings Recommendation: When I use the Auto ISO sensitivity control with my D800 I set my camera to Auto Minimum shutter speed. Why worry about having to adjust a setting just because I changed lenses? The camera is smart enough to know what to do and tries to protect me from losing sharpness from camera shake.

Note: Shutter-priority (S) and Manual (M) modes allow you to control the camera in a way that overrides certain parts of the Auto ISO sensitivity control.

In Manual mode (M), the camera relinquishes all control of the shutter and aperture. It can adjust only the ISO sensitivity by itself, so it can obey the Maximum sensitivity but the Minimum shutter speed is overridden and does not apply.

In Shutter-priority mode (S), the camera can control the aperture but the shutter speed is controlled only by the camera user. So, the Auto ISO sensitivity control can still control the Maximum sensitivity but has lost control over the Minimum shutter speed.

Also, it may be a good idea to enable High ISO NR—as discussed a few pages back—when you Auto ISO sensitivity control. This is especially true if you leave the camera set to the default Maximum sensitivity value of 6400. Otherwise, you may have excessive noise when the light drops.

When a flash unit is used, the value in Minimum shutter speed is ignored. Instead, the camera uses the value found in Custom setting e1 Flash sync speed.

If Auto is selected for Minimum shutter speed, the camera will decide which shutter speed to use as a minimum based on the focal length of the lens in use, if the lens is a CPU type; otherwise, for a non-CPU lens, the camera selects 1/30s as a Minimum shutter speed.

Enabling ISO-AUTO with External Controls

In case you like to use external controls to make adjustments when possible (don't we all), be aware that you can conveniently turn the Auto ISO sensitivity control on and off with the ISO button, the front Sub-command dial, and the Control panel. Figure 3.22G shows the controls. You will need to configure ISO-AUTO before you use the control or the camera will use factory defaults.

Figure 3.22G – Enabling Auto ISO sensitivity control with external camera controls

Here are the steps you'll use to manually enable or disable ISO-AUTO (figure 3.22G):

1. Hold down the ISO button above the Release mode dial (figure 3.22G, screen 1).
2. Rotate the front Sub-command dial to enable or disable ISO-AUTO, the Auto ISO sensitivity control (figure 3.22G, screen 2).
3. The ISO-AUTO symbol will show on the Control panel (figure 3.22G, screen 3).

When, Why, and How Should I Use ISO-AUTO?

How much automation do you need to produce consistently excellent images? Let's explore how and when automatic, self-adjusting ISO might improve or degrade your images. What is this feature all about? When and why should I use it? Are there any compromises in image quality when using this mode?

Normally, you set your camera to a particular ISO number, such as 200 or 400, and shoot your images. As the light gets darker, or in the deep shade, you might increase the ISO sensitivity to continue taking handheld images.

If you absolutely must get the shot, the Auto ISO sensitivity control will work nicely. Here are a few scenarios:

- **Scenario # 1:** Let's say you are a photojournalist and you're shooting flash pictures of the president as he disembarks from his airplane, walks into the terminal, and drives away in his limousine. Under these circumstances, you have little time to check your ISO settings or shutter speeds and are shooting in widely varying light conditions.
- **Scenario # 2:** You are a wedding photographer in a church that doesn't allow the use of flash. As you follow the bride and groom from the dark inner rooms of the church out into the lobby and finally up to the altar, your light conditions vary

constantly. You have no time to deal with the fluctuations in light by changing your ISO because things are moving too quickly.

- **Scenario # 3:** You are at a party, and you want some great pictures. You want to use flash, but the pop-up Speedlight may not be powerful enough to reach across the room at low ISO settings. You really don't want to be bothered with camera configuration at this time but still want some well-exposed images. Light will vary as you move around the room, talking, laughing, and snapping pictures.

These scenarios present excellent environments for the Auto ISO sensitivity control. The camera will use your normal settings, such as your normal ISO, shutter speed, and aperture, until the light will not allow those settings to provide an accurate exposure. Only then will the camera raise the ISO or lower the shutter speed to keep functioning within the shutter/aperture parameters you have set.

Look at Auto ISO as a failsafe for times when you must get the shot but have little time to deal with camera settings or when you don't want to vary the shutter/aperture settings but still want to be assured of a well-exposed image.

Unless you are a private detective shooting handheld telephoto images from your car or a photojournalist or sports photographer who must get the shot every time regardless of maximum quality, I personally would not recommend leaving Auto ISO sensitivity control set to On all the time. Use it only when you really need to get the shot under any circumstances!

Of course, if you are unsure of how to use the correct ISO for the light level due to lack of experience, don't be afraid to experiment with this mode. At the very worst, you might get noisier than normal images. However, it may not be a good idea to depend on this mode over the long term because noisy images are not very nice.

Are There Any Drawbacks to Using ISO-AUTO?

Maybe! It really depends on how widely the light conditions vary when you are shooting. Most of the time, your camera will maintain the normal range of ISO settings in Auto ISO sensitivity control, so your images will be their normal low-noise, sharp masterpieces. However, at times the light may be so low that the ISO may exceed low-noise range and will start getting into the noisier ranges above ISO 1600.

Just be aware that the Auto ISO sensitivity control can and will push your camera's ISO sensitivity into a range that causes noisier images when light levels drop, if you have allowed it. Use it with this understanding and you'll be fine.

The Auto ISO sensitivity control is yet another feature of our powerful Nikon cameras. Maybe not everyone needs this failsafe feature, but for those who do, it must be there. I will use it myself in circumstances where getting the shot is the most important thing and where light levels may get too low for normal ISO image-making.

Even if you think you might only use it from time to time, do learn how to use it for those times. Experiment with the Auto ISO sensitivity control. It's fun and can be useful!

Tightly Control How ISO-AUTO Works

It is an undocumented feature, but the normal ISO sensitivity setting (figure 3.22B) sets the minimum ISO the camera will use when the Auto ISO sensitivity control is enabled. The Maximum sensitivity setting (figure 3.22D) sets the maximum ISO it will use. With these two values, you can tightly control the range of ISO values your camera can use with Auto ISO sensitivity control turned on.

Of course, it always has the escape valve of dropping below the Minimum shutter speed if you constrain the camera too tightly. Be sure you understand how these features work together. Many people think they do when they really don't and may have some nasty surprises.

Multiple Exposure

(User's Manual – Page 195)

Multiple exposure is the process whereby you take more than one exposure on a single frame, or picture. Most of us will only do double exposures, which is two exposures on one frame.

Multiple exposure requires you to figure the exposure values carefully for each exposure segment so that in the final picture, all the combined exposures equal one normal exposure. In other words, if you are going to do a nonmasked double exposure, your background will need two exposures at half the normal exposure value to equal one normal exposure.

The D800 allows us to figure our own exposure settings and do them manually or gives us Auto gain to help us with exposure calculations.

There are really only four steps to setting up a Multiple exposure session. However, there are several Shooting Menu screens we'll use to do these four steps. The steps are as follows:

- Select the number of shots you want to take from the Shooting Menu screens.
- Set Auto gain to either On or Off according to how you want to control exposure.
- Choose whether you are shooting one image or a series of images.
- Take the picture.

Figure 3.23A – Setting up Multiple exposure basics

Use the following steps to configure one or a series of multiple exposures (figure 3.23A):

1. Select Multiple exposure from the Shooting Menu and scroll to the right (figure 3.23A, screen 1).
2. Select Number of shots and scroll right (figure 3.23A, screen 2).
3. Enter the number of shots you wish to take—any number between 2 and 10— and press the OK button (figure 3.23A, screen 3).
4. Select Auto gain and scroll right (figure 3.23A, screen 4).
5. Select On and press the OK button (figure 3.23A, screen 5).
6. This brings you back to the beginning and the Multiple exposure selection on the Shooting Menu (figure 3.23A, screen 6). At this point you must reenter the Multiple exposure system and choose whether you want one Multiple exposure or a series (figure 3.23B). Figure 3.23B takes up where figure 3.23A leaves off. It shows the final step of choosing how many multiple exposure images you want to take in this session.

Figure 3.23B – Choosing one multiple exposure or a series

7. Select Multiple exposure mode and scroll to the right (figure 3.23B, screen 1).
8. Choose On (series) if you want to take more than one distinct Multiple exposure image or On (single photo) for just one Multiple exposure picture.
9. Press the OK button and your camera is ready to take the multiple exposure.

Once you've selected the number of shots (step 2), the camera remembers the value and comes back to it for the next session. To repeat another Multiple exposure series with the same settings, you'll have to use the screens in figure 3.23B again. Start over with step 7 later. That prepares the camera to do the Multiple exposure series (or single photo) in the same way as last time. The camera remembers the previous settings until you reset them using the screens in figure 3.23A.

Understanding Auto Gain

Auto gain defaults to On, so you need to understand it well. Auto gain applies only if you want to make a number of exposure segments with the exact same exposure value for each. If you want to make two exposures, the camera will meter for a normal exposure and then divide the exposure in half for the two shots. For three shots, it will divide the exposure by 1/3, four shots by 1/4, eight shots by 1/8, and so forth.

In other words, it will divide the normal exposure for a single shot by the number you entered on the Number of shots screen so that when you are done, you have the equivalent of a single good exposure.

Here's another way of looking at it: If I want a two-shot Multiple exposure, I normally want the background to get 1/2 of a normal exposure in each shot so that it will appear normal in the final image. Auto gain does that automatically. If I need four shots, I want the background to get only 1/4 of a normal exposure for each shot so that I'll have a normally exposed background when the four shots are taken.

The reason I mention this in such a repetitive fashion is that it took me a little while to wrap my brain around the confusing presentation of this fact in the User's Manual. Whoever heard of *gain* meaning dividing something into parts? What I think the manual writer was trying to say is that each shot "gains" a portion of the normal exposure so that in the end, the exposure is complete and correct.

Auto gain is like an automatic normal-exposure "divider-upper" for multiple exposures. It divides the exposure into appropriate sections—so you won't have to fool with it.

When should one use Auto gain? Only when you have no need for controlling exposure differently for each frame but instead can use an exact division of similar exposures.

3

Figure 3.23C – Sample Multiple exposure images

Auto gain works fine if you're not using masks, where part of the image is masked off initially and later exposed. When you use a mask, you want a full normal exposure for each of the uncovered (nonmasked) sections of the image, so Auto gain will not work. In this case, you should use manual exposure, with Auto gain turned Off.

Note: You can assign the BKT button to allow you to select Multiple exposure settings with external camera controls (instead of bracketing). We will consider how in the chapter **Custom Setting Menu,** under the subheading **Custom Setting f8 – Assign BKT button.**

Settings Recommendation: Multiple exposure images can be a lot of fun to create (figure 3.23C). I often shoot Multiple exposure images with two people in the frame. One person leaves after the first half of the exposure is taken, while the other stays carefully still. When finished, you will have a normal picture of one person and the background, but the person that left halfway through the Multiple exposure will be ghosted. That means you'll be able to see the background right through her. It's even more fun if you have the person that leaves touch the other person during the first half of the Multiple exposure. Maybe have her put a hand on the other person's shoulder or wrap her arms around him.

If the person that stays for the entire exposure is very careful not to move at all, she will remain sharp and the image will certainly raise eyebrows later.

You can also do this with just one person, as the second picture in figure 3.23C shows. Just make sure she leaves halfway through the Multiple exposure.

Finally, be sure you are using a tripod when creating a Multiple exposure image unless you are masking part of the frame. Otherwise, the background will be completely blurred from camera movement between shots.

Interval Timer Shooting

(User's Manual – Page 201)

Interval timer shooting allows you set up your camera to shoot a series of images over time. Make sure you have a full battery or are connected to a full-time power source, such as the Nikon EH-5b AC adapter, for images taken over long periods.

Interval timer shooting is different than the setting covered next, *Time lapse photography*, in that it does not create a movie at the end of the image series. You simply have a series of images taken over a period of time when the camera is done with the Interval timer shooting session.

Let's examine how to configure the interval and how to start taking pictures.

Figure 3.24A – Interval timer shooting configuration

The screens in figure 3.24A look a little daunting, but it might help you to realize that the bottom half of screens 2 through 6 is informational in nature. It shows the settings you create with the top half of each screen.

There are three steps involved in configuring Interval timer shooting:

- Choose a start time (Start Time).
- Choose an interval (Interval).
- Choose the number of intervals and the number of shots per interval (Select no. of times x no. of shots).

Therefore, if I wanted to take a series of images starting at a particular time and shoot every 10 seconds (Interval) over a period of 30 seconds, (i.e., 3 intervals; number intervals), and make 2 images per interval (number of shots), I would set the following (get your camera and try these steps yourself so that it'll make sense to you):

1. Under Choose start time (figure 3.24A, screen 2), you could select Now, and the timer will start 3 seconds after you complete the remaining steps (3–5). If you would rather start at a future time, simply select Start time from screen 2 and scroll right. If you select Now, please skip step 2 below and go directly to step 3.

2. You will now see a Start time menu (figure 3.24A, screen 3) with the time in 24-hour (military) format:

   00:00

   Enter the time at which you want the intervals to begin. If I wanted to start at 3:30 PM, I would insert the following:

   15:30

   Once you've entered the time, scroll to the right.

3. You will now see the Interval screen with Hours : Minutes' Seconds" in the following format (figure 3.24A, screen 4):

   00 : 00' 00"

   The first two zeros represent the hours, the second set represents minutes, and the third set seconds. Since we want to start out with an Interval of 10 seconds, let's set the screen to look like this:

   00 : 00' 10"

   Scroll to the right to get to the next screen, screen 5.

4. Now we'll select the number of intervals (figure 3.24A, screen 5). This screen will say, Select no. of times x no. of shots in the format below. Number of intervals x number of shots = total shots.

   000 x 0 = 0000

   Set your camera so that it looks like this instead (figure 3.24A, screen 5):

   003 x 2 = 0006

   This means that there will be 003 intervals of 10 seconds each (set in step 3) and that the camera will take 2 pictures in each interval, for a total of 0006 pictures. In other words, 2 pictures will be taken every 10 seconds over a period of 30 seconds for a total of 6 images. Now scroll to the right to get to the next screen.

5. Select On from the final screen (figure 3.24A, screen 6) and press the OK button. A *Timer Active* message will appear on your camera's Monitor briefly. If you look at the Control panel you will see the word INTVL flashing. This will keep flashing as long as the Interval timer is in operation.

If you're shooting a timed interval during daylight hours, be sure to close the Viewfinder eyepiece shutter with the small lever to the left of the Viewfinder. Otherwise, changes in the light from behind the camera could cause the exposure to be inaccurate.

To pause timer operations or simply check on progress, open Interval time shooting from the Shooting Menu and select Pause from the menu, as shown in figure 3.24B. You will note the that Interval timer shooting is set to On in screen 1 and also that the In progress indicator (in green) is showing in screen 2. These indicate that Interval timer shooting is currently active. You can check the interval and number of shots information on the lower half of screen two.

Figure 3.24B – Pausing or resetting Interval timer shooting

If you want to modify the settings in the middle of the current interval, you can do so by selecting Off instead of Pause (figure 3.24B, screen 2), stepping back through the configuration screens, and then restarting the Interval timer. If you want to stop Interval timer shooting ahead of schedule, simply select Off.

Note: The number of intervals remaining will be displayed on the Control panel, in the same spot the shutter speed is normally displayed. The place that normally displays the aperture will instead display the number of shots remaining in the current interval setup.

Bracketing Info: Be sure to adjust any bracketing for the exposure, flash or Active D-Lighting (ADL) before you start Interval timer shooting. Bracketing overrides the number of shots, so you may not get what you expected if any kind of bracketing is active.

Settings Recommendation: Please learn to use this function! It is complicated, but if you read this section carefully and practice using Interval timer shooting as you read, you'll learn it quickly. This type of photography allows you to shoot things like flowers gradually opening or the sun moving across the sky. Have some fun with it!

Time-Lapse Photography

(User's Manual – Page 207)

Time-lapse photography is a close cousin to *Interval timer shooting* (last section). The primary difference is that Time-lapse photography is designed to create a silent time-lapse movie obeying the options selected in the final section of this chapter, **Movie Settings**.

During time-lapse photography, the camera automatically takes pictures at intervals you select during setup and later assembles them into a time-lapse movie.

Let's examine how to set up a short time-lapse sequence using Time-lapse photography.

Figure 3.25A – Configuring Time-lapse photography

Here are the steps to set up a Time-lapse photography movie (figure 3.25A):

1. Choose Time-lapse photography from the Shooting Menu and scroll to the right (figure 3.25A, screen 1).
2. Leave the Start choice set to Off because this is the initial configuration of the time-lapse sequence. Scroll to the right (figure 3.25A, screen 2).
3. Set the picture Interval in minutes and seconds. You can choose from 00:01 second to 10:00 minutes (figure 3.25A, screen 3). The hours column is not available to adjust from the Interval screen.
4. Choose a Shooting time over which the picture Interval will be executed. You can choose from 00:01 minute to 07:59 minutes (figure 3.25A, screen 4). The seconds column is not available.
5. Make sure your camera is on a tripod and ready for shooting the time-lapse sequence and then select On from the Start menu.

6. Press the OK button and the final screen will appear stating, *Starting time-lapse photography. Press OK to end before shooting is complete.* The time-lapse sequence has begun.

To interrupt the sequence and stop Time-lapse photography, simply press the OK button at any time.

Note: Before you start a time-lapse sequence, check the framing and exposure by taking a picture from the position you will use to capture the time-lapse movie. It is often best to shoot in Manual (M) exposure mode with everything preset to a particular aperture, shutter speed, and ISO sensitivity. This will prevent inconsistencies in exposure during the sequence. Additionally, it is a good idea to choose a White balance setting other than Auto to keep the colors the same across all the images in the the time-lapse movie.

If you have selected a long shooting time, you may want to consider connecting the camera to the optional Nikon EH-5b AC adapter for continuous power (you'll also need the EP-4B power connector if you do).

Time-lapse photography is not available (it's grayed out) if Shutter speed is set to Bulb, when you are in the middle of a bracket sequence, if the camera is connected via an HDMI cable to a device for movie recording, or when HDR, Multiple exposure, or Interval timer shooting is enabled.

Time-sequence length calculation: The total number of frames in the movie can be calculated by dividing the shooting time by the interval. Then you calculate the movie length by dividing the number of frames by the frame rate you've selected in *Shooting Menu > Movie settings > Frame/size/frame rate*. Remember, the Time-lapse photography system makes short movies based on the settings under *Shooting Menu > Movie settings*.

What you will see while shooting: While you're recording the time-lapse sequence, the word INTVL will flash on the Control panel. The time remaining in hours and minutes will show where the shutter speed normally appears, just before each frame is recorded. If you want to view the time remaining before a frame is fired, simply press the Shutter-release button halfway down and it will display in the shutter-speed area of the Control panel. No matter how you have Auto meter-off delay set, the exposure meter will not turn off during shooting.

If you want to see how things are progressing, simply press the MENU button and you can view the current sequence information on the bottom half of the screen. Unlike with Interval timer shooting, you cannot modify the settings while Time-lapse photography is running. To stop the sequence outright, press the OK button or turn the camera off.

A movie is made: When the sequence is complete, the camera will automatically assemble a short, silent movie based on the frame rates you selected in *Shooting Menu > Movie settings*. You can identify the time-lapse movie by the fact that it shows a Play button on the screen with the first frame of the movie sequence.

Settings Recommendation: This is a new functionality for Nikon D800 shooters. Instead of having to manually assemble frames from Interval time shooting into a movie, Time-lapse photography does it for us, based on normal camera movie settings. It is quite convenient for those of us who would like to experiment with or shoot interesting time-lapse sequences. Try shooting some short sequences of an event and see how easy it is!

Movie Settings

(User's Manual – Page 70)
Movie settings allow you to control how the camera records its main video Movies and Time-lapse photography sequences. This set of functions allows you to adjust four specific things about how the Movie mode works:

- *Frame size/frame rate* – Choose from seven frame size and rate combinations.
- *Movie Quality* – Select from High quality and Normal.
- *Microphone* – Change the sensitivity of the internal or external microphone, or turn it off.
- *Destination* – Select which memory card (SD or CF) will receive all Movies you create.

First, let's examine the seven frame rates and how to select your favorite.

Figure 3.26A – Frame size and rate selection

The following steps allow you to select a Frame size/frame rate for your next Movie (figure 3.26A).

1. Choose Movie settings from the Shooting Menu and scroll to the right (figure 3.26A, screen 1).

2. Select Frame size/frame rate and scroll to the right (figure 3.26A, screen 2).
3. Choose a size and rate for your movie from the list of seven Frame size/frame rate choices (figure 3.26A, screen 3).
4. Press the OK button to lock in the Movie size and rate.

Next, let's see about selecting High or Normal quality for the Movie. This affects the "bit rate" at which the movie is shot. Here is a list of frame size/frame rates and bit rates controlled by Movie quality:

Frame size	Frame rate	Bit Rate High Quality	Bit Rate Normal
1920×1080	30 fps	24 Mbps	12 Mbps
1920×1080	25 fps	24 Mbps	12 Mbps
1920×1080	24 fps	24 Mbps	12 Mbps
1280×720	60 fps	24 Mbps	12 Mbps
1280×720	50 fps	24 Mbps	12 Mbps
1280×720	30 fps	12 Mbps	8 Mbps
1280×720	25 fps	12 Mbps	8 Mbps

Table 3.1 – Frame size/frame rate and Movie quality bit rates

Figure 3.26B – Movie quality selection

Use the following steps to choose a Movie quality (figure 3.26B):

1. Choose Movie settings from the Shooting Menu and scroll to the right (figure 3.26B, screen 1).
2. Select Movie quality from the menu and scroll to the right (figure 3.26B, screen 2).
3. Choose High quality or Normal (figure 3.26B, screen 3).
4. Press the OK button to lock in the Movie quality.

Now, we'll look at choosing the most appropriate Microphone setting for your built-in mic, external accessory shoe mic, or external boom-mounted mic (such as the Nikon ME-1 stereo mic).

Figure 3.26C – Choosing a Microphone setting

The following steps allow you to select a Microphone setting for your next Movie (figure 3.26C).

1. Choose Movie settings from the Shooting Menu and scroll to the right (figure 3.26C, screen 1).
2. Select Microphone from the menu and scroll to the right (figure 3.26C, screen 2).
3. Choose Auto sensitivity, Manual sensitivity, or Microphone Off (figure 3.26C, screen 3). These settings are live so you can test them immediately.
4. Press the OK button to lock in the Microphone setting.

If you decide to use Manual sensitivity, you will need to use an extra screen that lets you choose a sound level manually, as seen in figure 3.26D.

Figure 3.26D – Choosing a Microphone setting manually

Use these steps to choose a sound level manually (figure 3.26D). See figure 3.26C to follow the flow to this screen series, which begins where figure 3.26C leaves off:

1. Choose Manual sensitivity from the menu and scroll to the right (figure 3.26D, screen 1).
2. Select a level for the microphone from the box by scrolling up or down with the Multi selector. You can choose from level 1 to level 20. The microphone is set to level 15 currently, the factory default (figure 3.26D, screen 2). These settings are live, so you will be able to test them immediately.

Finally, we'll examine the Movie setting called Destination (figure 3.26E). Destination lets you choose which memory card will receive and store your camera's video recordings. Just below the card slot selections you will see something like this:

02h 48m 56s. This is the total recording time the particular card will hold. If you're serious about shooting video with your camera, you'd better buy some high-capacity cards—you'll need them!

Figure 3.26E – Movie settings – Destination

Here are the steps to select a Destination for your Movies:

1. Choose Movie settings from the Shooting Menu and scroll to the right (figure 3.26E, screen 1).
2. Select Destination and scroll to the right (figure 3.26E, screen 2).
3. Select one of the two cards slots, SD card slot or CF card slot. Your movies will automatically flow to the card slot you have chosen (figure 3.26E, screen 3).
4. Press the OK button to use the card slot for Movies.

Note: The actual frame rate for 30 fps is 29.97 fps. For 24 fps it's 23.976, and for 60 fps it's 59.94 fps. It is important for you to know this because if you try to interface with some devices using anything but the exact frame rate, the device will not record the video.

The maximum length for any High-quality movie when recording to a memory card is 20 minutes. For Normal quality movies, the maximum recording length increases to 29 minutes, 59 seconds.

Using HDMI output, you can stream an endless stream of uncompressed, clean, broadcast-quality video, with no time limits. We will discuss Movies more deeply in the chapter called **Movie Live View.**

Settings Recommendation: When I shoot a movie, I normally select 1920×1080 at 24 fps because I have grown accustomed to the look of 1080p at 24 fps. You have many choices of broadcast-quality video available to you. If you want to save some card space, you may want to drop Frame size/frame rate down to 1280×720 at 30 fps. This provides extremely high-quality 720p HD video while taking up only a little more than half the space of full 1080p. To shoot video successfully, I suggest that you acquire at least some 16 GB cards, and even better, some 32 GB cards. Video uses a lot of storage space.

Author's Conclusions

Congratulations! You have fully configured one of the camera's four Shooting menu banks. Now, set up the rest of the banks according to your own ideas on how you want them to behave.

Using the camera's four Shooting menu banks allows you a great deal of flexibility in how your camera operates. You can switch between four different camera types, in a sense.

The upcoming information on the Custom setting banks will round out the major configuration of your camera for daily shooting. There are no direct connections between the four Shooting menu banks and the four Custom setting banks. You could create your own connection by naming them similarly. However, the combinations of how you configure this camera, and combine the banks, are virtually endless.

Custom Setting Menu

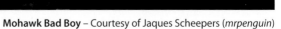

Mohawk Bad Boy – Courtesy of Jaques Scheepers (*mrpenguin*)

In chapter 3 we carefully considered the configurability of the Nikon D800 and its Shooting menu banks. Now we will continue with this process by examining the Custom settings banks in complete detail.

Let me start by clearly stating that the Shooting menu banks and Custom settings banks are separate entities, with different types of functions. I mentioned this in the preceding chapter but wanted to emphasize it here, too. There is no connection between them, although you could create an artificial connection by labeling the banks in a similar manner. However, it's only a label.

In my mind there is no clear difference between the settings in the two banks. In fact, in a recent camera (D8000), Nikon merged the Custom Settings with the Shooting Menu (and others). I think there is an awful lot of menu complexity in these pro-level cameras that could be rethought, and it probably will be in upcoming years.

I count no less than 54 Custom Settings in the D800. We've got a lot of ground to cover, and we will, in great detail. When finished with this chapter, you'll have a much deeper knowledge of this camera's inner workings and capabilities.

Without further ado, let's dive right into the settings and see what they do. First, we'll consider the process of renaming Custom settings bank A so that we'll know what style of shooting this bank is configured to support.

In the preceding chapter, we discussed how to rename a Shooting menu bank to describe its functionality. The process for changing the name of a Custom settings bank is exactly the same. If you're familiar with the process, you can just name your bank and skip this first section.

Figure 4.1A – Naming Custom settings bank A

Here are the steps to rename Custom settings bank A (figure 4.1A):

1. Notice that in the first screen of figure 4.1A, Custom settings bank has an A after it. This means that your camera is using bank A. If any letter other than A is showing, you are in a different Custom settings bank. Select Custom settings bank from the Custom Setting Menu and scroll to the right (figure 4.1A, screen 1).

2. Assuming that you have not yet renamed any of your Custom settings banks, you'll see the four blank default banks called A, B, C, and D, and a selection called Rename (figure 4.1A, screen 2). Set the bank to A, and scroll to the right.

3. Your screen will now look like the third screen in figure 4.1A. This is the bank rename screen. You'll see a series of characters on top, with a line of dashes below. The dashes are where we will put our text to rename the bank. Just after the small letter z there is a blank spot that represents a blank character for insertion in the line of text. Use the Multi selector to scroll through the numbers and letters to find the characters you want to use. Press the Multi selector center button to select a character. Keep selecting new characters until you have the entire bank name in place. If you make a mistake, hold down the Thumbnail/Playback zoom out button while using the Multi selector to move to the position of the error. Press the garbage can Delete button on the back of the camera to remove the bad character. For this example, I have named the bank General Purpose.

4. Press the OK button to save the new name.

Using the Information display edit screen to Access the Custom settings banks

If you would prefer to use a shortcut method of getting to the Custom settings banks, you can use the info button and Information display edit screen.

Figure 4.1B – Accessing Custom settings banks with the info button and Information display edit screen

Use these steps to quickly access the Custom settings banks:

1. Press the info button twice to bring up the Information display edit screen (figure 4.1B, screen 1).
2. Use the Multi selector to move to the Custom settings bank position, as shown in figure 4.1B, screen 2.
3. Press the OK button to open the Custom settings bank menu, which will show the main bank label screen.
4. Press the OK button to select a particular Custom settings bank or scroll to the right to enter the Rename screen. Follow the instructions connected with figure 4.1A, step 3, to rename a Custom settings bank.

Excellent! You've labeled bank A with a more meaningful name so you can quickly recognize this customizable bank of functions. I named bank A General Purpose on my camera to match the Shooting menu bank by the same name. Once again, this is completely optional.

Section One – a Autofocus

Custom Settings a1 to a8

You'll find eight distinct settings within the *a Autofocus* menu in the D800.

- **a1** – AF-C priority selection
- **a2** – AF-S priority selection
- **a3** – Focus tracking with lock-on
- **a4** – AF activation
- **a5** – AF point illumination
- **a6** – Focus point wrap-around
- **a7** – Number of focus points
- **a8** – Built-in AF assist illuminator

Custom Settings a1–a8 allow you to configure the autofocus system in various ways. The whole process is rather complex—and important for good photography. I thought autofocus and related functions important enough that I've included in this book an entire chapter dedicated to Autofocus (AF), AF-area modes, and Release modes. It covers autofocus and its supporting functions in much deeper detail. Please be sure to read that chapter well.

Custom Setting a1 – AF-C Priority Selection

(User's Manual – Page 281)

AF-C priority selection is designed to let you choose how your autofocus works when using Continuous-servo autofocus mode (AF-C).

Make sure you understand how this function works. If you configure this setting incorrectly for your style of shooting, it's entirely possible that a number of your pictures will be out of focus. Why?

Well, if you'll notice in figure 4.2, screen 3, there are three specific selections:

- **Release** – If the image must be taken, no matter what, then you will need to set AF-C priority selection to Release. This allows the shutter to fire every time you press the Shutter-release button, even if the image is not in focus. Releasing the shutter has "priority" over autofocus. If you are well aware of the consequences of shooting without a focus guarantee, then use this setting to make your camera take a picture every time you press the Shutter-release button. Your camera will shoot at its maximum frames per second (FPS) rate because it is not hampered by the time it takes to validate that each picture is in correct focus. You'll need to decide whether taking the image is more important than the image being in focus. We'll discuss why the Release and Release + focus functions exist in an upcoming section titled **Using Custom Settings a1 and a2.**

- **Release + focus** – This function slows the frame rate for improved focus when the light is low or the subject has little contrast with its surroundings, but it still allows the shutter to fire even if it cannot find a good focus point. Release still has priority over focus, but the camera tries to focus before releasing the shutter.

- **Focus** – This setting is designed to prevent your camera from taking a picture when the Viewfinder's green in-focus indicator is off. In other words, if the picture is not in focus, the shutter will not release. It does not mean that the camera will always focus on the correct subject. It simply means that your camera must focus on something before it will allow the shutter to release. Nikon cameras do a very good job with autofocus, so you can usually depend on the AF module to perform well. The Focus setting will drastically increase the chances that your image is in correct focus.

Figure 4.2 – Choosing a shutter-release priority for AF-C mode

Here are the steps to select a shutter-release priority when using AF-C mode (figure 4.2):

1. Select a Autofocus from the Custom Setting Menu and scroll to the right (figure 4.2, screen 1).
2. Highlight a1 AF-C priority selection and scroll to the right (figure 4.2, screen 2).
3. Choose one of the three settings from the menu, with full understanding of what may happen if you don't choose Focus. If you have the experience to use depth of field to cover autofocus, in case of slight focusing errors, or if you use the AF-ON button instead of the Shutter-release button for initiating autofocus, you may do well with AF-C priority selection set to Release or Release + focus. Test this carefully.
4. Press the OK button to select your shutter-release priority.

Settings Recommendation: Since I'm not a sports or action shooter, I choose Focus. Even if I were an action shooter, I would choose Focus. Read the section called **Using Custom Settings a1 and a2** before you make your final choice. The safe choice is Focus.

Custom Setting a2 – AF-S Priority Selection

(User's Manual – Page 282)

AF-S priority selection is very similar to AF-C priority selection. It too allows you to choose whether the camera will take a picture without something in focus. With this function, you set a shutter-release priority for Single-servo autofocus mode (AF-S). Set it wrong and many of your pictures may be out of focus. I choose Focus when using AF-S.

There are two modes to choose from (figure 4.3, screen 3):

*   ***Release*** – A photo can be taken at any time, even if not in focus. This can lead to images that are out of focus, unless you manually focus each time you take a picture. The camera's priority is releasing the shutter when you press the Shutter-release button, and it will do so even if nothing is in focus.
*   ***Focus (default)*** – The image must be in focus or the shutter will not release. This means that the shutter won't release unless the Viewfinder's green in-focus indicator is on. This is the closest thing to a guarantee that your image will be in focus when you press the Shutter-release button. However, if you are focused on the wrong part of your subject, the camera will still fire.

Figure 4.3 – Choosing a shutter-release priority for AF-S mode

Here are the steps to select a shutter-release priority when using AF-S mode (figure 4.3):

1. Select a Autofocus from the Custom Setting Menu and scroll to the right (figure 4.3, screen 1).
2. Highlight a2 AF-S priority selection and scroll to the right (figure 4.3, screen 2).
3. Choose one of the two settings from the menu, with full understanding of what may occur if you don't choose Focus (figure 4.3, screen 3).
4. Press the OK button to select your shutter-release priority.

Settings Recommendation: Once again, I choose Focus. I love pictures that are in focus, don't you? When I don't want the camera to care about autofocus over shutter release, I'll just flip the switch to manual on the camera or lens and focus where I want. Up next is the section called **Using Custom Settings a1 and a2.** Read it well!

Using Custom Settings a1 and a2

Before we proceed to the next Custom Setting, please consider the following special information.

Release priority vs. Focus priority – Two of the more important functions in this Custom Settings chapter are a1 and a2. I added this special section so you'll understand why you must pay very close attention to these two settings.

Focus priority simply means that your camera will refuse to take a picture until it can reasonably focus on something. Release priority means that the camera will take a picture when you decide to take it, whether anything is in focus or not!

Now, you might ask yourself, "Why is there such a setting as Release priority?"

Well, many professional photographers shoot high-speed events at high frame rates—taking hundreds of images—and use depth of field (or experience and luck) to compensate for less-than-accurate focus. They are in complete control of their camera's systems and have a huge amount of practice in getting the focus right where they want it to be.

There are valid reasons for these photographers not to use Focus priority. However, most of those same photographers do not let pressing the Shutter-release button halfway down start autofocus either because the focus could change every time the Shutter-release button is pressed. They set a4 AF activation so that the autofocus doesn't even activate until the AF-ON button is pressed. They then use the AF-ON button exclusively for autofocus and the Shutter-release button to take the picture. They separate the two functions instead of using the Shutter-release button for both.

You need to ask yourself, "What type of a photographer am I?"

If you are a pro shooting hundreds of pictures of fast race cars, Focus priority may not be for you. However, for the average photographer taking pictures of his kids running around the yard, deer jumping a fence, beautiful landscapes, flying birds, portraits, or a bride tossing a bouquet, Focus priority is usually the best choice. For most of us, it's better to have the camera refuse to take the picture unless it's able to focus on our subjects.

When you're shooting at a high frame rate, Focus priority may cause your camera to skip a series of out-of-focus images. It will slow your camera's frame rate so that it will not reach the maximum four frames per second in some cases. But, I have to ask, what is the point of several out-of-focus images mixed with the in-focus pictures? Why waste the card space, add shutter wear, and then have to weed through the slightly out-of-focus images? Especially with the image sizes the D800 creates!

Pay special attention to these two settings. You will need to decide—based on your style of shooting—whether you want your camera to refuse to take an out-of-focus image. If you set a1 and a2 to Focus priority and you try to take an out-of-focus image, the Shutter-release button will simply not release the shutter. The green in-focus indicator in the Viewfinder will have to be on before the shutter will release.

Settings Recommendation: I set both a1 and a2 to Focus priority. I'm not a high-speed shooter, so I don't need my camera to take a picture "no matter what." What good are out-of-focus images? We'll discuss this even more in the chapter titled **Autofocus, AF-Area, and Release Modes**.

Custom Setting a3 – Focus Tracking with Lock-On

(User's Manual – Page 283)

Focus tracking with lock-on allows you to select the length of time your camera will ignore an intruding object that blocks your subject.

In other words, let's say you are focused on a bird flying past you. As you pan the camera with the bird's movement, the autofocus system tracks it and keeps it in good focus. A road sign briefly interrupts the focus tracking as the bird moves behind it and then reemerges. How would you feel if the bright, high-contrast road sign grabbed the camera's attention and you lost tracking on the bird? That would be quite aggravating, wouldn't it?

The D800 provides Focus tracking with lock-on to prevent this from happening. The "lock-on" portion of this function helps your camera keep its focus on your subject, even if something briefly comes between the camera and subject. The camera locks on to your subject doggedly if this function is enabled.

Without Focus tracking with lock-on, any bright object that gets between you and your subject may draw the camera's attention and cause you to lose focus on the subject.

The camera provides a variable time-out period for the lock-on functionality. Lock-on time-out allows an object that stays between the camera and your subject for a predetermined length of time to attract the camera's attention. You can adjust this time-out according to the delay time period that works best for you. Plan to experiment a bit so that you can determine what is best for your style of shooting. The factory default is Normal, which I've determined from my own testing is about a one-second delay.

Figure 4.4 – Focus tracking with lock-on

Here are the steps to configure Focus tracking with lock-on (figure 4.4):

1. Select a Autofocus from the Custom Setting Menu and scroll to the right (figure 4.4, screen 1).
2. Highlight a3 Focus tracking with lock-on and scroll to the right (figure 4.4, screen 2).
3. Choose one of the six choices from the menu. Figure 4.4, screen 3, shows 3 (Normal), the factory default of about one second. The longest period, 5 (long), seems to provide only about two seconds of delay in my experience. Time each of these for yourself and see what you think.
4. Press the OK button to select the time-out period.

With Single-point AF, the camera will start the lock-on time-out as soon as the single AF point is unable to detect the subject.

With Dynamic-area AF or Auto-area AF and Focus tracking with lock-on enabled, I was amused at how adamant the camera was about staying with the current subject. I'd focus on a map on the wall and then cover most of the focusing points with the User's Manual. As long as I allowed at least one or two AF points to remain uncovered so the camera could see the map, the focus did not switch to the manual. I could just hear the D800 muttering, "*Hah, you can't fool me, I can still see a little edge of that map there, so I'm not changing focus!*"

Only when I stuck the D800 manual completely in front of the lens, covering all the AF points, did the camera decide to start timing the Focus tracking with lock-on time-out. After a second or two, the camera would give up on the map and focus on the manual instead.

Try this yourself! It's quite fun and will teach you something about the power of your camera's AF system.

Does Lock-On Cause Autofocus to Slow Down?

Some misunderstanding surrounds this technology. Because it is designed to cause the autofocus to hesitate for a variable time period before seeking a new subject, it may make the camera seem sluggish to some users.

But, this "sluggishness" is really a feature designed to keep you from losing your subject's tracked focus. Once the camera locks on to a subject's area of focus, it tries its best to stay with that subject even if it briefly loses the subject. This keeps the lens from racking in and out and searching for a new subject as soon as the previous subject is no longer under an AF point.

It also causes the camera to ignore other higher-contrast or closer subjects while it follows your original subject. You will have to judge the usefulness of this technology for yourself. I suggest that you go to some event or down to the lake and track moving objects with and without lock-on enabled. Your style of photography has a strong bearing on how you'll use—or whether you'll use—Focus tracking with lock-on.

Focus tracking with lock-on has little to do with how well the camera focuses. Instead, it is concerned with what it is focused on. Here are some good reasons to leave Focus tracking with lock-on enabled in your camera.

If Focus tracking with lock-on is set to Off, Dynamic-area AF and Auto-area AF will instantly react to something coming between your subject and the camera, even if it only appears in the frame for a moment. A good example of this is when you are tracking a moving subject and just as you are about to snap the picture, a closer or brighter object enters the edge of the frame and is picked up by an outside sensor. The camera may instantly switch focus to the intruding subject. When Focus tracking with lock-on is enabled, the camera will ignore anything that briefly gets between you and your subject.

When using Dynamic-area AF or Auto-area AF mode, I call turning off Focus tracking with lock-on "focus roulette!"

Configuring Custom setting a3 is not difficult. However, you'll need to decide just how long you want your camera to stay locked on to a subject's area before it decides that the subject is no longer available when something intrudes.

Settings Recommendation: I leave Focus tracking with lock-on enabled at all times. When I'm tracking a moving subject, I don't want my camera to be distracted by every bright object that gets in between me and the subject. In fact, the camera defaults to 3 (normal) from the factory. Nikon gives us variable focus lock time-outs so we can change how long the camera will keep seeking the old subject when we switch to a new one. I suggest you play around with this function until you fully understand how it works. Watch how long the camera stays locked on one subject's area before an intruding object grabs its attention. The time-out period seems shorter on the D800 than on previous Nikons I've worked with. Even the Long setting seems to give me only about two seconds of lock-on delay. You will have to decide which delay period is best for you. I choose 5 (Long).

This is one of those functions that people either love or hate. Personally, I find it quite useful for my type of photography. Try it and see what it does for you.

Custom Setting a4 – AF Activation

(User's Manual – Page 283)

AF activation allows you to choose whether you want the Shutter-release button to cause the camera to autofocus. If you leave this setting at the factory default, the AF system will be activated when you press the Shutter-release button halfway down or when you press the AF-ON button. You can also select the setting that allows only the AF-ON button to initiate autofocus and the Shutter-release button will not activate autofocus.

The primary purpose of this function is to allow a very experienced photographer to separate shutter release and autofocus operations. A sports photographer may only want to autofocus the camera when she presses the AF-ON button and not when she presses the Shutter-release button.

Various styles of photography require the photographer to find a good autofocus point with the AF-ON button and then fire many frames with the Shutter-release button with no danger of the camera changing the autofocus during shutter release.

Figure 4.5 – AF activation

Here are the steps used to configure AF activation (figure 4.5):

1. Select a Autofocus from the Custom Setting Menu and scroll to the right (figure 4.5, screen 1).
2. Highlight a4 AF activation and scroll to the right (figure 4.5, screen 2).
3. Choose one of the two choices from the menu. In figure 4.5, screen 3, Shutter/AF-ON has been selected.
4. Press the OK button to lock in the setting.

Here's a description of the two selections:

- **Shutter/AF-ON** – Autofocus will be activated if you press the Shutter-release button halfway or if you press the AF-ON button.
- **AF-ON Only** – Autofocus works only when you press the AF-ON button. The Shutter-release button will not activate autofocus; it will only start metering and release the shutter.

Settings Recommendation: I use Shutter/AF-ON myself because I'm primarily a nature shooter and don't need to separate autofocus from shutter release. I don't have many fast-moving subjects, other than flying birds or leaping deer. And with those, it just feels more natural to me to autofocus and fire the shutter with one button.

However, if I were shooting a high-speed event and wanted to maximize my camera's firing speed (frame rate), I wouldn't hesitate to use AF-ON only, and I would change Custom setting a1 – AF-C priority selection to Release priority. That would let me use my thumb to autofocus with the AF-ON button while my index finger is on the Shutter-release button firing bursts of images—using the Continuous high (CH) frame rate. I would autofocus only when needed and would use depth of field to cover small focus variations. That way, I could get as many pictures into my camera as possible for later publication choices.

Custom Setting a5 – AF Point Illumination

(User's Manual – Page 284)

AF point illumination helps you see the currently active AF points when you first start autofocus. You've seen the little squares—representing the active AF point or points—in the Viewfinder, when they briefly appear in red and then turn black. Sometimes the Viewfinder is dark, and it might be difficult to see a black square.

If AF point illumination is set to Off, you'll still have the black square that represents your selected AF point but may not be able to see it. If you set AF point illumination to Auto or On, the point will flash red when you first start autofocus or move the AF point with the Multi selector.

There are three selections on the AF point illumination screen. These affect how the AF points are displayed when active.

Figure 4.6 – AF point illumination

First, let's examine the steps to configure AF point illumination. Then we'll talk about how the settings work (figure 4.6).

1. Select a Autofocus from the Custom Setting Menu and scroll to the right (figure 4.6, screen 1).
2. Highlight a5 AF point illumination and scroll to the right (figure 4.6, screen 2).
3. Choose one of the three choices from the menu. In figure 4.6, screen 3, Auto has been selected.
4. Press the OK button to lock in the setting.

Here's a list of each selection and a description of its function:

- **Auto** – If the Viewfinder's background is dark, the selected AF point(s) will briefly flash red when you press the Shutter-release button or AF-ON button to start autofocus. If the background is bright, you'll have no trouble seeing your AF point's little black squares, so they don't flash red when you start autofocus.
- **On** – The selected AF point is highlighted in red when you start autofocus, regardless of the light level of the background.
- **Off** – The selected AF point does *not* light up in red when you start autofocus. It is always black.

Settings Recommendation: The simplest setting to use is Auto because that lets the camera determine whether there is enough light coming through the Viewfinder for you to see the AF point(s) at the start of autofocus. If you want to force the AF point(s) to flash each time you start autofocus or move the point(s) with the Multi selector, you can set AF point illumination to On. I wouldn't leave this set to Off unless I was in a consistently lighted studio where the Viewfinder has good contrast.

Custom Setting a6 – Focus Point Wrap-Around

(User's Manual – Pages 267, 272)

Focus point wrap-around allows you to control how AF point scrolling on the View-finder works. When you are scrolling your selected AF point to the right or left, or even up and down in the array of 51 points, it will eventually come to the edge of the Viewfinder area.

This setting allows you to set whether the AF point simply stops when it gets to the edge or scrolls to the opposite side. If you are scrolling the AF point to the left and it reaches the far left side of the screen, it will stop. If Focus point wrap-around is set to Wrap, the point will not stop and instead reappears on the right side of the screen. It "wraps" around. This setting works the same way in an up and down direction. If you scroll off the top of the sensor area, the AF point will reappear on the bottom when Wrap is enabled.

Figure 4.7 – Focus point wrap-around

Here are the steps used to configure Focus point wrap-around (figure 4.7):

1. Select a Autofocus from the Custom Setting Menu and scroll to the right (figure 4.7, screen 1).
2. Highlight a6 Focus point wrap-around and scroll to the right (figure 4.7, screen 2).
3. Choose one of the two choices from the menu. In figure 4.7, screen 3, No wrap has been selected.
4. Press the OK button to lock in the setting.

Here is a description of the two choices:

- **Wrap** – This setting allows the selected AF point to scroll off of the Viewfinder screen and then reappear on the other side.
- **No wrap (default)** – If you scroll the AF point to the edge of the screen, it stops there! You'll have to use the Multi selector to move the point in the opposite direction, back toward the middle.

Settings Recommendation: Wrapping the AF point around from one side to the other drives me bonkers. I don't like it on my computer screen or in my camera's Viewfinder. When the AF point gets to the edge, I want it to stop so that I can scroll back the other way with the Multi selector. However, I humbly submit that some people will simply adore having their AF point wrap to the other side of the Viewfinder. If that describes you, simply set it to Wrap. It's always No wrap for me!

Custom Setting a7 – Number of Focus Points

(User's Manual – Page 285)

Number of focus points allows you to adjust the distance the AF point moves when you move it around the screen with the Multi selector.

If you move your AF point often, it might get tiring to scroll through the full 51 focus points, one AF point jump at a time. In older Nikon cameras, we had a maximum of 11 sensors to scroll through, so it wasn't too bad. However, with 51 AF points, it could take longer than you want to scroll from one side of the viewfinder to the other. Or, you might just like the old way better!

Nikon has given you a choice. If you'd rather not scroll through 51 sensors, you can set Number of focus points to 11 sensors instead (figure 4.8A).

Figure 4.8A – 11 AF points vs. 51 AF points

In Figure 4.8A, the screen on the left shows the 11-point setting, while the right screen shows the 51-point setting.

This does *not* change the fact that there are 51 sensors available in Dynamic-area AF or Auto-area AF modes. It just means that the Multi selector will make the selected sensor move farther with each press. It skips over sensors when you scroll in Single-area AF and Dynamic-area AF modes. This means that you cannot choose "in-between" sensors as selected AF points, so you have a smaller choice of sensors to start autofocus.

When using Auto-area AF, the camera does not allow you to move the AF points. So this function does not affect the camera when Auto-area AF is selected.

If you are unhappy when scrolling through 51 points, change it to 11. You can always change it back!

Figure 4.8B – Number of focus points

Here are the steps to select one of the Number of focus points settings (figure 4.8B):

1. Select a Autofocus from the Custom Setting Menu and scroll to the right (figure 4.8B, screen 1).
2. Highlight a7 Number of focus points and scroll to the right (figure 4.8B, screen 2).
3. Choose one of the two choices from the menu. In figure 4.8B, screen 3, AF51 51 points has been selected.
4. Press the OK button to lock in the setting.

Here is a description of each Number of focus points selection:

- **51 points (default)** – Choose from any of the 51 focus points (AF points) when you are scrolling through them.
- **11 points** – Choose from only 11 focus points (AF points) when you are scrolling through them. The other AF points are still available for autofocus; you just can't scroll directly to them—some are skipped. That means the Multi selector will move the selected AF point around more quickly.

Settings Recommendation: I usually leave my camera set to 51 points for nature work because I have time to scroll among the AF points in an unhurried fashion. The only time I'll change that is when I need to shoot very quickly at an event that moves at a rapid pace, like a graduation ceremony or wedding. At these events I may not have time to scroll through all 51 points to select an AF point on the edge of the Viewfinder, so I'll set Number of focus points to 11 points.

Remember, setting it to 11 points does not change how many AF points are actually used by the camera. It only affects how fast you can move among the AF points when you use the Multi selector to scroll around. Some AF points are skipped during scrolling. You still get the benefit of the other 51 points, if they are set to be active.

Built-In AF-Assist Illuminator

(User's Manual – Page 286)

You've seen the very bright little light on the front of the D800, near the grip (figure 4.9A). Nikon calls this the Built-in AF-assist illuminator, and it lights up when the camera senses low-light conditions and when you're using certain AF-area modes (not all) to help with autofocus. Custom setting a8 allows you to control when that powerful little light comes on.

Figure 4.9A – Built-in AF-assist illuminator

Figure 4.9B – Built-in AF-assist illuminator settings

We'll look into the two modes of this setting, but first here are the steps to set the Built-in AF-assist illuminator to On or Off (figure 4.9B):

1. Select a Autofocus from the Custom Setting Menu and scroll to the right (figure 4.9B, screen 1).
2. Highlight a8 Built-in AF-assist illuminator and scroll to the right (figure 4.9B, screen 2).
3. Choose On or Off from the menu. In figure 4.9B, screen 3, On has been selected.
4. Press the OK button to lock in the setting.

Here are descriptions of how On or Off affects the AF-assist illuminator:

- **On (default)** – If the light level is low, the built-in AF-assist illuminator lights up to help light the subject enough for autofocus. This only works in certain modes:

a) Single-servo AF (AF-S) as a Focus mode at any time it's needed

b) Auto-area AF as an AF-area mode any time it's needed

c) Single-point AF and Dynamic-area AF as an AF-area mode if you are using only the center AF point as the selected sensor

d) When Continuous-servo AF (AF-C) is selected as a Focus mode, the built-in AF-assist illuminator becomes inactive.

- *Off* – The AF-assist illuminator does not light up to help you in low-light autofocus situations. The camera may not be able to autofocus in very low light.

Settings Recommendation: I leave Built-in AF-assist illuminator set to On most of the time. It is activated only when the light is low enough to need it. However, let me qualify this for specific circumstances. If you are trying to take pictures without being noticed, such as from across the room with a zoom lens or while doing street photography, you certainly don't want this extremely bright little light drawing attention when you start autofocus. Or, you may be shooting wildlife, such as a giant grizzly bear, and surely don't want to call attention to yourself by shining a bright light into the old bear's eyes. Use this feature when you don't mind others noticing you—especially if they are eight feet tall with claws—because it will draw attention immediately.

Section Two – b Metering/Exposure

Custom Settings b1 to b6

You'll find six settings within the *b Metering/exposure* menu in the D800:

- **b1** – ISO sensitivity step value
- **b2** – EV steps for exposure cntrl
- **b3** – Exp./flash comp. step value
- **b4** – Easy exposure compensation
- **b5** – Center-weighted area
- **b6** – Fine-tune optimal exposure

The first three settings in the Metering/exposure menu (b1, b2, b3) affect how your camera views steps in its EV range. Most people like to have their camera work very precisely, so they'll use the 1/3 step EV selection of b1, b2, and b3.

Others might not be as selective and would prefer to change sensitivity in 1/2 step EV, or even whole steps.

What Is EV?

EV simply means *exposure value*, which is an agreed-upon value of exposure metering. It is spoken of in full or partial EV steps, like 1/3, 1/2, or 1. It simply means different combinations of shutter speeds and apertures that give similar exposures. An EV step corresponds to a standard logarithmic "power-of-2" exposure step, commonly referred to as a *stop*. So, instead of saying 1 EV, you could substitute 1 stop. EV 0 (zero) corresponds to an exposure time of 1 second at an aperture of f/1.0 or 15 seconds at f/4. EV can be positive or negative. EV -6 equals 60 seconds at f/1.0. EV 10 equals 1/1000 seconds at f/1.0 or 1/60 seconds at f/4. The EV step system was invented in Germany back in the 1950s. Interesting, huh?

Custom Setting b1 – ISO Sensitivity Step Value

(User's Manual – Page 287)

ISO sensitivity step value allows you to change the way the camera handles its progression of exposure values for ISO. In other words, the camera's ISO "step" value is set with Custom setting b1. You can control the steps with the following values:

- 1/3 step EV (ISO steps 200, 250, 320, 400, etc.)
- 1/2 step EV (ISO steps 200, 280, 400, 560, etc.)
- 1 step EV (ISO steps 200, 400, 800, 1600, etc.)

If you are concerned with maximum ISO control, use the 1/3 step setting. It takes longer to scroll through the ISO selections if you manually set your ISO value in 1/3 steps. The 1/3 step setting is the factory default value for b1.

Figure 4.10 – ISO sensitivity step value

Here are the steps to change the ISO sensitivity step value (figure 4.10):

1. Select b Metering/exposure from the Custom Setting Menu and scroll to the right (figure 4.10, screen 1).
2. Highlight b1 ISO sensitivity step value and scroll to the right (figure 4.10, screen 2).

3. Choose one of the three items on the menu. In figure 4.10, screen 3, 1/3 step has been selected.
4. Press the OK button to lock in the setting.

Now, let's talk more about how to use the ISO sensitivity step value setting. With ISO sensitivity step value set to 1/3 step, hold down the ISO button on the top left of the camera and turn the rear Main command dial to the right. If your camera was set to ISO 100 initially, you'll see that the ISO number in the Control panel changes in the following pattern:

ISO sensitivity step value set to **1/3 step**:
100, 125, 160, 200, 250, 320, 400, 500, 640, etc.

ISO sensitivity step value set to **1/2 step**:
100, 140, 200, 280, 400, 560, 800, 1100, 1600, etc.

ISO sensitivity step value set to **1 step**:
100, 200, 400, 800, 1600, 3200, 6400, etc.

Settings Recommendation: I like the most control I can have over ISO sensitivity increments. I normally leave this set to the factory default of 1/3 step. This allows me to carefully fine-tune the ISO sensitivity value for precise exposures.

Custom Setting b2 – EV Steps for Exposure Cntrl

(User's Manual – Page 287)

EV steps for exposure cntrl refers to the number of steps in the shutter speed and aperture because those are your main exposure controls. It also encompasses the exposure bracketing system. Just as with the ISO sensitivity covered in the previous section, you can control the number of steps in the full range of exposure values.

Here are the three settings available for exposure control:

- 1/3 step (EV is 1/3 step; bracketing can be 1/3, 1/2, or 1 EV)
- 1/2 step (EV is 1/2 step; bracketing can be 1/2 or 1 EV)
- 1 step (EV and Bracketing are 1 step each)

Figure 4.11 – EV steps for exposure cntrl

Here are the steps used to adjust EV steps for exposure cntrl (figure 4.11):

1. Select b Metering/exposure from the Custom Setting Menu and scroll to the right (figure 4.11, screen 1).
2. Highlight b2 EV steps for exposure cntrl and scroll to the right (figure 4.11, screen 2).
3. Choose one of the three items on the menu. In figure 4.11, screen 3, 1/3 step has been selected.
4. Press the OK button to lock in the setting.

Now, let's examine the concept in more detail. All EV steps for exposure cntrl really means is that when you are adjusting the shutter speed or aperture manually, each will work incrementally in the following steps.

Shutter and Exposure (starting at a random shutter speed or aperture)

1/3 step EV:
Shutter:	1/100, 1/125, 1/160, 1/200, 1/250, 1/320, etc.
Aperture:	f/5.6, f/6.3, f/7.1, f/8, f/9, f/10, etc.

1/2 step EV:
Shutter:	1/90, 1/125, 1/180, 1/250, 1/350, 1/500, etc.
Aperture:	f/5.6, f/6.7, f/8, f/9.5, f/11, f/13, etc.

1 step EV:
Shutter:	1/60, 1/125, 1/250, 1/500, 1/1000, 1/2000, etc.
Aperture:	f/4, f/5.6, f/8, f/11, f/16, f/22, etc.

Bracketing

1/3 step EV	Bracket: 0.3, 0.7, 1.0 (or 1/3, 2/3, 1 EV steps)
1/2 step EV	Bracket: 0.5, 1.0 (or 1/2 and 1 EV steps)
1 step EV	Bracket: 1.0 (or 1 EV step)

Nikon chose to lump shutter speed, aperture, and bracketing all under Custom setting b2. The factory default value for EV steps for exposure cntrl is 1/3 step.

Settings Recommendation: Similar to ISO sensitivity step value, I keep EV steps for exposure cntrl set to 1/3 step. It's critical to control the EV steps with granularity, especially with exposure. It's best to increment the EV in small steps for use with the histogram.

Custom Setting b3 – Exp./Flash Comp. Step Value

(User's Manual – Page 287)

Exp./flash comp. step value is concerned with the granularity of exposure or flash compensation. Most of us will use the exposure or flash compensation system at one time or another.

Exposure compensation adjustments are made with the +/- Exposure compensation button on the top right of the camera, just behind the Shutter-release button. The Flash compensation button is right below the button that opens the pop-up Speedlight flash on the front of the camera. It has a small lightning bolt arrow icon.

Holding the +/- Exposure compensation button and turning the rear Main command dial allows you to adjust the exposure compensation. Holding the Flash compensation button and turning the front Sub-command dial allows you to adjust flash compensation.

Maybe the camera's light meter or flash is giving your images a little less exposure than you'd like, so you fine-tune by adding a little extra exposure with the +/- Exposure compensation or Flash compensation button. These buttons can be configured by setting b3 so that they allow you to adjust your camera in a finer (1/3 EV) or coarser way (1/2 or 1 EV) for exposure or flash compensation.

Exposure compensation can be added or subtracted in 1/3, 1/2, or 1 EV steps—for up to 5 EV (5 stops). Flash is a little less flexible with only +1.0 EV or -3.0 EV in 1/3, 1/2, or 1 EV step.

Figure 4.12 – Exp./flash comp. step value

Here are the steps used to adjust Exp./flash comp. step value (figure 4.12):

1. Select b Metering/exposure from the Custom Setting Menu and scroll to the right (figure 4.12, screen 1).
2. Highlight Exp./flash comp. step value and scroll to the right (figure 4.12, screen 2).
3. Choose one of the three items on the menu. In figure 4.12, screen 3, 1/3 step has been selected.
4. Press the OK button to lock in the setting.

Here is more information on the step values you can use with exposure or flash compensation, once you've selected your favorite increment (figure 4.12, screen 3):

- **1/3 step**: Exposure compensation of up to +/- 5.0 EV: 0.3, 0.7, 1.0, 1.3, 1.7, 2.0, 2.3, 2.7, 3.0, etc. Flash compensation is limited to +1.0 and -3.0 in 1/3 EV steps.
- **1/2 step**: Exposure compensation of up to +/- 5.0 EV: 0.5, 1.0, 1.5, 2.0, 2.5, 3.0, 3.5, 4.0, etc. Flash compensation is limited to +1.0 and -3.0 in 1/2 EV steps.
- **1 step**: Exposure compensation of up to +/- 5.0 EV: 1.0, 2.0, 3.0, 4.0, 5.0. Flash compensation is limited to +1.0 and -3.0 in 1 EV steps.

Settings Recommendation: The factory default for Exp./flash comp. step value is 1/3 step. Most shooters will leave it set to 1/3 step because that allows fine control over the amount of exposure or flash compensation. Like the two previous Custom settings (b1 and b2), b3 allows you to have fine or coarse control over compensation values. The 1/3 step EV setting seems to be the best for most of us.

Custom Setting b4 – Easy Exposure Compensation

(User's Manual – Page 288)

I had to do a bit of thinking to wrap my brain around *Easy exposure compensation*. The bottom line is that you can set the camera's exposure compensation without using the +/- Exposure compensation button. Instead, you can use the Command dial of your choice to dial in exposure compensation.

There are three settings in Easy exposure compensation, as follows: On (Auto reset), On, and Off.

Figure 4.13 – Easy exposure compensation

Here are the steps used to configure Easy exposure compensation (figure 4.13):

1. Select b Metering/exposure from the Custom Setting Menu and scroll to the right (figure 4.13, screen 1).
2. Highlight b4 Easy exposure compensation and scroll to the right (figure 4.13, screen 2).
3. Choose one of the three items on the menu. In figure 4.13, screen 3, Off has been selected.
4. Press the OK button to lock in the setting.

If you set the camera to On (Auto reset) or simply to On, you can use the Command dials to set exposure compensation instead of the +/- Exposure compensation button. Off means what it says: You will have to use the +/- Exposure compensation button.

Each exposure mode (P, S, A, M) reacts somewhat differently to Easy exposure compensation. Let's consider how the P-Program, S-Shutter-priority, and A-Aperture-priority modes act when you use the three settings. The M-Manual mode does not seem to be affected by Custom setting b4, although it does allow compensation with the normal +/- Exposure compensation button.

Here are the values and how they work:

- **On (Auto reset)** – Using the Sub-command dial in Program (P) or Shutter-priority (S) mode or the Main command dial in Aperture-priority (A) mode, you can dial in exposure compensation without using the normal +/- Exposure compensation button. The other Command dial will control the aperture or shutter speed, as it normally would. Once you allow the meter to go off, or turn the camera off, the compensation value you dialed in is reset back to 0. That's why it's called Auto reset. If you have already set a compensation value using the normal +/- Exposure compensation button, then the process of dialing in compensation with the Command dial simply adds or substracts compensation from the value you added with the normal +/- Exposure compensation button. When the meter resets, it returns back to the compensation value you added with the +/- Exposure compensation button and not to 0.
- **On** – This works the same way as On (Auto reset), except that the compensation you've dialed in does not reset but stays in place, even if the meter or camera is turned off.
- **Off** – Only the normal +/- Exposure compensation button applies exposure compensation.

Note: The granularity of Easy exposure compensation's EV step fine-tuning is affected by the Custom setting b3 1/3, 1/2, or 1 step setting. Also, the Command dials used to set compensation and change shutter speed and aperture can be swapped in *Custom Setting Menu > f9 Customize command dials > Change main/sub*, which we will consider later in this chapter.

When you adjust exposure compensation with either the normal +/- Exposure compensation button or with Easy exposure compensation, a +/- symbol will appear on the Control panel, in the Information display (open with info button), in the Viewfinder, and in Live view mode while exposure compensation is active.

Settings Recommendation: I have not found a use for this function. The normal +/- Exposure compensation button works fine for me. However, I have read in forums that some people really like this functionality because they can change the shutter speed and aperture with one Command dial, and dial in exposure compensation with the other.

I think I will keep on using what I am used to; however, why not experiment with this for a few minutes and see if you like dialing in compensation with the Command dials instead of the +/- Exposure compensation button? Nikon gives us a lot of choices!

Custom Setting b5 – Center-Weighted Area

(User's Manual – Page 289)

Center-weighted area allows you to control the area on the Viewfinder that has the greatest weight in metering a subject when the camera is in Center-weighted area metering mode. Years ago our cameras didn't have Matrix metering. Back in the good old days, we all had averaging meters, partially averaging meters, or none at all.

If you prefer not to use Nikon's built-in database of image scenes, otherwise known as Matrix metering, and you use Spot metering only as needed, you are most likely using the Center-weighted area meter. It's cool that Nikon gives us a choice. You have three meter styles in your camera, adding to its flexibility.

Figure 4.14A – Metering selector

On the camera's back, between the Viewfinder eyepiece and the AF-ON button, you'll find the AE-L/AF-L button (figure 4.14A). Surrounding the AE-L/AF-L button is a small knurled ring called the Metering selector. It has a white dot pointing to three symbols just above the ring. The right-hand symbol is the Center-weighted area meter (red arrow), the middle is the Matrix meter, and the left-hand symbol is the Spot meter. We are concerned with the Center-weighted area meter in this section.

The Center-weighted area meter can be configured to use a central area of the Viewfinder to do most of its metering, with less attention paid to subjects outside this area, or it can be set up to simply average the entire frame.

Here are the five settings used by the camera's Center-weighted area metering mode:

- 8 or 8 mm
- 12 or 12 mm
- 15 or 15 mm
- 20 or 20 mm
- Avg or Average

Figure 4.14B – Center-weighted area metering mode

Here are the steps used to choose a Center-weighted area metering mode (figure 4.14B):

1. Select b Metering/exposure from the Custom Setting Menu and scroll to the right (figure 4.14B, screen 1).
2. Highlight b5 Center-weighted area and scroll to the right (figure 4.14B, screen 2).
3. Choose one of the five items on the menu. In figure 4.14B, screen 3, 12 mm has been selected.
4. Press the OK button to lock in the setting.

Let's see how each setting works. Figure 4.14C shows the approximate size of the most sensitive area in the Viewfinder for each size of the Center-weighted area meter. The pink circle is the most sensitive area for metering, and it gets larger for each setting. In the final frame of figure 4.14C, all areas of the frame are equally sensitive and average the light values of everything seen in the Viewfinder.

Figure 4.14C – Center-weighted and Average-weighted areas shown in pink

When you are using the Center-weighted area metering mode, the metering system uses an invisible circle in the center of the Viewfinder to meter the subject (figure 4.14C). When it's set down to 8 mm, it's almost small enough to be a spot meter because the real Spot metering mode of the camera uses a 4 mm circle surrounding the currently selected AF point.

The Center-weighted area meter does *not* move around with the currently selected AF point point as the Spot meter does. Instead, it assigns the greatest weight to the center of the Viewfinder frame, and everything outside the circle in the center is not as important.

Each size increase from 8, 12, 15, to 20 mm will increase the sensitivity of the center of the Viewfinder so that more emphasis is given to a larger area in the middle.

If you select the Avg – Average setting, the entire Viewfinder frame is used to meter the scene. The camera takes an average of the entire frame by including all light and dark areas mixed together for an averaged exposure.

Note: If you use a non-CPU lens with the Center-weighted area meter, the camera selects the 12 mm circle automatically and it cannot be changed. The Average weighting works for both CPU and non-CPU lenses.

Settings Recommendation: When I use the Center-weighted area meter, I generally use the 20 mm setting to make the largest area of the center of the Viewfinder be the most sensitive section. Personally, I use 3D Matrix metering most of the time and have my camera's Fn button set up to switch to the Spot meter temporarily. That way, I am using Nikon's incredible 3D Color Matrix Metering III, with its ability to consider brightness, color, distance, and composition. Matrix gives me the best metering I've had with any camera yet! The Center-weighted area meter is still included in our modern cameras to make people who are used to using the older style meter more comfortable. Most of us will use Matrix metering these days.

Fine-Tune Optimal Exposure

(User's Manual – Page 290)

Nikon has taken the stance that users should be allowed to fine-tune most major camera systems. The exposure system is no exception. Fine-tune optimal exposure allows you to fine-tune the Matrix, Center-weighted area, and Spot metering systems by +1/-1 EV in 1/6 EV steps, independently.

In other words, you can force each of the three metering systems to add or deduct a little exposure from what it normally would use to expose your subject. This stays in effect with no further notice until you set it back to zero. It is indeed fine-tuning because the maximum 1 EV step up or down is divided into six parts (1/6 EV). If you feel that your camera is too conservative with the highlights, mildly underexposing, and you want to force it to add 1/2 step exposure, you simply add 3/6 EV to the compensation system for that metering system. (Remember basic fractions—where 1/2 equals 3/6?)

This works like the normal compensation system except it allows you only 1 EV of compensation. As screen 3 of figure 4.15A shows, an ominous-looking warning appears telling you that your camera will not show a compensation icon, as it does with the normal +/- Exposure compensation button, when you use the Fine-tune optimal exposure system. This simply means that while you have this fine-tuning system dialed in for your light meter, the camera will not remind you that it is fine-tuned by showing you a compensation icon. If it did turn on the compensation icon (+/- on the Control panel and in the Viewfinder), how could it show you the same icon when you are using normal compensation at the same time as meter fine-tuning?

This light meter fine-tuning applies only to the Custom setting bank you are currently working with. If you are working in bank A, banks B, C, and D are not changed.

Figure 4.15A – Fine-tune optimal exposure

1. Select b Metering/exposure from the Custom Setting Menu and scroll to the right (figure 4.15A, screen 1).
2. Select b6 Fine-tune optimal exposure and scroll to the right (figure 4.15A, screen 2).
3. Select Yes from the warning screen and scroll to the right (figure 4.15A, screen 3).
4. Select the metering system you want to adjust. In figure 4.15A, screen 4, you can see that I selected Matrix metering. Now, scroll to the right. All three meter fine-tuning operations work exactly the same way, and each meter can be adjusted independently of the other two. If you want to adjust a different meter besides Matrix metering, simply substitute one of the other two meter types in this step (Center-weighted metering or Spot metering).
5. Scroll up or down in 1/6 EV steps until you reach the fine-tuning value you would like to use (figure 4.15A, screen 5). I set +3/6, which is the equivalent of adding +1/2 EV of extra exposure to the Matrix metering system.

6. Press the OK button to lock in the fine-tuning value for the metering system you selected in step 4 only. *You must fine-tune each metering system separately.* Notice the red arrow in figure 4.15A, screen 6. It is pointing to an asterisk that shows, at a glance, that something in this menu has been fine-tuned. If you go into the menu system to see what is changed, it will show the fine-tuning fraction next to the meter that has been fine-tuned, as shown at the red arrow in figure 4.15B.

Figure 4.15B – Fine tuning the Matrix meter

That's all there is to it! Just remember that you have Fine-tune optimal exposure turned on because the camera will not remind you. Watch your histogram to make sure you're not regularly underexposing or overexposing images once you have the fine-tuning adjustment in place. If so, just go back in and adjust the fine-tuning up or down, or turn it off.

Settings Recommendation: Unless you have a good reason to adjust this, most of us will leave it alone. It certainly won't hurt anything to make a fine-tuning adjustment, if you feel confident that you really need it. I used to run +3/6 on my Nikon D300 a few years back. However, the Nikon D800 seems to have a significantly "hotter" meter, in that it tends—for me, anyway—to expose a little toward the bright side of the histogram, often even slightly clipping highlight values. If anything, with my D800, I might consider backing off exposure by -1/6 or maybe even as much as -3/6, merely as an experiment.

The point is, we have the ability to fine-tune our cameras to an amazing degree. Whether you need this now or not, you might later. Learn how it works and, as always, experiment with it to see if fine-tuning your light meter gives you better exposures.

Section Three – c Timers/AE Lock

Custom Settings c1 to c4

You'll find four settings within the *c Timers/AE lock* menu in the D800:

- **c1** – Shutter-release button AE-L
- **c2** – Auto meter-off delay
- **c3** – Self-timer
- **c4** – Monitor off delay

Custom Setting c1 – Shutter-Release Button AE-L

(User's Manual – Page 290)

Shutter-release button AE-L is designed to allow you to lock your camera's exposure when you press the Shutter-release button halfway down. Normally that type of exposure lock happens only when you press and hold the AE-L/AF-L button. However, when you have Shutter-release button AE-L set to On, your camera will act like you've pressed the AE-L/AF-L button every time you start autofocus and take a picture.

This function allows you to meter from one area of the scene and then recompose to another area without losing the meter reading from the first area, as long as you hold the Shutter-release button halfway down.

Looking at this another way, when you have Shutter-release button AE-L set to Off, exposure will lock only when you hold down the AE-L/AF-L button.

Figure 4.16 – Shutter-release button AE-L

Here are the steps used to configure Shutter-release button AE-L (figure 4.16):

1. Select c Timers/AE lock from the Custom Setting Menu and scroll to the right (figure 4.16, screen 1).
2. Highlight c1 Shutter-release button AE-L and scroll to the right (figure 4.16, screen 2).
3. Choose one of the two choices on the menu. In figure 4.16, screen 3, Off has been selected.
4. Press the OK button to lock in the setting.

Settings Recommendation: I use this feature only when I really need it, then turn it off. The rest of the time, I just use the AE-L/AF-L button to lock my exposure. I don't think I'd leave Shutter-release button AE-L turned on all the time because I might be holding the Shutter-release button halfway down to track a moving subject through light and dark areas.

For sunset shooters (or something similar) who like to include the sun in their image, this is a nice function. You can meter from an area of the sky that has the best color and then swing the camera around to include the sun in the shot. The camera will expose for the originally metered area as long as you hold the Shutter-release button halfway down. Normally, you'd just do this with the AE-L/AF-L lock button.

Custom Setting c2 – Auto Meter-Off Delay

(User's Manual – Page 291)

Auto meter-off delay controls the amount of time your camera's light meter stays on after you press the Shutter-release button halfway and then release it. The default value is 6 seconds.

When the light meter goes off, the various displays—like shutter speed and aperture—in the Control panel and Viewfinder do also.

If you would like your light meter to stay on longer for whatever reason, such as for multiple exposures, you can adjust it to the following settings:

- 4 s – 4 seconds
- 6 s – 6 seconds (default)
- 10 s – 10 seconds
- 30 s – 30 seconds
- 1 min – 1 minute
- 5 min – 5 minutes
- 10 min – 10 minutes
- 30 min – 30 minutes
- No limit – meter stays on until camera is turned off

Figure 4.17 – Auto meter-off delay

Here are the steps to set the Auto meter-off delay (figure 4.17):

1. Select c Timers/AE lock from the Custom Setting Menu and scroll to the right (figure 4.17, screen 1).
2. Highlight c2 Auto meter-off delay and scroll to the right (figure 4.17, screen 2).
3. Choose one of the nine choices on the menu. In figure 4.17, screen 3, 6 s has been selected. You can't see all the available selections in screen 3. Scroll down on your camera to find one more setting, No limit.
4. Press the OK button to lock in the setting.

Settings Recommendation: There are times when you want the light meter to stay on for a longer or shorter time than it normally does. When I'm shooting multiple exposures, I leave Auto meter-off delay set to No limit. However, when I'm shooting normally, it stays at either 6 s or 10 s. The longer the light meter stays on, the shorter the battery life, so extend the meter time only if you really need it. You can adjust it from 4 s to No limit. Easy enough!

Custom Setting c3 – Self-Timer

(User's Manual – Page 291)
The *Self-timer* setting is used to take pictures remotely or without touching the camera except to start the Self-timer operation. Hands-off shooting can reduce vibrations so that you have sharper pictures. Additionally, it gives you time to place yourself in group shots so there will be some pictures of you to look at later. Put yourself in front of the camera from time to time, or no one will remember what you look like!

Figure 4.18A – Self-timer selection on Release mode dial

To set the Self-timer, hold down the Release mode dial lock button and turn the Release mode dial until the little timer symbol (figure 4.18A) is directly above the white dash. When you press the Shutter-release button, the Self-timer will start its timed countdown and will flash the little AF-assist illuminator light (figure 4.9A) until just before the shutter fires. Additionally, if you have Custom setting d1 Beep set to On, the camera will beep about twice per second while counting down and speed up to about four times per second just before it fires the shutter.

Here are the three choices you have when configuring the Self-timer:

- **Self-timer delay** – This setting allows you to specify a delay before the camera's shutter fires so you have time to position yourself for the shot or allow vibrations to settle down. The time delay ranges from 2 to 20 seconds. This setting can be used instead of a remote release, and you won't have cables to trip over.
- **Number of shots** – Use this setting to choose how many shots will be taken for each cycle of the Self-timer. You can choose from one to nine shots in a row.
- **Interval between shots** – If you are taking more than one shot during a Self-timer cycle, this setting allows you to choose a time interval between each shot ranging from 1/2 second to 3 seconds. This lets you select a time that allows vibrations from the previous shot to settle down.

Now let's look at the screens and steps used to adjust each of these settings. First, we'll look at the Self-timer delay. Here is a list of the four available Self-timer delay settings:

- 2 s – 2 seconds
- 5 s – 5 seconds
- 10 s – 10 seconds (default)
- 20 s – 20 seconds

Figure 4.18B – Setting the Self-timer delay

Use the following steps to configure the Self-timer delay (figure 4.18B):

1. Select c Timers/AE lock from the Custom Setting Menu and scroll to the right (figure 4.18B, screen 1).
2. Highlight c3 Self-timer and scroll to the right (figure 4.18B, screen 2).

3. Select Self-timer delay from the menu and scroll to the right (figure 4.18B, screen 3).
4. Choose one of the four options from the menu (2 s to 20 s). Figure 4.18B, screen 4, shows that I selected 10 s.
5. Press the OK button to lock in the setting.

Next, let's look at how to configure the Number of shots for each Self-timer cycle.

Figure 4.18C – Setting the Number of shots

Use the following steps to configure the Number of shots:

1. Select c Timers/AE lock from the Custom Setting Menu and scroll to the right (figure 4.18C, screen 1).
2. Highlight c3 Self-timer and scroll to the right (figure 4.18C, screen 2).
3. Select Number of shots from the menu and scroll to the right (figure 4.18C, screen 3).
4. Choose the Number of shots, from 1 to 9, by scrolling up or down with the Multi selector. Figure 4.18C, screen 4, shows that I selected 1 shot.
5. Press the OK button to choose the setting.

Finally, let's look at how to configure the Interval between shots for each Self-timer cycle. Here is a list of the four available Interval between shots settings:

- 0.5 s – 1/2 second (default)
- 1 s – 1 second
- 2 s – 2 seconds
- 3 s – 3 seconds

Figure 4.18D – Setting the Interval between shots

Use the following steps to configure the Interval between shots:

1. Select c Timers/AE lock from the Custom Setting Menu and scroll to the right (figure 4.18D, screen 1).
2. Highlight c3 Self-timer and scroll to the right (figure 4. 18D, screen 2).
3. Select Interval between shots and scroll to the right (figure 4. 18D, screen 3).
4. Choose the Interval between shots, from 0.5 s to 3 s, by scrolling up or down with the Multi selector. Figure 4.18D, screen 4, shows that I selected 0.5 s (1/2 second).
5. Press the OK button to choose the setting.

Settings Recommendation: Often, if I don't want to take the time to plug in a remote release cable, I just put my camera on a tripod and set the Self-timer delay to 2 or 5 seconds. This lets the D800 make a hands-off exposure so I don't shake the camera or the tripod. If I must run to get into position for a group shot, I often increase the delay to at least 10 seconds to keep from looking like an idiot as I trip while running for position.

I can also control how many shots to take each time I use the Self-timer and how long to delay between those shots to allow vibrations to go away. I'm sure you'll agree that the Self-timer in your D800 is one of the most flexibile timers in a DSLR camera.

Another Way to Delay the Shutter Release

Many do not realize it, but you can also use the Mirror-up (MUP) function on the Release mode dial for even steadier timed releases. If you use a tripod and start an exposure with the camera set to Mirror-up, the camera will wait 30 seconds and then fire the shutter before lowering the mirror. Those concerned with maximum sharpness often use either Mirror-up or Self-timer delay to get the sharpest possible images.

Custom Setting c4 – Monitor Off Delay

(User's Manual – Page 292)

Monitor off delay lets you set a time-out for the Monitor on the back of the camera. You can select a variable timing for five individual functions that use the Monitor to display output. The Monitor will stay on until the time-out period expires. Here is a list of the individual functions:

- Playback
- Menus
- Information display
- Image review
- Live view

Figure 4.19A – Monitor off delay

Here are the steps to get to the screen for adjusting the time-outs. We'll consider each function individually (figure 4.19A).

1. Select c Timers/AE lock from the Custom Setting Menu and scroll to the right (figure 4.19A, screen 1).
2. Highlight c4 Monitor off delay and scroll to the right (figure 4.19A, screen 2).
3. Choose one of the five choices on the menu, as shown in figure 4.19A, screen 3. You can set the Monitor off delay for each specific display type. Let's examine each one.

Playback

First, let's look at setting a time-out for Playback. This is used when you are "playing back" images you have taken previously. This is not the Image review time-out, which is used when the camera displays a picture on the Monitor immediately after taking it. Playback is for when you are looking at a series of images on the Monitor for your own enjoyment and quality verification or when you are showing images to another person. The available time-out is from 4 s to 10 min.

Figure 4.19B – Monitor off delay – Playback

1. Figure 4.19B picks up where figure 4.19A leaves off. Select Playback from the c4 Monitor off delay screen (figure 4.19B, screen 1).
2. Choose from 4 seconds (4 s) to 10 minutes (10 min) delay time. The factory default of 10 s is selected (figure 4.19B, screen 2).
3. Press the OK button to lock in the setting.

Menus

Second, let's look at setting a time-out for using the Menus when you make adjustments to camera settings. How long do you want the time-out to be before the Monitor shuts off (4 s to 10 min)?

Figure 4.19C – Monitor off delay – Menus

1. Figure 4.19C picks up where figure 4.19A leaves off. Select Menus from the c4 Monitor off delay screen (figure 4.19C, screen 1).
2. Choose from 4 seconds (4 s) to 10 minutes (10 min) delay time. The factory default of 1 min is selected (figure 4.19C, screen 2).
3. Press the OK button to lock in the setting.

Information Display

Third, let's look at configuring a time-out for using the Information display that shows up when you press the info button. You can use the Information display as a larger reference for camera settings and adjustments before taking a picture and the Information display edit screen screen (by pressing the info button twice) to adjust several camera settings quickly. You can select from 4 s to 10 min.

Figure 4.19D – Monitor off delay – Information display

1. Figure 4.19D picks up where figure 4.19A leaves off. Select Information display from the c4 Monitor off delay screen (figure 4.19D, screen 1).
2. Choose from 4 seconds (4 s) to 10 minutes (10 min) delay time. The factory default of 10 s is selected (figure 4.19D, screen 2).
3. Press the OK button to lock in the setting.

Image Review

Finally, let's look at setting a time-out for Image review. When you take a picture and have *Playback Menu > Image review* set to On, the camera will display a picture on the Monitor for a specific period of time, controlled by the Image review time-out (2 s to 10 min).

Figure 4.19E – Monitor off delay – Image review

1. Figure 4.19E picks up where figure 4.19A leaves off. Select Image review from the c4 Monitor off delay screen (figure 4.19E, screen 1).
2. Choose from 2 seconds (2 s) to 10 minutes (10 min) delay time. The factory default of 4 s is selected (figure 4.19E, screen 2).
3. Press the OK button to lock in the setting.

Settings Recommendation: I set Monitor off delay to 1 min for Playback, Information display, and Image review on my D800. I set the Menu time-out to 5 min because I like to scroll around for longer periods as I set various settings in the menus.

If you want to conserve battery power, leave the Monitor off delay set to a low value like 4 to 20 seconds. The longer the Monitor stays on, the shorter the battery life, so extend the Monitor time only if you really need it. Like a small notebook computer screen, that big luxurious 3.2-inch VGA resolution Monitor pulls a lot of power. The Monitor and Control panel backlights are probably the biggest power drains in the entire camera.

However, you don't need to be overly concerned about this. As much image review (chimping) as I do, I can still shoot most of a day on one battery charge.

Section Four – d Shooting/Display

Custom Settings d1 to d12

Within the *d Shooting/display* menu, you'll find 12 settings in the D800, as follows:

- **d1** – Beep
- **d2** – CL mode shooting speed
- **d3** – Max. continuous release
- **d4** – Exposure delay mode
- **d5** – File number sequence
- **d6** – Viewfinder grid display
- **d7** – ISO display and adjustment
- **d8** – Screen tips
- **d9** – Information display
- **d10** – LCD illumination
- **d11** – MB-D12 battery type
- **d12** – Battery order

Custom Setting d1 – Beep

(User's Manual – Page 292)

The *Beep* setting allows your camera to make a beeping sound to alert you during the following events:

- Focus lock while in Single-servo AF (AF-S) mode
- Focus lock while in Live view mode
- Countdown in Self-timer mode operations
- At the end of Time-lapse photography
- Trying to take a picture with the memory card locked

You can set the camera to beep with a high- or low-pitched tone, and you can adjust the volume at which that tone sounds—or you can turn the beep sound off. When Beep is active, you'll see a little musical note displayed in the top Control panel and also in the Information display.

First let's examine how to set the Volume or disable Beep. It defaults to Off in the D800. The Volume settings under Beep in the Custom Setting Menu are 3, 2, 1, and Off (figure 4.20A).

Figure 4.20A – Choosing a Volume level for the camera's Beep

Use the following steps to select one of the d1 Beep Volume choices (figure 4.20A):

1. Select d Shooting/display from the Custom Setting Menu and scroll to the right (figure 4.20A, screen 1).
2. Highlight d1 Beep and scroll to the right (figure 4.20A, screen 2).
3. Select Volume from the menu and scroll to the right (figure 4.20A, screen 3).
4. Choose one of the four options from the list (1, 2, 3, or Off). In figure 4.20A, screen 4, Off is selected (factory default). You will hear a sample beep in each volume level as you choose it. The level 1 beep is rather quiet, so you may not hear it unless you hold your ear closer to the camera, while the level 3 beep is almost obnoxiously loud.
5. Press the OK button to lock in the setting.

Next, let's consider how to change the pitch of the beep. You have two pitch levels available: High (H) and Low (L). I compared them to my piano, and the Low (L) sound is F# just above middle C. The High (H) sound is almost three octaves higher. It is the B just before three octaves above middle C.

(You probably don't need that much information; however my somewhat compulsive personality requires that I give it to you. Notice that I didn't give you the decibel level of the three Beep volume levels. Wouldn't that be excessively excessive? Of course, with my trusty Radio Shack digital sound level meter, I do have that information. If you really want it, send me an e-mail.)

Getting back on track, here are the screens and steps to select a pitch for the beep.

Figure 4.20B – Choosing a Pitch for the camera's Beep

Use the following steps to select a Beep Pitch:

1. Select d Shooting/display from the Custom Setting Menu and scroll to the right (figure 4.20B, screen 1).
2. Highlight d1 Beep and scroll to the right (figure 4.20B, screen 2).
3. Select Pitch from the menu and scroll to the right (figure 4.20B, screen 3).
4. Choose one of the two options from the list (High or Low). In figure 4.20B, screen 4, High is selected (factory default). You will hear a sample beep in each pitch (B or F#) as you choose it.
5. Press the OK button to lock in the setting.

Settings Recommendation: I don't use Beep; it's turned Off on my D800. If I were using my camera in a quiet area, why would I want it beeping and disturbing those around me? I can just imagine me zooming in on that big grizzly bear, pressing the Shutter-release button, and listening to the grizzly roar his displeasure at my camera's beep. I want to live, so I turn off Beep. This is another function that you either love or hate. You can have it either way, but be careful around big wild animals when Beep is enabled. They might think you're calling them to supper, and you may be the main course.

However, you might want the reassurance of hearing a beep when AF has been confirmed or when the Self-timer is counting down. If so, turn it on. The AF-assist illuminator flashes during Self-timer operations, so I generally use that instead of Beep.

By the way, Beep is automatically disabled when you're using the new Q, or Quiet, shutter-release mode on the Release mode dial, regardless of how this setting is configured.

Custom Setting d2 – CL Mode Shooting Speed

(User's Manual – Page 293)

CL mode shooting speed controls how many frames-per-second (fps) the camera can take when set to Continuous low speed (CL) on the Release mode dial.

Figure 4.21A – CL mode on Release mode dial

CL mode is for those of us who would like to use a conservative frames-per-second rate. With the proper power, the camera can record 4 or 5 frames per second in FX mode. However, unless you are shooting race cars that are driving 200 mph, and unless you have large memory cards, you may not want 20 frames of the same subject a few milliseconds apart.

Figure 4.21B – CL mode shooting speed

Here are the steps used to configure CL mode shooting speed (figure 4.21B):

1. Select d Shooting/display from the Custom Setting Menu and scroll to the right (figure 4.21B, screen 1).

2. Highlight d2 CL mode shooting speed and scroll to the right (figure 4.21B, screen 2).

3. Choose one of the five choices on the list. In figure 4.21B, screen 3, 2 fps has been selected. If you set this setting to 4 fps, it will equal the CH setting on the Release mode dial. 5 fps is not available in FX mode unless you have an MB-D12 battery pack installed.
4. Press the OK button to lock in the setting.

As the last screen in figure 4.21B shows, you can adjust CL mode shooting speed so that your camera shoots at any frame rate from 1 to 5 fps. The default is 2 fps. Remember, you always have CH mode for when you want to blast off images like there's no end to your memory card(s) or when you want to impress bystanders with that extra-cool Nikon shutter clicking sound.

Note: When you are shooting Interval timer photography, this setting also sets the frame advance rate for single-frame.

Settings Recommendation: Use your favorite CL mode shooting speed, and grab a few, or many, frames with each press and hold of the Shutter-release button. I leave mine set at the default of 2 fps because that is reasonably fast yet not wasteful of card space. If you'd like, you can slow it all the way down to 1 fps and take only one picture each second that you hold the Shutter-release button down. You'll need to play around with this setting and decide for yourself what speed you like. Again, remember that you have both low (CL) and high (CH) speeds for the camera's shooting rate. This function is for the low speed setting (CL) found on the Release mode dial.

The D800 is not a very fast camera when it comes to frames per second, especially compared to a blazing-speed camera like the Nikon D4. In all honesty, this CL mode shooting speed function is not all that useful to me. If I need to shoot a series of images in rapid sequence, 4 fps is usually barely enough. However, for consistency's sake and for those who really need slower speeds, Nikon makes this function available.

Custom Setting d3 – Max. Continuous Release

(User's Manual – Page 293)
Max. continuous release sets the maximum number of images you can shoot in a single burst. It sounds like you can just start blasting away with your camera—shooting in a single burst until you have reached the number specified in figure 4.22, screen 3, which is up to 100 images.

While it is possible that you could reach 100 images in a single burst, it is improbable. Your camera is limited by the size of its internal memory buffer and the image format you are shooting.

There's a list in your camera User's Manual that specifies how large your camera's buffer is for each image type. In case you're interested in the raw buffer capacity data, the list is on page 436. Here is a summary of what the User's Manual reports concerning FX mode (there is some variation for changes in *Shooting Menu > Image area*):

- **NEF (RAW) files** – In FX mode (36×24 Image area), the memory buffer holds from 16 to 21 images, while in DX mode (24×16 Image area), the buffer holds 25 to 38 images, according to whether you are shooting in 12- or 14-bit color-depth and whether or not you are using compression.
- **TIFF files** – In FX mode (36×24 Image area), the memory buffer holds from 16 to 26 images, while in DX mode (24×16 Image area), the buffer holds 21 to 41 images, according to whether you are shooting L, M, or S size.
- **JPEG files** – In FX mode (36×24 Image area), the memory buffer holds 56 to 100 images, while in DX mode (24×16 Image area), the buffer holds 100 images, according to whether you are shooting in L, M, or S size; whether you are shooting in Fine, Normal, or Basic; and finally, whether you have selected Optimal quality or Size priority compression.

Note: All the preceding figures are approximate and will vary with the complexity of the subject matter in the image. Using or setting the following will cause the maximum number of images stored in the buffer to drop to a lower number:

- JPEG Optimal quality compression is On
- ISO sensitivity is set to Hi 0.3 or higher
- Enabling High ISO NR when Auto ISO sensitivity control is On
- Enabling High ISO NR when ISO sensitivity is set to ISO 1600 or higher
- Long exposure noise reduction is On
- Active D-Lighting is On
- Auto distortion control is On

Unless you are shooting the smaller JPEG normal or basic files, you'll fill up your camera buffer long before you reach the maximum of 100 shots specified by Max. continuous release.

Figure 4.22 – Max. continuous release

Here are the steps used to configure Max. continuous release (figure 4.22):

1. Select d Shooting/display from the Custom Setting Menu and scroll to the right (figure 4.22, screen 1).
2. Highlight d3 Max. continuous release and scroll to the right (figure 4.22, screen 2).
3. Use the Multi selector to scroll up or down and set the number of images you want in each burst. In figure 4.22, screen 3, 100 has been selected.
4. Press the OK button to lock in the setting.

Settings Recommendation: If you have a need to limit your camera to a maximum number of images in each shooting burst, simply change this number from its default of 100 images to whatever you feel works best for you. Personally, I want the buffer to hold as many images as it possibly can when I am blasting away in high-speed shooting modes, so I leave Max. continuous release set to 100.

However, you may want to artificially limit the camera to a maximum burst of 10 or 20 images, just so the buffer will not fill up and slow the camera way down. This also lets you maintain some control over your enthusiastic high-speed shooting. Do you really want dozens and dozens (and dozens) of pictures of those flying seagulls?

Custom Setting d4 – Exposure Delay Mode

(User's Manual – Page 293)

Exposure delay mode introduces a delay of 1 to 3 seconds after the Shutter-release button is pressed—and the reflex mirror raised—before the shutter is actually released. Hopefully, during the 1-second delay, camera vibrations will die down and the image will be sharper.

There are two settings available in Exposure delay mode (figure 4.23):

- **On** – The camera first raises the reflex (viewing) mirror and then waits 1, 2, or 3 seconds before firing the shutter, depending on the selection you choose, as shown in figure 4.23, screen 3. This allows the vibrations from the mirror movement to dissipate before the shutter fires. Of course, this won't be useful at all for shooting anything moving or for any type of action shots. But for slow shooters of static scenes, this is great and keeps you from having to use Mirror-up (MUP), which requires you to press the Shutter-release button twice to take a picture. It has the same effect as MUP but requires only one Shutter-release button press and a 1- to 3-second delay.
- **Off** – The shutter has no delay when this setting is turned off.

Figure 4.23 – Exposure delay mode

Here are the steps used to configure Exposure delay mode (figure 4.23):

1. Select d Shooting/display from the Custom Setting Menu and scroll to the right (figure 4.23, screen 1).
2. Highlight d4 Exposure delay mode and scroll to the right (figure 4.23, screen 2).
3. Choose one of the four choices on the list. In figure 4.23, screen 3, Off has been selected.
4. Press the OK button to lock in the setting.

Settings Recommendation: Exposure delay mode is very important to me. As a nature shooter, I use it frequently for single shots. When I'm shooting handheld—or on a tripod—and want a really sharp image, I use this mode to prevent the camera's internal reflex mirror movement from vibrating my camera and blurring my pictures. If you handhold your camera, shoot mostly static subjects, and want sharper pictures, this will help. On a tripod, this is a time-saver compared to Mirror-up (MUP) mode, which requires two Shutter-release button presses, or a 30-second delay.

Custom Setting d5 – File Number Sequence

(User's Manual – Page 294)

File number sequence allows your camera to keep count of the image file numbers for each picture you take, in a running sequence from 0001 to 9999. After 9999 pictures, it rolls back over to 0001. Or, you can cause it to reset the image number to 0001 when you format or insert a new memory card.

Here are the three settings, and an explanation of how each works:

- *On* (default) – Image file numbers start at 0001 and continue running in a sequence until you exceed 9999, at which point the image numbers roll over to 0001 again. The File number sequence continues even if a new folder is created, a new memory card is inserted, or the current memory card is formatted. If the file number exceeds 9999 during a shoot, the camera will create a brand-new folder on the same memory card and start writing the new images in numbered order from 0001 into the new folder. Similarly, if you accumulate 999 images in the current folder, the next image capture will result in the camera creating a new folder, but the file numbering will *not* be reset to 0001 unless that 999th image had a file number of 9999. No matter what you do with your memory cards, or how many folders you or the camera create, the File number sequence will continue incrementing until 9999 images have been taken. Only then will the File number sequence reset to 0001. In other words, File numbering continues from the last number used or the largest file number in the current folder, whichever is bigger, until 9999 images are reached, at which time the camera starts the numbering sequence over at 0001.

- *Off* – Whenever you format or insert a new a memory card, the number sequence starts over at 0001. If you exceed 999 images in a single folder, the camera creates a new folder and starts counting images at 0001 again.
- *Reset* – This is similar to the On setting. However, it is not a true running total to 9999 because the image number is dependent on the folder in use. The camera simply takes the last number it finds in the current folder and adds 1 to it, up to 999. If you switch to an empty folder, the numbering starts over at 0001. Because a folder cannot hold over 999 pictures, you will not exceed 999 images in any one folder. Each folder has its own number series and causes a File number sequence Reset.

Figure 4.24 – File number sequence

Here are the steps used to configure File number sequence (figure 4.24):

1. Select d Shooting/display from the Custom Setting Menu and scroll to the right (figure 4.24, screen 1).
2. Highlight d5 File number sequence and scroll to the right (figure 4.24, screen 2).
3. Choose one of the three choices on the list. In figure 4.24, screen 3, On has been selected. On is the best choice for most of us.
4. Press the OK button to lock in the setting.

Settings Recommendation: I heartily recommend that you set File number sequence to On, if it has been turned off. After much experience with Nikon DSLR cameras, and many years of storing thousands of files, I've found that the fewer number of files with similar image numbers, the better. Why take a chance on accidentally overwriting the last shooting session when copying files on your computer just because they have the same image numbers?

Plus, I like to know how many pictures I've taken with each camera. Since I use the *Shooting Menu > File naming* function to add my initials and a number reflecting the current number of times my camera has rolled over 9999 images (e.g., _1DY9999. NEF, _2DY9999.NEF, or _3DY9999.NEF), I'm better able to determine how many images I've taken with the camera. I just have to be careful to change the 1DY to 2DY when the image File number sequence rolls over from 9999 to 0001.

How Many Images?

The User's Manual describes an unusual situation that few of us will ever see. However, just in case you leave your frame rate set to CH and never let up on the Shutter-release button, you might want to read this paragraph carefully.

Each time you exceed 999 images in a folder, the camera will create a new folder. If your current folder is number 999 and has either 999 images or an image is numbered 9999, your camera will stop responding to Shutter-release button presses. I guess it figures that you've taken quite enough images in this session! The only way you'll get your camera to take more pictures is to set File number sequence to Reset (Custom setting d5) and format or insert a new memory card.

Basically, you should never number a folder as high as 999 (999ND800) and then shoot over 999 images or let the camera's running total of images exceed 9999 in a folder numbered 999.

When you manually create a folder with Storage folder numbering (*Shooting Menu > Storage folder* setting), please keep your folder numbers lower than 999 if you are going to shoot more than 999 images that day or if your number sequence in that folder is about to exceed 9999. Read this paragraph over 999 times and you'll understand just what I'm talking about. ☺

Custom Setting d6 – Viewfinder Grid Display

(User's Manual – Page 295)
A few years ago, the 35mm film Nikon N80/F80 was released with a viewfinder grid display, and I was hooked. Later, as I bought more professional cameras, I was chagrined to find that they did not have the on-demand gridlines that I had grown to love.

With the D800, you have not only a Viewfinder grid display, but also Live view (LV) gridlines. The best of both worlds! There are only two selections in Viewfinder grid display:

- *On* – Gridlines are displayed in the Viewfinder and on the Monitor in LV mode.
- *Off* – No gridlines are displayed.

Figure 4.25 – Viewfinder grid display

Here are the steps used to enable/disable the Viewfinder grid display (figure 4.25):

1. Select d Shooting/display from the Custom Setting Menu and scroll to the right (figure 4.25, screen 1).
2. Highlight d6 Viewfinder grid display and scroll to the right (figure 4.25, screen 2).
3. Choose On or Off from the list. In figure 4.25, screen 3, On has been selected.
4. Press the OK button to lock in the setting.

Settings Recommendation: I use these gridlines to line up things as I shoot so that I won't have weird tilted horizons and such. Many of us tend to tilt the camera one way or another, and gridlines help us see that we've tilted the frame.

I especially enjoy shooting with gridlines enabled when I'm down at the beach. Who needs tilted ocean views? When you're shooting architecture, the gridlines are invaluable for making sure buildings, walls, and doors are correctly oriented with the edge of the frame. There are lots of ways to use the Viewfinder grid display.

If you set Viewfinder grid display to On, I doubt you'll turn it back Off. The nice thing is that you can turn the gridlines On and Off at will. You don't have to buy an expensive viewfinder replacement screen for those times you need gridlines. Good stuff, Nikon!

Custom Setting d6 – ISO Display and Adjustment

(User's Manual – Page 295)

The *ISO display and adjustment* setting modifies how the D800 shows you the ISO sensitivity in the Control panel and Viewfinder, where you can normally see the frame count, or how many pictures you have left to take before the memory card is full. You can use ISO display and adjustment to modify the readout so the ISO sensitivity is shown instead of the frame count. There are three settings:

- **Show ISO sensitivity** – This setting displays the ISO sensitivity, instead of the frame count, in the Control panel.
- **Show ISO/Easy ISO** – This setting affects how you adjust the ISO sensitivity as well as how it is displayed. It works like Show ISO sensitivity in that it replaces the frame count with the ISO sensitivity value. It also adds a way to change the

ISO sensitivity while taking pictures. Normally you would use *Shooting Menu >
ISO sensitivity settings* or press the ISO button and turn the rear Main command
dial to change the ISO sensitivity. However, when you enable Show ISO/Easy ISO,
the camera lets you adjust the ISO sensitivity with either the rear Main command
dial or front Sub-command dial alone, without using the ISO button, according
to which exposure mode you are using. This applies only when you use the P,
S, or A modes on the Mode dial. Normally, when you have the camera in P or
S mode, you control the aperture (P mode) or shutter speed (S mode) with the
rear Main command dial. The front Sub-command dial does nothing. When you
set the camera to Show ISO/Easy ISO, the front Sub-command dial now sets the
ISO sensitivity when the P or S mode is set. Likewise, when the camera is set to
A mode, you normally control the aperture with the front Sub-command dial,
and the rear Main command dial does nothing. When you enable Show ISO/Easy
ISO in A mode, the camera lets you adjust ISO sensitivity with the unused rear
Main command dial, and you continue to control the aperture with the front
Sub-command dial. Basically, for photographers who need to adjust ISO sensi-
tivity quickly while shooting, this can be very convenient. M mode on the Mode
dial is not affected by this setting.

- **Show frame count** (default) – This is the default setting and leaves the camera
functioning as normal, with the frame count showing in the Control panel and
Viewfinder.

Figure 4.26 – Using ISO display and adjustment

Use the following steps to select an ISO display and adjustment setting (figure
4.26):

1. Select d Shooting/display from the Custom Setting Menu and scroll to the right
   (figure 4.26, screen 1).
2. Highlight d7 ISO display and adjustment and scroll to the right (figure 4.26,
   screen 2).
3. Choose one of the three settings from the menu. In figure 4.26, screen 3, Show
   frame count is selected.
4. Press the OK button to lock in the setting.

Settings Recommendation: I find little use for this setting because the ISO button is so easily available. My slow and deliberate tripod-based style of nature shooting rarely requires changing ISO sensitivity from its low settings (ISO 50–100). However, I recognize that many people need to change ISO sensitivity on the fly and may not want to use the Auto ISO sensitivity control, which adjusts ISO sensitivity automatically, within bounds, to get the shot.

This feature shows how interested Nikon is in giving us very fine control over our cameras. You can use automatic methods or control everything manually. ISO display and adjustment basically gives you manual control over a feature that most people would manage with Auto ISO sensitivity control.

If you are an action shooter and find yourself in varying light levels where you want to maintain fast manual control over ISO sensitivity, maybe you should learn to use this feature.

Custom Setting d8 – Screen Tips

(User's Manual – Page 295)

Screen tips allows you to enable small, helpful tips on the camera's Information display edit screen. This display is accessed by pressing the camera's info button *twice*. Pressing the info button once brings up only a summary display—you can't edit anything. Pressing it twice shows a similar screen that allows you to change several settings. It's a shortcut screen with settings that are accessed frequently, such as the Shooting menu bank and Custom settings bank settings.

Figure 4.27A, screen 1, shows the screen that appears when you press the info button once (Information display screen). Screen 2 shows the screen that appears when you press the info button twice (Information display edit screen).

I have Screen tips enabled on my D800 camera, so you can see the small Screen tip for changing the Color space (red arrow in figure 4.27A, screen 2).

Figure 4.27A – Information display and Information display edit screens, with Screen tips enabled

If you press the OK button when you have one of the settings highlighted on the Information display edit screen—as figure 4.27A, screen 2, shows for Color space—the camera will switch to a normal text menu and allow you to modify the setting. If you disable Screen tips, the little white tip bar shown at the red arrow in screen 2 will not be displayed.

Figure 4.27B – Enabling Screen tips

Here are the steps to configure Screen tips (figure 4.27B):

1. Select d Shooting/display from the Custom Setting Menu and scroll to the right (figure 4.27B, screen 1).
2. Highlight d8 Screen tips and scroll to the right (figure 4.27B, screen 2).
3. Choose On or Off from the list. In figure 4.27B, screen 3, On has been selected.
4. Press the OK button to lock in the setting.

Settings Recommendation: This is a helpful function that gives you "tool tips" for using the Information display edit screen. I would leave this set to the factory default of On. These little tips don't get in the way of anything and help remind you which setting you are looking at on the Information display edit screen.

Custom Setting d9 – Information Display

(User's Manual – Page 296)

The *Information display* setting allows your camera to automatically sense how much ambient light is in the area where you are shooting. If the ambient light is bright, the color of the physical Information display screen will also be bright so it can overcome the ambient light.

To open the Information display screen, press the stand-alone info button. The Information display screen shows the current shooting information. As I mentioned, the extremely cool thing about this Information display screen is that it can adjust its color and brightness according to the ambient light the camera senses through its lens.

Figure 4.28A – Dark-on-light and Light-on-dark display screens

Figure 4.28A shows the difference between the light and dark screens, which you can select by using one of the two Manual settings or using Auto to allow the camera to select a screen automatically. In figure 4.28A, screen 1 is the Dark-on-light screen and screen 2 is the Light-on-dark screen.

Try this: With your lens cap off, your camera turned on, and nothing displayed on the rear Monitor, press the info button. If there's dim to bright ambient light, you'll see a light-blue information screen with black characters. Now, go into a dark area or put your lens cap on and cover the Viewfinder eyepiece with your hand. You'll see that anytime there is very little ambient light, the camera changes the Information display screen to light gray characters on a dark blue background. This assures that you won't be blinded when you need to see the shooting information in a dark area. This may not impress you much, but I'm easily entertained!

As shown in figure 4.28B, image 3, there are two available selections for the Information display setting:

- **Auto** – The D800 decides through its capless lens or uncovered Viewfinder eyepiece how much ambient light there is and changes the color and contrast of the Information display screen accordingly.
- **Manual** – The Manual setting allows you to select the light or dark version of the Information display screen manually. If you choose Manual, you can see in figure 4.28C, screen 4, that you have two options: B Dark on light (light blue screen) and W Light on dark (dark blue screen).

Figure 4.28B – Setting Information display to Auto

Use the following steps to configure the Information display setting for Auto:

1. Select d Shooting/display from the Custom Setting Menu and scroll to the right (figure 4.28B, screen 1).
2. Highlight d9 Information display and scroll to the right (figure 4.28B, screen 2).
3. In figure 4.28, screen 3, Auto is selected. The camera will choose the light-blue or dark-blue screen depending on the ambient light level.
4. Press the OK button to lock in the setting.

Figure 4.28C – Setting Information display to Manual

If you want to manually select the screen color for your camera's Information display screen, use the following steps:

1. Select d Shooting/display from the Custom Setting Menu and scroll to the right (figure 4.28C, screen 1).
2. Highlight d9 Information display and scroll to the right (figure 4.28C, screen 2).
3. Choose B Manual and scroll to the right (figure 4.28C, screen 3).
4. The next screen shows the B Dark on light and W Light on dark choices. In figure 4.28C, screen 4, B Dark on light is selected, so the light-blue screen will be displayed when I press the info button.
5. Press the OK button to lock in the setting.

Settings Recommendation: I leave Information display set to Auto because it seems to work very well at automatically selecting the proper screen for current light conditions.

If you want to impress your friends and make your enemies envious, just show them how cool your camera is when it's smart enough to adjust its screen color to the current light conditions. I warned you that I'm easily entertained, didn't I?

Custom Setting d10 – LCD Illumination

(User's Manual – Page 296)

The *LCD illumination* setting gives you a simple way to set how the illumination of the Control panel LCD backlight works. When it's on, the Control panel lights up in yellowish green. Here are the two choices and how they work:

- **Off** (default) – If you leave LCD illumination set to Off, the Control panel will not turn on its backlight unless you tell it to by moving the Power switch to the backlight setting. If you move the Power switch all the way to the right, the Control panel will light up (figure 4.29A).
- **On** – This setting makes the Control panel illumination come on anytime the exposure meter is active. If you shoot in the dark and need to refer to the Control panel often, then switch this setting to On.

Figure 4.29A – Backlight position of the Power and backlight switch

Figure 4.29B – LCD illumination

Use the following steps to configure the LCD illumination setting:

1. Select d Shooting/display from the Custom Setting Menu and scroll to the right (figure 4.29B, screen 1).
2. Highlight d10 LCD illumination and scroll to the right (figure 4.29B, image 2).
3. Choose either On or Off from the menu. In figure 4.29B, image 3, Off is selected.
4. Press the OK button to lock in the setting.

Settings Recommendation: This setting will affect the battery life because backlights pull a lot of power, so I don't suggest using the On setting unless you really need it. You have the Power switch (On/Off/Backlight)—surrounding the Shutter-release button—to manually turn on the Control panel light when needed.

Custom Setting d11 – MB-D12 Battery Type

(User's Manual – Page 297)

MB-D12 battery type applies only when you choose to use AA-sized batteries of various types in your optional MB-D12 battery pack. It does not apply when you are using normal Nikon EN-EL3e, EN-EL4, or EN-EL4a li-ion batteries because they're intelligent and communicate with the camera.

If you have an MB-D12 and plan on using cheap AA batteries, then you'll need to tell the camera what type of AA batteries you're using for this session. It certainly is *not* a good idea to mix AA battery types.

These are the battery types the camera will accept (figure 4.30):

- LR6 (AA alkaline)
- HR6 (AA Ni-MH)
- FR6 (AA lithium)

Figure 4.30 – MB-D12 battery type

Here are the steps used to configure the MB-D12 battery type (figure 4.30):

1. Select d Shooting/display from the Custom Setting Menu and scroll to the right (figure 4.30, screen 1).
2. Highlight d11 MB-D12 battery type and scroll to the right (figure 4.30, screen 2).
3. Choose one of the three choices on the list. In figure 4.30, screen 3, LR6 (AA alkaline) has been selected.
4. Press the OK button to lock in the setting.

Settings Recommendation: Nikon allows but does not recommend using certain AA batteries, such as alkaline (LR6). Its primary objection to this type is that they do not work well at lower temperatures. In fact, once the ambient temperature drops below 68 degrees F (20 degrees C), an alkaline battery starts losing its ability to deliver power and will die rather quickly. You may not get as many shots out of a set of AA batteries, so your cost of shooting may rise.

However, AA batteries are readily available and relatively low cost, so some people like to use them, especially in an emergency. If you do choose to use AA batteries, I recommend sticking with lithium types (FR6). That is the same type of cell used in the normal Nikon EN-EL15 batteries and is not affected as much by a low ambient temperature. You can also use the Ni-MH (HR6, nickel-metal hydride) batteries safely because they are not as temperature sensitive and provide consistent power.

Custom Setting d12 – Battery Order

(User's Manual – Page 298)

Battery order lets you choose the order in which you want the available batteries to be used—camera's battery first or those in the MB-D12 battery pack first.

Here are the two menu choices:

- Use MB-D12 batteries first
- Use camera battery first

Figure 4.31 – Battery order

Here are the steps used to configure the Battery order (figure 4.31):

1. Select d Shooting/display from the Custom Setting Menu and scroll to the right (figure 4.31, screen 1).
2. Highlight d12 Battery order and scroll to the right (figure 4.31, screen 2).
3. Choose one of the two settings on the list. In figure 4.31, screen 3, Use MB-D12 batteries first has been selected.
4. Press the OK button to lock in the setting.

Settings Recommendation: Which battery do you want to draw down first? Personally, I like to use the MB-D12 batteries first and have my camera's internal battery available as a backup. That way, if I remove the MB-D12, my camera won't suddenly go dead due to a depleted battery. Nikon thinks the same way, evidently, because the camera defaults to Use MB-D12 batteries first.

Section Five – e Bracketing/Flash

Custom Settings e1 to e7

Within the *e Bracketing/flash* menu, you'll find seven settings in the D800:

- **e1** – Flash sync speed
- **e2** – Flash shutter speed
- **e3** – Flash cntrl for built-in flash
- **e4** – Modeling flash
- **e5** – Auto bracketing set
- **e6** – Auto bracketing (Mode M)
- **e7** – Bracketing order

Custom Setting e1 – Flash Sync Speed

(User's Manual – Page 299)

Flash sync speed lets you select a basic flash synchronization speed from 1/60 s to 1/250 s. The D800 has a more flexible Flash sync speed than many cameras. Or, if you prefer, you can use the two Auto FP modes of your camera—1/250 s (Auto FP) or 1/320 s (Auto FP). These Auto FP modes are available only with certain external Speedlights and not with the built-in pop-up Speedlight.

At press time, six Nikon Speedlights can be used with the D800 in Auto FP high-speed sync mode:

- SB-910
- SB-900
- SB-800
- SB-700
- SB-600
- SB-R200

Auto FP high-speed sync enables the use of fill flash even in bright daylight with wide aperture settings. It allows you to set your camera to the highest shutter speed available, up to 1/8000s, and still use the external flash unit to fill in shadows. See the upcoming section titled Auto FP High-Speed Sync Review, where we discuss how this works. Here are your choices (figure 4.32, screen 3):

- 1/320 s (Auto FP)
- 1/250 s (Auto FP)
- 1/250 s
- 1/200 s
- 1/160 s
- 1/125 s
- 1/100 s
- 1/80 s
- 1/60 s

Figure 4.32 – Flash sync speed

Here are the steps used to adjust your camera's Flash sync speed (figure 4.32):

1. Select e Bracketing/flash from the Custom Setting Menu and scroll to the right (figure 4.32, screen 1).
2. Highlight e1 Flash sync speed and scroll to the right (figure 4.32, screen 2).
3. Choose one of the nine choices on the list—1/60 s to 1/320 s (Auto FP). In figure 4.32, screen 3, 1/320 s (Auto FP) has been selected.
4. Press the OK button to lock in the setting.

When you're using Auto FP mode, the output of your flash is reduced but doesn't cut off the frame for exposures using a shutter speed higher than the normal flash sync speed (X Sync). Why? Let's review.

Auto FP High-Speed Sync Review

In a normal flash situation, with shutter speeds of 1/250 of a second and slower, the entire shutter is fully open and the flash can fire a single burst of light to expose the subject. It works like this: There are two shutter curtains in your camera. The first shutter curtain opens, exposing the sensor to your subject. The flash fires, providing correct exposure, and then the second shutter curtain closes. For a very brief period, the entire sensor is uncovered. The flash fires during the time when the sensor is fully uncovered.

However, when your camera's shutter speed goes above 1/250 of a second, the shutter curtains are never fully open for the flash to expose the entire subject in one burst of light. The reason is that at higher shutter speeds, the first shutter curtain starts opening and the second shutter curtain quickly starts following it. In effect, a slit of light is scanning across the surface of your sensor, exposing the subject. If the flash fired normally, a flash of light would expose the width of that slit between the shutter curtains, but the rest of the sensor would be blocked by the curtains. You would have a band of correctly exposed image, and everything else would be underexposed.

What happens to your external Nikon Speedlight to allow it to follow that slit of light moving across the sensor? It changes from a normal flash unit into a pulsing strobe unit. Have you ever danced under a strobe light? A strobe works by firing a series of light pulses. Similarly, when your camera's shutter speed is so high that the Speedlight cannot fire a single burst of light for correct exposure, it can use its Auto FP high-speed sync mode and fire a series of light bursts over and over as the shutter curtain slit travels in front of the image sensor. The Speedlight can fire thousands of bursts per second. To a photographer or subject, it still looks like one big flash of light, even though in reality it is hundreds or thousands of bursts of light, one right after the other.

When you are in Auto FP mode, you'll see something like this on your Speedlight's LCD monitor:

- TTL FP
- TTL BL FP

This tells you that the camera and Speedlight are ready for you to use any shutter speed you'd like and still get a good exposure. Even with wide open apertures!

You can safely leave your camera set to 1/320 s Auto FP or 1/250 s Auto FP all the time because the high-speed sync mode does not kick in until you raise the shutter speed above the maximum setting of 1/250 s. Below that shutter speed, the flash works in normal mode and does not waste any power by pulsing the output.

This pulsing of light reduces the maximum output of your flash significantly but allows you to use any shutter speed you'd like while still firing your external Speedlight. The higher the shutter speed, the lower the flash output. In effect, your camera is depending on you to provide enough ambient light to offset the loss in power. I've found that even my powerful SB-900 Speedlight can provide only enough power to light a subject out to about 8 feet (2.4 m) when using a 1/8000s shutter speed. With shutter speeds that high, there needs to be enough ambient light to help the flash light the subject unless you are very close to the subject.

However, now you can use wide apertures to isolate your subject in direct sunlight—which requires high shutter speeds. The flash will adjust and provide great fill light if you're using Auto FP high-speed sync mode.

Note: If your flash fires at full power in normal modes, it will blink the flash indicator in the Viewfinder to let you know that all available flash power has been dumped and you need to check to see if the image is underexposed. When the camera is firing in Auto FP high-speed sync mode, that doesn't happen. You'll get no warning in the Viewfinder if the image does not have enough light. Check the camera's histogram often to validate your exposures when using Auto FP.

Special Shutter Speed Setting X + Flash Sync Speed

When using Manual (M) or Shutter-priority auto (S) exposure modes, there is still one more setting below 30 seconds and bulb, named X + Flash sync speed. This special setting allows you to set the camera to a known shutter speed and shoot away. You will see X 250 if *Custom Setting Menu > e1 Flash sync speed* is set to 1/250 s. Whatever Flash sync speed you select will show up after the X. If you select a Flash sync speed of 1/125 s, then X 125 will show up as the next setting below bulb. Selecting a Flash sync speed of 1/60 s means that X 60 will show up below bulb.

The shutter speed will not vary from your chosen setting. The camera will adjust the aperture and flash when in Shutter-priority auto (S) mode, or you can adjust the aperture while the flash controls exposure in Manual (M) mode.

This special X-Sync mode is not available in Aperture-priority auto (A) or Programmed auto (P) modes because the camera controls the shutter speed in those two settings. Primarily, you'll use this setting when you are shooting in Manual or in Shutter-priority auto and want to use a known X-Sync speed.

Settings Recommendation: I leave my camera set to 1/320 s (Auto FP) as shown in figure 4.32, screen 3, all the time. The camera works just as it normally would until one of my settings takes it above 1/250s shutter speed, at which time it starts pulsing the light to match the shutter curtain travel. Once again, you won't be able to detect this high-frequency strobe effect because it happens so fast it seems like a single burst of light.

Just remember that the flash loses significant power (or reach) at higher shutter speeds because it is forced to work so hard. Be sure you experiment with this to get the best results. You can use a big aperture like f/1.4 to have very shallow depth of field in direct bright sunlight because you can use very high shutter speeds. This will allow you to make images that many others simply cannot create. Learn to balance the flash and ambient light in Auto FP high-speed sync mode. All this technical talk will make sense when you see the results. Pretty cool stuff!

Custom Setting e2 – Flash Shutter Speed

(User's Manual – Page 300)

Flash shutter speed controls the minimum shutter speed your camera can use in various flash modes. You can select between 30 seconds (30 s) and 1/60 of a second (1/60 s). Whereas the previous function, Flash sync speed, controls the fastest shutter speed available, Flash shutter speed controls the slowest shutter speed available in specific modes.

Let's consider each mode and its minimum shutter speed:

- ***Front-curtain sync, Rear-curtain sync, or Red-eye reduction*** – In Programmed auto (P) mode or Aperture-priority auto (A) mode, the slowest shutter speed can be selected from the range of 1/60 of a second (1/60 s) to 30 seconds (30 s) (figure 4.33). Shutter-priority (S) mode and Manual (M) mode cause the camera to ignore Flash shutter speed, and the slowest shutter speed is 30 seconds (30 s).

Which Flash Units for Auto FP High-Speed Sync Mode?

If you are using the camera's built-in pop-up Speedlight, or the small Nikon SB-400, your camera's maximum flash shutter speed is limited to 1/320s. If you use the external Speedlights SB-910, SB-900, SB-800, SB-700, SB-600, and SB-R200, you can use any shutter speed and the flash will adjust (pulse) to match lighting needs. With the larger Speedlights, you'll need to learn how to balance ambient light with light from the flash when using shutter speeds higher than 1/250s. Just remember that your flash unit's range will be seriously reduced at higher shutter speeds.

- *Slow sync, Red-eye reduction with slow sync,* or *Slow rear-curtain sync* – These three modes ignore Flash shutter speed, and the slowest shutter speed is 30 seconds (30 s).

Figure 4.33 – Flash shutter speed

Here are the steps to set the Flash shutter speed minimum (figure 4.33):

1. Select e Bracketing/flash from the Custom Setting Menu and scroll to the right (figure 4.33, screen 1).
2. Highlight e2 Flash shutter speed and scroll to the right (figure 4.33, screen 2).
3. Choose one of the settings on the list—1/60 s to 30 s. In figure 4.33, screen 3, 1/60 s has been selected. Remember that slower shutter speeds can cause subject ghosting when flash is used in high ambient light conditions.
4. Press the OK button to lock in the setting.

Custom setting e2 is only partially used by the flash modes because the default is preset to 30 seconds in Shutter-priority and Manual modes.

Settings Recommendation: I normally use 1/60 s. Shutter speeds lower than 1/60 s can cause ghosting if the ambient light is too high. The subject can move after the flash fires but with the shutter still open and with enough ambient light to record a blurred ghost effect. You'll have a well-exposed picture of the subject with a ghost of him also showing in the image. Use slower shutter speeds only when you are sure that you'll be in dark conditions and the flash will provide the only lighting—unless you're shooting special effects, like a blurred aftereffect following your subject to imply movement.

Custom Setting e3 – Flash Cntrl for Built-in Flash

(User's Manual – Page 301)

Flash cntrl for built-in flash provides four distinct ways to control the pop-up Speedlight's flash output. This setting does not apply to flash units you attach via the Accessory shoe (hotshoe) on top of the camera. It is only for the pop-up flash.

Additionally, the built-in flash can be used to control multiple groups or banks of standalone Speedlight flash units. When you use the flash in this manner, you are using it in Commander mode.

Figure 4.34A – Flash cntrl for built-in flash – TTL mode

Here are the steps used to configure Flash cntrl for built-in flash (figure 4.34A):

1. Select e Bracketing/flash from the Custom Setting Menu and scroll to the right (figure 4.34A, screen 1).
2. Highlight e3 Flash cntrl for built-in flash and scroll to the right (figure 4.34A, screen 2).
3. Choose one of the four choices on the list. In figure 4.34A, screen 3, TTL has been selected. The other choices will be detailed in figures 4.34B, 4.34C, and 4.34D. Those three figures start where figure 4.34A leaves off.
4. Press the OK button to lock in the setting.

Let's consider each of these modes.

TTL

Also known as iTTL, this mode is the standard way to use the camera for flash pictures (figure 4.34A). TTL (through the lens) and allows very accurate and balanced flash output using a pre-flash method to determine correct exposure before the main flash burst fires. This is a completely automatic mode and will adjust to distances along with the various shutter speeds and apertures your camera is using.

M – Manual

This mode allows you to manually control the output of your flash (figure 4.34B). The range of settings can go from Full power to 1/128. At full power, the built-in Speedlight has a Guide Number of 12/39 (m/ft, ISO 100, 20°C/68°F).

Figure 4.34B – Flash cntrl for built-in flash – Manual mode

RPT – Repeating Flash

This setting turns your flash into a strobe unit that you can see pulsing (unlike Auto FP high-speed sync mode), allowing you to get creative with stroboscopic multiple flashes (figure 4.34C). Using the screen on the right in figure 4.34C (screen 2), you can use the Multi selector to scroll up and down to set the values or left and right to move between Output, Times, and Frequency. Press the OK button when you have it configured.

Figure 4.34C – Flash cntrl for built-in flash – Repeating flash mode

There are three settings, as shown in Figure 4.34C, screen 2:

- **Output** – You can vary the power of the flash from 1/4 to 1/128 of the full power. The more power the flash uses, the fewer times it can fire. Here is a table of how many times the built-in pop-up flash can fire using the different Output levels:

  1/4: 2 times
  1/8: 2–5 times
  1/16: 2–10 times
  1/32: 2–10 or 15 times
  1/64: 2–10, 15, 20, 25 times
  1/128: 2–10, 15, 20, 25, 30, 35 times

- **Times** – This setting controls the number of times the flash will strobe per second, between 2 and 10 in one-step increments and then from 10 to 35 (at 1/128) in five-step increments. Refer to the preceding table to set the number of times the flash can fire. Increasing the flash power output (going toward 1/4) will lower the number of times, while decreasing the power (going toward 1/128) will increase the number of times the flash can fire. As you change the Output amount, you'll see the Times maximum change.
- **Frequency** – This lets the flash fire a series of pulses for each of the times it fires, from 1 pulse to 50 pulses.

How Does Repeating Flash Work, Technically?

If you have Output set to 1/128, Times set to 5, and Frequency set to 50, that means the camera will fire its built-in pop-up Speedlight at 1/128 of the full power, five times, with each flash burst divided into 50 pulses. Therefore, the flash will pulse a total of 250 times at 1/128 power for a 1-second exposure, or 4 times for a 1/60-second exposure.

C – Commander Mode

This mode allows your camera to become a commander, or controller, of up to two banks of an unlimited number of external CLS-compatible Speedlight flash units, with four available channels (figure 4.34D).

In figure 4.34D, screen 2, you'll see Built-in flash, Group A and B, and a Channel setting. Following Built-in flash and Group A and B, you'll see Mode and Comp. settings. Use the Multi selector to move around and modify settings on this screen.

Figure 4.34D – Flash cntrl for built-in flash – Commander mode

Built-in flash – This lets you set the pop-up flash to one of three settings. The settings do not affect any of the flash units the Commander mode is controlling in Group A or B:

- **TTL** – Otherwise known as i-TTL mode, this is a completely automatic mode that does monitor pre-flashes to determine correct exposure for the pop-up flash. You can set compensation (Comp.) from +3.0 to -3.0 EV in 1/3 EV steps.
- **M** – This allows you to choose a manual flash level from 1/1 (full power) to 1/128 (1/128 of the full power).
- **- - -** I call this the double-dash mode. This disables the pop-up flash from adding light to the image. The primary light burst from the pop-up flash will not fire. However, the pop-up flash still must fire the monitor pre-flashes to determine a correct exposure and to communicate with any flash units out there in Group A or Group B that it is "commanding."

Group A and **B** – These banks represent groups of an unlimited number of remote mode (slaved) Speedlights that your camera can control and fire under the Nikon Creative Lighting System (CLS). Each group has four settings that apply to each flash unit in the bank:

- **TTL** – This works like Built-in flash except that it causes all flash units being controlled in each group to use TTL (i-TTL) for the group. You can also set compensation (Comp.) between +3.0 and -3.0 EV in 1/3 EV steps. Comp. will affect all flash units in the group, or bank.
- **AA** – This stands for Auto aperture and is only available when your D800 is controlling a top-end Speedlight flash unit in slave mode on a bank. This is an older technology that does not use the newer i-TTL exposure technology. It is included for those who are used to using the older style of exposure. You can safely ignore this mode and use TTL instead and you'll get better exposures. If you really want to use AA mode, that's fine. It works like TTL mode but with less accurate exposures. You can set compensation (Comp.) between +3.0 and -3.0 EV in 1/3 EV steps. Comp. will affect all flash units in that group or bank.
- **M** – This allows you to choose a manual flash level between 1/1 (full power) and 1/128 (1/128 of the full power) for each of the flash units being controlled by a particular group. If you like to shoot manually for ultimate control, the camera gives you a way to control multiple groups of flash units manually.
- **- - -** The flash units in the group do not fire. Double-dash mode disables an entire group so that you can concentrate on configuring the other group. Then you can turn the disabled group back on and configure it too. Or, you can just use one group of slaved Speedlights (A or B) and disable the other.

Channel – This one channel controls all slaved flash units. You must match the Channel number for the camera and each flash unit. This is the channel on which communications flow to all grouped, remote flashes. You have a choice of four Channel numbers, 1 to 4. This allows you to use your flash units near another photographer who is also controlling groups without firing the other person's flash units accidentally. You just each choose a different channel.

An upcoming chapter of this book, **Speedlight Flash,** is devoted to using Nikon's Creative Lighting System (CLS) and covers each of the Commander modes and flash unit types in more detail than the summary found here.

Commander Mode Notes

When you're using multiple flash units under the control of your camera in Commander mode, it is important that you understand the following points.

First, the camera communicates with the remote slaved flash groups (A and B) during the monitor pre-flash cycle, so the pop-up flash must be raised in Commander mode in order to communicate with the remote flash units.

Second, each remote flash unit has a little round photocell sensor on its side that picks up the monitor pre-flashes from your camera's pop-up flash. Make sure those little sensors are not blocked or exposed to direct, very bright light while in use or they may not be able to see the monitor pre-flashes from your camera.

Third, if you want to prevent the monitor pre-flashes from appearing in photographs, or causing people to squint, you need to purchase the optional SG-3IR infrared panel for the pop-up flash. This infrared panel makes the monitor pre-flashes mostly invisible to humans and imaging sensors, yet the remote flash units can still see them and react properly. Nikon says this in the User's Manual (page 306) about using the built-in flash in Commander mode: *"To prevent timing flashes emitted by the built-in flash from appearing in photographs taken at short range, choose low ISO sensitivities or small apertures (large f-numbers) or use an optional SG-3IR infrared panel for the built-in flash. An SG-3IR is required for best results with rear-curtain sync, which produces brighter timing flashes."*

Fourth, don't position any of the remote flash units more than 33 feet (10.05 m) from the camera. That's the maximum distance Nikon supports for the D800 pop-up flash in Commander mode.

If these issues bother you, then invest in the Nikon SU-800 Wireless Infrared Controller unit that replaces the pop-up flash/Commander mode combo. You mount it onto the Accessory shoe and let it control the remote slaves out to 66 feet (20.10 m) without some of the issues just mentioned.

Custom Setting e4 – Modeling Flash

(User's Manual – Page 307)

Modeling flash lets you fire a pulse of flashes to help you see how the light is wrapping around your subject. It works like modeling lights on studio flash units except it pulses instead of shines. You can press the Depth-of-field preview button to see the effect if you set Modeling flash to On.

This function works with Nikon's main Speedlight flash unit group: SB-910, SB-900, SB-800, SB-700, SB-600, and SB-R200. It also works with the pop-up flash for limited periods. The SB-400 flash unit does not work with Modeling flash.

Figure 4.35 – Modeling flash

Here are the steps used to configure Modeling flash (figure 4.35):

1. Select e Bracketing/flash from the Custom Setting Menu and scroll to the right (figure 4.35, screen 1).
2. Highlight e4 Modeling flash and scroll to the right (figure 4.35, screen 2).
3. Choose one of the two settings on the list. In figure 4.35, screen 3, On has been selected.
4. Press the OK button to lock in the setting.

Here's what each of the settings for Modeling flash accomplishes:

*   ***On*** – This setting allows you to see (somewhat) how your flash will light the subject. If you have this setting turned On, you can press the Depth-of-field preview button to strobe the pop-up flash, or any attached/controlled external Speedlight unit, in a series of rapid pulses. These pulses are continuous and simulate the lighting that the primary flash burst will give your subject. The Modeling flash can be used for only a few seconds at a time to keep from overheating the flash unit, so look quickly.
*   ***Off*** – This means that no Modeling flash will fire when you press the Depth-of-field preview button.

Settings Recommendation: I often forget that I have this turned on and when I want to check my actual depth of field on a product shot. When I press the Depth-of-field preview button, I get the modeling light instead of depth of field. I don't find this feature to be particularly useful, and it often startles me. You might like it if you do a lot of studio-style flash photography that requires a modeling light. Give it a try, but be prepared—the pulsing of the flash sounds like an angry group of hornets about to attack your face.

Custom Setting e5 – Auto Bracketing Set

(User's Manual – Pages 132, 307)

Auto bracketing set lets you choose how bracketing works for each of the camera's bracketing methods. You can set up bracketing for the exposure system (AE), flash, White balance, and Active D-Lighting (D800 only).

Let's start by reviewing the five types of bracketing on the D800. I'll explain how to use bracketing in an upcoming section:

- **AE & flash** – When you set up a session for bracketing, the camera will cause any type of normal pictures you take to be bracketed, whether they are standard exposures or you are using flash. See how to bracket in the next section.
- **AE only** – Your bracketing settings will affect only the exposure system and not the flash.
- **Flash only** – Your bracketing settings will affect only the flash system and not the exposure.
- **WB bracketing** – White balance bracketing works the same as exposure and flash bracketing, except it is designed for bracketing color in mired values, instead of bracketing light in EV step values. WB bracketing is not available with image quality settings of NEF (RAW) or NEF (RAW) + JPEG.
- **ADL bracketing** – In this case, you are bracketing Active D-Lighting (ADL) in up to five separate exposures. The next higher level of ADL is used on each selected exposure.

AE & Flash Bracketing (Includes AE Only and Flash Only)

Figure 4.36A – Auto bracketing set

Here are the steps used to select an Auto bracketing set type (figure 4.36A):

1. Select e Bracketing/flash from the Custom Setting Menu and scroll to the right (figure 4.36A, screen 1).
2. Highlight e5 Auto bracketing set and scroll to the right (figure 4.36A, screen 2).
3. Choose one of the five choices on the list. In figure 4.36A, screen 3, AE & flash has been selected. See the following instructions for using external camera controls to configure the five bracketing modes (figures 4.36B to 4.36F).
4. Press the OK button to lock in the setting.

Now, let's look into how the various bracketing systems work. Using figure 4.36B as a guide, you'll use the BKT button (1) and the Main command dial (2) or Sub-command dial (3) to change the bracketing values.

Exposure Bracketing (AE and Flash Combinations)

Figure 4.36B – Controls for Auto bracketing: (1) BKT button, (2) Main command dial, (3) Sub-command dial

Here are the steps to configure AE and flash bracketing combinations (figure 4.36A and figure 4.36B):

1. Choose AE & flash, AE only, or Flash only from the Auto bracketing set screen (figure 4.36A, screen 3).
2. Next, press and hold the BKT button (figure 4.36B, number 1, red arrow) and turn the rear Main command dial (figure 4.36B, number 2, red arrow) to select the number of shots in the bracket (up to 9). You can also select the side of normal exposure on which the camera will take the shots.
   When you hold down the BKT button, you will see symbols on your camera's Control panel similar to the ones shown in figure 4.36C, except that the symbols may be 0F and 1.0 (if not previously changed) and there may be no lines hanging below the - .... 0 .... + scale. You will set both of those values as you create the bracket. You can identify that bracketing is active by the BKT symbol on the Control panel.

Figure 4.36C – Auto bracketing (AE & flash)

The number of shots appears on the top left of the Control panel, as shown in each screen in figure 4.36C, as 5F, --2F, and +3F. You can shoot up to 9 frames (9F) in an AE & flash, AE only, or Flash only bracket.

The number of small vertical lines hanging below the - .... 0 .... + scale equals the number of shots in the bracket. The position of those lines represents the EV spread of the shots in the bracket. In figure 4.36C, screen 1, for instance, you can count five lines hanging below the -/+ scale and there is one stop of exposure between each line. Those five shots are represented by the 5F in screen 1.

3. The front Sub-command dial (figure 4.36B, number 3) controls the EV steps between each exposure in the bracket. This value appears on the top right of each screen in figure 4.36C as 1.0, 0.3, and 0.3. While holding the BKT button, rotate the front Sub-command dial to change the EV value of each image in the bracket, in steps of 1/3, 1/2, or 1 EV. The EV step value is set in *Custom Setting Menu b2 > EV steps for exposure cntrl.* (You can use *Custom Setting Menu > e7 Bracketing order* to set the order of the exposures. We'll discuss this in a later section titled **Custom Setting e7 – Bracketing Order**. The default order is *normal > underexposed > overexposed*. You can change it to *underexposed > normal > overexposed* if you'd like.)

Figure 4.36C, screen 1, shows a five-shot bracket on the camera's Control panel with both over- and underexposure of 1.0 EV step per image. You can tell by the 5F at the top left of the Control panel along with the number of lines hanging below the scale. The 1.0 means that there is 1.0 EV step (1 stop) between each exposure in the bracket. The fact that the 5F has no plus or minus sign in front of it tells us that the bracket uses exposures that are normal, overexposed, and underexposed.

Figure 4.36C, screen 2, shows a two-image bracket with 0.3 EV steps (1/3 stop) between each exposure. Notice the minus signs before the 2F symbol (--2F). This means that the bracket is configured to take only normal and underexposed shots—no overexposed ones. The bracketed images are on the minus side of the -/+ scale.

Figure 4.36C, screen 3, represents a three-image bracket at 0.3 EV steps per exposure, in the normal and overexposure direction only (+3F).

4. Take the bracketed picture series, including however many shots you have dialed into the bracket (2F to 9F). As you take each image, one of the lines that hang down below the -/+ scale will disappear. When they are all gone, your bracket is complete. If you have your camera set to one of the Continuous release modes (CL or CH), and hold down the Shutter-release button, the camera will fire off only the number of images in the bracketed series and then stop firing.

Note about flash bracketing: If you are using a Speedlight flash unit to light the bracketed series, it may or may not be able to keep up with bracketed shots taken in Continuous-release mode. If you fully dump the flash power between shots, you'll have to wait for the next shot. Also, the pop-up flash simply does not recycle fast enough to be able to shoot continuously while flash bracketing, so you'll have to take each shot individually.

Here's a short review:

- BKT button plus rear Main command dial = number of exposures
- BKT button plus front Sub-command dial = EV step value of bracketed exposures (1/3, 1/2, or 1 EV step)

Settings Recommendation: I normally bracket with a 1 EV step value (1 stop) so that I can get a good spread of light values in high dynamic range (HDR) images. In most cases, I will do a three- to five-image bracket, with one or two images overexposed and one or two images underexposed by 1 stop. This type of bracketing allows me to combine detail from the highlight and dark areas in-computer for the HDR exposures everyone is experimenting with these days.

In figure 4.36D you will find a sample five-image bracket with 1.0 EV step between each exposure. I combined the five images using *Photomatix Pro* software (**http://www.hdrsoft.com**) and was pleased with the final result. The image on the next page (figure 4.36D) was created with a bracketed series of five shots—the images underneath the main image—using the same settings shown on the Control panel in figure 4.36C, screen 1.

WB Bracketing

(User's Manual – Page 137)

The process for *WB bracketing* (white balance bracketing) is similar to the process for flash or exposure bracketing, even using the same controls (figure 4.36B).

If you want to bracket your camera's white balance, you must set *Custom Setting Menu > e5 Auto bracketing set* to WB bracketing (figure 4.36A, screen 3). This means that AE or flash bracketing will not work during the time that Custom setting e5 is set to WB bracketing.

Figure 4.36D – Five-image bracket combined in Photomatix Pro to a single HDR image

It may be a good idea to review the previous section, **Exposure Bracketing (AE and Flash Combinations)**, if you've not read it yet because WB bracketing is so similar. WB bracketing does not work when your camera is in NEF (RAW) and NEF (RAW) + JPEG modes. White balance information is stored with the RAW image but is not directly applied to the image. You can change the White balance after the fact when you are shooting RAW, so bracketing a RAW image makes no sense.

Use figure 4.36A as reference screens to select WB bracketing, and then use these steps to bracket the white balance:

1. Using figure 4.36A as a guide, set your camera to WB bracketing (figure 4.36A). You can identify that WB bracketing is in effect by looking for the WB-BKT symbol on the Control panel.

Figure 4.36E – Auto bracketing (WB)

2. Using the controls shown in figure 4.36B, choose the number of shots in the bracket (3F, A3F, or b3F) , as shown in the Control panel screens in figure 4.36E. Press and hold the BKT button while turning the Main command dial left or right, up to nine shots total (9F). The 3F symbol shows the number of images (3), as do the lines hanging below the -/+ scale—just below the WB-BKT symbol.

3. You control the white balance color differences by bracketing toward amber or blue (A or b). Change the mired number by holding the BKT button while turning the Sub-command dial left or right, up to three maximum (figure 4.36B). Each increment of color difference is called a *mired* and is controlled by the number at the top right of the Control panel screens in figure 4.36E. Each number represents multiple mired. Choose 1, 2, or 3, where 1=5 mired, 2=10 mired, and 3=15 mired. Figure 4.36E, screen 1, shows a 5 mired difference (1), screen 2 shows a 15 mired difference (3), and screen 3 shows a 10 mired difference (2).

   Figure 4.36E, screen 1, shows a three-image bracket on the camera's Control panel, with each image having a 5 mired difference (1) in color. One has more amber, one is normal, and one has more blue (3F).

   Figure 4.36E, screen 2, shows a three-image bracket with a 15 mired difference (3) between each image, in the amber direction only (A3F).

   Figure 4.36E, screen 3, shows a three-image bracket with a 10 mired color difference (2) in the blue direction only (b3F).

   If you do not see an A (A3F) or b (b3F) in the image number position at top left, it simply means that the bracket goes in both directions, such as *amber > normal >blue* or *normal>amber >blue*, according to how you have *Custom Setting Menu > e Bracketing/flash > e7 Bracketing order* set.

4. Take the bracketed picture series. Interestingly, you do this by taking **one** picture. The camera takes that picture, reapplies the color filtration for each image in the bracket, and then saves each image as a separate image file with a new consecutive file number and bracketed color value. This works very differently from AE or flash bracketing, where you have to fire off each individual frame of the bracket. WB bracketing is very easy because you only have to set the bracket in the Control panel and take one picture. However many images (up to nine) are in the bracket simply appear on your memory card. Nikons are fun!

Here's a short review:

- BKT button plus rear Main command dial = number of exposures (2F to 9F)
- BKT button plus front Sub-command dial = 5, 10, or 15 mired steps (1–3)

Settings Recommendation: Personally, I prefer to use RAW mode and make minor or major color adjustments in the computer post-processing stage. However, you may want to use WB bracketing while shooting JPEGs because it degrades the image when you modify and resave a JPEG file. Only people with extreme concern over color balance will find WB bracketing useful. Most of us won't worry about it.

What Is Mired?

Changes to mired simply modify the color of your image, in this case toward amber (reddish) or blue. In effect, changing mired toward amber or blue warms or cools the image. The color changes are applied directly to the image by the camera when shooting JPEGs or are saved as markers when shooting RAW images. You don't have to worry about mired values unless you are a color scientist. You can just determine whether you like the image the way it is or would prefer that it be warmer or cooler and bracket accordingly. WB bracketing toward the A direction warms the image, while the b direction cools it. Technically, a mired is calculated by multiplying the inverse of the color temperature by 106. I'd rather let my camera figure mired values and then judge them with my eye, wouldn't you? Remember, if you shoot in RAW, you can modify color values later in your computer. Otherwise, they are applied permanently to JPEG files.

ADL Bracketing

(User's Manual – Page 141)

ADL bracketing (ADL stands for Active D-Lighting) is designed to let you shoot a normal image and then a series of up to four additional images with Active D-Lighting applied to each at progressively higher levels.

As you set ADL bracketing from two to five shots, you are setting the camera to switch to a higher ADL level for each consecutive shot. The progressive levels are Off, Low, Normal, High, and Extra High.

Here are the steps to use ADL bracketing:

1. Using figure 4.36A as a guide, set your camera to ADL bracketing. You can identify that ADL bracketing is active by the ADL- and BKT symbols on the Control panel.
2. Using the controls shown in figure 4.36B, hold down the BKT button and turn the rear Main command dial to select the number of frames you want in the

bracket (one to five images). You'll see AdL on the top left of the Control panel and the number of frames in the bracket series on the top right (5F).

Figure 4.36F shows a bracket of five frames (5F), which means that the camera will use all five available levels of Active D-Lighting (Off, Low, Normal, High, and Extra high) as the five images are taken (Auto Active D-Lighting is ignored). You'll be able to see hanging lines under the +/- scale for only four of the shots—an arrow points to the right for the fifth. *Custom Setting Menu > e Bracketing/flash > e7 Bracketing order* does not apply to ADL bracketing.

Figure 4.36F – ADL bracketing

3. Take the bracketed series of however many levels of ADL bracketing you selected (2F to 5F). If you use Continuous-release mode (CL or CH), you can shoot the number of frames in your bracket by holding down the Shutter-release button. Once the bracket is complete, the camera will stop firing. As each shot is taken, you'll see one of the vertical lines just under the -/+ scale disappear.

Settings Recommendation: This is a great way to capture very important shots and try to get extra shadow detail and highlight protection in some of them. You may not need ADL bracketing on all shots, but on very important images where you are slightly off on your exposure selection, ADL will help to open shadows and mildly protect the highlights.

Of course, if you shoot in RAW mode, you can apply ADL in-computer. I don't bracket ADL very often, but I'm glad to know it's there when I need it.

One final note about bracketing of any type: *Turn it off when you're done!* I often forget and then wonder why my camera keeps under- and overexposing a series of images. Only after wasting several images do I realize that I left bracketing turned on. You'll see what I mean if you use AE & flash bracketing often, as I do.

Custom Setting e6 – Auto Bracketing (Mode M)

(User's Manual – Page 308)

Auto bracketing (Mode M) is a series of four selections that let you, or the camera, control the flash, shutter speed, and aperture in various ways during a bracketing operation, but only when the camera is set to Manual (M) exposure mode. This gives you a little finer control over manual camera settings while you are taking several exposures within a bracket of images.

Here is a list of the four settings under Auto bracketing (Mode M) and what each does. The camera controls the selected setting when you are using Manual (M) exposure mode while bracketing. These functions are dependent on how *Custom Setting Menu > e Bracketing/flash > e5 Auto bracketing set* is configured.

- **Flash/speed** – This setting allows you to control the aperture for best depth of field while still using bracketing. The camera will control the shutter speed. If *Custom Setting Menu > e Bracketing/flash > e5 Auto bracketing set* is configured to AE & Flash, the camera will vary the shutter speed and flash level to expose the bracketed images while you control the aperture. If e5 Auto bracketing set is set to AE only, then the camera will vary only the shutter speed to get the exposures.

- **Flash/speed/aperture** – This setting is for those who want the camera to control the shutter speed, aperture, and flash while still using bracketing. If *Custom Setting Menu > e Bracketing/flash > e5 Auto bracketing set* is configured to AE & Flash, the camera will vary the shutter speed, aperture, and flash level to expose the bracketed images. If e5 Auto bracketing set is set to AE only, then the camera will vary the shutter speed and aperture to get the exposures.

- **Flash/aperture** – This setting is for those who want to control the shutter speed for best action shots while still using bracketing. The camera will control the aperture and flash. If *Custom Setting Menu > e Bracketing/flash > e5 Auto bracketing set* is configured to AE & Flash, the camera will vary the aperture and flash level to expose the bracketed images. If e5 Auto bracketing set is set to AE only, then the camera will vary only the aperture to get the exposures.

- **Flash only** – This setting is for those who want to control only the flash while using bracketing. The camera will only vary the flash level to get the bracketed exposures. AE only obviously does not apply with this setting.

Note: Flash bracketing is performed only with i-TTL or AA flash control. If any setting other than Flash only is selected and the flash is not used, the ISO sensitivity will be fixed at the value for the first shot regardless of the setting selected for Auto ISO sensitivity control.

Figure 4.37 – Auto bracketing (Mode M)

Here are the steps used to configure Auto bracketing (Mode M):

1. Select e Bracketing/flash from the Custom Setting Menu and scroll to the right (figure 4.37, screen 1).
2. Highlight Auto bracketing (Mode M) and scroll to the right (figure 4.37, screen 2).
3. Choose one of the four settings on the list. In figure 4.37, screen 3, Flash/speed has been selected.
4. Press the OK button to lock in the setting.

Settings Recommendation: Because I am mostly a nature shooter, I often leave my camera set to Flash/speed so that the camera will control the shutter speed when I take a series of bracketed images, but I'll control the aperture. That way I can choose how much depth of field I want to allow in my images.

If I were shooting important action shots and wanted to bracket, I'd select Flash/aperture so that the camera would control the aperture and flash while I controlled the shutter speed for action.

If I were letting only my Speedlight flash control the exposure, as with indoor shots, I might use Flash only during the bracket.

Finally, if I wanted to let the camera alone decide how to get the best exposure during the bracket, I might use Flash/speed/aperture. Then all I have to do is take pictures and let the camera do the rest. This seems to me to be a small violation of the principle of manual exposure, though.

Custom Setting e7 – Bracketing Order

(User's Manual – Page 308)

Bracketing order allows you to choose the order of your exposure settings (normal, overexposed, and underexposed) during a bracketing operation. There are two bracketing orders available in the D800. They allow you to control which images are taken first, second, and third in the bracketing series.

Here are the three values in the bracket order and what they each mean:

*   **MTR** = Metered value (normal exposure)
*   **Under** = Underexposed
*   **Over** = Overexposed

Next, let's see how these are used during bracketing:

*   ***MTR > under > over*** – With this setting, the normal exposure (MTR) is taken first, followed by the underexposed image, then the overexposed image. If you are taking a group of five images in your bracket (Custom setting e5), the camera will take the images like this: normal exposure > most underexposed > least underexposed > least overexposed > most overexposed. For WB bracketing, the pattern is normal > amber > blue. This does not apply to ADL bracketing.

- **Under > MTR > over** – Using this order for bracketing means that a five-image bracket will be exposed in the following manner: most underexposed > least underexposed > normal exposure > least overexposed > most overexposed. For WB bracketing, the pattern is amber > normal > blue. This does not apply to ADL bracketing.

Figure 4.38 – Bracketing order

Finally, let's look at the steps to actually configure the Bracketing order (figure 4.38):

1. Select e Bracketing/flash from the Custom Setting Menu and scroll to the right (figure 4.38, screen 1).
2. Highlight e7 Bracketing order and scroll to the right (figure 4.38, screen 2).
3. Choose one of the two bracketing orders on the list. In figure 4.38, screen 3, MTR > under > over has been selected.
4. Press the OK button to lock in the setting.

Settings Recommendation: I leave Bracketing order set to MTR > under > over, so that when the images are displayed in series by the camera, I can see the normal exposure (MTR) first and then watch how it varies as I scroll through the bracketed images. It gets confusing to me if there are nine images in a bracket and I am trying to figure out which one is the MTR image, as I would with the other bracketing order.

If that doesn't suit you, change it to the other direction, Under > MTR > over. The normal exposure will be in the middle of the bracket instead of at the beginning. Some prefer the more natural flow of that bracketing order (under to over).

Section Six – f Controls

Custom Settings f1 to f13

Within the *f Controls* menu you'll find 13 settings in the D800:

- **f1** – ☀ Switch (Backlight)
- **f2** – Multi selector center button
- **f3** – Multi selector
- **f4** – Assign Fn button
- **f5** – Assign preview button
- **f6** – Assign AE-L/AF-L button
- **f7** – Shutter spd & aperture lock
- **f8** – Assign BKT button
- **f9** – Customize command dials
- **f10** – Release button to use dial
- **f11** – Slot empty release lock
- **f12** – Reverse indicators
- **f13** – Assign MB-D12 AF-ON

☀ Switch (Backlight)

(User's Manual – Page 309)

The *Backlight switch* control position has been on the Power switch for many generations of Nikon cameras—controlling the backlight for the Control panel. However, with the D800, the Power switch's Backlight switch position can potentially control two functions. One is for the Control panel backlight, and the other is for the Information display (rear Monitor) backlight.

Figure 4.39A – Backlight switch position on Shutter-release button

When you push the switch, as shown in figure 4.39A, you'll turn on the backlight for just the Control panel or both the Control panel and the Information display, according to how you have the Backlight switch function configured. In figure 4.39A, the top red arrow shows the direction to push the Power switch for the backlight position, and the bottom red arrow points to the tiny icon on the camera's Power switch.

The Control panel and Information display have different backlight time-outs controlled by separate functions. The Control panel backlight time-out is controlled by *Custom Setting Menu > c Timers/AE lock > c2 Auto meter-off delay*. The Information display backlight time-out is controlled by *Custom Setting Menu > c Timers/AE lock > c4 Monitor off delay > Information display*. You can set these two time-outs first, and when you activate the Backlight switch, both timers will start counting down separately, with one important caveat. When you are using the Information display screen on the rear Monitor, it keeps the light meter active for as long as it displays. Therefore, if you have *Custom Setting Menu > c Timers/AE lock > c4 Monitor off delay > Information display* set to a long value, such as 1 min (one minute), the Information display will time-out first at the end of its 1 min delay, and then the Control panel backlight will start its countdown, using the delay set in *Custom Setting Menu > c Timers/AE lock > c2 Auto meter-off delay*.

This sounds a bit confusing, but just think of it this way: Because the Control panel time-out is tied in with the light meter time-out, the Control panel backlight will stay on longer than the Information display by the amount you have set in *Custom Setting Menu > c Timers/AE lock > c2 Auto meter-off delay*. If that value is the default of 6 s (6 seconds), that means the Control panel backlight will time-out 6 seconds after the Information display times out.

Figure 4.39B – Backlight switch

Here are the steps to select what the Backlight switch controls (figure 4.39B):

1. Select f Controls from the Custom Setting Menu and scroll to the right (figure 4.39B, screen 1).
2. Highlight ☀ switch and scroll to the right (figure 4.39B, screen 2).
3. Choose one of the two types on the list. In figure 4.39B, screen 3, LCD backlight (Control panel backlight only) has been selected.
4. Press the OK button to lock in the setting.

Settings Recommendation: While this function could be useful if one uses the Information display frequently, I suspect that many D800 users do not depend on the Information display as often as those who own lower-cost Nikons. The lower-end cameras are more and more Information display-centered, since many of their users came over from the point-and-shoot world and expect that easy, shortcut style of camera configuration.

Only recently has Nikon added more functionality to the Information display on the D800-level cameras, which sets a pattern that will only grow in future cameras. How long will it be before we have touch-screen technology?

In any case, I still mostly use the Backlight switch setting to turn on the backlight for the Control panel only. I would rather simply press the info button when I want access to the Information display on the rear Monitor.

Multi Selector Center Button

(User's Manual – Page 309)

Multi selector center button determines how the unlabeled button in the center of the Multi selector works in three different camera modes.

The three modes that affect how the Multi selector center button works are as follows:

- **Shooting mode** is in force when you are actually using the camera to take pictures through the Viewfinder.
- **Playback mode** is in use when you are examining already-taken pictures on the rear Monitor.
- **Live view** is used when you are in Live view mode taking pictures with the Monitor instead of the Viewfinder.

Figure 4.40A – Multi selector center button

Figure 4.40A shows an arrow pointing to the Multi selector center button on the back of the camera. Let's examine each mode in detail.

Shooting Mode

First, let's see how pressing the Multi selector center button works in the Viewfinder-based Shooting mode. Following are the screens and steps used to configure what the Multi selector center button does (figure 4.40B).

Figure 4.40B – Multi selector center button (Shooting mode)

1. Select f Controls from the Custom Setting Menu and scroll to the right (figure 4.40B, screen 1).
2. Highlight f2 Multi selector center button and scroll to the right (figure 4.40B, screen 2).
3. Select Shooting mode and scroll to the right (figure 4.40B, screen 3).
4. Choose one of the three choices on the list. In figure 4.40B, screen 4, Select center focus point has been chosen.
5. Press the OK button to lock in the setting.

There are three selections in Shooting mode, as follows (figure 4.40B, screen 4):

- **Select center focus point** – Often when shooting, you'll be using the Multi selector with your thumb to move the selected focus point (AF point) around the Viewfinder to focus on the most appropriate area of your subject. When you are done, you have to scroll the AF point back to the center. Not anymore! If Select center focus point is chosen, the focus point pops back to the center point of the Viewfinder when you press the Multi selector center button. This is the default action of the button.
- **Highlight active focus point** – Sometimes, when the Viewfinder is showing a confusing subject, it may be a little hard to see the small black AF point bracket. When Highlight active focus point is selected and you press the Multi selector center button, the AF point lights up in red for easy viewing in its current location.
- **Not used** – This does what it says—nothing happens when you press the Multi selector center button in Shooting mode.

Playback Mode

Now, let's examine how the Multi selector center button can be used in Playback mode. Playback mode is used when you are examining images on the camera's Monitor after you have taken them.

Figure 4.40C – Multi selector center button (Playback mode)

Use these steps to set up the Multi selector center button (figure 4.40C):

1. Select f Controls from the Custom Setting Menu and scroll to the right (figure 4.40C, screen 1).
2. Highlight f2 Multi selector center button and scroll to the right (figure 4.40C, screen 2).
3. Select Playback mode and scroll to the right (figure 4.40C, screen 3).
4. Choose one of the four options on the list. In figure 4.40C, screen 4, View histograms has been chosen. If you choose Zoom on/off, you'll need to scroll to the right and select one of the three subsettings (use figure 4.40F in the upcoming section called **Zoom on/off**). If you select Choose slot and folder, you'll also need to be aware of some additional screens your camera will present (use figure 4.40G in the upcoming section called **Choose slot and folder**).
5. Press the OK button to lock in the setting.

There are four selections in Playback mode, as follows (figure 4.40C, screen 4):

Thumbnail on/off

This feature allows you to switch from viewing one image on your camera's Monitor to viewing multiple thumbnails instead. It's a toggle, so you can press the Multi selector center button to turn thumbnail view on and off. Figure 4.40D shows Thumbnail on/off as selected.

Figure 4.40D – Multi selector center button (Playback mode – Thumbnail on/off)

Use the following steps to configure and use Thumbnail on/off (figure 4.40D):

1. Figure 4.40D continues where figure 4.40C leaves off. Select Thumbnail on/off from the Playback mode menu (figure 4.40D, screen 1).
2. Press the OK button to select the setting.
3. Now, when you press the Playback button and view a picture, like the picture of my Jeep shown in figure 4.40D, screen 2, you can then press the Multi selector center button to get a thumbnail view of the image you have on the Monitor currently along with the three surrounding images (figure 4.40D, screen 3).

View histograms

I discovered this really cool View histograms feature while I was writing another book and now immediately switch my Nikons to this setting when I get a new one. When the Multi selector center button function is set to View histograms, I can have an image open on my Monitor, and then press and hold the Multi selector center button to view a luminance histogram. This saves a lot of scrolling around through the data, RGB histograms, and information screens. It's a quick histogram view that disappears when the Multi selector center button is released. Great feature! Let's see how to configure and use it.

Figure 4.40E – Multi selector center button (Playback mode – View histograms)

Use the following steps to configure and use View histograms (figure 4.40E):

1. Figure 4.40E continues where figure 4.40C leaves off. Select View histograms from the Playback mode menu (figure 4.40E, screen 1).

2. Press the OK button to select the setting.
3. Now, when you press the Playback button and view a picture, like the picture of my Jeep shown in figure 4.40E, screen 2, you can then press the Multi selector center button to get a luminance histogram of the image you have on the Monitor currently (figure 4.40D, screen 3). This is an extremely convenient setting for those who use the histogram regularly.

Zoom on/off

If you want to zoom into your image on the Monitor without using the normal zoom in and out buttons, this is a good feature for you. If you have an image showing on the Monitor and Zoom on/off is selected, when you press the Multi selector center button the image jumps immediately to one of three levels of zoom, skipping the middle steps. It is like a toggle switch because pressing the Multi selector center button a second time takes you back to a normal full-screen view.

Here is a description of the three levels of zoom available under this setting (Low to High):

- **Low magnification** seems to be the same as viewing the image at about 100 percent pixel-peeping level. Pressing the Playback zoom in button eight times brings you to the same 100 percent level.
- **Medium magnification** is for viewing the image at about 200 percent. This is like pressing the Playback zoom in button nine times.
- **High magnification** is around the 400 percent viewing level, or like pressing the Playback zoom in button 10 times.

Figure 4.40F – Multi selector center button (Playback mode – Zoom on/off settings)

Use the following steps to configure and use Zoom on/off (figure 4.40F):

1. Figure 4.40F continues where figure 4.40C leaves off. Select Zoom on/off from the Playback mode menu (figure 4.40F, screen 1).
2. Select Low magnification, Medium magnification, or High magnification from the Zoom on/off list (figure 4.40F, screen 2).
3. Press the OK button to select the setting.
4. Now press the Playback button to display a picture on the Monitor (as shown in figure 4.40F, screen 3, where you can see my Jeep again in normal full-screen mode).
5. Now press the Multi selector center button and the camera will immediately zoom in to view the picture on the Monitor at 100, 200, or 400 percent. Screens 4, 5, and 6 in figure 4.40F match the zoom levels selectable in screen 2: Low magnification, or 100 percent view (screen 4); Medium magnification, or 200 percent view (screen 5); and High magnification, or 400 percent view (screen 6).

Note: The zoom display centers on the focus point used to take the image. If you are using Thumbnail view, you can select from a series of images on the Monitor. When you have one of the images selected, even though it is not full size, you can press the Multi selector center button and the image is enlarged to whichever of the three zoom magnification levels you previously selected. When you press the button again, the camera switches back to Thumbnail view.

Choose slot and folder
When you select Choose slot and folder, you will have a memory card slot selection screen available while you are examining an image in Playback mode. To open the slot selection screen, press the Multi selector center button.

Figure 4.40G – Multi selector center button (Playback mode – Choose slot and folder)

Use the following steps to configure and use Choose slot and folder (figure 4.40G):

1. Figure 4.40G continues where figure 4.40C leaves off. Select Choose slot and folder from the Playback mode menu (figure 4.40G, screen 1).
2. Press the OK button to select the setting.

3. Now, when you press the Multi selector center button with an image showing on the Monitor, you will be presented with the screen shown in figure 4.40G, screen 2. Choose a card type, SD card slot or CF card slot, and then scroll to the right.

4. You will see a screen showing you the folders that can be found on the card slot you selected in the previous step (Figure 4.40G, screen 3). Select one of the folders, if there is more than one available, and press the OK button.

5. The camera will now show images from the folder you have selected. If you have *Playback Menu > Playback folder* set to All or ND800, the camera will switch folders, and even memory cards, when it gets to the end of the current folder. If *Playback Menu > Playback folder* is set to Current, the camera will show only the images in the current folder and will display no other images from any other folder or card.

Note: If there is only one folder on the current memory card, this setting will have little effect except to display the one folder. You cannot choose a memory card with no folders on it; the selection for that card slot will be grayed out. The same applies if you try to select a memory card slot with no card in the slot.

Live View

When shooting still images in Live view mode, you can assign one of three different settings to the Multi selector center button.

Figure 4.40H – Multi selector center button (Live view mode)

Use the following steps to choose how the Multi selector center button functions in Live view mode (figure 4.40H):

1. Select f Controls from the Custom Setting Menu and scroll to the right (figure 4.40H, screen 1).
2. Highlight f2 Multi selector center button and scroll to the right (figure 4.40H, screen 2).
3. Select Live view and scroll to the right (figure 4.40H, screen 3).
4. Choose one of the three settings on the list. In figure 4.40H, screen 4, Select center focus point has been chosen. Please refer to the list following these steps to decide which functionality you like best. If you select Zoom on/off, there will be another screen presented to you so that you can choose a magnification level for the Zoom on/off function. Figure 4.40I shows the screen with magnification choices.
5. Press the OK button to lock in the setting.

Here are descriptions of each of the functions available:

- **Select center focus point** – When you are using Live view, you can scroll the little contrast-detection focus square to any point of the Monitor for excellent focusing with the AF-ON button or Shutter-release button (halfway down). Unfortunately, moving the little focus square around the screen is time-consuming. If you want to return the focus square to the center of the screen at any time and have this Select center focus point mode selected, just press the Multi selector center button and the focus square pops to the middle of the Monitor.

- **Zoom on/off** – The Live view contrast-detection autofocus system allows you to zoom into your subject quite deeply so that you can focus very accurately. You could use the Playback zoom in button or Thumbnail/Playback zoom out button to zoom in and out, or you can configure this function and use the Multi selector center button to zoom in and out instead. With Zoom on/off, you can select one of three levels of magnification for focusing in Live view mode. When you want to zoom into the live image to focus on your subject in a very accurate way, simply press the Multi selector center button and the camera will immediately jump to a zoom position of what I percieve to be about 50 percent for Low magnification, 100 percent for Medium magnification, and 400 percent for High magnification. Use the screens found in figure 4.40I to select a magnification level (Low, Medium, or High magnification). Figure 4.40I starts where figure 4.40H leaves off. This works similarly to functions found under the *Playback mode > Zoom on/off* (figure 4.40F) except it is working with a live subject on the Monitor in Live view.

Figure 4.40I – Multi selector center button (Live view mode – Zoom on/off)

- **Not used** – If you press the Multi selector center button while in Live view, it has no effect.

Settings Recommendation: I have my camera set so that when I press the Multi selector center button in Shooting mode, it jumps to the center AF point. It saves time because I don't have to scroll back manually.

When I press the Multi selector center button in Playback mode, I have the camera show me a luminance histogram. I absolutely adore being able to see a histogram for an image I just took by pressing the Multi selector center button instead of scrolling to the histogram screen. This saves time by letting me see my camera's histogram when I need it most, right after taking the picture.

When using Live view mode, I leave my camera set to Select center focus point because it takes so long to scroll the little focus square around the Monitor. I find it quite nice to be able to pop the focus square to the center by pressing the Multi selector center button.

Custom Setting f3 – Multi Selector

(User's Manual – Page 310)

The *Multi selector* function allows you to set the camera's Multi selector so that any usage of it turns the light meter on or resets its delay back to the value found in *Custom Setting Menu > c Timers/AE lock > c2 Auto meter-off delay*. This allows the light meter to stay on after you've used the Multi selector until the Auto meter-off delay time-out expires.

Figure 4.41 – Multi selector

Here are the steps used to configure the Multi selector function (figure 4.41):

1. Select f Controls from the Custom Setting Menu and scroll to the right (figure 4.41, screen 1).
2. Highlight f3 Multi selector and scroll to the right (figure 4.41, screen 2).
3. Choose one of the two selections from the list. In figure 4.41, screen 3, Reset meter-off delay has been selected.
4. Press the OK button to lock in the setting.

Here is an explanation of what these two selections accomplish:

- **Reset meter-off delay** – This setting is a handy way to turn on the exposure meter without pressing the Shutter-release button halfway down. Maybe you'd like to meter the subject but not cause autofocus to start, so instead of using the Shutter-release button to turn the meter on, you can use the Multi selector. I find this to be a useful function for another reason. I'll often want to move an AF point around the Viewfinder, but the light meter has gone off, so it won't move. I have to press the Shutter-release button halfway down to activate the meter and then scroll the AF point around the Viewfinder. When Reset meter-off delay is selected, any usage of the Multi selector causes the light meter to come on. Custom setting c2 (Auto meter-off delay) controls how long it stays on; the default is 6 seconds.
- **Do nothing** – If the light meter is off, it stays off when you press the Multi selector.

Settings Recommendation: I have been leaving my camera set to Reset meter-off delay so that any use of the Multi selector will keep my camera's meter from going off. The only drawback is shorter battery life because this will tend to keep the meter on longer. Of course, the D800 is quite good at managing its battery. It has to be now that the new Japanese Electrical Appliance and Material Safety Law requires smaller batteries in our cameras.

Custom Setting f4 – Assign Fn Button
Custom Setting f5 – Assign Preview Button
Custom Setting f6 –Assign AE-L/AF-L Button
(User's Manual – Pages 311, 315)

Assign Fn button, Assign preview button, and Assign AE-L/AF-L button are all discussed in this one section. All three work exactly the same way, so instead of repeating the same instructions three times, I chose to explain them once.

When I speak of the **Selected button**, I am talking about the camera button you want to configure—Fn, Preview, or AE-L/AF-L. When you see the words **Selected button** in bold italics, please mentally replace this with the button name you want to configure.

You can assign various camera functions to any of the three buttons mentioned. After we consider each of the screens used to assign the various functions, we'll look at each function in detail in the section **Assignable Function List**. There are a lot of different functions to select from.

The screens, steps, and settings we are about to review are designed to let you customize the usage of the ***Selected button*** alone or the ***Selected button*** + Command dials.

Here are the screens and steps used to configure Assign Fn button, Assign preview button, and Assign AE-L/AF-L button (figures 4.42A to 4.42C):

Figure 4.42A – Assign Fn button

Figure 4.42B – Assign preview button

Figure 4.42C – Assign AE-L/AF-L button

Remember that the next nine steps are designed to explain any of the three buttons to which you can assign a function. **Selected button** represents the button you are currently assigning. For example, Preview button press is represented by **Selected button** press.

1. See figures 4.42A to 4.42C for individual button assignment screens:
   figure 4.42A = Fn button
   figure 4.42B = Preview button (a.k.a., Depth-of-field preview button)
   figure 4.42C = AE-L/AF-L button
2. Select f Controls from the Custom Setting Menu and scroll to the right (figure 4.42A, 4.42B, or 4.42C, screen 1).
3. Highlight (f4, f5, f6) Assign **Selected button** (Fn, Preview, or AE-L/AF-L) and scroll to the right (figure 4.42A, 4.42B, or 4.42C, screen 2). This is where you choose which button you are working with and select it for function assignment.
4. Choose **Selected button** press and the scroll to the right (figure 4.42A, 4.42B, or 4.42C, screen 3). The next step makes an assignment for when you simply press the button.
5. Select one of the functions from the list. This will assign the function you choose to a single button press of the **Selected button** you are configuring (figure 4.42A, 4.42B, or 4.42C, screen 4). See the upcoming section **Assignable Function List** for an explanation of each function.
6. Press the OK button to lock in the assignment for **Selected button** press.
7. Now you'll highlight **Selected button** + command dials and scroll to the right (figure 4.42A, 4.42B, or 4.42C, screen 5). The next step makes an assignment for when you press and hold the button and then rotate one of the Command dials.

8. Choose one of the functions to assign to the ***Selected button*** + command dials (figure 4.42A, 4.42B, or 4.42C, screen 6). The upcoming section **Assignable Function List** will explain what each one does.

9. Press the OK button to lock in the setting for ***Selected button*** + command dials.

Now, let's look at the **Assignable Function List** to see what amazing powers we can give each of the assignable buttons on our cameras.

Assignable Function List

Let's review each of the functions you can assign to the ***Selected button*** press. Then we'll look at the ones you can assign to the ***Selected button*** + command dials.

Please review the functions that have a double asterisk (**) carefully. Setting those functions will disable functionality in another part of the camera.

Note: The camera's User's Manual has information for these assignments on pages 311 through 314.

Selected button press

- ***Preview**** – Normally, the depth of field function is controlled by the Depth-of-field preview button. Some users may not like the location of the Depth-of-field preview button, and—since it is also configurable—decide to switch the FN button (for instance) with the Depth-of-field preview button. Then, when Preview is selected in one of these Custom settings, the FN button will activate Depth-of-field preview instead. Setting this function disables other functionality in the D800. Please see the important note marked with two asterisks (**) at the end of this section.

- ***FV lock**** – If you set ***Selected button*** to FV lock, the button will cause the built-in Speedlight or the external Speedlight to emit a monitor pre-flash and then lock the flash output to the level determined by the pre-flash until you press the ***Selected button*** a second time. Setting this function disables other functionality in the D800. Please see the important note marked with two asterisks (**) at the end of this section.

- ***AE/AF lock*** – Enabling this function causes AE (exposure) and AF (focus) to lock on the last meter and autofocus system reading while the ***Selected button*** is held down.

- ***AE lock only*** – This allows you to lock AE (exposure) on the last meter reading when you hold down the ***Selected button***.

- ***AE lock (Reset on release)**** – Enabling this function causes AE (exposure) to lock on the last meter reading when the ***Selected button*** is pressed once. It stays locked until you press the ***Selected button*** again. Releasing the shutter resets the AE Lock just as pressing the ***Selected button*** a second time does. If the light meter goes off, it will also reset this function. Setting this function disables other functionality in the D800. Please see the important note marked with two asterisks (**) at the end of this section.

- **AE lock (Hold)**** – Enabling this function causes AE (exposure) to lock on the last meter reading when the **Selected button** is pressed once. It stays locked until you press the **Selected button** again. In other words, the **Selected button** toggles AE lock. This is similar to AE lock (Reset on release) except that releasing the shutter *does not reset* the AE lock hold. You must press the **Selected button** again to release AE lock. Setting this function disables other functionality in the D800. Please see the important note marked with two asterisks (**) at the end of this section.

- **AF lock only** – When set, this function locks the AF system (focus) on the last autofocus reading while you hold down the **Selected button**.

- **AF-ON (Assign AE-L/AF-L button only)** – If you set AE-L/AF-L button press to AF-ON, then the AE-L/AF-L button duplicates the functionality of the AF-ON button and will initiate autofocus. AF-ON cannot be assigned to the other two buttons (Fn and Preview). It doesn't even appear in their lists of functions.

- **Flash off** – This is a temporary way to disable the flash when you want to leave your flash turned on and still be able to take a non-flash picture. While you hold down the **Selected button**, the flash is disabled.

- **Bracketing burst** – Normally, during a bracketing sequence with the shutter's Release mode set to Single Frame Release Mode—the S next to CL and CH on the Release mode dial—you have to press the Shutter-release button once for each of the images in the bracket. The only way to shoot all the images in the bracketed series without letting up on the Shutter-release button is to set the Release mode dial to CL or CH. If you set Bracketing burst, you can hold down the **Selected button** while also holding down the Shutter-release button and the camera will take all the images in the bracket without letup. This seems a bit redundant to me. I think I'd rather just set the Release mode to CL–Continuous-low or CH–Continuous-high release mode and take the bracketed burst. This applies to AE, Flash, and ADL bracketing, which take one image for each shutter release. WB bracketing is mentioned in the manual too, but because it takes the entire bracket in one shutter release, what's the point? If you use this function for WB bracketing and hold down the Shutter-release button, you'll create multiple groups of bracketed images on your memory card. Remember, WB bracketing takes the entire bracket in one shutter press. Multiple shutter releases will capture numerous multi-image WB brackets. Be careful with this function when using WB bracketing.

- **Matrix metering** – If you do not use Matrix metering as your primary metering system but want to use it occasionally, this setting allows you to turn on Matrix metering while you hold down the **Selected button**. When you release the **Selected button**, the camera returns to your customary meter type, such as Spot or Center-weighted metering.

- **Center-weighted** – If you normally use Matrix or Spot metering as your primary metering system, you can temporarily use Center-weighted metering by holding down the **Selected button**. When you release the button, the camera returns to your customary meter type, such as Spot or Matrix.

- **Spot metering** – If you normally use a metering system other than Spot metering, you can temporarily switch to Spot by holding down the **Selected button**. When you release the button, the camera returns to your customary meter type, such as Center-weighted or Matrix.

- **Playback**** – This function causes the **Selected button** to act as if you had pressed the Playback button. Nikon included this so that you could play back images when using a big telephoto lens that requires two hands to use. Setting this function disables other functionality in the D800. Please see the important note marked with two asterisks (**) at the end of this section.

- **Access top item in MY MENU** – You can press the **Selected button** to jump directly to the top item in My Menu. This allows you to quickly modify a favorite menu item.

- **+NEF (RAW)**** – If you are a regular JPEG shooter and have JPEG fine, normal, or basic selected as your normal image capture format, you can use the **Selected button** to temporarily switch to NEF (RAW) mode. Once you take the RAW format picture, the camera switches back to JPEG. If you decide not to take the NEF (RAW) picture, just press the **Selected button** again to return to JPEG mode. Setting this function disables other functionality in the D800. Please see the important note marked with two asterisks (**) at the end of this section.

- **Viewfinder virtual horizon**** – You can press the **Selected button** to display a Virtual horizon indicator on the right and bottom sides of the Viewfinder. Setting this function disables other functionality in the D800. Please see the important note marked with two asterisks (**) at the end of this section.

- **None** (default) – When this setting is enabled, the **Selected button** does nothing.

** Important note: If you decide to use this particular function (marked with **), please realize that it will disable the **Selected button** + command dials feature of the camera. You'll see a warning on the screen when you set it, but by then it will have turned the **Selected button** + command dials to None. If you then go back and try to set a value under **Selected button** + command dials, the camera will give you a warning and set the **Selected button** function to None. They cannot be used at the same time.

Selected button + command dials

- *Choose image area* – You may press the ***Selected button*** and rotate either of the Command dials to choose from the camera's various image areas. Your choices are FX (36x24) 1.0x, 1.2x (30x20) 1.2x, DX (24x16) 1.5x, and 5:4 (30x24). Figure 4.42D shows the Control panel icons you'll see when you use Choose image area. You can see the Image area selections scroll by in the following formats as you turn a Command dial: 36 - 24 equals 36x24 mm *(FX or 1.0x)*, 30 - 20 equals 30x20 mm *(1.2x)*, 24 - 16 equals 24x16 mm *(DX or 1.5x)*, and 30 - 24 equals 30x24 mm *(5:4)*.

  Note: You can also choose the Image area from a special menu screen that is not available for any of the other **Selected button** + command dials selections. Figure 4.42E shows the screen you can use to select an Image area. Use the following menu path to get to this screen: *Custom Setting Menu > f controls > fN Assign **Selected button** > **Selected button** + command dials > Choose image area.* I used a menu screen from *f4 Assign Fn button > Fn button + command dials* as an example.

Figure 4.42D – Choose image area – 30x24 mm (5:4) is selected

Figure 4.42E – Choose image area by menu selection

- *Shutter speed & aperture lock* – Simply press the **Selected button** and rotate the front Main command dial to lock in the camera's shutter speed when you are using Shutter-priority (S) and Manual (M) modes. Or, you can press the Selected button and turn the front Sub-command dial to lock in the aperture setting when using Aperture-priority (A) and Manual (M) modes.

- ***1 step spd/aperture*** (not available for AE-L/AF-L + command dials) – If you set *Custom Setting Menu > b Metering/exposure > b2 EV steps for exposure cntrl* to 1/3 step you can change your camera's shutter speed and/or aperture in 1/3 EV steps while in Aperture-priority (A), Shutter-priority (S), and Manual (M). However, you may want to use larger EV steps occasionally. By setting 1 step spd/aperture, you can hold down the ***Selected button*** and the camera will allow you to change the shutter speed or aperture in 1 step increments instead of the normal 1/3 step. Example shutter speeds in 1/3 EV steps are 1/60, 1/80, 1/100, 1/125, 1/160. Example shutter speeds in 1 EV step are 1/60, 1/125, 1/250, 1/500, 1/1000.
- ***Choose non-CPU lens number*** – If you have configured non-CPU lenses under *Setup Menu > Non-CPU lens data* you'll be able to hold down the ***Selected button*** while rotating the front Sub-command dial to scroll through a list of up to nine non-CPU lenses. Figure 4.42F shows the Control panel icons you will see when you use Choose non-CPU lens number**.** The number 35 shown in figure 4.42F is the focal length of one of my registered non-CPU lenses—my AI Nikkor 35mm f/2—and the F2 represents the maximum aperture. The n-1 represents the lens numbers *(*n-1 through n-9*)* that are registered with the camera.

Figure 4.42F – Choose non-CPU lens number

Figure 4.42G – Active D-Lighting – Auto

- ***Active D-Lighting*** – Press the ***Selected button*** and rotate either of the Command dials to adjust Active D-Lighting (ADL) to one of its six settings: Off (oFF), Low (L), Normal (n), High (H), Extra high (HP), and Auto. Figure 4.42G shows the Control panel icons you will see when you use Active D-Lighting as described here. You will see the symbols that represent the various settings, such as Auto**,** H, and HP, scroll by as you turn either of the Command dials.
- ***None*** – Nothing happens when you hold down the ***Selected button*** and rotate the Command dials.

Using the Information display edit screen to Assign Buttons

Interestingly, you can also use the camera's info button and Information display edit screen to initiate assignments to the Fn button, Preview button, and AE-L/AF-L buttons. Use the following screens to do it, referring back to the previous section, **Assignable Function List**, for selections.

Figure 4.42H – *Selected button* assignment from the Information display edit screen

Use the following steps to access the Information display edit screen and initiate changes to the *Selected button* assignments (figure 4.42H):

1. Press the info button twice to open the Information display edit screen.
2. You will see screens as shown in figure 4.42H. Scroll around with the Multi selector and choose the button you want to assign (positions shown in figure 4.42H).
3. When you have selected the correct button assignment screen, simply press the OK button to open the actual assignment menus, which are identical to the menus covered in figures 4.42A, 4.42B, and 4.42C (starting with screen 3 in each) including all the functions listed in the **Assignable Function List**. Basically, the Information display edit screen allows you to skip the first two menu items on the Custom Setting Menu and jump directly to the assignment screen (screens 3–6) in figures 4.42A, 4.42B, and 4.42C. This may save you a little time in the field.

Settings Recommendation: There are so many available functions here that I'm loathe to recommend anything definitively. However, I will tell you how I set mine, and you can experiment and see if that suits your style. If not, you've got a lot of choices!

Darrell's favorites:

- *Assign Fn button press* – Spot metering (my normal meter is Matrix)
- *Assign Fn button + command dials* – Active D-Lighting
- *Assign preview button press* – Preview (Depth-of-field preview)
- *Assign preview button + command dials* – None (I don't use this)
- *Assign AE-L/AF-L button press* – AE lock only
- *Assign AE-L/AF-L button + command dials* – Choose non-CPU lens number

Custom Setting f7 – Shutter Spd & Aperture Lock

(User's Manual – Page 316)

Shutter spd & aperture lock is an interesting function that allows you to lock the shutter speed at the currently selected value when shooting in Shutter-priority (S) or Manual (M) mode. You can also lock the aperture at its current value when you are shooting in Aperture-priority (A) or Manual (M) mode. This function does not apply to and will not work when shooting in Programmed auto (P) mode.

Figure 4.43 – Selecting Shutter spd & aperture lock

Use the following steps to keep your shutter speed or aperture from changing, according to which exposure mode you are using (figure 4.43):

1. Select f Controls from the Custom Setting Menu and scroll to the right (figure 4.43, screen 1).
2. Highlight f7 shutter spd & aperture lock and scroll to the right (figure 4.43, screen 2).
3. Select Shutter speed lock or Aperture lock (according to which exposure mode you are currently using) and scroll to the right (figure 4.43, screen 3).
4. Choose either On or Off from the list. In figure 4.43, screen 4, Off has been chosen for Aperture lock. I didn't show the screens for Shutter speed lock since they work exactly the same way as Aperture lock.
5. Press the OK button to lock in the shutter speed or aperture.

Settings Recommendation: If I were shooting in a studio, under carefully controlled lighting, and wanted to lock the shutter speed or aperture to a value that will not change throughout the session, this function will do the job well. It can be a protection for when you do not want a value to change.

Shooting out in the field with varying light conditions may make this function much less useful, so many of us will never use it. Your style of shooting will govern whether this function has any value for you.

Custom Setting f8 – Assign BKT button

(User's Manual – Pages 316, 132, 197, 176)

Assign BKT button allows you to either leave bracketing assigned to the BKT button or to assign Multiple exposure or HDR (high dynamic range), instead of bracketing, to the BKT button. Bracketing is fully described in the previous section **Custom Setting Menu – e5 Auto bracketing set**, in case you want to review it.

In the chapter titled **Shooting Menu**, we covered how to do multiple exposures and shoot HDR (high dynamic range) images based on Shooting Menu settings. Let's see how to change BKT button's assignment to initiate one of these functions.

Figure 4.44A – Assign BKT button

Use these steps to change the assignment of the BKT button from Bracketing to Multiple exposure or HDR (figure 4.44A):

1. Choose f controls from the Custom Setting Menu and scroll to the right (figure 4.44A, screen 1).
2. Select f8 Assign BKT button from the menu and scroll to the right (figure 4.44A, screen 2).
3. Choose Auto bracketing, Multiple exposure, or HDR (high dynamic range) from the list (figure 4.44A, screen 3).
4. Press the OK button to select the setting.

You can manage all three of these functions—Auto bracketing, Multiple exposure, and HDR (high dynamic range)—using external camera controls and the Control panel. We covered the normal use of the BKT button (exposure bracketing) in a previous section of this chapter, **Custom Setting e5 – Auto bracketing set**, so we won't review it here. However, we need to examine the Control panel screens for Multiple exposure and HDR (high dynamic range).

First let's look into the Control panel icons and what they mean for Multiple exposure (figure 4.44B). You may want to review the section titled **Multiple**

Exposure in the **Shooting Menu** chapter to make sure you understand what each part of this function does.

Figure 4.44B – Multiple exposure using the BKT button

Press the BKT button and rotate the rear Main command dial until you see the symbols shown in figure 4.44B. Here is what each symbol means, and how to use it, referenced by the numbers in red:

1. This symbol shows the number of shots in the Multiple exposure. Hold down the BKT button and turn the front Sub-command dial to select between 2 and 10 exposures for the Multiple exposure.
2. The tiny symbol L informs you that you have selected On (series), meaning you will take a series of multiple-exposure images, not just one. If the L is not displayed, you have selected On (single photo) and will take only a single Multiple exposure. Hold down the BKT button and turn the rear Main command dial to toggle the symbol—and the functionality it represents—On or Off.
3. The symbol AG stands for Auto Gain. It is displayed if you have Auto gain set to On in *Shooting Menu > Multiple exposure > Auto gain*. You cannot turn AG on or off by using external camera controls. You must use the Shooting Menu instead.
4. This symbol is displayed to let you know you have enabled Multiple exposure. Hold down the BKT button and rotate the rear Main command dial until the symbol appears on the Control panel.

Now, we will examine how you can use external camera controls to enable and change the HDR (high dynamic range) function.

Figure 4.44C – HDR using the BKT button

Hold down the BKT button and turn the rear Main command dial to select HDR (high dynamic range) and control the number of two-shot HDR brackets you will shoot—one or a series. Hold down the BKT button and turn the front Sub-command dial to control the exposure difference between each shot in the two-shot HDR bracket (1 to 3 stops or Auto). You should review the section titled **HDR (High Dynamic Range)** in the **Shooting Menu** chapter to make sure you understand what each part of this function does. Here is what the numbers mean:

1. This number (3.0) represents the exposure differential between the shots in the two-shot bracket. In this case a 3-stop exposure difference will be made between the two pictures that will later be combined into one HDR image. You can select: Auto, 1, 2, or 3 (stops). Hold down the BKT button and rotate the front Sub-command dial to change the exposure differential.
2. The HDR symbol appears when you hold down the BKT button and rotate the rear Main command dial, enabling HDR (high dynamic range).
3. The small L symbol appears when you continue holding down the BKT button and rotating the rear Main command dial. When the L is displayed, you have selected On (series). When the L is not displayed, you have selected On (single photo).

Settings Recommendation: I usually leave the BKT button set to bracketing because I do a lot of bracketing when I'm out shooting high-contrast landscape scenes. However, if you do more multiple exposures or two-picture HDR than bracketing, why not assign the BKT button to one of those two alternate functions? Nikon gives us some excellent personal customizability with this camera.

Custom Setting f9 – Customize Command Dials

(User's Manual – Page 317)

Customize command dials does exactly what it sounds like—it lets you change how the Command dials operate. There are several operations you can modify:

- Reverse rotation
- Change main/sub
- Aperture setting
- Menus and playback

Let's examine each of these items and the screens and steps used to change them.

Figure 4.45A – Customize command dials

Use the following steps to change the functionality of the Command dials (figure 4.45A):

1. Select f Controls from the Custom Setting Menu and scroll to the right (figure 4.45A, screen 1).
2. Highlight f9 Customize command dials and scroll to the right (figure 4.45A, screen 2).
3. Choose one of the four selections from the list. In figure 4.45A, screen 3, Reverse rotation has been selected.
4. Scroll to the right and use the screens and steps under each of the following sections to configure the various functions (figures 4.45B to 4.45E).

Reverse Rotation

Reverse rotation allows you to change what happens when you rotate the Command dials in a certain direction. You can reverse Command dial operations with this setting. There are two selections:

- **Exposure compensation** – When you press and hold the Exposure compensation button and turn the Sub-command dial clockwise, it decreases the amount of compensation. If you place a check mark in this box and select Done, the camera will increase the amount of compensation when you turn the Sub-command dial clockwise.

- **Shutter speed/aperture** – Normally, when the D800 is set to Aperture-priority (A) or Manual (M) mode and you rotate the Sub-command dial clockwise, the aperture gets smaller. If you put a check mark next to Shutter speed/aperture and select Done, the aperture will get larger when you turn the Sub-command dial clockwise. The same goes for shutter speed in Shutter-priority (S) and Manual (M) modes. Normally, turning the rear Main command dial clockwise slows down the shutter speed. If you put a check mark next to Shutter speed/aperture and select Done, the shutter speed will get faster when you turn the Main command dial clockwise. Finally, when you override the aperture setting in Programmed auto (P) mode by turning the Main command dial clockwise, instead of decreasing the size of the aperture, it increases it.

Figure 4.45B – Customize command dials (Reverse rotation)

Here are the steps to change the rotation direction of the Command dials (figure 4.45B):

1. Continuing from figure 4.45A, screen 3, select Reverse rotation and scroll to the right (figure 4.45B, screen 1).
2. Using the Multi selector, highlight Exposure compensation or Shutter speed/aperture and scroll to the right to set a check mark in the corresponding small check box (figure 4.45B, screen 2). In figure 4.45B, screen 3, I have placed a check mark in both of the selections.
3. Scroll up to Done (figure 4.45B, screen 4) and press the OK button to lock in the setting.

Settings Recommendation: I leave the Command dials rotation set to factory default. I find life confusing enough without my camera working backwards. Of course, if you come from a different camera brand than Nikon—having been drawn by the siren call of 36 megapixels—and are used to the dials working in the opposite direction, you may feel more comfortable reversing them on your D800.

Change Main/Sub

Change main/sub allows you to swap the functionality of the two Command dials. The rear Main command dial will take on the functions of the front Sub-command dial and vice versa. Here are the three setting variations:

- **On** – By selecting On, you reverse the functionality of the two Command dials so that the Sub-command dial controls shutter speed while the Main command dial controls aperture.

- **On (Mode A)** – This special mode sets the camera so that the Main command dial on both the camera body and the MB-D12 battery pack (if mounted) controls the aperture when using Aperture-priority (A) mode only.
- **Off** – The functionality of the Command dials is set to the factory default. The Main command dial controls the shutter speed while the Sub-command dial controls the aperture.

Figure 4.45C – Customize command dials (Change main/sub)

Here are the steps to swap the functionality of the Command dials (figure 4.45C):

1. Continuing from figure 4.45A, screen 3, select Change main/sub and scroll to the right (figure 4.45C, screen 1).
2. Select one of the three settings from the list (figure 4.45C, screen 2). Off is selected in screen 2.
3. Press the OK button to lock in the setting.

Settings Recommendation: I leave the Command dials set to factory default (Off). I've been using Nikons for too many years to change Command dial functionality now. However, you may have valid reasons for swapping the Command dial functionality. If so, it's very easy.

Aperture Setting

There are two selections that allow you to modify how the camera treats CPU lenses that have aperture rings on them (non-G lenses):

- **Sub-command dial** – This is the factory default setting. The aperture is set using the Sub-command dial. You could reverse this functionality so that the Main command dial controls the aperture instead. See the previous section **Change Main/Sub**. If you select this setting and are using a non-G lens with an old-style aperture ring, you will need to set and lock it (if available) to the smallest aperture and then use the Sub-command dial to change apertures.
- **Aperture ring** – This setting allows those with older non-G type lenses with a CPU to use the lens's aperture ring to adjust the aperture instead of using the Sub-command dial. The EV increments will be displayed in only 1 EV steps when

this is active. If you are using a G-type lens with no aperture ring, you clearly can't set the aperture with a nonexistent aperture ring, so the camera ignores this setting.

Note: When a non-CPU lens is used, the aperture ring must always be used to set the aperture instead of the Sub-command dial.

Figure 4.45D – Customize command dials (Aperture setting)

Here are the steps to change the style of Aperture setting (figure 4.45D):

1. Continuing from figure 4.45A, screen 3, select Aperture setting and scroll to the right (figure 4.45D, screen 1).
2. Select Sub-command dial or Aperture ring from the list (figure 4.45D, screen 2).
3. Press the OK button to lock in the setting.

Settings Recommendation: I leave Aperture setting set to Sub-command dial. I have some older AF Nikkors that I still like using, so I keep them locked at their smallest aperture settings and use the Sub-command dial to change their apertures. I don't adjust apertures with the old aperture ring on the lens unless I'm using older non-CPU, manual focus AI or AI-S lenses.

Menus and Playback

Menus and playback is designed for those who do not like to use the Multi selector for viewing image Playback or Info screens. It also allows you to use the Command dials for scrolling though menus. There are two selections for how the menus and image playback work when you would rather not use the Multi selector:

- **On** – While viewing images during playback, turning the Main command dial to the left or right scrolls through the displayed images. Turning the Sub-command dial left or right scrolls through the data and histogram screens for each image. While viewing menus, turning the Main command dial left or right scrolls up or down in the screens. Turning the Sub-command dial left or right scrolls left or right in the menus. The Multi selector button works normally, even when this is set to On. This setting simply allows you two ways to view your images and menus instead of one. Also, when you are using thumbnail viewing of multiple images on the Monitor, turning the rear Main command dial moves left and right in the list of thumbnail images, while the front Sub-command dial moves up and down in the list of thumbnails.

- **On (image review excluded)** – This works exactly the same as On, with one exception. When you use On alone (previous setting) and take a picture, the picture will show up on the Monitor and you can then use the Command dials to review images other than the one you just took. However, if you select On (image review excluded) instead of just On, you will not be able to examine other images with the Command dials when an image pops up for review after you take it. In other words, image review with the Command dials is excluded just after you take a picture. You can view only the picture you just took unless you use the Multi selector, not the Command dials, to scroll through the other images taken previously. You can still use the Command dials for Playback image review (after pressing the Playback button)—just not immediately after taking an image, when it first pops up on the Monitor.
- **Off** – This is the default action. The Multi selector is used to scroll through images and menus.

When using either of these settings, you can press the OK button or the Multi selector center button to make a selection.

Figure 4.45E – Customize command dials (Menus and playback)

Here are the steps used to configure Menus and playback (figure 4.45E):

1. Continuing from figure 4.45A, screen 3, select Menus and playback and scroll to the right (figure 4.45E, screen 1).
2. Select one of the three settings from the list (figure 48E, screen 2). On is selected in screen 2.
3. Press the OK button to lock in the setting.

Settings Recommendation: I have my D800 set to On for Menus and playback. I like the fact that I can use the Multi selector or the Command dials to move around in my camera's menus and images. Try this one out; you may like it too!

Custom Setting f10 – Release Button to Use Dial

(User's Manual – Page 318)

Release button to use dial allows those who don't like to or cannot hold down buttons and turn a Command dial at the same time to change to an easier method. This function may be very useful to people with limited hand strength, allowing them operate the camera more easily.

There are two settings under this function. Let's examine them and then look at the screens and steps to modify Release button to use dial:

- **Yes** – This setting changes a two-step operation into a three-step operation. Normally, you would press and hold down a button while rotating a Command dial. When you select Yes under Release button to use dial, the camera allows you to press and release a button, rotate the Command dial, then press and release the button again. The initial button press locks the button so that you do not have to hold your finger on it while turning the Command dial. Once you have changed whatever you are adjusting, you must press the button a second time to unlock it.
- **No** – This is the default setting. You must press and hold a button while rotating the Command dials in order to change camera functionality.

If the exposure meter turns off or you press the Shutter-release button halfway while the Yes operation is active, you must press the original button again to restart the action. You can set the exposure meter to No limit or a longer time-out in *Custom Setting Menu > c Timers/AE lock > c2 Auto meter-off delay* to prevent the exposure meter from turning off after a few seconds. This may make the function more useful if you have weak hands or must move slowly.

Figure 4.46 – Release button to use dial

Here are the steps to configure Release button to use dial (figure 4.46):

1. Select f Controls from the Custom Setting Menu and scroll to the right (figure 4.46, screen 1).
2. Highlight f10 Release button to use dial and scroll to the right (figure 4.46, screen 2).

3. Choose Yes or No from the list. In figure 4.46, screen 3, No has been selected.
4. Press the OK button to lock in the setting.

Settings Recommendation: I haven't found this function useful for myself. However, a person with certain physical disabilities may find this to be a very useful function.

Custom Setting f11 – Slot Empty Release Lock
(User's Manual – Page 319)

Slot empty release lock defaults to locking the shutter when you try to take an image without a memory card inserted in the camera. By enabling it, you *can* take pictures without a memory card but cannot save them later.

This function exists so that when you have your camera tethered to your computer using Nikon Camera Control Pro 2 software (not included), you can send pictures directly to the computer, bypassing the memory card.

You can allow the camera to take pictures with no card inserted when you select the OK Enable release setting. Here is a description of both settings:

*   **LOCK Release locked** – When you choose this default setting, your camera will refuse to release the shutter when there is no memory card present.
*   **OK Enable release** – Use this setting if you want to use the optional Camera Control Pro 2 software to send images from the camera directly to the computer.

Figure 4.47 – Slot empty release lock

Here are the steps used to configure Slot empty release lock (figure 4.47):

1. Select f Controls from the Custom Setting Menu and scroll to the right (figure 4.47, screen 1).
2. Highlight f11 Slot empty release lock and scroll to the right (figure 4.47, screen 2).
3. Choose one of the two settings from the list. In figure 4.47, screen 3, LOCK Release locked has been selected.
4. Press the OK button to lock in the setting.

Settings Recommendation: I tried using the OK Enable release setting as an experiment. I found that there is no real reason to use this setting other than when the camera is tethered to a computer. You cannot save the images in the memory buffer to a memory card later.

Being the stubborn sort, I wanted to test this to the limit. Without a memory card present, I went around the house taking pictures until I eventually ran out of internal camera buffer memory.

The Monitor displayed DEMO on each image I took while the cards were out of the camera, and I could scroll around in the pictures normally. When I ran out of memory buffer space the camera simply started deleting the first picture in the series to make room for the new last image.

Okay, maybe I can just shoot some images, turn the camera off, and then insert a memory card to write the buffer out to the memory card? No! As soon as I turned off the camera to insert a memory card, it flushed the buffer and no images were left.

Hmm, maybe I can just shoot some images and, without turning off the camera, insert a memory card? No, again! Even though I had several images waiting around in buffer memory, as soon as I inserted the card, the camera switched to the inserted card and dumped the buffer again, deleting my lovely buffer images in the process.

I can find no way to write any of the images in the buffer out to a memory card later. If you are the curious type, I hope this saves you some time.

Custom Setting f12 – Reverse Indicators

(User's Manual – Page 319)

Reverse indicators lets you change the direction of your camera's exposure displays. Normally, anytime you see the exposure indicators in your camera's Control panel, Viewfinder, or the Information display, the - is on the left and the + is on the right. See Figure 4.48A, where I show the Information display and the exposure indicator therein. The first image shows the normal direction. The second image shows the Information display with the exposure indicators reversed (see red arrows).

Figure 4.48A – Reversed indicators on the Information display (see red arrows)

Figure 4.48B – Reverse indicators

Here are the steps to reverse the direction of all camera exposure indicators (figure 4.48B):

1. Select f Controls from the Custom Setting Menu and scroll to the right (figure 4.48B, screen 1).
2. Highlight f12 Reverse indicators and scroll to the right (figure 4.48B, screen 2).
3. Choose one of the two selections from the list. In figure 4.48B, screen 3, the reversed exposure indicator direction has been selected. Set it back to factory default it with the other selection.
4. Press the OK button to lock in the setting.

Settings Recommendation: Nikon changed the game on us with the D800. For as long as I can remember, my Nikons have had their exposure indicators in the +/- direction, not -/+. Inexplicably, Nikon changed it. Could it be that Nikon realized the D800 would be so desirable that many photographers using other camera brands would migrate over and they may be used to reversed-direction exposure meters? Maybe.

At first this aggravated me to no end and I changed it back to the +/- setting. However, after thinking about it for a while, I realized that the histogram works in a -/+ direction, with dark on the left and bright on the right. I use the histogram frequently, so I changed it back to the factory default of -/+. I have now used it this way for several weeks and it is beginning to make sense and feel more natural.

If you feel uncomfortable seeing the meter indicator working "backwards," you may want to change the exposure indicator to the "correct" direction. If you do change it, you may also want to reverse the Exposure compensation direction with *Custom Setting Menu > f controls > f9 Customize command dials > Reverse rotation > Exposure compensation* (see the previous section **Custom Setting f9 – Customize Command Dials**). Otherwise, you will notice that the Exposure compensation setting works backwards from the reversed direction of the exposure indicator. It's a good thing we still have a choice about reversing things!

Custom Setting f13 – Assign MB-D12 AF-ON

(User's Manual – Page 320)

The *Assign MB-D12 AF-ON* setting lets you assign a different use for the AF-ON button built into the optional MB-D12 battery pack than the one on the camera's body. There are eight distinct functions you can assign to the MB-D12's AF-ON button, as follows:

- **AF-ON** – This causes the camera to initiate autofocus when you press the AF-ON button on the MB-D12. It is the normal setting for the AF-ON button.
- **FV lock** – If you set the AF-ON button on the MB-D12 to FV lock, the button will cause the built-in Speedlight or an external Speedlight to emit a monitor pre-flash. It will lock the flash output to the level determined by the preflash until you press the AF-ON button on the MB-D12 a second time.
- **AE/AF lock** – Enabling this function causes AE (exposure) and AF (focus) to lock on the last meter and autofocus system reading while the AF-ON button on the MB-D12 is held down.
- **AE lock only** – This allows you to lock AE (exposure) on the last meter reading when you hold down the AF-ON button on the MB-D12.
- **AE lock (Reset on release)** – AE (exposure) locks when the MB-D12's AF-ON button is pressed once and released. AE remains locked until the AF-ON button is pressed and released a second time, the exposure meter turns off, or the shutter is released.
- **AE lock (Hold)** – Enabling this function causes AE (exposure) to lock on the last meter reading when the AF-ON button on the MB-D12 is pressed and released once. It stays locked until you press the AF-ON button again or the exposure meter goes off.
- **AF lock only** – This function locks the AF (focus) system on the last autofocus reading while you hold down the AF-ON button on the MB-D12.
- **Same as Fn button** – This setting allows you to set the AF-ON button on the MB-D12 so it executes whatever function you assigned to the camera's Fn button in *Custom Setting Menu > f controls > f4 Assign Fn button*.

Figure 4.49 – Assign MB-D12 AF-ON

Use the following steps to select an AF-ON setting for the MB-D12 battery pack (figure 4.49):

1. Select f Controls from the Custom Setting Menu and scroll to the right (figure 4.49, screen 1).
2. Highlight f13 Assign MB-D12 AF-ON button and scroll to the right (figure 4.49, screen 2).
3. Choose one of the selections from the list. In figure 4.49, screen 3, AF-ON is selected.
4. Press the OK button to lock in the setting.

Settings Recommendation: I generally leave AF-ON assigned to this button because I like to focus with AF-ON sometimes. You can assign any one of the eight functions listed to this button. If you don't want to use AF-ON, then assign your favorite instead.

Section Seven – g Movie

Custom Settings g1 to g4
Within the *g Movie* menu you'll find four settings in the D800:
* **g1** – Assign Fn button
* **g2** – Assign preview button
* **g3** – Assign AE-L/AF-L button
* **g4** –Assign shutter button

Custom Setting g1 – Assign Fn Button
(User's Manual – Page 321)
Assign Fn button lets you choose how the Fn button works in Movie live view mode only. Following are the four choices:

* ***Power aperture (open)*** – By selecting this function, you ask the camera to open the aperture to a larger setting when you press the Fn button. It does so automatically without you having to turn any dials; just pressing the Fn button "powers" it open smoothly. Most of us will use the function in conjuction with *Power aperture (close)* under *Custom Setting Menu > g Movie > g2 Assign preview button > Preview button press*. Unfortunately, this does not work *while* a movie is actually being recorded, only before the Movie-record button is pressed. You can set your aperture only before the recording begins with this function. During a movie recording session, you *can* change the aperture manually by turning the front Sub-command dial, and the camera will adjust the ISO sensitivity to keep

the exposure accurate. However, when you do adjust the aperture manually, you can hear an audible clicking noise for each aperture change that will be picked up by the microphone, even the isolated Nikon ME-1 external mic when it's mounted in the accessory shoe. It is best to set the camera's aperture before the movie. If you are recording with a boom mic, it is unlikely that it will pick up the aperture-changing click. **Note**: Power aperture is available only in Aperture-priority (A) and Manual (M) modes.

- *Index marking* – If you have Index marking enabled while you are recording a movie, you can set an index mark at the current frame position by pressing the Fn button. This index mark does not actually appear in the movie itself. It is, however, available when you are viewing and editing movies.

- *View photo shooting info* – This function allows you to view shooting information for still images when using Movie live view mode. The resulting still images have a slightly reduced image size and a different ratio, which we will discuss in a moment. Normally, when in Movie live view mode, the camera displays the shutter speed, aperture, and ISO sensitivity (recording information) for a potential movie at the bottom of the Monitor. When you press the Fn button, the camera displays the shutter speed, aperture, and ISO sensitivity (shooting information) for still image creation instead. The camera will happily take still images when you are using Movie live view mode. However, please note that there are some image size and ratio differences when taking a still image using Movie live view instead of Live view photography mode. When you are using Live view photography mode, a normal Large FX image is $7,360 \times 4,912$ (36.2 MP); however, while in Movie live view, a Large still image is $6,720 \times 3,776$ (25.3 MP). When using Movie live view, the camera switches its thinking and formats over to the HD world, which is one of the reasons this camera is called an HD-SLR, not just a D-SLR. Instead of the 3:2 aspect ratio used by Live view photography mode, the still image from Movie live view uses a 16:9 ratio. It is still a fully usable image at 25.3 MP. The ratio matches the look of an HDTV (16:9) instead of a normal picture format. You could use this mode for still images when you know the pictures will be displayed on an HDTV because it will match the HD ratio without the blank space on the sides you will find when displaying a normal 3:2 image on a modern monitor. Test this for yourself on a newer LCD or LED computer monitor and you will see how much more closely the 16:9 format matches the monitor's display size. See the section **Image Area** in the chapter titled **Shooting Menu** for more detail on image aspect ratios.

- *None* – Pressing the Fn button when in Movie live view mode does nothing.

Figure 4.50 – Assign Fn button for Movie live view mode

Use these steps to assign the previously mentioned functions to the Fn button (figure 4.50):

1. Select g Movie from the Custom Setting Menu and scroll to the right (figure 4.50, screen 1).
2. Highlight g1 Assign Fn button and scroll to the right (figure 4.50, screen 2).
3. Highlight Fn button press and scroll to the right (figure 4.50, screen 3).
4. Choose one of the four selections from the list. In figure 4.50, screen 3, Power aperture (open) is selected.
5. Press the OK button to lock in the setting.

Settings Recommendation: I enjoy using the Power aperture (open) setting because it is a useful function for me before I start creating a movie. However, if I didn't shoot many movies but used the 25.3 MP 16:9 still images provided by Movie live view mode, I would select View photo shooting info so I could more easily validate my exposure information. The Index marking function is very useful for those who want to mark certain locations in a movie for future editing purposes.

Custom Setting g2 – Assign Preview Button

(User's Manual – Page 322)

Assign preview button lets you choose how the Depth-of-field preview button works in Movie live view mode only. Following are the four choices:

- **Power aperture (close)** – By selecting this function, you ask the camera to close (stop down) the aperture to a smaller setting when you press the Depth-of-field preview button. It does so automatically without you having to turn any dials; just pressing the Depth-of-field preview button automatically closes the aperture while you hold the button down. Most of us will use the function in conjuction with Power aperture (open) under *Custom Setting Menu > g Movie > g1 Assign Fn button > Fn button press*. As mentioned in the previous section, this does not work while a movie is actually being recorded, only before the Movie-record button is pressed. You can set your aperture only before the recording begins with this function. **Note**: Power aperture is available only in Aperture-priority (A) and Manual (M) modes.

- **Index marking** – If you have Index marking enabled while you are recording a movie, you can set an index mark at the current frame position by pressing the Depth-of-field preview button. This index mark does not actually appear in the movie itself. It is, however, available when you are viewing and editing movies.

- **View photo shooting info** – This function allows you to view shooting information for still images when using Movie live view mode. Normally, the camera displays the shutter speed, aperture, and ISO sensitivity (recording information) for a potential movie at the bottom of the Monitor. When you press the Depth-of-field preview button, the camera displays the shutter speed, aperture, and ISO sensitivity (shooting information) for still image creation instead.

- **None** – Pressing the Fn button when in Movie live view mode does nothing.

Figure 4.51 – Assign preview button for Movie live view mode

Use these steps to assign the previously mentioned functions to the Depth-of-field preview button (figure 4.51):

1. Select g Movie from the Custom Setting Menu and scroll to the right (figure 4.51, screen 1).
2. Highlight g2 Assign preview button and scroll to the right (figure 4.51, screen 2).
3. Highlight Preview button press and scroll to the right (figure 4.51, screen 3).
4. Choose one of the four selections from the list. In figure 4.51, screen 3, Power aperture (close) is selected.
5. Press the OK button to lock in the setting.

Settings Recommendation: Because I use the sister function (g1 Assign Fn button) with an assignment of Power aperture (open), the Power aperture (close) function is a natural complement. I enjoy using the Power aperture (close) setting because it is a useful function for me before I start creating a movie. However, as I mentioned in the preceding section, if I didn't shoot many movies but used the 25.3 MP 16:9 still images provided by Movie live view mode, I would select View photo shooting info so I could easily validate my exposure information. Again, the Index marking function is very useful for those who want to mark certain locations in a movie for future editing purposes.

Custom Setting g3 – Assign AE-L/AF-L Button

(User's Manual – Page 323)

Assign AE-L/AF-L button lets you choose how the AE-L/AF-L button works in Movie live view mode only. Following are the seven choices:

- ***Index marking*** – If you have Index marking enabled while you are recording a movie, you can set an index mark at the current frame position by pressing the AE-L/AF-L button. This index mark does not actually appear in the movie itself. It is, however, available when you are viewing and editing movies.
- ***View photo shooting info*** – This function allows you to view shooting information for still images when using Movie live view mode. Normally, the camera displays the shutter speed, aperture, and ISO sensitivity (recording information) for a potential movie at the bottom of the Monitor. When you press the AE-L/AF-L button, the camera displays the shutter speed, aperture, and ISO sensitivity (shooting information) for still image creation instead.
- ***AE/AF lock*** – Enabling this function causes AE (exposure) and AF (focus) to lock on the last meter and autofocus system reading while the AE-L/AF-L button is held down.
- ***AE lock only*** – This allows you to lock AE (exposure) on the last meter reading when you hold down the AE-L/AF-L button.

- *AE lock (Hold)* – This function causes AE (exposure) to lock on the last meter reading when the AE-L/AF-L button is pressed and released once. It stays locked until you press the AE-L/AF-L button again or the exposure meter goes off.
- *AF lock only* – This function locks the AF (focus) system on the last autofocus reading while you hold down the AE-L/AF-L button.
- *None* – Pressing the AE-L/AF-L button when in Movie live view mode does nothing.

Figure 4.52 – Assign AE-L/AF-L button for Movie live view mode

Use these steps to assign the previously mentioned functions to the AE-L/AF-L button (figure 4.52):

1. Select g Movie from the Custom Setting Menu and scroll to the right (figure 4.52, screen 1).
2. Highlight g3 Assign AE-L/AF-L button and scroll to the right (figure 4.52, screen 2).
3. Highlight AE-L/AF-L button press and scroll to the right (figure 4.52, screen 3).
4. Choose one of the seven selections from the list. In figure 4.52, screen 3, AE lock (Hold) is selected.
5. Press the OK button to lock in the setting.

Settings Recommendation: Sometimes when you are making movies, the light will suddenly change levels drastically when the subject moves near a window or a bright lamp in the room. The surroundings will go dark, including the subject, while the camera adjusts to the much brighter light source. To prevent that from happening, it is a good idea to use AE lock (hold). With a single touch of the AE-L/AF-L button, I can lock the camera at a correct exposure for the subject. If the subject walks in front of a bright window, the details outside the window will be blown out but the subject will still be properly exposed. The camera does not change exposure levels when a sudden bright light is temporarily introduced.

However, what if I need to walk from a darker room into a bright room, or even go outside with my subject? I simply press the AE-L/AF-L button again, allow the camera to adjust to the new light source, and then press it once more to lock the exposure again. Many videographers use a similar method. I find AE lock (Hold) to be the most useful function to assign to the AE-L/AF-L button.

Of course, since there are seven functions, you should read about each one and experiment with when and why you might use it. You will likely need all of them at one time or another.

Custom Setting g4 – Assign Shutter Button

(User's Manual – Page 324)

Assign shutter button lets you choose how the Shutter-release button works in Movie live view mode only. Following are the two choices:

- **Take Photos** – If you are in the middle of recording a movie and you absolutely must have a Large FX still image of something going on in the frame, you can acquire a 16:9 aspect ratio image by pressing the Shutter-release button all the way down. The camera will stop recording the movie and take a still image with a pixel ratio of 6,720 × 3,776 (25.3 MP). This image will closely match the format of an HDTV and modern computer monitor, being shorter and wider than a normal 3:2 aspect ratio FX image.

- **Record movies** – If you are going to shoot movies for a while instead of taking still images, you can select this setting and the camera will enter Movie live view mode whenever you press the Shutter-release button halfway down. Once in Movie live view mode, you can focus by pressing the Shutter-release button halfway down again. Then press the Shutter-release button all the way down to start recording the movie. To stop recording the movie, simply press the Shutter-release button all the way down again. To stop Movie live view mode, press the LV button. When you have this function selected, the camera behaves more like a true movie camera than a still camera. You cannot, of course, take still images when using this function because the Shutter-release button is set to enter, focus, start, and stop movie recording.

Figure 4.53 – Assign shutter button for Movie live view mode

Use these steps to assign the previously mentioned functions to the Shutter-release button (figure 4.53):

1. Select g Movie from the Custom Setting Menu and scroll to the right (figure 4.53, screen 1).
2. Choose g4 Assign shutter button and scroll to the right (figure 4.53, screen 2).
3. Choose one of the two selections from the list. In figure 4.53, screen 3, Take photos is selected.
4. Press the OK button to lock in the setting.

Settings Recommendation: If you use the Record movies function, the camera's brain becomes focused on recording video and turns off almost everything that has to do with still image creation. You can't take pictures, measure preset white balance, take dust off reference photos, do interval timer photography, or do most other things related to still imagery. If you think you might need to stop a movie and take a picture, don't use Record movies; use Take photos instead. You can still shoot a video, but you have the ability to stop the video and get a quick still image.

If you bought the Nikon D800 to take advantage of its superior, clean, uncompressed, broadcast-quality video, you will most likely set the Record movies function and never look back. However, if you are like most of us and want the D800 for both video and still images, Take photos is the best setting.

Author's Conclusions

Using the Shooting Banks and Custom Banks Together

Now that you have set up and named one of the Custom settings banks, you are ready to make your camera act like a chameleon (or herd of chameleons). It is time to configure all the Custom settings banks with different shooting styles in mind. Once you have each Shooting menu bank and Custom settings bank configured, you can use them together.

Often, I use a combination of Shooting menu bank A and Custom settings bank A. But nothing prevents you from using Shooting menu bank B with Custom settings bank D, or Shooting menu bank C with Custom settings bank A. Choose whatever combination you'd like to use. That's where the camera's extreme flexibility comes in.

Maybe you have Shooting menu bank A set for Best Quality JPEGs and are shooting them with Custom settings bank A, which is set for no focus tracking. Suddenly, a flock of geese flies by and you realize you must use focus tracking to accurately capture the one big fat goose you like. You simply press the MENU button, scroll to Custom settings bank B, and you are set. (You did configure Custom settings bank B for focus tracking, right?)

Or, maybe while you're using Shooting menu bank A for Fine-quality JPEGS, an incredibly beautiful rainbow appears. You quickly switch to Shooting menu bank C, where you've previously set lossless RAW mode for maximum quality.

Get the point? Your camera can change the way it shoots on the fly, in much less time than it takes to talk about it. Now that you've read this over, set up a few banks on your camera. Give it some serious thought and then do it. Think of the ways you most often take pictures, and configure your D800 for each of those ways. Your camera will be customized to you!

Now, let's move into the next menu system—the Setup Menu—and configure the camera's basic setup. This menu is very important for initial camera configuration, but only a few of its functions are used after initial setup.

Setup Menu

5

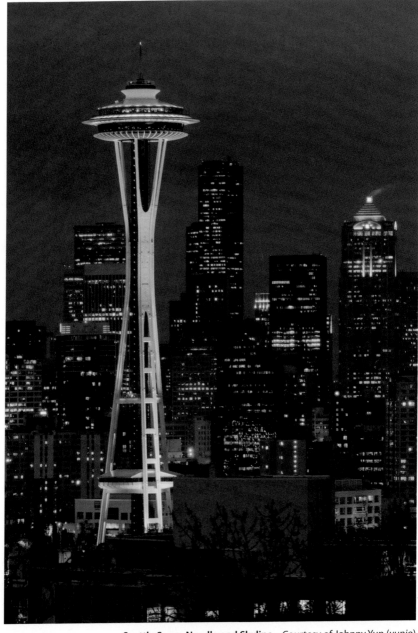

Seattle Space Needle and Skyline – Courtesy of Johnny Yun (*yunjo*)

The Setup Menu contains a series of settings for basic camera configuration not directly related to taking pictures. It covers things like how bright you'd like the Monitor, battery information, firmware version, the default language, image sensor cleaning, and many other basic settings.

These menus are most likely the first you'll use when you prepare your new D800. You'll have to set the Time zone and date, Language, and Copyright information (for embedding in images), among other things.

Following is a list of the 21 functions available in the Setup Menu:

- **Format memory card** – This function allows you to delete all images from your camera's memory card(s).
- **Monitor brightness** – Choose the brightness level for the Monitor on the back of your camera.
- **Clean image sensor** – This function allows immediate cleaning of the imaging sensor to remove dust spots, or you can configure the camera to clean the sensor at startup and shutdown.
- **Lock mirror up for cleaning** – You can safely lock the mirror up and open the shutter so you can manually clean the sensor with a brush, blower, or chemicals and swabs.
- **Image Dust Off ref photo** – You can create a dust off reference photo to help remove a dust spot from images accidentally taken with some dust on the sensor. This requires the use of a program like Nikon Capture NX 2 to actually remove the dust with the reference photo as a guide.
- **HDMI** – You can select various HDMI sync rates for interfacing with an HDTV or monitor.
- **Flicker reduction** – If you often shoot under fluorescent or mercury-vapor lights while making a movie, this function allows you to choose a frequency that matches the local electrical power supply to reduce flickering.
- **Time zone and date** – Set the Time zone, Date and time, Date format, and Daylight saving time in your camera.
- **Language** – Choose the language you would like your camera to use from a list of 24 languages. Menus and screens will be displayed in the chosen language.
- **Auto image rotation** – This function adds camera orientation information to each image so it will display correctly on your camera's Monitor and later on your computer's monitor.
- **Battery info** – This function gives you information about the battery's current charge, the number of pictures taken with the battery on the current charge, and the useful life remaining in the battery (battery age) before you should dispose of it.

- **Wireless transmitter** – This function allows you to adjust the settings for connecting the camera to a wireless network using an optional Nikon WT-4A wireless transmitter.
- **Image comment** – Add a comment (up to 36 characters) that embeds itself in the internal metadata of each image. This can help you protect yourself from image theft or simply add pertinent personal or location information to each image.
- **Copyright information** – You can add two items of information, including Artist (36 characters) and Copyright (54 characters). This function is designed for those who use their images commercially. It allows you to embed specific identity information into the picture's internal metadata.
- **Save/load settings** – This function allows you to save the current menu configuration of most internal camera settings to a memory card for transfer to a computer. You can back up complex configurations and restore them to the camera when needed.
- **GPS** – If you own a GPS that can be connected to the Nikon D800—such as the Accessory-shoe mounted Nikon GP-1 or another GPS unit—this function allows you to record Latitude, Longitude, Altitude, Heading, and UTC (Coordinated Universal Time) into the metadata of each image.
- **Virtual horizon** – This function displays a virtual horizon on the camera's Monitor. This display shows tilt to the left or right and forward or backward. This is an excellent tool for leveling the camera on a tripod and prevents having to use an Accessory-shoe mounted bubble level.
- **Non-CPU lens data** – This function lets you select from a series of nine non-CPU lenses, such as AI and AI-S Nikkor lenses from the 1970s to the 1980s. Each lens is registered within the camera with its own number so you can select it and use it later.
- **AF fine-tune** – You can fine-tune the autofocus for up to 20 of your AF-S lenses. The camera will detect which lens you have mounted and correct for front or back focus according to your settings.
- **Eye-Fi upload** – You can use an Eye-Fi Connect, Mobile, or Pro wireless SD card to transmit images from your D800 to your home computer and/or online services (e.g., Flickr). Or you can use the Eye-Fi Pro X2 cards to transmit images directly to your Wi-Fi–enabled computer using Ad hoc transfer. You'll have menu access to enable or disable uploading along with connectivity information.
- **Firmware version** – Discover the current firmware version installed in your camera. Firmware is the camera's operating system software that is embedded on in-camera memory chips. It can be upgraded when Nikon releases new firmware specific to your camera.

Let's examine each of these settings in detail.

Format Memory Card

(User's Manual – Page 326)

Format memory card allows you to prepare your memory card(s) for use in your camera. This is the best way to prepare the memory card, and it should be done before using a new one.

Interestingly, formatting a memory card doesn't actually remove any images from the card. Instead, it removes their entries in the memory card's file allocation table (FAT) so they can no longer be seen or found by the camera. However, you could use card recovery software to rescue the images if you do not write anything new to the card after you format it. That's a good thing to remember in case you ever accidentally format a card with images you wanted to keep.

The D800 has two memory card slots, the CF card slot and SD card slot. You have to format each of them separately. There are two ways to format a memory card. First, you can use the *Setup Menu > Format memory card* function; second, you can use external camera controls. We'll look at both methods in this section.

Let's see how it is done with the Setup Menu by looking at the screens and steps for card formatting.

Figure 5.1A – Format memory card with Setup Menu screens

Use the following steps to format a memory card (figure 5.1A):

1. Select Format memory card from the Setup Menu and scroll to the right (figure 5.1A, screen 1).
2. Next, you'll see a screen that asks you to select the card you want to format (figure 5.1A, screen 2). You have a choice of SD card slot or CF card slot. Choose the one you want to format, and scroll to the right. You'll need to repeat this action to format the second card.

3. The next screen makes it very clear with an ominous-sounding message that you are about to delete all the images on the card you have selected for formatting. The screen presents a big red exclamation point and the message *All images on memory card will be deleted. Ok?* If you have decided not to format the card, just select No and press the OK button; otherwise, continue with step 4 (figure 5.1A, screen 3).

4. Select Yes from the screen with the warning that all images will be deleted (figure 5.1A, screen 4).

5. Press the OK button to start the format. When you press the OK button, you'll see two screens in quick succession (figure 5.1A, screens 5 and 6). The first will say, *Formatting memory card*. A few seconds later—when the card has been successfully formatted—you'll briefly see a final screen that says, *Formatting complete*. Then the camera switches back to the Setup Menu's first screen. The card is now formatted and you can take lots of pictures.

Camera Button Format Method

This is the fastest method to format the memory card, and it is not very difficult. The camera defaults to formatting the primary card slot, not the secondary slot. You can select the secondary slot instead, as I'll describe in the upcoming step-by-step method. Figure 5.1B shows the buttons and Control panel screens used to format the card. Notice how the two buttons are marked with the red FORMAT symbol.

Figure 5.1B – Format memory card with camera controls

To complete the memory card formatting process, follow these steps (figure 5.1B):

1. Hold down the Delete/Format button and MODE/Format button at the same time for more than two seconds (figure 5.1B, screens 1 and 2), until *For* starts flashing on the Control panel (figure 5.1B, screen 3, red arrow on left).

2. While you're still holding down the two buttons and *For* is flashing, you can rotate the Main command dial with your thumb to select either CF or SD on the Control panel (screen 3, red arrow on right). It's a three-finger operation, but it's easier than it sounds. You can see in figure 5.1B, screen 3, that I selected the CF card slot.

3. While *For* is still flashing in the Control panel, quickly release and instantly repress the Delete/Format button and MODE/Format button together. You'll see *For* showing on the Control panel where the image count normally appears (figure 5.1B, screen 3, bottom right corner where my D800 says [1.1]^K). The format operation is in process while *For* appears in the image count location. Do not turn your camera off during a format. When *For* changes back to the image count number, the format operation is complete. You can repeat the operation for the other slot on the D800 if needed.

Settings Recommendation: Both the *Setup Menu > Format memory card* and camera button format methods are easy to use. Most people learn to use the button press method because it's so fast. However, I sometimes use the *Setup Menu > Format memory card* method immediately after viewing images on the Monitor for verification of previous transfer to my computer. If it's safe to format the card, I quickly switch to the Setup Menu to format because I'm already looking at the Monitor. It's a good idea to learn how to use both methods.

Monitor Brightness

(User's Manual – Page 326)

Monitor brightness is more important than many people realize. If the Monitor is too dim, you'll have trouble seeing your images in bright light. If it is too bright, you might allow some images to be underexposed because they look fine on the Monitor. Even a seriously underexposed image may look okay on a screen that is too bright.

The D800 allows you to adjust the brightness of the Monitor manually, or you can let the camera sense the amount of ambient light with its Ambient brightness sensor (figure 5.2A, red arrow) and adjust itself accordingly.

If you adjust it manually, you can select from 10 levels of brightness, varying from -5 to +5.

Figure 5.2A – Ambient brightness sensor on back of D800

Auto Monitor Brightness Level Adjustment

With *Auto*, you can use the following screens and steps to set the camera so that it senses the ambient light and changes the camera's Monitor intensity to match. This works like the light sensor in many of today's smartphones. When it is dark, the Monitor will dim to a level that is not blinding. If it's very bright, the Monitor will increase its intensity to help overcome the ambient light.

Figure 5.2B – Monitor brightness level adjustment – Auto

Use the following steps to let your camera decide how bright and saturated the Monitor appears (figure 5.2B):

1. Select Monitor brightness from the Setup Menu and scroll to the right (figure 5.2B, screen 1).
2. Choose Auto from the Monitor brightness menu (figure 5.2B, screen 2). The camera will use its Ambient brightness sensor (figure 5.2A) to decide when to increase or decrease the brightness of the Monitor.
3. Press the OK button to lock in the setting.

Manual Monitor Brightness Level Adjustment

With *Manual*, you can adjust the brightness of the Monitor manually. Most people have grown accustomed to this way of dealing with the Monitor's intensity level. If you want to adjust this frequently, just add this function to My Menu in your camera. We will discuss how to add items to My Menu in the chapter **My Menu and Recent Settings**.

Figure 5.2C – Monitor brightness level adjustment – Manual

Use the following steps to manually adjust the brightness of your Monitor (figure 5.2C):

1. Select Monitor brightness from the Setup Menu and scroll to the right (figure 5.2C, screen 1).
2. Choose Manual and scroll to the right (figure 5.2C, screen 2).
3. Use the Multi selector to scroll up or down through the values -5 to +5, scrolling to the minus side to dim the Monitor or to the plus side to brighten it (figure 5.2C, screen 3). Now, use the gray-level bars (dark to light) as a guide to adjust the brightness. Adjust until you can make a distinction between the last two dark bars on the left. That may be the best setting for your camera in the current ambient light. The brightness defaults to 0 (zero), which is right in the middle.
4. Press the OK button when you've found the value you like best.

Settings Recommendation: I tried the Auto setting for a while but disliked the Monitor dimness I was seeing in interior shots. It seemed a little too dim to me. Try the Auto setting and see if you like it. I'm sure it will work for many photographers.

I use the manual adjustment and generally leave it at the zero setting unless I need the extra brightness on a sunny day. If you choose to set your camera to a level brighter than 0, be sure to check the histogram frequently to validate your exposures. Otherwise, you may find that you are mildly underexposing images because they look fine on the Monitor due to the extra brightness. That's one reason I examine the histogram often.

Some photographers run their monitor at -1 to keep the images from appearing artificially bright. This is a setting where experimentation is required. Letting the Monitor run too brightly might mask those times when the camera needs help. The bright screen can fool you. Use your histogram!

Clean Image Sensor

(User's Manual – Page 394)

Clean image sensor is Nikon's helpful answer to dust spots on your images that are due to a dirty imaging sensor. Dust is everywhere and will eventually get on your camera's sensor. Well, it doesn't really get on the sensor itself because there are filters in front of the sensor. The D800 cleans the sensor by vibrating the entire sensor unit, which includes the low-pass filter in front of the sensor. These high-frequency vibrations will dislodge dust and make it fall off the filter so you won't see it as spots on your pictures.

The vibration cleaning method seems to work pretty well. Of course, if sticky pollen or other wet dust gets into the camera, the vibration system won't be able to remove it. Then it may be time for brush or wet cleaning.

Clean Now

Clean now allows you to clean the imaging sensor at any time. If you detect a dust spot, or just get nervous because you are in a dusty environment with your D800, you can simply select Clean now and the camera will execute a sensor cleaning cycle.

Figure 5.3A – Clean now screens

Use the following steps to clean the camera's sensor immediately (figure 5.3A):

1. Select Clean image sensor from the Setup Menu and scroll to the right (figure 5.3A, screen 1).
2. Select Clean now from the menu and press the OK button (figure 5.3A, screen 2).
3. Step 2 starts the automatic cleaning process. A screen will appear that says, *Cleaning image sensor* (figure 5.3A, screen 3). When the process is complete, another screen will appear that says, *Done* (figure 5.3A, screen 4). Then the camera switches back to the Setup Menu.

Now, let's look at how to select an active method for regular sensor cleaning.

Clean at Startup/Shutdown

For preventive dust control, many people set their cameras to clean the sensor at startup, shutdown, or both. There are four selections for startup/shutdown cleaning:

- Clean at startup
- Clean at shutdown
- Clean at startup and shutdown
- Cleaning off

These settings are self-explanatory. I find it interesting that I don't detect any startup or shutdown delay when using the startup/shutdown cleaning modes. I can turn my camera on and immediately take a picture. The cleaning cycle seems to be very brief, or at least interruptible, in this mode.

Figure 5.3B – Clean at startup/shutdown screens

Use the following steps to choose a Clean at startup/shutdown method (figure 5.3B):

1. Select Clean image sensor from the Setup Menu and then scroll to the right (figure 5.3B, screen 1).
2. Choose Clean at startup/shutdown from the menu and scroll to the right (figure 5.3B, screen 2).
3. Select one of the four methods shown in figure 5.3B, screen 3. I chose Clean at startup & shutdown.
4. Press the OK button to lock in your choice.

Nikon suggests that you hold the camera at the same angle as when you are taking pictures (bottom down) when you use these modes to clean the sensor.

Lock Mirror Up for Cleaning

(User's Manual – Page 397)

Lock mirror up for cleaning is for those times when the high-frequency vibration method of cleaning your D800's sensor does not dislodge some stickier-than-normal dust. You may have to clean your sensor more aggressively.

In many cases, all that's needed is to remove the dust with a puff of air from a dust blower. I remember having to do this with my Nikon D100 in 2002, and I was always afraid I might ruin the shutter if I did it incorrectly. With the D100, I had to hold the shutter open in bulb mode with one hand while I blew dust off the sensor with a blower in the other hand.

The D800 helps out by providing the Lock mirror up for cleaning mode so you can more safely blow a stubborn piece of dust off the low-pass filter. Using this function is much safer for blowing dust off the sensor; you can use both hands while the battery power holds the reflex mirror up and the shutter open.

Figure 5.4A – Lock mirror up for cleaning

Use the following steps to select this mode for manual sensor cleaning (figure 5.4A):

1. Select Lock mirror up for cleaning from the Setup Menu and scroll to the right (figure 5.4A, screen 1).
2. Press the OK button with Start highlighted (figure 5.4A, screen 2).
3. You'll see a message screen telling you that as you press the Shutter-release button the camera will raise the mirror and open the shutter (figure 5.4A, screen 3).
4. Remove the lens and press the Shutter-release button once. The sensor will now be exposed and ready for cleaning. Be careful not to let new dirt in while the sensor is open to air.
5. Clean the sensor with proper fluids and pads (i.e., Eclipse fluid and PEC*PADs).
6. Turn the camera off and put the lens back on.

Make sure you have a fresh battery in the camera because that's what holds the shutter open for cleaning. It must have a 60 percent or greater charge or the camera will refuse to allow you to start the process.

Settings Recommendation: You'll need a good professional sensor-cleaning blower, such as my favorite, the Giottos Rocket-air blower with a long tip for easy insertion (figure 5.4B). I bought by Rocket-air blower from the Nikonians PhotoPro-Shop (**http://www.PhotoProShop.com**).

Figure 5.4B – Giottos Rocket-air blower

If an air blower fails to remove stubborn dust or pollen, you will have to either have your sensor professionally cleaned or do it yourself. Nikon states that you will void your warranty if you touch the low-pass filter in front of the sensor. However, many people still wet or brush clean their D800's sensor. I've done it myself, although I'll never admit it! (Oops!)

If all of this makes you nervous, then send your camera off to Nikon for approved cleaning, or use a professional service. Fortunately, a few puffs of air will often remove dust too stubborn for the high-frequency vibration methods. It helps to have the proper tools, such as the Giottos Rocket-air blower from the Nikonians PhotoProShop.

Image Dust Off Ref Photo

(User's Manual – Page 327)

You may go out and do an expensive shoot only to return and find that some dust spots have appeared in the worst possible places in your images. If you immediately create an *Image Dust Off ref photo*, you can use it to remove the dust spots from your images and then clean the camera's sensor for your next shooting session.

When you use the following instructions to create the Image Dust Off ref photo, you'll be shooting a blank, unfocused picture of a pure white or gray background. The dust spots in the image will then be readily apparent to Nikon Capture NX 2 software. Yes, you must use Nikon's software to automatically batch-remove dust spots from a large number of images.

When you load the image to be cleaned into Capture NX 2, along with the Image Dust Off ref photo, the software will use the Image Dust Off ref photo to remove the spots in your production image.

The position and amount of dust on the low-pass filter may change. You should take Image Dust Off ref photos regularly and use one that was taken within one day of the photographs you wish to clean up.

Finding a Subject for the Dust-Off Reference Photo

First, you'll need to select a featureless subject to make a photograph for the Image Dust Off ref photo. The key is to use a material that has no graininess, such as a bright, well-lit white card. I tried using plain white sheets of paper held up to a bright window, but the resulting reference photo was unsatisfactory to Capture NX 2. It gave me a message that my reference photo was too dusty when I tried to use it.

After some experimentation, I finally settled on three different subjects that seem to work well:

- A slide-viewing light table with the light turned on
- A computer monitor with a blank white word processor document
- A plain white card in the same bright light in which your subject resides

All of these were bright and featureless enough to satisfy both my camera and Capture NX 2. The key is to photograph something fairly bright, but not too bright. You may need to experiment with different subjects if you don't have a light table or computer.

Now, let's prepare the camera for the actual reference photo.

Figure 5.5A – Image Dust Off ref photo settings

Here are the steps you'll use to create an Image Dust Off ref photo (figure 5.5A) :

1. Select Image Dust Off ref photo from the Setup Menu and scroll to the right (figure 5.5A, screen 1).
2. Choose Start and press the OK button (figure 5.5A, screen 2). Afterward, you'll see the characters *rEF* in the Viewfinder and on the Control panel. This simply means that the camera is ready to create the image. (There is also a Clean sensor and then start selection. However, since I want to remove dust on current pictures, I won't use this setting. It might remove the dust bunny that is imprinted on the last 500 images I just shot! I'll clean my sensor after I get a good Image Dust Off ref photo. Choose Clean sensor and then start only if the Image Dust Off ref photo will not be used with existing images!)
3. When the camera is ready, hold the lens about 4 inches (10 cm) away from the blank subject. The camera will not try to autofocus during the process, which is good because you want the lens at infinity. You are not trying to take a viewable picture; you're creating an image that shows where the dust is on the sensor. Focus is not important, and neither is minor camera shake. If you try to take the picture and the subject is not bright enough, too bright, or too grainy (not featureless), you will see the screen shown in figure 5.5B. If you are having problems with too much brightness, use a gray surface instead of white. Most of the time this error is caused by insufficient light.

Figure 5.5B – Image Dust Off ref photo failure

4. If you don't see the screen in figure 5.5B and the shutter fires, you have successfully created an Image Dust Off ref photo. You will find the image shown in
   figure 5.5C on your camera's Monitor. A file that's approximately 7 MB—mine
   was 6718 KB (6.7 MB)—is created on your camera's memory card with a filename
   extension of .ndf instead of the normal .nef, .tif, or .jpg (an example filename
   is DSC_1234.NDF). This NDF file is basically a small database of the millions of
   clean pixels in your imaging sensor and a few dirty ones. You cannot display the
   Image Dust Off ref photo on your computer. It will not open in Nikon Capture
   NX 2 or any other graphics program that I tried. It is used only as a reference by
   Capture NX 2 when it's time to clean images.

Figure 5.5C – Successful Image Dust Off ref photo

White Card Tip

Remember, all your camera needs to create an Image Dust Off ref photo is a
good look at its imaging sensor so it can map the dirt spots into an NDF file (ref
photo file). If you get the warning screen shown in figure 5.5B that says exposure
settings are not appropriate, change the exposure settings and try again with a
nice bright, clean, white surface. Put the lens very close to the surface, and make
sure it is not in focus. Nikon recommends less than 4 inches (10 cm). You might
even want to manually set the lens to infinity if you are having problems with
this. When you've found your favorite white or gray surface for Image Dust Off
ref photos, keep it safe and use it consistently.

Where to Store the Reference Photo

Copy the NDF file from your camera's memory card to the computer folder containing the images that have dust spots on them, the ones for which you created this Image Dust Off ref photo. You can now use Nikon Capture NX 2 to remove the dust spots from all of the images represented by the Image Dust Off ref photo. That process is beyond the scope of this book, but there are many good Nikon Capture NX 2 books on the market that explain it well.

HDMI

(User's Manual – Page 256)

HDMI (which stands for high-definition multimedia interface) allows you to display your images and video on a high-definition television (HDTV), external video monitor, or computer monitor with an HDMI connection. You can also use the HDMI port to stream clean, uncompressed, broadcast-quality video to an external video recording device.

You'll need an HDMI Type-A to HDMI Type-C cable, which is not included with the camera but is available from many electronics stores. This cable is also known as a mini-HDMI–to–HDMI A/V HD cable.

Figure 5.6A gives you a closeup look at both ends of the cable. The smaller end (mini-HDMI Type-C) goes into the HDMI port under the rubber flap on your camera, and the other end (HDMI Type-A) plugs into your HD device. The HDMI setting has two options, Output resolution and Advanced, which we'll discuss next.

Figure 5.6A – HDMI connectors

Output Resolution

You can select one of the following formats for output to your HDMI device:

- *Auto (default)* – This allows the camera to select the most appropriate format for displaying your image on the currently connected device.
- *480p (progressive)* – 640 × 480 progressive format.
- *576p (progressive)* – 720 × 576 progressive format.

- **720p (progressive)** – 1280 × 720 progressive format.
- **1080i (interlaced)** – 1920 × 1080 interlaced format.

Figure 5.6B – Selecting an HDMI Output resolution

Use the following steps to select an Output resolution (figure 5.6B):

1. Select HDMI from the Setup Menu and scroll to the right (figure 5.6B, screen 1).
2. Choose Output resolution from the menu and scroll to the right (figure 5.6B, screen 2).
3. Select one of the five output resolutions (figure 5.6B, screen 3). I chose 1080i (interlaced) as an example. You might want to try Auto at first to see if the camera and display device will interface by themselves. If not, read the user's manual for the display device to find out what output resolution works best with it. Set the camera accordingly.
4. Press the OK button to lock in your selection.

HDMI and the Live View Modes

You can use the HDMI port to display camera output on external devices for both Live view photography and Movie live view modes. There are some differences, though, in how the camera outputs the resulting video stream.

Figure 5.6C – Live view photography and Movie live view modes

- **Live view photography mode** – While you're using Live view photography mode (figure 5.6C), the camera obeys the settings shown in Output resolution (figure 5.6B), which are Auto to 1080i (interlaced).

- *Movie live view mode* – When you use Movie live view mode (figure 5.6C) for recording or playback, according to page 257 of the User's Manual, the camera automatically chooses the Auto setting from Output resolution (figure 5.6B), "regardless of the option selected" in HDMI Output resolution. It then obeys the settings found in *Shooting Menu > Movie settings > Frame size/frame rate*.

   If you are having problems interfacing the camera to a device, you can override the Auto setting and use the normal HDMI Output resolution settings to connect. We will discuss this in much greater detail in the chapter titled **Movie Live View**.

Advanced

With the large variety of display and recording devices available, your camera has to deal with all sorts of video standards. For instance, *Output range* controls how color is displayed on the receiving device, and *Output display size* sets frame coverage for horizontal and vertical output. Also, when you're streaming video to an external device, you must decide whether the camera's Monitor displays the output too (stays on). The *Advanced* settings allow you to control these items. Let's examine each setting on the Advanced menu.

Figure 5.6D – Using Advanced HDMI settings

Use the following steps to open the Advanced menu (figure 5.6D):

1. Select HDMI from the Setup Menu and scroll to the right (figure 5.6D, screen 1).
2. Choose Advanced from the menu and scroll to the right (figure 5.6D, screen 2).
3. Select one of the three settings from the Advanced menu and scroll to the right (figure 5.6D, screen 3).
4. Refer to figures 5.6E, 5.6F, and 5.6G for details on the configuration of each item.

Output Range

Output range allows you to adjust the level of colors sent to a recording or display device. When you are outputting video to a device, such as an HDTV or recorder, the device may not accept normal *Full range* RGB with a color range of 0 to 255 correctly. Some devices accept only *Limited range* RGB input in the range of 16 to

235 color levels (YCbCr). If you try to send Full range RGB video output to a Limited range YCbCr device, you may end up with washed-out, grayish blacks and blown-out, featureless whites.

The solution is to match the correct output to the correct device type. If you see the problems just described when the camera is set to Full range (RGB), try the Limited range (YCbCr) setting instead. Or, you could try the Auto setting to see if the camera can detect what the display or recording device requires.

Again, we will discuss this in deeper detail in the upcoming chapter **Movie Live View**.

Figure 5.6E – Selecting an Output range

Use the following steps to select Full range or Limited range output (figure 5.6E continues from figure 5.6D):

1. Select Output range from the Advanced menu and scroll to the right (figure 5.6E, screen 1).
2. Select Auto, Limited range, or Full range from the Output range menu. Auto (factory default) is selected in figure 5.6E, screen 2.
3. Press the OK button to select the Output range.

Output Display Size

At times, the *Output display size* may not match the display device well. In that case, you can reduce the Output display size from 100% to 95%, to help the display fit better. I plugged my D800 into a Vizio 32-inch HDTV and found that the output from the camera on the TV was a little bit too tall. I changed Output display size to 95% and it fit perfectly.

You can do this while viewing the live output on the HDTV by opening the *Setup Menu > HDMI > Output display size* setting and making the change. Let's see how to modify the Output display size.

Figure 5.6F – Changing the Output display size

Use the following steps to change the Output display size (figure 5.6F continues from figure 5.6D):

1. Select Output display size from the Advanced menu and scroll to the right (figure 5.6F, screen 1).
2. Select 95% or 100% from the Output display size menu. 100% (factory default) is selected in figure 5.6F, screen 2).
3. Press the OK button to select the Output display size.

Live View On-Screen Display

Live view on-screen display is the setting you'll use when you want the streaming video output from the camera to have no shooting information overlays. When Live view on-screen display is set to Off, the camera outputs clean, uncompressed video with nothing but the video coming out of the camera.

If you choose On, the camera will stream video with the same information you see on the the Monitor, which may include shooting information such as aperture, shutter speed, ISO sensitivity, metering mode, gridlines, sound input levels, focus mode, Picture Control type, image size, image quality, image area, and so forth.

If you want to output clean, overlay-free, uncompressed, broadcast-quality video, choose Off for this setting.

Figure 5.6G – Choosing a Live view on-screen display mode

Use the following steps to change the Live view on-screen display (figure 5.6G continues from figure 5.6D):

1. Select Live view on-screen display from the Advanced menu and scroll to the right (figure 5.6G, screen 1).

2. Select On or Off from the Live view on-screen display menu. Off (factory default) is selected in figure 5.6G, screen 2.
3. Press the OK button to lock in the setting.

We have examined only how to select and set the modes, with some basic reasons why we decided to use each mode. Shooting video is new to many photographers, so the chapter **Movie Live View** will provide much-needed detail.

Flicker Reduction

(User's Manual – Page 329)
Flicker reduction allows you to attempt to match the camera's recording frequency to that of the local AC power supply so that when you use Live view photography or Movie live view modes under fluorescent or mercury-vapor lighting, you can minimize flickering.

Start out by trying the Auto setting to see if the camera can determine the best setting. If not, there are two things you can do. First, try using the 50 Hz and 60 Hz settings individually to see if one helps. If the subject is especially bright, which makes flicker worse, Nikon recommends closing down the aperture.

Second, use a shutter speed that is close to the frequency of the local power supply. For a 60 Hz supply, use 1/30 s, 1/60 s, or 1/125 s. For a 50 Hz supply, use 1/25 s or 1/50 s.

In some cases, flicker can be impossible to remove completely; however, these methods may help you reduce it. Let's see how to choose a Flicker reduction frequency.

Figure 5.7 – Selecting a Flicker reduction frequency

Use the following steps to select a setting in hopes of reducing flicker (figure 5.7):

1. Select Flicker reduction from the Setup Menu and scroll to the right (figure 5.7, screen 1).
2. Choose Auto, 50 Hz, or 60 Hz from the menu (figure 5.7, screen 2).
3. Press the OK button to lock in your setting.

Settings Recommendation: This function is somewhat limited because there are only two settings: 50 Hz or 60 Hz. However, it could help to control the flickering that looks like dark horizontal bands moving through the movie. Experiment to see if it helps to switch between the two settings when you detect flickering under fluorescent or mercury-vapor lighting. The best solution is to stay away from those types of lighting when shooting videos.

Time Zone and Date

(User's Manual – Page 329)

Time zone and date allows you to configure the Time zone, Date and time, Date format, and Daylight saving time for your camera.

If you haven't set the time and date, you'll see the word CLOCK flashing on the Control panel. In addition to the main li-ion battery pack, the camera has a built-in clock battery that is not user replaceable. The built-in battery charges itself from the main camera battery pack. If CLOCK is blinking in the Control panel, it can also mean that the internal battery is exhausted and the clock has been reset.

It takes about two days of having a charged battery in the camera to fully charge the separate built-in clock battery. When the clock battery is fully charged, the clock will remain active without a main camera battery for up to three months.

Let's examine how to set the various parts of Time zone and date. You may have already done this when you first received your camera. We discussed this briefly in the first chapter.

Time Zone

The *Time zone* screen used to set the local time zone displays a familiar world map from which you will select the area of the world where you are using the camera. Figure 5.8A shows the Time zone configuration screens.

As an example, New York is in the Eastern Time zone (ET). You'll need to select your Time zone by choosing it from the map (figure 5.8A, screen 3). I hope you remember your geography lessons! Fortunately, the camera displays some major city names below the Time zone map in case you don't recognize your location.

Figure 5.8A – Time zone settings

Use the following steps to set the Time zone (figure 5.8A):

1. Select Time zone and date from the Setup Menu and scroll to the right (figure 5.8A, screen 1).
2. Choose Time zone from the menu and scroll to the right (figure 5.8A, screen 2).
3. To set the Time zone, use the Multi Selector to scroll left or right until your location is under the vertical yellow bar or you see the nearest city marked with a small red dot (figure 5.8A, screen 3).
4. Press the OK button to lock in the Time zone.

Date and Time

Figure 5.8B shows the three *Date and time* configuration screens. The final screen allows you to select the year, month, and day (Y, M, D) and the hour, minute, and second (H, M, S).

Figure 5.8B – Date and time settings

Use the following steps to set the Date and time (figure 5.8B):

1. Select Time zone and date from the Setup Menu and scroll to the right (figure 5.8B, screen 1).
2. Choose Date and time from the menu and scroll to the right (figure 5.8B, screen 2).
3. Using the Multi Selector, scroll left or right until you've selected the value you want to change. Then scroll up or down to change the value. The Y M D settings on the left in 5.8B, screen 3, are for the year, month, and day. The H M S settings on the right are for the hour, minute, and second.
4. Press the OK button to lock in the Date and time.

Note: The 24-hour military-style clock is used for the time setting. To set the clock to 3 p.m., you would set the H and M settings to 15:00. Please refer to the following 12 - to 24-Hour Time Conversion Chart.

12- to 24-Hour Time Conversion Chart

A.M. Settings:

12:00 a.m. = 00:00 (midnight)	06:00 a.m. = 06:00
01:00 a.m. = 01:00	07:00 a.m. = 07:00
02:00 a.m. = 02:00	08:00 a.m. = 08:00
03:00 a.m. = 03:00	09:00 a.m. = 09:00
04:00 a.m. = 04:00	10:00 a.m. = 10:00
05:00 a.m. = 05:00	11:00 a.m. = 11:00

P.M. Settings:

12:00 p.m. = 12:00 (noon)	06:00 p.m. = 18:00
01:00 p.m. = 13:00	07:00 p.m. = 19:00
02:00 p.m. = 14:00	08:00 p.m. = 20:00
03:00 p.m. = 15:00	09:00 p.m. = 21:00
04:00 p.m. = 16:00	10:00 p.m. = 22:00
05:00 p.m. = 17:00	11:00 p.m. = 23:00

Note: There is no 24:00 time (midnight). After 23:59 comes 00:00.

Date Format

Date format gives you three different ways to format the camera's date, as follows:

- **Y/M/D** – Year/Month/Day (2013/12/31)
- **M/D/Y** – Month/Day/Year (12/31/2013)
- **D/M/Y** – Day/Month/Year (31/12/2013)

Figure 5.8C – Date format settings

Here are the steps to set the Date format (figure 5.8C):

1. Select Time zone and date from the Setup Menu and scroll to the right (figure 5.8C, screen 1).
2. Choose Date format from the menu and scroll to the right (figure 5.8C, screen 2).

3. Choose your favorite Date format from the menu (figure 5.8C, screen 3). I selected M/D/Y Month/Day/Year.
4. Press the OK button to lock in the Date format.

Daylight Saving Time

Many areas of the world observe daylight saving time. On a specified day in spring of each year, many people set their clocks forward by one hour. Then in the fall they set them back, leading to the clever saying "spring forward, fall back." If you set *Daylight saving time* to On, the camera will change the time automatically and save you the trouble.

Figure 5.8D – Daylight saving time settings

Here are the steps to enable or disable Daylight saving time (figure 5.8D):

1. Select Time zone and date from the Setup Menu and scroll to the right (figure 5.8D, screen 1).
2. Choose Daylight saving time from the menu and scroll to the right (figure 5.8D, screen 2).
3. Figure 5.8D, screen 3, shows you the two choices for Daylight saving time: On or Off. If you select On, your camera will automatically spring forward and fall back. Select Off if you don't observe daylight saving time or if you'd rather change the time yourself.
4. Press the OK button to lock in the setting.

Settings Recommendation: This series includes the first settings you'll modify when you get a brand-new D800 camera. It is important that all these items are set correctly because this informatoin is written into the metadata of each image you make. Daylight saving time is optional but very convenient.

Language

(User's Manual – Page 330)

Language is a function that lets the camera know what language you prefer for the camera's menus, screens, and messages. Nikon is an international company that sells cameras and lenses around the world. For that reason, the D800 can display its screens and menus in 24 languages.

Figure 5.9 – Language selection

Use the following steps to select your preferred Language (figure 5.9):

1. Select Language from the Setup Menu and scroll to the right (figure 5.9, screen 1).
2. Choose your preferred Language (figure 5.9, screen 2).
3. Press the OK button to lock in your choice.

The camera should come preconfigured for the main language that is spoken where you live. If you prefer a different one, use this setting to select it.

Auto Image Rotation

(User's Manual – Page 331)

Auto image rotation is concerned with how vertical images are displayed on your camera's Monitor and later on your computer. Horizontal images are not affected by this setting. The camera has a direction-sensing device, so it knows how the camera was oriented when a picture was taken.

Depending on how you have Auto image rotation set, how the *Playback Menu > Rotate tall* setting is set, and the direction in which you hold your camera's hand grip, the camera will display a vertical image either as an upright portrait image, with the top of the image at the top of the Monitor, or lying on its side in a horizontal direction, with the top of the image to the left or right on the Monitor. The two selections in the menu are as follows:

- **On** – With Auto image rotation turned On, the camera stores orientation information within each image, primarily so the image will display correctly in computer
  software such as Nikon Capture NX 2, Lightroom, Aperture, and Photoshop. In
  other words, the camera records, as part of the image metadata, whether you
  were holding your camera horizontally or vertically (hand grip down) or even
  upside-down vertically (hand grip up). The image will display in the correct orientation on your camera's Monitor only if you have *Playback Menu > Rotate tall*
  set to On. Auto image rotation lets the image speak for itself as to orientation,
  while Rotate tall lets the camera listen to the image and display it in the proper
  orientation.
- **Off** – If Auto image rotation is turned Off, the vertical image will be displayed as
  a horizontal image lying on its side in your computer software. The top of the
  image will be on the left or right according to how you held the hand grip—up
  or down—when you took the picture. The camera does not record orientation
  information in the image metadata. It will display images horizontally even if
  you have the *Playback Menu > Rotate tall* function set to On.

Figure 5.10 – Auto image rotation settings

Use the following steps to set the Auto image rotation function (figure 5.10):

1. Select Auto image rotation from the Setup Menu and scroll to the right (figure
   5.10, screen 1).
2. Choose On or Off from the menu (figure 5.10, screen 2).
3. Press the OK button to lock in your selection.

If you're shooting in one of the Continuous frame advance modes (CL or CH), the
position in which you hold your camera for the first shot sets the direction in which
images are displayed.

Settings Recommendation: If you want your images to be displayed correctly on
your camera's Monitor and in your computer, you need to be sure that Auto image
rotation is set to On. I always keep mine set that way.

Battery Info

(User's Manual – Page 332)

The *Battery info* screen (figure 5.11A, screen 2) will let you know how much battery charge has been used (Charge), how many images have been taken with this battery since the last charge (No. of shots), and how much life the battery has before it will no longer hold a good charge (Battery age).

Figure 5.11 – Battery info screen

Here are the steps to examine the Battery info (figure 5.11A):

1. Select Battery info from the Setup Menu and scroll to the right (figure 5.11A, screen 1).
2. The next screen is the Battery info screen. It is just for information, so there's nothing to set (figure 5.11A, screen 2).
3. When you've finished examining your camera's Battery info, press the OK button to exit.

The D800 goes a step further than most cameras. Not only does it inform you of the amount of charge left in your battery, it also lets you know how much life is left. After some time, all batteries weaken and won't hold a full charge. The Battery age meter will tell you when the battery needs to be completely replaced. It shows five stages of battery life, from 0 to 4, so you'll be prepared to replace the battery before it gets too old to take many shots.

Battery Info When Using an MB-D12 Battery Pack

If you are using a battery in your MB-D12 battery pack in addition to the one in the camera, the Battery info screen will display as a split screen. The left side of the screen shows information for the battery in the camera, and the right side shows information for the battery in the MB-D12 battery pack (figure 5.11B).

Additionally, when you are using a larger Nikon D4 EN-EL18 battery in the MB-D12, you will see a fourth item—besides Charge, No. of shots, and Battery age—on the Battery info screen. You will see calibration information (not shown). Calibration (CAL) shows up on the screen when the battery needs to be recalibrated with a Nikon MH-26 battery charger. This ensures that the battery's Charge level can be reported accurately after repeated use and recharging. When Calibration is not required, a long dash (—) will appear instead of CAL.

Figure 5.11B – Battery info screen with MB-D12 mounted

Settings Recommendation: It's important to use Nikon brand batteries in your D800 so they will work properly with the camera. Aftermarket batteries may not charge correctly in the D800 battery charger. In addition, they may not report correct Battery age information. There may be an aftermarket brand that works correctly, but I haven't found it. Instead, I use the batteries designed by Nikon to work with this camera. I am a bit afraid to trust a camera that costs this much to a cheap aftermarket battery of unknown origin.

Wireless Transmitter

(User's Manual – Page 245)

The *Wireless transmitter* menu system is concerned with having the WT-4 wireless transmitter attached to the D800. Using the WT-4, you can send images wirelessly to a computer or printer. You can also use Nikon Camera Control 2 software to control the D800 remotely.

Here are the four Wireless transmitter modes in the D800 with a WT-4 transmitter attached:

- *Transfer mode* – Using this mode, you can upload new or existing images to a computer or even to a File Transfer Protocol (FTP) server.
- *Thumbnail select mode* – This allows someone to preview the images you are shooting on a remote computer. They can select the ones they like and upload them to the computer. Sports shooters love this!
- *PC mode* – This might have been called Studio mode instead. It allows studio artists to control their D800 from a computer using the Nikon Camera Control Pro 2 software.
- *Print mode* – This allows someone shooting near a network to print the images on a networked printer.

Figure 5.12 – Initial WT-4 Wireless transmitter configuration screens

It is beyond the scope of this book to discuss the full configuration of a WT-4 wireless transmitter, which is an external device with a rather complex setup. However, the opening screens are provided in case you want to use them to get started. Refer to your WT-4 Transmitter user's manual to continue.

For those on a limited budget, there is a low-cost alternative to the expensive WT-4 Wireless transmitter—the Eye-Fi Pro X2 card, which we will consider next.

Low-Cost Wireless Image Transmission

If you need to wirelessly transmit images between your camera and computer but cannot afford the expensive WT-4 or WT-4A transmitters, please read the upcoming section called **Eye-Fi Upload**. Eye-Fi cards allow limited-range (50 to 90 feet) wireless transmission of images between your camera and a Wi-Fi network access point.

If you use the Eye-Fi Pro X2 8GB SD/SDHC card, you can even do direct-to-computer, Ad hoc wireless transmission of images, even in locations where there are no wireless Internet access points. The card in the camera directly transfers image files to the computer (Ad hoc). Again, we will discuss this low-cost wireless solution in greater detail in the upcoming **Eye-Fi Upload** section.

Image Comment

(User's Manual – Pages 170, 333)

Image comment is a useful setting that allows you to attach a 36-character comment to each image you shoot. The comment is embedded in the picture's internal metadata and does not show up on the image itself. I attach the comment "Photo by Darrell Young" to my images.

You could include information containing your copyright here even though the camera has a place to put Copyright information (next section).

Use the following steps to create an Image comment (figure 5.13):

1. Select Image comment from the Setup Menu and scroll to the right (figure 5.13, screen 1).
2. Select Input comment from the menu and scroll to the right (figure 5.13, screen 2).

Figure 5.13 – Attaching an Image comment

3. In figure 5.13, screen 3, you'll see a series of letters, numbers, and symbols on top and a rectangle with tiny lines at the bottom. The little lines are where you will put the text of the comment you want to attach to the image. There is a blank spot just after the lowercase *z*, which represents a blank space that you can insert in the line of text. Notice that lowercase letters follow the uppercase letters. Use the Multi Selector to scroll through the numbers and letters to find the characters you want to use, and press the Multi Selector center button to insert a character. If you make a mistake, hold down the checkered Thumbnail/Playback zoom out button while using the Multi Selector to move to the position of the error. Push the Delete button and the character will disappear.

4. Press the OK button when you are finished entering the comment.

5. The camera will switch back to the Image comment screen (figure 5.13, screen 4). You need to put a check mark in the Attach comment check box so the comment will attach itself to each image. To check the box, highlight the Attach comment line and scroll to the right or press the OK button to place a check mark in the box. You'll see a check mark appear as soon as you scroll to the right (figure 5.13, screen 5, red arrow).

6. Scroll up to Done and press the OK button to save the new comment (figure 5.13, screen 6).

Settings Recommendation: You can use this comment field for any text you want to add to the internal metadata of the image. There is another Setup Menu selection called Copyright information (next section) that allows you to add your personal copyright. I added basic "who took it" information here because I am worried about image theft. You may want to add other text—as the camera provides a specific Copyright information screen—such as information to identify the shoot. Remember, you are limited to 36 characters in the comment.

Copyright Information

(User's Manual – Page 334)

Copyright information allows you to embed Artist and Copyright data into each image. Refer to figure 5.14 and use the following steps to add personal information to your camera. Your Artist name and Copyright information will then be written into the metadata of each of your images.

Figure 5.14 – Copyright information settings

Here are the steps to enter your Artist and Copyright information (figure 5.14):

1. Select Copyright information from the Setup Menu and scroll to the right (figure 5.14, screen 1).
2. When you arrive at the screen with Done at the top, scroll to the right (figure 5.14, screen 2).
3. Scroll down to Artist and scroll to the right (figure 5.14, screen 3).
4. You'll now see the Artist data input screen with all the available characters to choose from (figure 5.14, screen 4). Add your name here, with a maximum of 36 characters. Use the Multi Selector to scroll around within the characters. Lowercase characters follow the uppercase letters. Select a character by pressing the Multi selector center button. Correct errors within the text you've already entered by holding down the Thumbnail/Playback zoom out button

and scrolling left or right with the Multi Selector. Remove a character that's already in the name area by scrolling to it and pressing the Delete button. Press the OK button when you have entered your name.

5. Now scroll down to the Copyright line on the Copyright information screen and scroll to the right (figure 5.14, screen 5).

6. Add your name using the method and controls described in step 4 (figure 5.14, screen 6).

7. Scroll down to the Attach copyright information line (figure 5.14, screen 7). Notice that there is no check mark in the little box (figure 5.14, screen 7, red arrow).

8. Now scroll to the right or press the OK button and you'll see a tiny check mark appear in the box (figure 5.14, screen 8, red arrow).

9. Finally, scroll up to Done on the Copyright information screen (figure 5.14, screen 9).

10. Press the OK button to save your Artist and Copyright information.

Settings Recommendation: Be sure to add your name in both the Artist and Copyright sections of this function. With so much intellectual property theft going on these days, it's a good idea to identify each of your images as your own. Otherwise, you may post an image on Flickr or Facebook to share with friends and later find it on a billboard along the highway. With the Artist and Copyright information embedded in the image metadata, you will be able to prove that the image is yours and charge the infringer.

Embedding your personal information is not a foolproof way to identify your images because unscrupulous people may steal them and strip the metadata out of them. However, if you do find one of your images on the front page of a magazine or on someone's website, you can at least prove that you took the image and have some legal recourse under the Digital Millennium Copyright Act (DMCA). When you've taken a picture, you own the copyright to that image. You must be able to prove you took it. This is one convenient way.

You'll have even more power to protect yourself if you register your images with the US Copyright Registry at the following web address: **https://copyright-center.com/**.

If you sell your camera, or loan it to someone, be sure to remove the Artist and Copyright information to prevent misuse of your name.

Save/Load Settings

(User's Manual – Page 335)

Do you have your D800 set up exactly the way you like it? Have you spent hours and hours reading this book and the User's Manual, or simply exploring menus, and finally got all the settings in place? Are you worried that you might accidentally reset your camera or that it could lose its settings in one way or another? Well, worry no more! *Save/load settings* writes configuration settings to the memory card, allowing you to back up camera settings to your computer.

When you have your camera configured to your liking, or at any time during the process, simply use the Save/load settings function to save the camera configuration to your memory card. It creates a 2 KB file named NCSETUP8.BIN in the root directory of your memory card. You can then save that file to your computer's hard drive and have a backup of your camera settings.

Figure 5.15 – Save/load settings

Here are the steps to save or load the camera's settings (figure 5.15):

1. Choose Save/load settings from the Setup Menu and scroll to the right (figure 5.15, screen 1).
2. Select Save settings or Load settings from the Save/load settings menu, and then follow one of these two easy procedures (figure 5.15, screen 2):
3. a. **Save settings** – Select Save settings and press the OK button. Your most important camera settings will be saved to your memory card. Afterward, copy the settings file (NCSETUP8.BIN) to your computer for safekeeping. **Warning**: You may notice in figure 5.15, screen 2, that the Load settings selection is grayed out. If Load settings is not grayed out when you get ready to save the settings, be careful—you are about to overwrite previously saved settings that are currently on the memory card. The only time you'll see Load settings not grayed out is when an NCSETUP8.BIN file already exists on the memory card.
4. b. **Load settings** – Insert a memory card with a previously saved NCSETUP8.BIN file in the card's root directory, select Load settings, and press the OK button. The settings you previously saved will be reloaded into the D800 and will overwrite your current settings without prompting you for permission, so be sure that you are ready to have the settings overwritten. If you change the name of the NCSETUP8.BIN file, the D800 will not be able to reload your settings.

Here is a list of settings that are saved or loaded when you make use of one of these functions. It doesn't save or load every setting in the D800, only the ones listed here:

Playback Menu

- Playback display options
- Image review
- After delete
- Rotate tall

Shooting Menus (all four banks included)

- Shooting menu bank
- Extended menu banks
- File naming
- Primary slot selection
- Secondary slot function
- Image quality
- Image size
- Image area
- JPEG compression
- NEF (RAW) recording
- White balance (includes fine-tuning adjustments and presets d-1 to d-4)
- Set Picture Control
- Color space
- Active D-Lighting
- Vignette control
- Auto distortion control
- Long exposure NR
- High ISO NR
- ISO sensitivity settings
- Movie settings

Custom Settings (all four banks included)

- All Custom Settings

Setup Menu

- Clean image sensor
- HDMI
- Flicker reduction
- Time zone and date (except Date and time)
- Language
- Auto image rotation
- Copyright information
- GPS
- Non-CPU lens data
- Eye-Fi upload

My Menu and Recent Settings
- My Menu (includes all items you've entered)
- All Recent Settings
- Choose tab

Settings Recommendation: This function is a great idea. After using my camera for a few days and getting it set up just right, I save the settings file to my computer for safekeeping. Later, if I change things extensively for some reason and then want to reload my original settings, I just put the backed-up settings file on a memory card, pop it into the camera, select Load settings, and I'm back in business.

GPS

(User's Manual – Page 218)
Nikon has wisely included the ability to geotag your images with global positioning system (GPS) location data by providing an easy-to-use interface for various GPS devices.

Now when you shoot a spectacular travel image, you can rest assured that you'll be able to find that exact spot next year. With the Nikon GP-1 GPS (or an aftermarket brand), the D800 will record the following GPS information about your location into the metadata of each image:

- Latitude
- Longitude
- Altitude
- Heading
- UTC (time)

Using a GPS Unit with Your D800
The GPS unit you choose must be compatible with the National Marine Electronics Association NMEA0183 data format version 2.01 or 3.0.

I use a Nikon GP-1 GPS unit on my D800. It's small, easy to carry and store, and works very well. I have other Nikon DSLRs too, and this GPS unit works on all of them, with the proper cables. In figure 5.16A, you can see a Nikon GP-1 attached to the camera's Accessory shoe. You can also see the GP1-CA10 cable plugged into the 10-pin connector on the front of the camera. I deliberately put the curl in the cable to keep it from sticking out awkwardly.

Figure 5.16A – Nikon D800 with a Nikon GP-1 GPS unit, GP1- CA10 cable, and MC-DC2 remote release cable

The GP1-CA10 cable will interface with Nikon cameras that have a 10-pin port on the body, such as the D200, D300, D300S, D700, D800, D800E, D2X, D3, D3S, D3X, and D4. The GP-1 GPS unit also comes with a GP1-CA90 cable to interface with Nikon cameras such as the D3100, D3200, D5000, D5100, and D7000, so it is a useful device for almost any of your newer Nikons.

You can also get an optional Nikon MC-DC2 remote release cable that plugs directly into the GP-1 GPS unit for hands-off, vibration-free photography. The MC-DC2 remote release cable can be used to fire the shutter on any Nikon DSLR or HD-SLR that can interface with the GP-1 GPS unit. You can see the MC-DC2 remote release cable on the left side of the camera in figure 5.16A. It is plugged into the GP-1 GPS unit on the opposite side of where the GP1-CA10 cable plugs in.

Note: The Nikon GP-1 GPS unit doesn't have a built-in digital compass, so it will not report Heading information to the camera. Other GPS units do have the built-in compass and will report the Heading. If that is important to you, please investigate the Geotagger Pro GPS unit at **https://www.photoproshop.com/.**

Preparing the Camera for GPS Usage

There are several screens used in setting up the D800 for GPS use. First, you have to make a decision about the exposure meter when a GPS unit is plugged into the camera. While the GPS is plugged in, the camera's exposure meter must be active to record GPS data to the image. You should do one of two things:

- Set the exposure meter to stay on for the entire time that a GPS is plugged in. This, of course, will increase battery drain, but it keeps the GPS locked to the satellites (no seeking time).
- Press the Shutter-release button halfway down to activate the exposure meter before finishing the exposure. If you push the Shutter-release button down quickly and the GPS is not active and locked, it won't record GPS data to the image. The meter must be on before the GPS will seek satellites.

Auto Meter-Off

Figure 5.16B shows the screens used to set the meter to stay on the entire time the GPS is connected or to shut down after the Auto meter-off delay expires (Custom setting c2). You can select either Enable or Disable. Here's what each setting in *Auto meter-off* does:

- **Enable** (default) – The meter turns off after the *Custom Setting Menu > c Timers/ AE lock > c2 Auto meter-off* delay expires (default 6 seconds). GPS data will be recorded only when the exposure meter is active, so allow some time for the GPS unit to reacquire a satellite signal before taking a picture. This is hard to do when c2 Auto meter-off is set to Enable. You just about have to stand around with your finger on the Shutter-release button trying to keep the meter active. I suggest using Disable, as described next.
- **Disable** – The exposure meter stays on the entire time a GPS unit is connected. As long as you have a good GPS signal, you will be able to record GPS data at any time. This is the preferred setting for using the GPS for continuous shooting. It does use extra battery life, so you may want to carry more than one battery if you're going to shoot all day. Turn the camera off between locations.

Figure 5.16B – Setting an Auto meter off delay for GPS usage

Here are the steps to configure the GPS settings (figure 5.16B):

1. Choose GPS from the Setup Menu and scroll to the right (figure 5.16B, screen 1).
2. Select Auto meter-off and scroll to the right (figure 5.16B, screen 2).
3. Select Enable or Disable (figure 5.16B, screen 3). Use Disable for more reliable GPS usage, with somewhat greater battery drain. It is a good idea to carry

multiple batteries if you are shooting all day with a Nikon GP-1 GPS unit or other GPS unit attached.

4. Press the OK button to lock in the setting.

Position

There is also a *Position* setting, as shown in figure 5.16C, screen 2. If your GPS unit is not attached to the camera, the Position selection is grayed out. When a GPS is attached, the next screen after Position shows the actual GPS location data being detected by the D800 (figure 5.16C, screen 3).

Figure 5.16C – GPS Position information screen

To validate that the GPS is picking up GPS location data, examine the Position screen by using the following steps (figure 5.16C):

1. Choose GPS from the Setup Menu and scroll to the right (figure 5.16C, screen 1).
2. Select Position from the GPS menu and scroll to the right (figure 5.16C, screen 2).
3. Examine the Position screen to see the five items provided from the GPS satellite data (figure 5.16C, screen 3). Notice that my Nikon GP-1 GPS unit did not give me Heading information. Other GPS units will give you that information, as discussed previously.

When the camera establishes communication with your GPS unit, three things happen:

- Position information appears on the GPS Position screen (figure 5.16C, screen 3).
- A small GPS symbol will display on the Control panel and Information display, just under the shutter speed indicator. It will blink when acquiring a GPS signal lock and stop blinking when at least three global positioning satellites are acquired.
- An additional data information display screen will be displayed when you are using the Playback button to review the captured images. You can press up or down with the Multi Selector button to scroll through the image data screens on the Monitor. One of them will be similar to the screen shown in figure 5.16D, which is a picture of the GPS data screen from a picture I took of a tree.

Figure 5.16D – GPS Information display screen (Playback)

Note: The Nikon GP-1 GPS unit will blink its rear LED light in red while acquiring satellites and shine solid green when locked onto three satellites. Allow a few seconds for the GPS to acquire satellites when the camera has been turned off. If you are a significant distance from where you last used the GP-1 GPS unit, it may require up to a minute or two to acquire a satellite lock. Once the GP-1 has a local satellite lock and you turn the camera off, the GPS unit will reacquire the signal in just a few seconds when the camera is turned back on.

Use GPS to Set Camera Clock

The D800 has a cool feature designed to let the GPS satellite keep your camera's time accurate: the *Use GPS to set camera clock* function. The camera can query the GPS satellite and set the camera's clock. If you use GPS a lot, you might want to leave this on. The clock in the Nikon D800 is not as accurate as a wristwatch, for instance, and will tend to lose accuracy more quickly. It's a good idea to set the camera's clock from time to time. This is an easy way to accomplish that for GPS users.

Figure 5.16E – Using GPS to set camera clock

Here are the steps to enable Use GPS to set camera clock:

1. Choose GPS from the Setup Menu and scroll to the right (figure 5.16E, screen 1).
2. Select Use GPS to set camera clock and scroll to the right (figure 5.16E, screen 2). Select Yes to enable the setting or No if you want to check the clock yourself from time to time (figure 5.16E, screen 3).
3. Press the OK button to save the setting.

Using the GPS

If the GPS icon is flashing on the Control panel and Information display screen, it means that the GPS is searching for a signal. If you take a picture with the GPS icon flashing, no GPS data will be recorded. If the GPS icon is not flashing (solid), it means that the D800 is receiving good GPS data and is ready to record data to a picture. If the D800 loses communication with the GPS unit for more than two seconds, the GPS icon will disappear. Make sure the icon is displayed and isn't flashing before you take pictures!

If you want the GPS Heading information to be accurate, keep your GPS unit pointing in the same direction as the lens. Some aftermarket GPS units also contain a digital compass, unlike the Nikon GP-1. Point the GPS in the direction of your subject and give it enough time to stabilize before you take the picture or the Heading information will not be accurate. This does not apply to the Nikon GP-1 GPS unit, which has no digital compass. It records only Latitude, Longitude, Altitude, and UTC time, not the Heading.

The Nikon GP-1 GPS unit mounts either onto the camera's Accessory shoe (figure 5.16A) or on the camera's strap, with the included GP1-CL1 strap adapter.

Note: You can also attach some external handheld GPS units through an optional (and pricey) Nikon MC-35 cable, which uses a D-sub 9-pin connector. You must find a handheld GPS unit with a cable that will connect to the 9-pin connector on the MC-35, which is not as easy as it used to be because many handheld units use USB cables connections now.

A handheld unit I have personally used successfully is the Garmin eTrex Legend GPS unit. You can pick up a new Garmin eTrex Legend GPS unit for around US$150 on Amazon.com. It can be used with the Nikon MC-35 cable to interface with your camera, and when it's disconnected from the camera, it can keep you from getting lost while hiking to and from that special scenic spot. To interface a handheld unit with the Nikon D800, you will need to use NMEA mode at 4800 baud. Refer to the GPS unit's user's manual for more information on setting the mode and baud rate. As mentioned previously, the GPS unit you choose must be compatible with the National Marine Electronics Association NMEA0183 data format version 2.01 or 3.0.

Settings Recommendation: Get the Nikon GP-1 GPS unit from one of many vendors, or get the Geotagger Pro GPS from the Nikonians PhotoProShop (www.Photo-ProShop.com). Either unit is easy to use, foolproof, and has all the cables you need for interfacing with your camera.

If you choose the Nikon GP-1 GPS unit, the only other cable you'll need to buy is the optional MC-DC2 shutter-release cable (coiled on the left in figure 5.16A). I use the tiny Nikon GP-1 GPS unit constantly when I'm shooting nature images so I can remember where to return in the future. After you start using a GPS unit, you'll find it hard to stop.

Virtual Horizon

(User's Manual – Page 337)

Virtual horizon is a function that allows you to level your camera when it's on a tripod. This particular Virtual horizon function is not for Live view photography or Movie live view still image or video use. All this function does is bring up the Virtual horizon indicator on the camera's Monitor so that you can use it to help level your camera on a tripod or other stable shooting base.

The Live view photography and Movie live view modes have a similar version of this Virtual horizon that you can see through for live usage. That Virtual horizon is available by pressing the info button repeatedly until the Virtual horizon shows up as one of several overlays available in either of those Live view modes.

Let's see how to use the convenient Virtual horizon to level your camera. No more need for those Accessory-shoe mounted bubble levels!

Figure 5.17A – Virtual horizon

Here are the steps to use the Virtual horizon:

1. Choose Virtual horizon from the Setup Menu and scroll to the right (figure 5.17A, screen 1).
2. The next two screens (figure 5.17A, screens 2 and 3) show the Virtual horizon indicator. You can use it to level the camera on your tripod or even handheld if you would like. The indicator shows left and right tilts, along with forward and backward tilts. Figure 5.17, screen 2, indicates that the camera is tilted to the right with the lens point slightly downward. Screen 3 shows that the camera is level.

Settings Recommendation: This is a very convenient function because it allows me to level my when I am using a tripod without breaking out the old Accessory-shoe bubble level. I suggest adding this function to the My Menu section of your camera. That way, you will have it available whenever you want to use it, without digging through menus to find it. We will discuss how to add items to My Menu in the chapter titled **My Menu and Recent Settings**.

Viewfinder Virtual Horizon

Although not directly related to the graphical Virtual horizon function for the camera's Monitor, there is another function called *Viewfinder virtual horizon* that is available to you. You can use it to see a somewhat different-looking Virtual horizon indicator in the camera's Viewfinder by assigning one of the assignable buttons to Viewfinder virtual horizon. Let's use the Fn button as an example. We covered how to assign different functionality to the Fn button in the chapter **Custom Setting Menu** in the section **Custom Setting f4 – Assign Fn button**.

Figure 5.17B – Viewfinder virtual horizon

If you go to *Custom Setting Menu > f Controls > f4 Assign Fn button > Fn button press* (or another button) and choose Viewfinder virtual horizon, you will see another type of Virtual horizon on the bottom and the right side of your camera's Viewfinder when you press the button you've assigned it to (figure 5.17B, red arrows).

The Viewfinder virtual horizon is showing level in figure 5.17B. Once it's assigned to a button, you can activate the Viewfinder virtual horizon with a press of that button. When it shows in the Viewfinder, it will register left and right tilt, along with forward and backward tilt, by changing the look of the two indicators at the red arrows' tips.

Non-CPU Lens Data

(User's Manual – Page 159)
Non-CPU lens data helps you use older non-CPU Nikkor lenses with your camera. Do you still have several older AI or AI-S Nikkor lenses? I do! The image quality from the older manual-focus (MF) lenses is excellent.

Since the D800 is positioned as a pro-level camera, it must have the necessary controls to use both auto focus (AF) and manual focus (MF) lenses. Many photographers on a budget use the older MF lenses to obtain professional-level image quality without having to break the bank on expensive lens purchases. You can buy excellent AI and AI-S Nikkor lenses on eBay for US$100–$300 and have image quality that only the most expensive zoom lenses can produce.

Lens manufacturers like Zeiss and Nikkor are still making MF lenses, and because some of them do not have a CPU (electronic chip) that communicates with the camera, it's important to have a way to let the D800 know something about the lens in use.

This Non-CPU lens data function allows you to do exactly that. You can store information for up to nine separate non-CPU lenses within this section of the D800.

Here is a detailed analysis of the Non-CPU lens data screen selections (figure 5.18A, screen 2):

- **Done** – When you have completed the setup of a particular lens, or several lenses, simply scroll to this selection and press the OK button. Your lens data will be saved within the D800. Later, you can put a non-CPU lens on your camera and select it from the list of nine lenses. You can use external camera controls (an assigned button) or the Non-CPU lens data menu to change to your current lens.
- **Lens number** – Using the Multi Selector, you can scroll left or right to select one of your lenses. There are nine lens records available. When you select a Lens number here, the focal length and maximum aperture of that lens will show up in the Focal length and Maximum aperture fields. If you haven't stored information for a particular Lens number, you'll see double dashes – – in the Focal length and Maximum aperture fields.
- **Focal length (mm)** – This field contains the actual focal length in millimeters (mm) of the Lens in use. You can select focal lengths from 6 mm to 4000 mm. Hmm, I didn't know they even made a 4000 mm lens. I want one!
- **Maximum aperture** – This field is for the Maximum aperture of the lens. You can enter an f-stop number from F1.2 to F22. Remember, this is for the maximum aperture only (largest opening or f-stop). When you've entered a maximum aperture, the camera will be able to determine the other apertures by your use of the aperture ring on the lens. (Remember those?)

Figure 5.18A – Non-CPU lens data

Use the following steps to configure (save) each of your non-CPU lenses for use with your D800:

1. Select Non-CPU lens data from the Setup Menu and scroll to the right (figure 5.18A, screen 1).
2. Scroll down to Lens number and scroll left or right until you find the number you want to use for this particular lens (figure 5.18A, screen 2).
3. Scroll down to Focal length (mm) and scroll left or right to select the focal length of the lens. If you are configuring a non-CPU zoom lens, select the widest setting. This works because the meter will adjust for any light falloff that may occur as the lens is zoomed out.
4. Scroll down to Maximum aperture and scroll left or right to select the maximum aperture of the lens. If you are configuring a variable-aperture zoom lens, select the largest aperture the lens can use. This works because the meter will adjust for the variation in the aperture.
5. Scroll to Done and press the OK button to store the setting.

When you're done entering data for your non-CPU lenses, don't forget to use the Done selection to save your work! The Done selection allows you to either select a lens or save changes to one or all nine of your lenses. In other words, you can use the set of screens in figure 5.18A to both input and select a non-CPU lens.

When you have selected a lens for use, the *Setup Menu > Non-CPU lens data* selection will show the number of the lens you've selected. It will be in the format of No. 1 to No. 9. In figure 5.18A, screen 1, you can see the lens selection (No. 1) at the end of the Non-CPU lens data line. That's my beloved AI Nikkor 35mm f/2 lens!

Selecting a Lens by Using the Non-CPU Lens Menu

When it's time to shoot pictures, follow these steps to select a non-CPU lens:

1. Open the Non-CPU lens data screen (figure 5.18A, screen 2).
2. Select a lens by scrolling left or right on the Lens number field.
3. Scroll up to the Done selection and press the OK button.

Selecting a Non-CPU Lens with External Camera Controls

The D800 allows you to customize its buttons to do things the way you want them to be done. You may have only one or two non-CPU lenses, so it may be sufficient to use the Non-CPU lens data menu to select a lens. However, if you have a large selection of non-CPU lenses, you may wish Nikon had provided more than nine lens selections in the Non-CPU lens data menu.

Since I use several older manual-focus AI Nikkor lenses, I use the Custom Setting Menu's assign button functions to map *Custom Setting Menu > f Controls > f4 Assign Fn button > Fn button + command dials* to Choose non-CPU lens number, for selecting Non-CPU lens data on the fly. Then I can simply hold down the Fn button and turn either of the Command dials to select one of the nine non-CPU lenses I have already registered with the camera.

Here are the steps to select a non-CPU lens using external camera controls:

1. On the bottom right of figure 5.18B, you will see n – 1. That is where you choose the actual lens by its assigned number. You'll see n–1 to n–9 scroll by as you rotate whichever Command dial is most convenient to you.
2. In figure 5.18B, the number on the top left applies to the focal length of the currently selected lens, in this case, 35mm (35).
3. The number on the top right of figure 5.18B shows the maximum aperture of the currently selected non-CPU lens (F2).
4. Hold down the button you've assigned (I use Fn) and turn a Command dial until the number of your lens appears (n -1 to n - 9), and then release the button. Now your camera knows which lens is mounted.

Figure 5.18B – Non-CPU lens data with external controls

This is a really quick way to change the camera's Non-CPU lens data settings after you mount a different non-CPU lens.

Settings Recommendation: I like using the Fn button + command dial setting to select my non-CPU lenses. This is very fast and easy in the field. Or, you can simply use the *Setup Menu > Non-CPU lens data* function to select a lens with menus. Play with both and learn how to use each. They'll both come in handy for different times.

AF Fine-Tune

(User's Manual – Page 338)
One thing that really impresses me about the D800 is its ability to be fine-tuned in critical areas like metering and autofocus. With many older cameras, if an AF lens had a back focus problem, you just had to tolerate it or send it off to be fixed. Now, with *AF fine-tune*, you can adjust your camera so the lens focuses where you want it to focus.

Nikon has made provisions for keeping a table of up to 20 lenses you have fine-tuned for better focus. The idea behind fine-tuning is that you can push the focus forward or backward in small increments, with up to 20 increments in each direction.

When the little round, green AF indicator comes on in your camera's Viewfinder and AF fine-tune is enabled for a lens you've already configured, the actual focus is moved from its default position forward or backward by the amount you've specified. If your lens has a back focus problem and you move the focus a little forward, the problem is solved. There are four selections on the AF fine-tune menu:

- AF fine-tune (On/Off)
- Saved value
- Default
- List saved values

Figure 5.19A – Fine-tuning the focus of a lens

Use the following steps to start the process of fine-tuning a lens (figure 5.19A):

1. Choose AF fine-tune from the Setup Menu and scroll to the right (figure 5.19A, screen 1).
2. Select AF fine-tune (On/Off) from the menu and scroll to the right (figure 5.19A, screen 2).
3. The next four subsections show the screens to configure AF fine-tune (figures 5.19B to 5.19E). Each of the following figures continues where figure 5.19A, screen 2, left off.

AF Fine-Tune (On/Off)

Figure 5.19B shows the AF fine-tune (On/Off) screen and its selections. The two values you can select are as follows:

- **On** – This setting turns the AF fine-tune system on. Without this setting enabled, the D800 focuses like a factory default D800. Set AF fine-tune (On/Off) to On if you are planning to fine-tune a lens now. Press the OK button to save the value.
- **Off** – This default setting disables the AF fine-tune system.

Figure 5.19B – Enabling or disabling AF fine-tune

Saved Value

With an autofocus lens mounted, *Saved value* allows you to control the amount of front or back focus fine-tuning you would like to input for the listed lens. At the top left of figure 5.19C, screen 2, just under the words Saved value, you'll see the focal length of the lens that is mounted on your camera, the maximum aperture, and the number assigned to the lens. If you're configuring a lens for the first time, you'll see No. – –. You can fine-tune a maximum of 20 lenses. After you save a lens configuration, a number will appear in place of the dashes (No. 1 to No. 20).

Figure 5.19C – Fine-tuning a lens with a Saved value

To the right of the lens information is a scale that runs from +20 on the top to -20 on the bottom. The yellow pointer on the right starts out at 0. You can move this yellow pointer up or down to change the amount of focus fine-tuning you need for this lens. Moving the pointer up on the scale pushes the focal point away from the camera, and moving it down pulls the focal point toward the camera. I set my 50mm F1.4 lens to +5 forward focus, as shown in figure 5.19C, screen 2. When you set the fine-tuning amount you need, press the OK button.

Default

The *Default* configuration screen looks a lot like the Saved value screen, except there is no lens information listed. This Default value will be applied to all AF lenses you mount on your camera. If you are convinced that your particular camera always has a back or front focus problem and you are not able or ready to ship it off to Nikon for repair, you can use the Default value to push the autofocus in one direction or the other until you are satisfied that your camera is focusing the way you'd like. *Again, this will affect all autofocus lenses you mount on your camera.*

Figure 5.19D – Setting a Default fine-tune adjustment for all lenses

As shown in figure 5.19D, screen 2, to set an *AF fine-tune > Default*, use the scale that runs from +20 on the top to -20 on the bottom. The yellow pointer starts at 0. You can move this yellow pointer up or down to change the amount of focus fine-tuning you need for whatever lens you currently have on the D800 if no value already exists in the Saved value for the lens. Moving the pointer up on the scale pushes the focal point away from the camera (front focus), and moving it down pulls the focal point toward the camera (back focus). When you are done, press the OK button.

Note: You could use this Default value as a value for any of your AF lenses that do not have a Saved value. I tested this with a different lens (not shown) by setting a Saved value of +1 for my AF-S Nikkor 24-120 mm lens. While the 24-120 mm lens was still mounted, I set a value of -2 for the Default value. When I removed the 24-120 mm lens and mounted an AF Nikkor 60 mm micro lens, the +1 in the Saved value field disappeared, but the -2 in the Default field stayed put. So it appears that you can use the Default field either for all AF lenses that have no Saved value or for a currently mounted AF lens that you want to adjust but not save a value for.

List Saved Values

Notice in figure 5.19E that there are several screens used to configure the list of saved values. *List saved values* helps you remember which lenses you've fine-tuned. It also allows you to set an identification number (00–99) for a particular lens out of the 20 lenses you can register.

Figure 5.19E – Assigning an AF fine-tune lens number to one of your 20 lenses

Many people use the last two digits of the lens's serial number as the List saved values number for that lens. Alternatively, you can select a sequential number from

00–99. In figure 5.19E, screen 2, you'll see the 50/1.4 lens listed; this screen will show a list of all lenses for which you have saved values. Notice in the third screen that there is a little box in the middle after No. Use the Multi Selector to scroll up or down in that box, from 00 to 99. That way, you can set whatever number you want to use for each particular lens.

Note: With AF fine-tune enabled, the lens may not be able to focus at the minimum focus distance or at infinity. Test this carefully! Fine-tuning is not applied to any lenses when you're using Live view photography mode. If you use teleconverters, you will need to store a value for the lens itself and the lens with the teleconverter mounted.

Settings Recommendation: AF fine-tune is good to have. If I buy a new lens and it has focus problems, I don't keep it. Back it goes to the manufacturer for a replacement. However, if I buy a used lens or have had one long enough to go out of warranty and it later develops front or back focus problems, the camera allows me to fine-tune the autofocus for that lens. A pro-level camera has these little necessities to keep you out of trouble when shooting commercially.

Eye-Fi Upload

(User's Manual – Page 339)
Eye-Fi upload allows you to use an Eye-Fi card to send images you take from your camera to your computer, either through a local Wi-Fi Internet connection or directly to the computer with an Ad hoc Wi-Fi connection.

Eye-Fi upload appears on the Setup Menu of your D800 *only* when you have an Eye-Fi card inserted. Otherwise, the camera does not even show the Eye-Fi Upload menu selection between AF fine-tune and Firmware version on the Shooting Menu.

Figure 5.20A – Eye-Fi Pro X2 8 GB Wi-Fi card

The Eye-Fi company makes several of these SD cards with built-in Wi-Fi transmitters. Figure 5.20A shows my Eye-Fi Pro X2 8 GB high-speed Class 6 SD card.

With an Eye-Fi card inserted and Eye-Fi software installed on a computer with a wireless network connection, you can take pictures that are automatically transferred to your computer. You can also simultaneously transfer images to file-sharing websites like Flickr and Facebook (and many more).

Most lower-cost Eye-Fi cards require a wireless network to transfer the images. However, Eye-Fi's X2 Pro cards will do Ad hoc transfers, meaning that they don't need a wireless network connection and will send pictures directly to a computer with wireless capability. In effect, the Eye-Fi card becomes a wireless (Wi-Fi) transmitter that can talk directly to a Wi-Fi–enabled computer, without an intervening network.

At the time of this writing, only one card—the Eye-Fi Pro X2 8 GB—will transfer images directly to a computer without a wireless network as an intermediary. The other cards cost less but require a wireless network connection to move images.

Eye-Fi names its cards that are capable of Ad hoc transfer with the Pro moniker. The other cards have names like Connect X2, Mobile X2, Geo X2, and Explore X2. Only the Pro X2 cards can do the no-network-required, direct-to-computer Ad hoc file transfers. Because memory card prices are extremely volatile, I'm sure that the capacities and card names will change quickly.

For more information on Eye-Fi cards, see the website at the following location: **http://www.eye.fi**.

Enabling Eye-Fi Uploads on the D800

An Eye-Fi card does not use any more battery life than a normal SD card until you enable Wi-Fi. Unless you are currently shooting images for transfer, I wouldn't leave the Eye-Fi upload feature (Wi-Fi) enabled. Why waste battery life out in the woods where there are no wireless networks? To make it really convenient to access the Eye-Fi upload function for quick enabling—only when needed—I simply added it to My Menu in the D800. We'll examine how to do that in the chapter, **My Menu and Recent Settings**.

Figure 5.20B – Enabling Eye-Fi (Wi-Fi)

Here are the steps to Enable or Disable Eye-Fi upload (figure 5.20B):

1. Choose Eye-Fi upload from the Setup Menu and scroll to the right (figure 5.20B, screen 1).
2. Select Enable or Disable from the Eye-Fi upload screen (figure 5.20B, screen 2).
3. Press the OK button to lock in the setting.

Note: You may download additional information on the Eye-Fi card in a document called **Eye-Fi Card Information** from this book's downloadable resources on the Web at the following locations:

http://www.Nikonians.org/NikonD800
http://rockynook.com/NikonD800

According to the User's Manual, "As of September 2011, the camera supports 8 GB SDHC Pro X2 Eye-Fi cards." The D800 may or may not support the other non-pro cards. It probably will, but there are no guarantees for the non-pro cards.

Settings Recommendation: I wanted to buy a nice Nikon WT-4A transmitter until I saw the price. Whew! I think I'd rather buy that AF-S Nikkor 200-400 mm f/2.8 ED VR lens I crave mightily. So instead, I bought an Eye-Fi card for about one-eighth of the price of the WT-4A. It doesn't give me the large wireless range and multiple modes the powerful WT-4A transmitter offers, but I can shoot an event within 50 to 90 feet of my notebook computer and have immediate wireless Ad hoc file transfer capability.

Because even the low-priced Eye-Fi cards have the ability to use an existing Wi-Fi connection to transfer images through the Internet to a home computer, you could do a photographic walkabout downtown, stop in at a McDonalds for a burger or Starbucks for a coffee, and use its wireless connection to transfer images to your home computer while you eat. I really like this little Eye-Fi card!

Firmware Version

(User's Manual – Page 340)
Firmware version is a simple informational screen, like the Battery info screen. It shows you which version of the camera's operating system (firmware) you are running. My camera is currently running version A1.00, B1.00, and L1.004.

Figure 5.21 – Viewing the camera's Firmware version

Here are the steps to see the Firmware version of your camera (figure 5.21):

1. Choose Firmware version from the Setup Menu and scroll to the right (figure 5.21, screen 1).
2. Examine the Firmware version (figure 5.21, screen 2).
3. Select Done and press the OK button.

Upgrading Your Camera's Firmware

From time to time, Nikon releases firmware upgrades for its cameras. You may want to install the upgrades for the D800 because they often fix bugs, speed things up, and even add features to your camera.

When you are ready to upgrade your camera's firmware, you can learn how to do it by going to the downloadable resources website for this book and downloading the document called **Firmware Upgrade**:

http://www.Nikonians.org/NikonD800
http://rockynook.com/NikonD800

Author's Conclusions

Whew! The D800 may seem like a complicated little beast, but that's what you get when you fold medium-format, pro-level functionality into a relatively small DSLR body. For as complex as it is, I'm certainly delighted with it.

Next, we'll consider how to use the camera's Retouch Menu to adjust images without using a computer. If you are in the field shooting RAW files and you need a quick JPEG, black-and-white version of a file, or red-eye reduction, the Retouch Menu has you covered.

You can even do things like red-eye correction, color balance changes, filtration, cropping, and image resizing—all without touching a computer. Let's see how!

Retouch Menu

6

Two Leopards Descending – Courtesy of David Hays (*Haysys*)

Retouching allows you to modify your images in-camera. If you like to do digital photography but don't particularly like to adjust images on a computer, these functions are for you! Obviously, the camera's Monitor is not large enough to allow you to make heavily creative changes to an image—as you could do within Nikon Capture NX 2, Lightroom, Aperture, or Photoshop—but it's surprising what you can accomplish with the Retouch Menu.

The D800 has 20 Retouch Menu selections. The following is a list of each function and what it does:

- **D-Lighting** – This feature opens up detail in the shadows and tends to protect highlight details from blowing out. This is similar to the *Shooting Menu > Active D-Lighting* function, but it's applied *after* the image is taken.
- **Red-eye correction** – This removes the unwanted red-eye effect caused by light from a flash reflecting back from the eyes of your human subjects.
- **Trim** – This feature creates a trimmed (cropped) copy of a selected photograph. You can crop the image according to several aspect ratios, including 1:1, 3:2, 4:3, 5:4, and 16:9.
- **Monochrome** – You can convert your color images into monochrome. There are three tints available, including Black-and-white (grays), Sepia (golden), and Cyanotype (bluish).
- **Filter effects** – There are seven filter effects that can be applied to an image to change its appearance. The seven filters are Skylight, Warm filter, Red intensifier, Green intensifier, Blue intensifier, Cross screen, and Soft.
- **Color balance** – To change the color balance of your image, you can increase or decrease the amount of Green, Blue, Amber, and Magenta.
- **Image overlay** – This creates a new image by overlaying two existing NEF (RAW) files. Basically, you can combine two RAW images to create special effects—such as adding an image of the moon into a separate landscape picture.
- **NEF (RAW) processing** – You can create highly specialized JPEG images from your NEF (RAW) files without using your computer.
- **Resize** – You can take a full-size image and convert it into several smaller sizes. This is useful if you would like to send an image via e-mail or if you need a smaller image for other reasons.
- **Quick retouch** – The camera automatically tweaks the image with enhancements to saturation and contrast. In addition, when a subject is dark or is backlit, the camera applies D-Lighting to open up shadow detail.
- **Straighten** – You can straighten an image with crooked horizons by rotating it in-camera. The camera will trim (crop) the edges of the image to create a normal image perspective, without the tilt.

- **Distortion control** – You can remove barrel and pincushion distortion that affects the edges of the image. You can cause the camera to make automatic adjustments or you can do it manually. The camera automatically trims (crops) the edges of the image after adjustment.
- **Fisheye** – This feature allows you to incrementally bulge images from their centers to get that strange fisheye effect you often see while looking through a door peephole. It provides a very distorted image that will make your friends either laugh or chase you. Warning: This effect can be dangerous to use on wives, sisters, and girlfriends! (Don't ask me how I know!)
- **Color outline** – This creates an outline effect, as if you had traced an underlying image on paper with a pencil. The effect is in monochrome, contrary to the name of the function. Nikon provides this effect to "create an outline of a photograph to use as a base for painting."
- **Color sketch** – This effect is very similar to Color outline; the main difference is that it is in pastel color. It sketches the edges of the subjects in your image and colorizes them in a way similar to using colored pencils or crayon. You can control the vividness of the color and the contrast of the line edges.
- **Perspective control** – This is a useful control that helps adjust perspective distortion out of an image. It's useful for pictures of things like buildings, which can have a falling-over-backward effect when shot with a wide-angle lens. The camera automatically crops the edges of the image to allow the distortion to be removed.
- **Miniature effect** – This effect allows you to create a reverse diorama (an image taken from a high vantage point of a real scene with a very limited band of sharpness) to make the image look fake. The image may be of a real subject, like a city shot from the top of a tall building; however, the Miniature effect causes the scene to look artificial, as if small models of reality were used.
- **Selective color** – You can use this function to create photographs with certain elements in color and the rest black-and-white. Imagine a bright red rose with nothing in the image in color except the rose petals. You can selectively choose a color with an eyedropper icon, and only that color will show in the image.
- **Edit movie** – You can shorten a movie by cropping out a small section from a large movie file.
- **Side-by-side comparison** – You can compare a retouched image—created via the Retouch Menu—with the original image. The images are presented side by side so you can see before and after effects.

The Retouch Menu is the fifth menu down the menu selection bar, just below the Setup Menu. Its icon resembles a palette and paintbrush. Unless you have some images on one of the camera's memory cards, the Retouch Menu is grayed out and unavailable, for obvious reasons. No images, no retouching!

Figure 6.1 shows a sample of the results from only one of the 20 functions available in the Retouch Menu. I was shooting RAW files in the Great Smoky Mountains in Tennessee and decided to create a JPEG from one of my images immediately. Having no computer handy, I simply used the NEF (RAW) processing function to convert the image to JPEG. Fast and easy!

Figure 6.1 – Cascades in Great Smoky Mountains National Park, Tennessee, United States. An image converted from NEF (RAW) to JPEG using the Retouch Menu. Nikon D800, AF-S Nikkor 50mm f/1.4G lens at f/13, on tripod, Aperture-priority mode, LS (Landscape) Picture Control, 1-second exposure at ISO 50. Hoya circular polarizer used to remove reflections from the water. Active D-Lighting set to Normal.

Retouched Image File Numbering

When you use Retouch Menu items, the D800 does not overwrite your original file. It always creates a JPEG file with the next available image number. The retouched image will be numbered as the last image on the memory card. If you have 100 images on your card and you are retouching image number DSC_0047, the new JPEG image will be numbered DSC_0101 (it will be the 101st image).

Accessing the Retouch Functions – Two Methods

There are two methods for accessing the Retouch Menu. You can use the main Retouch Menu—under the MENU button—to choose an image to work with, or you can display an image on the Monitor in Playback mode and press the OK button to open the Retouch Menu.

They work basically the same, except the Playback Retouch Menu leaves out the step of choosing the image (since there is already an image on the screen), and it has fewer retouch selections. The most comprehensive retouch selections are available under the Retouch Menu.

Since both the Playback Retouch Menu and Retouch Menu methods have the same functions, we'll discuss them as if you were using the Retouch Menu. However, in case you decide to use the Playback method, let's discuss it briefly.

Playback Retouching

Use the following steps if you want to work with an image that you are viewing on your camera's Monitor—what I call Playback retouching:

1. Press the Playback button and choose a picture by displaying it on the Monitor (figure 6.2A, images 1 and 2). You now have a picture ready for retouching.
2. Press the OK button to open an abbreviated Retouch Menu (figure 6.2A, screen 3).
3. Select one of the Playback Retouch Menu items (figure 6.2A, screen 4).

Figure 6.2A – Playback Retouch Menu

Remember that some of the Retouch Menu options are not available under the Playback Retouch Menu.

The following descriptions require that you select a Retouch Menu function and then select an image to which you want to apply the effect.

Limitations on Previously Retouched Images

Sometimes there are limitations imposed when you are working on an image that has already been retouched. You may not be able to retouch a previously retouched image with another Retouch Menu function.

When using the Playback retouch method, certain menu items will be grayed out because they cannot be applied to an already retouched image. If you use the Retouch Menu directly, any images that are overlaid with a box containing a yellow X cannot be retouched again with the current retouch function (figure 6.2B, red arrow).

Figure 6.2B – Cannot be retouched

Using Retouch Menu Items Directly

D-Lighting
(User's Manual – Page 344)
D-Lighting allows you to reduce the shadows in an image and maybe even rein in the highlights a bit, lowering the overall image contrast. It works like Active D-Lighting except that it is applied to the image after it is taken.

Remember that Retouch Menu effects are applied to a copy of the image, so your original picture is safe and untouched. In figure 6.3, you can see that I retouched an image that was about one stop underexposed. I used High D-Lighting and brought out the shadow detail.

Figure 6.3 – D-Lighting

Use the following steps for applying D-Lighting to an image (figure 6.3):

1. Select D-Lighting from the Retouch Menu and scroll to the right (figure 6.3, screen 1).
2. Select the image you want to modify and press the OK button (figure 6.3, screen 2).
3. Using the Multi selector to scroll up or down, choose the amount of D-Lighting you want for the chosen image. You'll choose from Low, Normal (or medium), and High D-Lighting (figure 6.3, screen 3). When the image on the right of the side-by-side comparison images looks the way you want it to, press the OK button to save the new file.
4. The D800 will display a brief *Image saved* notice between screens 3 and 4, and then display the new file on the Monitor. The retouched image will have a small palette-and-paintbrush icon to show that it has been retouched (figure 6.3, screen 4, red arrow). The original image is still available for future retouching.

Settings Recommendation: There is no one setting that is correct for all images. I often use Normal (medium) to see if an image needs more or less D-Lighting, and then change to High or Low if needed. Remember that any amount of D-Lighting has the potential to introduce noise in the darker areas of the image, so the less D-Lighting you use, the better.

Red-Eye Correction

(User's Manual – Page 345)

Red-eye correction attempts to change bright red pupils—caused by flash exposure reflection—back to their normal dark color. Red-eye makes a person look like one of those aliens with glowing eyes from a science fiction show.

If you've used flash to create a picture, the Red-eye correction function will work on the image if it can detect any red eye. If it can't detect red eye in the image, you will briefly see a screen that says *Unable to detect red-eye in selected image.*

The camera will not let you select an image that was not taken with flash. Each image not taken with flash will have a box with a yellow *X*, signifying that the image cannot be selected for this function.

Use the following steps to execute the Red-eye correction function (figure 6.4):

1. Select Red-eye correction from the Retouch Menu and scroll to the right (figure 6.4, screen 1).
2. Select the image you want to modify and press the OK button (figure 6.4, screen 2).
3. You'll see an hourglass on the Monitor while the camera detects and removes red eye (figure 6.4, screen 3). This can take several seconds.
4. Press the OK button to save the file with a new file number as a retouched image (figure 6.4, screen 4, red arrow) or press the Playback button to cancel. After Red-eye correction is complete, you can use the Playback zoom in button to zoom in on the image and see how well it worked. Zoom back out with the checkered Thumbnail/Playback zoom out button.

Figure 6.4 – Red-eye correction

Settings Recommendation: I've found that the Red-eye correction function works pretty well as long as the subject is fairly large in the frame. I have tried Red-eye correction on smaller subjects, such as in larger groups of people, and sometimes it works and other times it doesn't. When the subject is smaller, the eyes are much smaller too. The camera may struggle to find red eye in very tiny subjects. I've had it correct one eye that was closer to the camera (and therefore larger) and not the other. I would rate this function as quite helpful but not always completely effective. It's a good function to have for quick red-eye correction on critical images you need to use immediately.

Trim

(User's Manual – Page 346)

The *Trim* function allows you to crop an image in-camera, change its aspect ratio, and save the file as a new image. Your original image is not modified. This is a useful function if you need to remove distracting elements from the background.

Figure 6.5 – Trim function

Use the following steps to Trim an image in-camera (figure 6.5):

1. Select the Trim function from the Retouch Menu and scroll to the right (figure 6.5, screen 1).
2. Select the image you want to modify and press the OK button (figure 6.5, screen 2).
3. You'll see a screen that has an area of the image outlined in yellow (figure 6.5, screen 3). Use the checkered Thumbnail/Playback zoom out button to make the size of the yellow crop outline smaller or the Playback zoom in button to enlarge the outline. Use the Multi selector to move the yellow selection rectangle in any direction within the frame until you find the best crop.
4. Select the aspect ratio of the cropped image by rotating the rear Main command dial. Your choices are 3:2, 4:3, 5:4, 1:1 (square), or 16:9. Figure 6.5, screen 3 (red arrow), shows that the 16:9 aspect ratio is selected.
5. When you have the cropped area correctly sized and the aspect ratio set, press the OK button to save the image with a new file name (figure 6.5, screen 4).

Settings Recommendation: This is a very useful function for cropping images without a computer. The fact that you have multiple aspect ratios available is just icing on the cake. The D800 has some useful aspect ratios, including a square (1:1) and an HD format (16:9).

Monochrome

(User's Manual – Page 253)

The *Monochrome* function in the D800 is fun to play with and can make some nice images. Converting the images to one of the three monochrome tones is a good starting point for creative manipulation.

The three options for the Monochrome function are as follows:

- Black-and-white (grays)
- Sepia (golden tone)
- Cyanotype (blue tone)

Figure 6.6A – Monochrome images

Figure 6.6A shows a sample of the three monochrome tones you can use to convert a normal color photo. I chose the Darker setting on the Sepia and Cyanotype versions to show their maximum effects. Notice in screen 1 that the Black-and-white version has no darkness or lightness setting because the D800 provides only one level. However, for Sepia and Cyanotype, you can fine-tune the tint from lightly saturated to very saturated in three levels. The three images in figure 6.6A are at the Darker (most saturated) maximum.

Use the following steps to create a Monochrome image from one of your color images (figure 6.6B):

1. Select Monochrome from the Retouch Menu and scroll to the right (figure 6.6B, screen 1).
2. Select a Monochrome tone—Black-and-white, Sepia, or Cyanotype (figure 6.6B, screen 2). I selected Black-and-white.
3. Select the image you want to modify (figure 6.6B, screen 3).
4. For a Black-and-white image, you cannot adjust the level of lightness or darkness. For Sepia and Cyanotype, you can use the Multi selector to saturate or

desaturate the tone. Scroll up or down and watch the screen until the tint is as dark or light as you want it to be. You can cancel the operation by pressing the Playback button. Figure 6.6B, screen 4 displays the final, adjusted image.

5. Press the OK button to save the new image with a new file name. A screen that says *Image saved* will appear briefly, and then the final image will appear with a retouch icon in the top left of the Monitor (not shown).

Figure 6.6B – Monochrome (Black-and-white) image creation

Settings Recommendation: I normally use the Black-and-white conversion when I need an immediate Monochrome image. However, it's a lot of fun to make the image look old-fashioned with either Sepia or Cyanotype. New Sepia-toned images can look very old if you dress people accordingly (figure 6.6C).

Figure 6.6C – Sample Sepia image conversion (border from Photoshop manipulation)

Filter Effects

(User's Manual – Page 348)

The D800 allows you to add various filter effects to any image. You can intensify the image colors in certain ways and add starburst effects to points of light. You can even experiment with a soft filter effect for a dreamy look.

Here is a list of the effects that are available:

- Skylight
- Warm filter
- Red intensifier
- Green intensifier
- Blue intensifier
- Cross screen (starburst filter)
- Soft

Figure 6.7A shows a red, green, and blue (RGB) test subject. Let's use this subject to compare the changes made by each filter effect, and in the end we will look at the changes all together.

Figure 6.7A – RGB test subject: my Lego blocks again

Skylight Filter Effect

The *Skylight* filter effect is rather mild and removes the blue effect caused by atmospheric diffraction in distant scenes. Basically, by using this effect you will make the image slightly less blue.

Figure 6.7B – Skylight filter effect

Use the following steps to choose the Skylight filter effect (figure 6.7B):

1. Select Filter effects from the Retouch Menu and scroll to the right (figure 6.7B, screen 1).
2. Select Skylight and scroll to the right (figure 6.7B, screen 2).
3. Choose an image and press the OK button (figure 6.7B, screen 3).
4. You will see the image with the Skylight effect added (figure 6.7B, screen 4). Press the OK button to save the image with a new file name or press the Playback button to cancel.

Warm Filter Effect

The *Warm filter* filter effect adds a mild red cast to the image to make it appear a little warmer.

Figure 6.7C – Warm filter effect

Here's how to set the Warm filter effect (figure 6.7C):

1. Select Filter effects from the Retouch Menu and scroll to the right (figure 6.7C, screen 1).
2. Select Warm filter and scroll to the right (figure 6.7C, screen 2).
3. Choose an image and press the OK button (figure 6.7C, screen 3).
4. You will see the image with the Warm filter effect added (figure 6.7C, screen 4). Press the OK button to save the image with a new file name or press the Playback button to cancel.

Red Intensifier Filter Effect

The *Red intensifier* filter effect intensifies the reds in an image. There are three levels of intensity.

Figure 6.7D – Red intensifier filter effect

Here's how to set the Red intensifier filter effect (figure 6.7D):

1. Select Filter effects from the Retouch Menu and scroll to the right (figure 6.7D, screen 1).
2. Select Red intensifier and scroll to the right (figure 6.7D, screen 2).
3. Choose an image and press the OK button (figure 6.7D, screen 3).
4. You will see a new image with the Red intensifier effect added (figure 6.7D, screen 4). You can control the intensity of this effect by using the Multi Selector to scroll up or down when the image is on the screen. The default level of intensity is applied first. You can scroll up for the maximum effect and scroll down for the minimum effect.
5. Press the OK button to save the image with a new file name or press the Playback button to cancel.

Green Intensifier Filter Effect

The *Green intensifier* filter effect intensifies the greens in an image. There are three levels of intensity.

Here's how to set the Green intensifier filter effect (figure 6.7E):

1. Select Filter effects from the Retouch Menu and scroll to the right (figure 6.7E, screen 1).
2. Select Green intensifier and scroll to the right (figure 6.7E, screen 2).
3. Choose an image and press the OK button (figure 6.7E, screen 3).

4. You will see a new image with the Green intensifier effect added (figure 6.7E, screen 4). You can control the intensity of this effect by using the Multi Selector to scroll up or down when the image is on the screen. The default level of intensity is applied first. You can scroll up for the maximum effect and scroll down for the minimum effect.

5. Press the OK button to save the image with a new file name or press the Playback button to cancel.

Figure 6.7E – Green intensifier filter effect

Blue Intensifier Filter Effect

The *Blue intensifier* filter effect intensifies the blues in an image. There are three levels of intensity.

Figure 6.7F – Blue intensifier filter effect

Here's how to set the Blue intensifier effect (figure 6.7F):

1. Select Filter effects from the Retouch Menu and scroll to the right (figure 6.7F, screen 1).
2. Select Blue intensifier and scroll to the right (figure 6.7F, screen 2).
3. Choose an image and press the OK button (figure 6.7F, screen 3).
4. You will see a new image with the Blue intensifier effect added (figure 6.7F, screen 4). You can control the intensity of this effect by using the Multi Selector to scroll up or down when the image is on the screen. The default level of intensity is applied first. You can scroll up for the maximum effect and scroll down for the minimum effect.
5. Press the OK button to save the image with a new file name or press the Playback button to cancel.

Let's take a look at the filters side by side to compare their effects (figure 6.7G).

Figure 6.7G – Filter effects compared

I increased the filter effects to their maximum settings (Darker) in screens 4 through 6 to give you a better view of the effect. It can be hard to show effects like this in a book due to the subtlety of the color shift. I can say from personal observation that there is a distinct effect for each of the intensifier filters in particular. They do intensify the individual color without adding a strong cast to the overall image.

Cross Screen Filter Effect

The *Cross screen* filter effect adds a starburst to any points of light. There are four adjustments for this effect, along with Confirm and Save commands.

Figure 6.7H – Cross screen filter effect

To create the Cross screen filter effect, use the following steps (figure 6.7H):

1. Select Filter effects from the Retouch Menu and scroll to the right (figure 6.7H, screen 1).
2. Select Cross screen and scroll to the right (figure 6.7H, screen 2).
3. Choose an image with the Multi selector and press the OK button to select it (figure 6.7H, screen 3).
4. Now follow steps 5 through 10. Step 5 and figure 6.7I starts where figure 6.7H, screen 3, leaves off.

   Note: Through this upcoming series of Cross screen effect pictures (figures 6.7I–6.7M), you will not see a change in the appearance of the candle until the end when I apply the Confirm step. At that point, all the settings are applied and the appearance changes to its final form, ready for the Save step.

5. The first adjustment is the Number of points (4, 6, or 8) in the starburst (figure 6.7I). Scroll to the right to select the Number of points. In the image on the right, you can see that an icon with the number of rays in the starburst is provided along with a numeral. I selected 8 points. Press the OK button to lock in your selection. You will follow the same procedure for the next three adjustments, which are Filter amount, Filter angle, and Length of points.

Figure 6.7I – Cross screen filter effect – Number of points

6. The second adjustment is the Filter amount (figure 6.7J). This adjustment affects the brightness of the light source(s). The more Xs, the brighter the light source. I selected the maximum level, as you can see in screen 2.

Figure 6.7J – Cross screen filter effect – Filter amount

7. Select the angle of the starburst rays with the Filter angle adjustment (figure 6.7K). You can rotate the rays in a clockwise direction until the starburst is at the angle you prefer.

Figure 6.7K – Cross screen filter effect – Filter angle

8. Select the length of the starburst rays with the Length of points adjustment (figure 6.7L). I wanted the longest rays, so I selected the bottom setting, shown in screen 2.

Figure 6.7L – Cross screen filter effect – Length of points

9. Select Confirm to see the effect applied to your image (figure 6.7M). This is like an update button. You can change the adjustments in steps 5 through 8 multiple times and Confirm them each time to see the updated image until you're happy with the effect. Screens 1 and 2 of figure 6.7M show the image before and after I selected Confirm.

Figure 6.7M – Cross screen filter effect – Confirm

10. Select Save and press the OK button (figure 6.7N, screen 1). After a moment you'll see a screen that says *Image saved* (figure 6.7N, screen 2). Then you'll see the full-size image in normal Playback mode (figure 6.7N, screen 3). Notice the retouch icon at the top left of the image, which tells you that the image has been retouched. This is the final, fully retouched version of the image (screen 3).

Figure 6.7N – Cross screen filter effect – Save

Soft Filter Effect

The *Soft* filter effect is designed to give your subject that dreamy look popularized by old movies, where the beautiful woman looks soft and sweet. You can select from three levels of softness: Low, Normal, and High.

Figure 6.7O – Soft filter effect samples

Figure 6.7O shows small versions of the original image and the three softness settings. The images are in this order: 1 = Original, 2 = Low, 3 = Normal, 4 = High.

This is an interesting effect. Even though the overall image has a softness to
it after the effect has been applied, the subject is still somewhat sharp. It doesn't
look like the image is soft because it's not in focus or the camera moved. It's like a
softness has been overlaid on the image, and the original image is still sharp. You'll
have to see this misty look in a full-size image to see what I mean.

Figure 6.7P – Soft filter effect settings

Use the following steps to select one of the Soft filter levels for your image (figure
6.7P):

1. Select Filter effects from the Retouch Menu and scroll to the right (figure 6.7P,
   screen 1).
2. Choose Soft from the menu and scroll to the right (figure 6.7P, screen 2).
3. Select the image to which you want to apply the Soft filter effect and press the
   OK button (figure 6.7P, screen 3).
4. You'll see the word Normal surrounded by yellow (figure 6.7P, screen 4, red
   arrow). Use the Multi selector to scroll up or down and select one of the softness
   levels (Low, Normal, or High). The small image on the left is the original image,
   and the one on the right is the adjusted image. You can easily see the softness
   vary as you select different levels.
5. Press the OK button to save the new image and display it on the Monitor.

Settings Recommendation: In comparing the levels of softness, I tend to like the
Normal setting best. Low looks like I made a mistake, and High is too soft. Compare
the three levels and see which works best for you.

Color Balance

(User's Manual – Page 349)

Color balance lets you deliberately add various tones to your pictures. You can visually add a mild or strong color cast. You might want to warm things up a bit by adding a touch of red or cool things down with a touch of blue. Or you could get creative and add various color casts to an image for special effects.

You can tone the image with the following color casts:

- Green
- Blue
- Amber
- Magenta

Figure 6.8A – Color balance samples

Figure 6.8A shows four samples of the colors used for tinting. Notice the red arrow in screen 1 that points to the color box. You move the little black square around in the color box to add tints to the image. In screens 1 though 4 you can see that I moved the tiny black square into different areas of the color box. The small picture above the color box shows how the final image will look. You can return the square to the center of the color box to neutralize any tints.

On the right side of each screen you can see the RGB histograms for the image. As you make color changes, you will see the color shift in the histograms. Be careful not to over- or underexpose any of the colors (clip them off on the right or left) or you will lose detail in that particular color channel (R, G, or B). We'll discuss the histogram in more detail in the chapter **Metering, Exposure Modes, and Histogram**.

Figure 6.8B – Color balance settings

Use the following steps to modify the Color balance in your image:

1. Select Color balance from the Retouch Menu and scroll to the right (figure 6.8B, screen 1).
2. Select the image you want to modify and press the OK button (figure 6.8B, screen 2).
3. Use the Multi selector to move the black indicator square in the center of the color box toward whatever color makes you happy (figure 6.8B, screen 3). Watch the histograms as they display the changing color relationships between the red, green, and blue color channels. You can see the color changes or casts as they are applied to the small version of your image in the upper-left corner of the screen (screen 3).
4. Press the Playback button to cancel or the OK button to save the image with a new file name (figure 6.8B, screen 4).

Note: If you zoom in with the Playback zoom in button, the camera will update the histogram to reflect only what can be seen on the Monitor. This is a nice way to get a histogram for only a portion of your subject.

Settings Recommendation: This is a cool function for persnickety people, and I'm one of them! If you like to fine-tune the color of your pictures—but hate using the computer—here's your control. You can introduce almost any color tint into the image by moving the black square in any direction within the color box, using combinations of colors to arrive at one that pleases you. This also allows you to overcome current color casts caused by various lighting-source color temperatures. Very flexible camera, eh?

Image Overlay

(User's Manual – Page 350)

The *Image overlay* function is a nice way to combine two RAW images as if they were taken as a multiple exposure. Basically, you can select a couple of NEF (RAW) shots and combine them into a new overlaid image.

The results can be a lot like what you get when using *Shooting Menu > Multiple exposure*, but Image overlay gives you a visual way to overlay two separate images instead of shooting multiple exposures on one picture.

The results can be high quality because the overlay is done using RAW image data. You can vary the density of each image, with a review display (overlay) showing how the combined image will appear, before you make the final combination of the two images.

Figure 6.9 – Image overlay settings

Use the following steps to do an Image overlay (figure 6.9):

1. Select Image overlay from the Retouch Menu and scroll to the right (figure 6.9, screen 1).
2. Select the RAW Image 1 box (outlined in yellow in figure 6.9, screen 2) from the combination screen and press the OK button to open the selection screen.
3. Select an image from the selection screen (figure 6.9, screen 3). Press the OK button again to return to the combination screen with an image selected in the

Image 1 position (figure 6.9, screen 4). You can vary the gain of the first image by using the Multi selector to scroll up or down in the X1.0 field (figure 6.9, screen 4). The X1.0 setting is variable from X0.1 to X2.0. It lets you control how bright or dark (dense) an image is so it can more closely match the density of the other image in the overlay. X1.0 is normal image density, as shown.

4. Use the Multi selector to move the yellow box to the RAW Image 2 position (figure 6.9, screen 5). Press the OK button again and select the second picture from the image selection screen (figure 6.9, screen 6).

5. Press the OK button to insert the image into the Image 2 position (figure 6.9, screen 7). As mentioned in step 3, you can use the X1.0 field to vary the density of an image, in this case the second image in the overlay (figure 6.9, screen 7). Try to match the density of Image 1 as much as possible to provide a realistic overlay.

6. Use the Multi selector to move the yellow box to the Preview area. You will see two selections below it: Overlay and Save. Choose one of them and press the OK button (figure 6.9, screen 8).

   a. If you select Overlay, the D800 will temporarily combine the images and you will see another screen that displays a larger view of the new image (not shown). You can press the OK button to save the image with a new file name, or you can press the checkered Thumbnail/Playback zoom out button to return to the previous screen.

   b. If you choose Save instead of Overlay and press the OK button, the D800 immediately combines the two images and saves the image with a new file name without letting you review the image first. Basically, the Save selection saves now, and Overlay gives you a preview of the combination so you can modify or save it.

Settings Recommendation: This is an easy way to overlay images without a computer. There are some drawbacks, though. One image may have a strong background that is impossible to remove no matter how much you adjust the gain or image density (X0.1 to X2.0). This is a situation in which a computer excels because you can use software tools like masking in Capture NX 2 or Photoshop to remove parts of the background and make a more realistic overlay. However, if you must combine two images in the field, you have a way to do it in-camera.

NEF (RAW) Processing

(User's Manual – Page 353)

NEF (RAW) processing is a function that allows you to convert a RAW image into a JPEG inside the camera. If you normally shoot in RAW but need a JPEG quickly, this is a great function. It works only on images taken with the D800, so you can't insert a card from a different Nikon and expect to process its images.

There is quite a comprehensive catalog of things you can do to an image during NEF (RAW) processing. A RAW file is not yet an image, so the camera settings you used when you took the picture are not permanently applied. In effect, when you use NEF (RAW) processing, you are applying camera settings to the JPEG image after the fact, and you can change the settings you used when you originally took the picture.

You can apply settings just before you take a picture through the Shooting Menu or by using external camera controls. However, with NEF (RAW) processing, the settings are applied to the image after the fact instead of while shooting. See the chapter titled **Shooting Menu** for a thorough explanation of each setting.

Here's a list of post-shooting adjustments you can make with NEF (RAW) processing, with basic explanations of each function:

- *EXE* – This simply means execute. When you select this and press the OK button, all your new settings will be applied to a new JPEG image, and it will be saved to the memory card with a separate file name.
- *Image quality* – With NEF (RAW) processing, you are converting a RAW file to a JPEG file, so the camera gives you a choice of FINE, NORM, or BASIC. These are equivalent to the *Shooting Menu > Image quality* settings called JPEG fine, JPEG normal, or JPEG basic.
- *Image size* – This lets you select how large the JPEG file will be. Your choices are L, M, or S, which are equivalent to the Large (36.2 megapixels), Medium (20.3 megapixels), and Small (9.0 megapixels) *Shooting Menu > Image size* settings.
- *White balance* – This lets you change the White balance of the image after you have already taken the image. You can select from a series of symbols that represent various types of White balance color temperatures. As you scroll up or down in the list of symbols, notice that the name of the corresponding White balance type appears just above the small picture. You can see the effect of each setting as it is applied.
- *Exposure compensation* – This function allows you to brighten or darken the image by applying -/+ Exposure compensation to it. You can apply compensation up to 2 EV in either direction (+2.0 to -2.0 EV).
- *Picture control* – With this setting you can apply a different Picture Control than the one with which you took the image. It shows abbreviations for each Nikon Picture Control (SD, NL, VI, MC, PT, or LS) plus any Custom Picture Controls you might have created with the designations of C-1, C-2, C-3, and so forth.
- *High ISO NR* – You can change the amount of High ISO noise reduction applied to the image. The camera offers you H, N, L, and Off settings, which are equivalent to the *Shooting Menu > High ISO NR* settings called High, Normal, Low, and Off.

- **Color space** – You can change which Color space is applied to the image. You can choose from the camera's two Color space settings, sRGB or Adobe RGB. Adobe RGB is abbreviated as Adobe in this setting. This is equivalent to the *Shooting Menu > Color space* setting.

- **Vignette control** – This allows you to reduce the light falloff on the corners and edges of the frame, common when using a full-frame sensor with certain lenses. You have four choices: Off, Low (L), Normal (N), and High (H).

- **D-Lighting** – This lets you manage the level of contrast in the image by brightening the shadows and protecting the highlights. You have four choices: Off, Low (L), Normal (N), and High (H).

Figure 6.10A – NEF (RAW) processing

Now, let's look at the steps you can use to convert a file from NEF (RAW) to JPEG in-camera (figures 6.10A–6.10N):

1. Select NEF (RAW) processing from the Retouch Menu and scroll to the right (figure 6.10A, screen 1).

2. Select a RAW image with the Multi selector and press the OK button (figure 6.10A, screen 2). Only NEF (RAW) images will show in the list. Now we'll look at each setting shown in figure 6.10A, screen 3. The following steps and figures (6.10B to 6.10N) begin where figure 6.10A, screen 3 leaves off.

3. Select one of the Image quality settings—FINE, NORM, or BASIC—from the Image quality menu (figure 6.10B, screen 2). FINE gives you the best possible quality in a JPEG image. Press the OK button to save the setting and return to the main NEF (RAW) processing configuration screen. You can cancel the operation with the Playback button. You can zoom in to check the image quality with the Playback zoom in button.

Figure 6.10B – NEF (RAW) processing – Image quality

4. Select one of the Image size settings from the Image size menu (figure 6.10C, screen 2):

   - L – Large (7360×4912; 36.2 MP)
   - M – Medium (5520×3680; 20.3 MP)
   - S – Small (3680×2456; 9.0 MP)

   When you've selected a setting, press the OK button to return to the main NEF (RAW) processing configuration screen. You can cancel the operation with the Playback button or zoom in to check the image quality with the Playback zoom in button.

Figure 6.10C – NEF (RAW) processing – Image size

5. Select one of the White balance settings for your new JPEG (figures 6.10D to 6.10G). You can choose from AUTO, Incandescent, Fluorescent, Direct sunlight, Flash, Cloudy, Shade, K - Choose color temp., or PRE - Preset manual. Please review the chapter titled **White Balance** for detailed information on each of these selections. The Fluorescent, K, and PRE settings have an additional screen with choices you must select. AUTO is selected in this example (figure 6.10D, screen 2). We won't consider how to select each individual White balance setting because they work the same as AUTO (three screens). However, because Fluorescent, K, and PRE are different, we will look at each of those settings individually (four screens).

Figure 6.10D – NEF (RAW) processing – White balance

   a. **Fluorescent** – You must choose a type of fluorescent light. There are seven choices, with names like Sodium-vapor lamps, Warm-white fluorescent, Cool-white fluorescent, etc. Each choice has a number assigned to it. Figure 6.10E, screen 3, shows Cool-white fluorescent, which is number 4 on the list. Scroll to the right to move to the fine-tuning screen, where you can adjust the color tint of the image by moving the black dot in the color box (figure 6.10E, screen 4). Press the OK button to save the setting, or press the Playback button to cancel.

Figure 6.10E – NEF (RAW) processing – White balance – Fluorescent

b. *K - Choose color temp.* – You can choose a color temperature from the list shown in figure 6.10F, screen 3. Remember that color temperatures change how the image color looks by warming it (reddish) or cooling it (bluish). The list ranges from 2500K (cool) to 10000K (warm). You can also use the fine-tuning screen to modify the color's base, if you'd like (figure 6.10F, screen 4). Press the OK button to save the setting or the Playback button to cancel.

Figure 6.10F – NEF (RAW) processing – White balance – K-Choose color temp.

c. **PRE - Preset manual** – With this setting you can choose an already-saved White balance that you previously obtained while letting the camera measure the ambient light reflected from a gray or white card (the PRE method). See the chapter titled **White Balance** for information on doing ambient light (PRE) readings. You can choose from up to four previous PRE readings that are stored in memory locations d-1 to d-4 (figure 6.10G, screen 3). As you scroll through the list of settings, you'll be able to see the color temperature of the image change. Select the setting you want to use and press the OK button to return to the main NEF (RAW) processing configuration screen. You can fine-tune the colors of the individual White balance by using the settings shown in figure 6.10G, screen 4. You'll see your fine-tuning adjustment change the color temperature of the image. If you don't want to fine-tune the White balance, simply press the OK button when you get to the fine-tuning screen. The camera will return to the main NEF (RAW) processing configuration screen. You can cancel the operation with the Playback button.

Figure 6.10G – NEF (RAW) processing – White balance – PRE-Preset manual

6. Now you have an opportunity to lighten or darken the image by selecting an Exposure compensation value of +/- 2.0 EV steps (figure 6.10H, screen 2). In screen 1 of figure 6.10H, you can see that the image is a little overexposed because my D800 tends to shoot a little hot some of the time. In screen 2, you can see that I removed one stop of light (-1.0 EV). The image looks about right at that setting. When your image looks just right, press the OK button to save the setting and return to the main NEF (RAW) processing configuration screen. You can cancel the operation with the Playback button.

Figure 6.10H – NEF (RAW) processing – Exposure compensation

7. Next, you can apply a Nikon Picture Control or one of your own Custom Picture Controls, if you have created any (figure 6.10I, screen 2). You can make the image sharper and give it more contrast, give it more or less color saturation, or even change it to monochrome. In fact, you can even modify the current Picture Control's settings by using the fine-tuning screen (figure 6.10I, screen 3). Choose from SD-Standard, NL-Neutral, VI-Vivid, MC-Monochrome, PT-Portrait, LS-Landscape, or any of your custom controls (C-1 to C-9) that appear farther down the list than this screen shot shows (figure 6.10I, screen 2).

You can scroll to the right with the Multi selector if you want to fine-tune the image (figure 6.10I, screen 3). Scroll up or down to select one of the settings— Sharpening, Contrast, Brightness, and so forth—and then scroll left or right (-/+) to modify the selected setting. If you make a mistake and want to start over, press the Delete button and the camera will display a screen that says *Selected Picture Control will be reset to default settings. OK?* Choose Yes or No and press the OK button. When a Picture Control is adjusted so that it's different from the factory default, an asterisk will appear next to its name in all menus. The Monochrome (MC) Picture Control not only lets you adjust things like Sharpening, Contrast, and Brightness in the fine-tuning screen, it also gives you toning (tint) controls like the *Shooting Menu > Set Picture Control* function.

When the image looks just right, press the OK button to save the setting and return to the main NEF (RAW) processing configuration screen. You can cancel the operation with the Playback button.

Figure 6.10I – NEF (RAW) processing – Picture Control

8. If the image needs high ISO noise reduction, you can apply it now (figure 6.10J, screen 1). You have a choice of four settings: High (H), Normal (N), Low (L), or Off (figure 6.10J, screen 2). Choose one and press the OK button to save the setting and return to the main NEF (RAW) processing configuration screen. You can cancel the operation with the Playback button.

Figure 6.10J – NEF (RAW) processing – High ISO NR

9. Color space lets you choose one of the camera's two color space settings, sRGB or AdobeRGB (figure 6.10K, screen 2). Choose one and press the OK button to save the setting and return to the main NEF (RAW) processing configuration screen. You can cancel the operation with the Playback button. As a comparative test, why not look carefully at your picture while you switch back and forth between sRGB and AdobeRGB. You will find that AdobeRGB has a smoother look, if not quite as saturated, when your subject has a good range of colors. AdobeRGB has a wider color gamut and is best for commercial printing, whereas sRGB may do better with computer and Internet display and home printing on basic inkjet printers.

Figure 6.10K – NEF (RAW) processing – Color space

10. Vignette control lets you choose a level for edge and corner light falloff correction (figure 6.10L, screen 2), as is sometimes needed on an FX-sized imaging sensor with certain lenses. You have a choice of four settings: High (H), Normal (N), Low (L), or Off. Choose one and press the OK button to save the setting and return to the main NEF (RAW) processing configuration screen. You can cancel the operation with the Playback button.

Figure 6.10L – NEF (RAW) processing – Vignette control

11. D-lighting (figure 6.10M) is very similar to *Shooting Menu > Active D-Lighting* in that it restores shadow detail and protects highlights in your images. However, D-Lighting is applied after the fact. Active D-Lighting is applied at the time the image is taken. Otherwise, they are basically the same thing. You can select from high (H), normal (N), low (L), or Off (figure 6.10M, screen 2). Press the OK button to set the D-Lighting level, or press the Playback button to cancel.

Figure 6.10M – NEF (RAW) processing – D-Lighting

12. When you are finished with NEF (RAW) processing, scroll down to the EXE (execute) selection and press the OK button (figure 6.10N, screen 1). An hourglass will appear for a few seconds while the new JPEG is being created with your carefully crafted settings. An *Image saved* screen will appear briefly (figure 6.10N, screen 2), indicating that the new JPEG has been saved on the memory card with a new file name, and the image will be displayed on the Monitor (figure 6.10N, screen 3). You can cancel the operation with the Playback button.

Figure 6.10N – NEF (RAW) processing – EXE

This is a nice way to create specialized JPEG images from NEF (RAW) files without using a computer. How much longer will it be until our cameras come with keyboard, monitor, and mouse ports? They are powerful graphics processing computers after all! (Hmmm, Angry Birds on a 3.2-inch Monitor wouldn't be too bad.)

Settings Recommendation: NEF (RAW) processing is a complex, multistep process because you're doing a major conversion from NEF (RAW) to JPEG in-camera, without using your computer. You're in complete control of each level of the conversion and can even replace the camera settings you originally used when you took the picture. If you want to simply convert the image without going through all these steps, just choose the EXE selection first and press the OK button. That will convert the image immediately with the camera settings you used to take the picture.

Resize

(User's Manual – Page 355)

The *Resize* function allows you to convert an image from a full-size 36.2M (7360×4912) picture to a smaller one, with four available megapixel sizes. This function seems to be designed so you can create images that can easily be e-mailed or used on a website or blog. There are three selections:

- *Select image* – This selection allows you to choose one or more images for resizing.
- *Choose destination* – This selection allows you to choose a destination for the resized pictures.
- *Choose size* – You can choose from four image sizes:
  - 1920×1280; 2.5M
  - 1280×856; 1.1M
  - 960×640; 0.6M
  - 640×424; 0.3M

Figure 6.11A – Resize – Choose destination

Let's examine the steps for resizing images (figure 6.11A):

1. Select Resize from the Retouch Menu and scroll to the right (figure 6.11A, screen 1). Although it seems out of order, select Choose destination and scroll to the

right (figure 6. 11A, screen 2). Select either SD card slot or CF card slot to be a destination for the resized images and press the OK button (figure 6.11A, screen 3). This selection will be grayed out if one of the memory card slots is empty. In that case, the destination will be the single card slot that contains a card. Skip this step if you are using only one memory card.

2. Next, select Choose size and scroll to the right (figure 6.11B, screen 2). You will see four sizes, from 2.5M to 0.3M (figure 6.11B, screen 3). These are the actual megapixel sizes available for images after you save them. Select a size and press the OK button.

Figure 6.11B – Resize – Choose size

3. Next, choose Select image and scroll to the right (figure 6.11C, screen 2). You'll see six image thumbnails. Use the Multi selector to scroll around in this group of thumbnails and press the Thumbnail/playback zoom out button to select an image you want to resize. You can select as many images as you'd like, and each of them will be resized. A tiny resize symbol will appear in the top-right corner of each thumbnail you select (figure 6.11C, screen 3, red arrow). Notice that the top three images in the list of six images have been selected.

Figure 6.11C – Resize – Select image

4. When you have selected the images, press the OK button. A screen will appear with a message asking, *Create resized copy? N images* (figure 6.11C, screen 4). Select Yes and press the OK button to create the resized images. An hourglass will be displayed on the Monitor while the images are resized, and then an *Image saved* screen will briefly appear (figure 6.11C, screen 5). The last image in the group of resized images will appear on the Monitor (figure 6.11C, screen 6). The resized images will look just like the originals except they'll each have a retouch icon in the top-left corner (figure 6.11C, screen 6).

Settings Recommendation: I use this function when I'm in the field and want to make a small image to send via e-mail. The full-size JPEG file is too large to send through some e-mail systems. It's nice to have a way to reduce image size without having to find a computer. Please notice that this function does not reduce the image size by cropping, like the Trim function we studied earlier. Instead, it simply reduces the image size in the same aspect ratio as the original, except it has fewer megapixels.

Quick Retouch

(User's Manual – Page 357)

If you want to adjust an image without much effort so that all parameters are within viewable range, use the *Quick retouch* function. It creates a new copy of an existing image with "enhanced saturation and contrast," according to the User's Manual. D-Lighting is automatically applied to your old image, and the new image is supposed to look better. You can scroll up and down in the preview screen to see the range of enhancements that can be applied when the new image is created.

Figure 6.12 – Quick retouch of an image

Here are the steps to use Quick retouch (figure 6.12):

1. Select Quick retouch from the Retouch Menu and scroll to the right (figure 6.12, screen 1).
2. You'll see the images on your memory card(s) that are eligible for Quick retouch. Use the Multi selector to scroll to an image you want to retouch, and press the OK button to select it (figure 6.12, screen 2).
3. Use the Multi selector to scroll up or down, and then select High, Normal, or Low (figure 6.12, screen 3). You can preview the effect of your changes on the image by looking at the before and after images. I chose Normal.
4. Press the OK button when you're satisfied with the look. The new image will be created and displayed on the Monitor (figure 6.12, screen 4).

Settings Recommendation: This function can give some images a little more snap. I use Quick retouch only if I am going to give someone an image directly out of the camera and want to enhance it a little first. This function can be used for quick saturation and contrast enhancements.

Straighten
(User's Manual – Page 357)

Straighten is another excellent and useful function. Often, I'll be shooting a landscape or ocean view handheld, and in my excitement I'll forget to level the horizon. With Straighten I can adjust the image to level before anyone else sees it.

You can rotate an image up to 5 degrees clockwise or counterclockwise. You use the Multi selector to scroll right or left through a graduated scale line. Each increment is equal to about 0.25 degrees. As you rotate the image, the camera will automatically trim the edges so that the picture looks normal. Of course, this means you are throwing away some of the image and making it smaller. However, it's better for the image to be a little smaller and have a nice level horizon, don't you think?

Here are the steps to straighten an image (figure 6.13):

1. Select Straighten from the Retouch Menu and scroll to the right (figure 6.13, screen 1).
2. You'll see the images on your memory card(s). Use the Multi selector to scroll to the one you want to straighten and press the OK button to select it (figure 6.13, screen 2).
3. Now, rotate the image to the left (counterclockwise) or right (clockwise) in 0.25 degree increments using the Multi selector. The little yellow pointer moves as you press the Multi selector to the left or right (figure 6.13, screens 3 and 4, red arrows).
4. When you are happy with the new image, press the OK button to save it or the Playback button to cancel (figure 6.13, screen 5).

5. An *Image saved* screen will briefly appear between screens 5 and 6 (not shown).
6. Finally, you will see the newly saved image on the Monitor (figure 6.13, screen 6).

Figure 6.13 – Straighten an image

Settings Recommendation: This is a handy function to level an image—as long as it is not tilted more than 5 degrees—without using a computer. Some of us tend to tilt our cameras just a little when we take pictures. Use this function to save embarrassment later.

Distortion Control

(User's Manual – Page 358)

The *Distortion control* function is a companion to the Straighten function. Whereas the Straighten function is concerned with leveling the image left to right, the Distortion control function is concerned with barrel and pincushion distortion. Barrel distortion causes the edges of a subject to bow outward, like a barrel. Pincushion distortion is the opposite: the edges bow inward, like an hourglass. Using this control will remove some of the edge of the image as distortion compensation takes place. There are two settings in the Distortion control function: Auto and Manual.

Auto Distortion Control

You can use this setting only if you have a D or G lens on your D800. Select Auto when you want the camera to automatically make rough distortion adjustments. Then you can fine-tune the adjustments yourself if you think the new image needs it.

Figure 6.14A – Auto Distortion control

Here are the steps to let the camera make an Auto distortion adjustment (figure 6.14A):

1. Select Distortion control from the Retouch Menu and scroll to the right (figure 6.14A, screen 1).
2. Choose Auto from the menu to let the camera make automatic distortion adjustments (figure 6.14A, screen 2).
3. Next you'll see the images on your memory card. Use the Multi selector to select the one you want to fix and press the OK button (figure 6.14A, screen 3).
4. The camera will automatically make its best adjustment and then display the adjusted image (figure 6.14A, screen 4). The red arrow in screen 4 points to the yellow adjustment pointer, which will be centered. If you are not satisfied with the camera's Auto adjustment, use the Multi selector to move the yellow pointer along the scale to the left to remove pincushion distortion (add barrel) or to the right to remove barrel distortion (add pincushion). Screens 5 and 6 in Figure 6.14A show the maximum settings (red arrows).
5. When you are happy with the appearance of the image, press the OK button to save it or the Playback button to cancel (not shown).

The effect is not easy to see in these small images or on the Monitor of the camera. However, if you look closely at figure 6.14A, screen 5, and compare it to screen 6, you can see a slight difference. Greater adjustments should be made on a computer with full-sized images.

Manual distortion adjustments work the same way, except the camera does not make an Auto adjustment before displaying an image that you can manually adjust.

Manual Distortion Control

You are in control of this operation. You can adjust the image until you think it looks good, without interference from the camera. It makes no initial distortion adjustment as Auto does.

Figure 6.14B – Manual Distortion control

Here are the steps to manually correct distortion (figure 6.14B):

1. Select Distortion control from the Retouch Menu and scroll to the right (figure 6.14B, screen 1).
2. Choose Manual from the menu and scroll to the right (figure 6.14B, screen 2).
3. You'll see the images on your memory card. Use the Multi selector to scroll to the one you want to fix and press the OK button (figure 6.14B, screen 3). You can zoom in to check the image with the Playback zoom in button.
4. The image will be displayed with the yellow pointer centered under the scale (figure 6.14B, screen 4, red arrow). No adjustment has been made at this point. Move the yellow pointer along the scale to the left to remove pincushion distortion (add barrel) or to the right to remove barrel distortion (add pincushion). Full barrel distortion correction is applied in figure 6.14B, screen 5 (red arrow). As with the Auto distortion adjustment, the Manual distortion adjustment is rather minor.
5. When you are happy with the appearance of the image, press the OK button to save it or the Playback button to cancel. You'll see the new adjusted image on the Monitor.

Settings Recommendation: This function is only somewhat useful because it does not allow for larger corrections. However, it does allow minor distortion correction for images with just a little distortion. If you have no computer available and need to use an image with a touch of distortion quickly, this function may be helpful.

Fisheye

(User's Manual – Page 261)

The *Fisheye* function is quite fun! You can distort your friends and make hilarious pictures that will make everyone laugh (well, maybe not everyone). Although the results are not true circular fisheye images, they do have a similar distorted appearance.

Figure 6.15A – Fisheye distortion samples

Figure 6.15A shows two samples of the Fisheye setting. Notice the small yellow pointer at the bottom under the scale. When it's all the way to the left, the image appears normal. The farther right you move it, the more distorted the image. (Can you detect trouble brewing with wives and girlfriends? I carefully used a picture of my son to stay out of trouble!)

Figure 6.15B – Fisheye settings

Here are the steps to use Fisheye to distort one of your images (figure 6.15B):

1. Select Fisheye from the Retouch Menu and scroll to the right (figure 6.15B, screen 1).

2. You'll see the images on your camera's memory card(s). Scroll to the one you want to distort and press the OK button to select it (figure 6.15B, screen 2).
3. Now press the Multi selector to the right and watch the yellow pointer move and the distortion grow (figure 6.15B, screen 3).
4. When you have found the perfect distortion amount (to the max, right?), simply press the OK button to save the image or the Playback button to cancel (figure 6.15B, screen 4).

Settings Recommendation: Be careful with this one! If you publish many pictures of your friends with this effect, I'm afraid they'll start running when they see you with your camera.

Color Outline

(User's Manual – Page 359)

Have you ever wanted to convert one of your images to a cartoon or a line drawing? This retouch setting creates an interesting outline effect on the distinct lines or color changes in your image. Figure 6.16A shows an original image and the image after Color outline was applied. The final image is not actually in color; it is black-and-white to allow an artist to fill (computer), draw (colored pencils and crayons), or paint (oil and watercolor) a print's colors.

Figure 6.16A – Color outline sample

You can convert an image to a color outline, open it in Photoshop, and use the fill functions to add cartoon colors between the lines (like the Color sketch function, coming up next). Or you can post-process the image into a fine-art line tracing. This is an unusual functionality and shows the direction that our highly computerized cameras are going. They have computer power built in, so why not make use of it in new and fun ways?

Notice in figure 6.16A that the camera did not pick up the background. This is because the background is blurred from my using a large aperture. There are no strong edges in the background for an outline to be applied to. From this you can see that if you want to eliminate the background in your image, you can use a large aperture or telephoto lens to blur the background and the camera will ignore it.

Figure 6.16B – Color outline settings

Here are the steps to create a Color outline (figure 6.16B):

1. Choose Color outline from the Retouch Menu and scroll to the right (figure 6.16B, screen 1).
2. Select an image from the list of thumbnails. You can either press the OK button to start the conversion to outline form or press the Playback zoom in button to check the image (figure 6.16B, screen 2). If you press the OK button, you will see an hourglass for a few seconds while the image is converted.
3. After conversion, press the OK button to save the new image or the Playback button to cancel (figure 6.16B, screen 3). The new image will appear on the Monitor (figure 6.16B, screen 4).

Settings Recommendation: The Color outline setting gives you the opportunity to be creative and have some fun with your images. It creates a very sparse image that resembles a line drawing. You could use this as a basis for a painting, hand coloring, or just to have a cool-looking image that most cameras won't make.

Color Sketch

(User's Manual – Page 359)

With the *Color sketch* function, you can create a copy of your image that looks (somewhat) like a sketch made with colored pencils or crayons. This function is similar to Color outline except it uses pastel colors instead of a gray scale. Figure 6.17A shows an image before and after Color sketch was applied.

You can convert an image to a Color sketch and change the Vividness (pastel color saturation) and Outlines (line and color contrast) until you get the look you want. The converted image in figure 6.17A uses both settings set to maximum.

Figure 6.17A – Color sketch sample

Figure 6.17B – Color sketch settings

Use the following steps to create a Color sketch (figure 6.17B):

1. Choose Color sketch from the Retouch Menu (figure 6.17B, screen 1).
2. Select an image and press the OK button (figure 6.17B, screen 2).
3. You can now set the Vividness, or color saturation, of the pastel colors (figure 6.17B, screen 3).
4. Next, you will choose an Outlines setting, which will change the contrast of the lines and colors (figure 6.17B, screen 4).
5. I set both Vividness and Outlines to the plus side, or maximum (figure 6.17B, screen 5). Press the OK button to make the new image or press the Playback button to cancel.
6. You will see an *Image saved* screen between screens 5 and 6 (not shown), and then the new image will appear on the Monitor (figure 6.17B, screen 6).

Settings Recommendation: Like Color outline, the Color sketch function lets you play around with the post-processing computer in your camera. Occasionally, I like to play with these functions. Are they really useful? Well, I guess it depends on how often you need a Color outline or Color sketch. Maybe you have a great use for them in mind?

Perspective Control

(User's Manual – Page 360)

When you use a wide-angle lens to take a picture from the base of a tall object, like a building, the object will look like it is falling over backward. You can correct the problem with large-format view cameras using their rise, fall, shift, tilt, and swing controls. Nikon makes perspective-control lenses that perform some of the functions of a view camera, namely tilt and shift—for a significant investment, of course.

Nikon has given D800 users some image correction capability with the Straighten, Distortion control, and *Perspective control* functions. We discussed the first two earlier in this chapter. Now let's see how to use Perspective control.

Perspective control allows you to stretch the left, right, top, or bottom of an image in a way that tends to twist leaning objects so they appear straighter in the corrected image. Figure 6.18A, screen 3, shows yellow pointers and their indicators (identified by the red arrows). You can move these pointers to change the perspective of the image by tilting the top toward or away from you or rotating the image to the left or right. This is a powerful control because it can help give certain images a much better perspective.

Figure 6.18A – Adjusting an image with Perspective control

Use the following steps to configure Perspective control (figure 6.18A):

1. Select Perspective control from the Retouch Menu and scroll to the right (figure 6.18A, screen 1).
2. Choose an image from the list of thumbnails and press the OK button (figure 6.18A, screen 2).
3. You will see gridlines for edge comparison and two slider controls that are operated by the Multi selector (figure 6.18A, screen 3). Move the yellow pointer on the vertical scale up or down to tilt the top of the image toward you or away from you. Slide the yellow pointer on the horizontal scale to the left or right to turn the left or right edge toward you or away from you.
4. When the image looks the way you want it, press the OK button to save the image or the Playback button to cancel.

Figure 6.18B shows what happens to the image when you use the vertical slider on the left side. Notice how the top of the subject leans either toward you or away from you (forward-to-backward tilt) according to how the vertical slider is positioned.

Figure 6.18B – Tilting the top of the image

Figure 6.18C shows how the image swings to the left or right as you move the horizontal slider on the bottom. Can you see how powerful this functionality is to control perspective? The camera automatically crops off the top and bottom of the stretched ends to keep the image looking like a normal rectangle, so the final image will be smaller.

Figure 6.18C – Rotating the sides of the image

Settings Recommendation: Learn to use this rather powerful function! You now have excellent Perspective control, with no additional lens purchases! Add Straighten for leveling horizons (rotating the image), Distortion control for removing barrel and pincushion distortion, and finally Perspective control to remove angle distortion, and you have the basics of a graphics software program built right into the camera.

Remember that you can convert RAW files to JPEG with NEF (RAW) processing and use Print set (DPOF) to create a print order and print directly to a PictBridge printer. Why do we need a computer? What an amazing camera!

Miniature Effect

(User's Manual – Page 361)

Miniature effect is unusual because it allows you to create a reverse diorama. A diorama is a small 3-D model that looks like the real thing. You may have seen a city diorama, where there are tiny detailed houses and cars and even figures of people. A diorama is often used to make a movie when the cost would be too high to use real scenes.

The reason I call the Miniature effect a reverse diorama is that the camera takes a real image and uses a very narrow band of sharpness with a very shallow depth of field to make the subject look like a diorama.

Figure 6.19A is a sample Miniature effect image I took while looking at a train depot from a bridge over the tracks. It's best to shoot this type of image from a high vantage point so it looks like a real miniature.

Figure 6.19A – Miniature effect reverse diorama

The camera added extra saturation to the image to make the train cars look unreal. Notice how there is a band of sharpness running horizontally across the middle of the image on this Miniature effect application. That very shallow depth of field in a full-sized image makes it look fake. Depth of field is usually that narrow in closeup and macro shots only.

Figure 6.19B – Miniature effect settings

Here are steps to create your own Miniature effect reverse diorama:

1. Select Miniature effect from the Retouch menu and scroll to the right (figure 6.19B, screen 1).
2. Choose an image shot from a high vantage point that would make a good reverse diorama and press the OK button (figure 6.19B, screen 2).
3. Notice the yellow rectangle in figure 6.19B, screen 3. This band represents a horizontal, movable band of sharpness. You can move it up or down on the screen with the Multi selector until you find the optimum place to put the sharpness. Everything above and below the band is blurry. If you are working with a vertical image, the band will be vertical instead of horizontal. In other words, it is across the image, left to right, no matter what direction you hold the camera when using the horizontal setting. You can change the band of sharpness from horizontal to vertical by pressing the Thumbnail/Playback zoom in button (figure 6.19B, screen 4, red arrow). After you position the band where you want it, press the OK button to save the image.
4. An hourglass will appear while the Miniature effect is applied, and then an *Image saved* screen will appear briefly. You will now see the new Miniature effect image on the Monitor (figure 6.19B, screen 6). It is saved with a new file name on your memory card.

Settings Recommendation: To get good use out of this function, you'll need to be looking down on your subject—for example, from a bridge, the top of a building, or an airplane (unless you are shooting a vertical reverse diorama). It's a lot of fun to make these images, although it's difficult to make one look realistic. Next time you are high above a real scene with lots of detail, try shooting a Miniature effect image for fun.

Selective Color

(User's Manual – Page 362)

Selective color allows you to create black-and-white still images with selective colors left in. We have all seen pictures of a lovely red rose with only the petals having color while the rest of the image is black-and-white. Well, the Nikon D800 goes a step farther than that and allows you to create black-and-white images with up to three selective colors. Let's see how to do it.

Figure 6.20 – Using Selective color

Use these steps to create black-and-white images with up to three selective colors included (figure 6.20):

1. Select Selective color from the Retouch menu and scroll to the right (figure 6.20, screen 1).
2. Choose an image to use as a base and press the OK button (figure 6.20, screen 2).
3. Turn the rear Main command dial to select one of the color boxes, as shown at the top left of figure 6.20, screen 3, where you will store the colors you want to remain in your black-and-white image. You will need to turn the Main command dial multiple times in either direction to get it to skip over a color box with its up/down adjustments and move to the next box.

4. Use the Multi selector to scroll the yellow selection box to the location from which you want to choose a color and then press the Multi selector center button to choose it. You can zoom in with the Playback zoom in button to select a color more precisely from a small section of the subject. Zoom back out with the Thumbnail/Playback zoom out button.

5. In figure 6.20, screen 3, you will note that I have chosen the color of my subject's forehead for one of the available color choices. The first color box contains the selected color (see arrow). In figure 6.20, screen 4, you can see that I chose a second color to keep in the image, based on her brown hair. Pressing the Multi selector center button captured the hair color and stored it in the second color box (red arrow). Figure 6.20, screen 5, shows that I chose the color of the subject's blouse (red arrow), storing it in the third color box (red arrow).

6. As shown in figure 6.20, screen 6, you can adjust the range of similar colors in any of the color boxes by highlighting its up/down selector with the rear Main command dial and then using the Multi selector to raise or lower the number from as low as 1 to as high as 7. The higher the number, the more similar colors—to the shade in the color box—the camera will allow into the image. In my opinion, the interface for moving around among the color boxes needs improvement. It is slow and clunky.

7. Once you have finished configuring the Selective color system, you can press the OK button to save the image. Figure 6.20, screen 7, shows the hourglass that stays on the screen for a few seconds while the camera removes the colors you have disallowed. A screen with the words *Image saved* will appear briefly (figure 6.20, screen 8). The final image will then appear on the Monitor, having been saved under a new file name (figure 6.20, screen 9).

User's Manual Error Notice (Manual # 6MB12211-02): The "En" User's Manual, on page 363, in step 5, indicates that one can record a Selective color movie in addition to still images, as with the Nikon D5100. The actual text in step 5 says "Press [up] or [down] to increase or decrease the range of similar hues that will be included in the final photograph or movie." However, I have found no way to record a new movie with Selective colors nor to adjust an old one to display only Selective colors. The inclusion of the words "or movie" is an error in the manual. Maybe Nikon was going to have Selective color movies in the D800 originally and decided not to at the last minute, or the folks who wrote the manual copied the Selective color section of the D5100 manual and forgot to remove the word movie in step 5. I contacted NikonUSA about this apparent error, and after discussion and testing, it was validated that the D800 cannot create Selective color movies, only still images. The technician made a note of the typo in the manual.

Settings Recommendation: Selective color still images are a lot of fun. You can shoot images and later remove most of the colors for fine art black-and-white images. Other than the clunky interface surrounding the color boxes, this function is a useful one. You may want to spend a few minutes learning to use it and then see if you can make some art.

Edit Movie

(User's Manual – Page 63)

Edit movie gives you a two-step process to cut a section out of the middle of a movie created with your D800, or you can remove a beginning or ending segment. In addition, you can save an individual frame as a still image from anywhere in the movie.

There are two individual parts to the process of editing a movie—choosing a start point and choosing an end point. You can use one or the other, or both. When you finalize one of the Start point and/or End point selections, the camera saves the file as a new movie with a new file name. This tends to create a bunch of smaller movies on your memory card that you'll need to delete, taking care that you don't delete the wrong one.

There are two parts to Edit movie:

- **Choose start/end point** – This allows you to delete frames from the beginning or the end of your movie and choose a new starting or ending point.
- **Save selected frame** – You can take a low-resolution 16:9 ratio (up to 2.07 megapixel) JPEG snapshot of any frame in the movie.

Choose Start/End Point

Method 1 – Editing a Movie from the Playback Retouch Menu

Let's examine the steps to remove a portion—select the start or end—of a movie segment (figure 6.21A). I refer to these steps as Method 1 because we will later look at an even more precise but slow variation, which I call Method 2.

Here are the steps to use Method 1:

1. Choose a movie to play by pressing the Playback button and scrolling with the Multi selector until a movie is showing on the Monitor (figure 6.21A, screen 1).
2. Press the Multi selector center button to play the movie (figure 6.21A, screen 2). When the movie gets to the point where you want to cut it, press down on the Multi selector, which pauses the movie.
3. Select Choose start/end point and scroll to the right (figure 6.21A, screen 3).
4. Choose Start point or End point from the menu (figure 6.21A, screen 4). If you choose Start point, you will be removing a segment from the front of the movie file. Choosing End point lets you cut off the end of the movie file.

5. When you choose a Start point or End point to cut the movie and press the OK button, a screen showing the new length of the movie will appear. In the bottom-left corner, you will see the length indicator showing the new length (figure 6.21A, screen 5, red arrow). When this screen is active, you can toggle between the Start point or End point selection by pressing the Protect/Picture Control/Help button (looks like a key, right below the MENU button). This allows you to cut both ends of the movie in one operation by toggling the Start point/End point selection to End point and scrolling backward with the Multi selector until you have removed some of the end of the movie.

Figure 6.21A – Edit movie

6. Press up on the Multi selector to cut the movie to the new length. A screen offering to Save as new file, Overwrite existing file, Cancel, or Preview will appear (figure 6.21A, screen 6). Choose one of the options. Here is a list of what each option on the menu does:

- **Save as new file** – If you choose Save as new file, the camera will both retain the old, longer movie and create the new, shorter movie with its own new file name.
- **Overwrite existing file** – If you choose Overwrite existing file (be careful), the camera will overwrite the older, long movie with the new, shorter one.

- ***Cancel*** – If you choose Cancel, the camera returns to the location shown in figure 6.21A, screen 5, and awaits further input from you.
- ***Preview*** – If you select Preview, the camera will play the movie from or to the position of the new cut point. In other words, it plays what would become the new, shorter movie if you save it. When the Preview movie is finished playing, the camera will return to the menu as shown in figure 6.21A, screen 6, and await further input.

7. Figure 6.21A, screen 6, shows that I chose Save as new file, and the camera saved the file. Screen 8 appears briefly with the word *Done*, and then the camera displays the new, shorter movie on the Monitor. You can tell it is a cut movie by the frame and scissors symbol in the left corner, after the movie camera icon (figure 6.21A, screen 9, red arrow).

Method 2 – Editing a Movie Directly from the Main Retouch Menu

You can start this entire process directly from the Retouch Menu. The steps are basically the same except that you choose a movie from a list of movies in the Retouch Menu instead of starting with a movie on the Monitor.

Figure 6.21B – Edit movie directly from the Retouch Menu

Following are the steps to choose a new start and end point for a movie directly from the Retouch Menu (figure 6.21B):

1. Choose Edit movie from the Retouch Menu and scroll to the right (figure 6.21B, screen 1).
2. Select Choose start/end point from the Edit movie menu and scroll to the right (figure 6.21B, screen 2).
3. Choose a movie from the list of movies and press the OK button to select it. You can briefly zoom in on the movie to make sure it is the one you want to edit by pressing and holding the Playback zoom in button (figure 6.21B, screen 3).
4. When a screen similar to the one in figure 6.21B, screen 4, appears, either press the Multi selector center button to start playing the movie or manually scroll to the right with the Multi selector to move the left Start point selector to the right (figure 6.21B, screen 4, red arrow).
5. The Start point selector will move to the right as you select footage to remove by either letting the movie play or by manually scrolling with the Multi selector (figure 6.21B, screen 5, red arrow). If you are playing the movie, simply press down on the Multi selector to pause the video once it has reached the position you want to be the new beginning of the movie. If you are scrolling through frames manually with the Multi selector, stop when you find the frame you want to use as the beginning frame for the new shorter movie (figure 6.21B, screen 5).
6. If you want to remove footage from the end of the movie, press the Protect/ Picture Control/Help button to toggle to the End point selector (figure 6.21B, screen 6, red arrow). Press left on the Multi selector to scroll the End point selector to the left until you have found the frame you want to use as the last frame of the movie.
7. Press up on the Multi selector and the menu will pop open, allowing you to save the new, shorter movie. See step 6 in the steps for Method 1 for a full explanation of what each menu choice does.
8. Once you have chosen to save the file, screens 8 and 9 of figure 6.21B will appear in rapid sequence. The final screen, screen 9 in the figure, is the new, shorter movie, saved under a new file name—as shown by the frame and scissors symbol at the red arrow point.

Note: Your movie must be at least two seconds long when you're done or the camera will refuse to cut any more frames; it will give you a terse message informing you that it cannot edit the movie. Also, if you try to clip a movie by pressing up on the Multi selector when a movie is displayed for edit and the Start point or End point selectors have not been moved, the camera will refuse to let you edit and you will see the message Cannot edit movie.

Settings Recommendation: I have presented the two main methods of editing or trimming a movie. Method 1 is what the User's Manual proposes, and it seems somewhat easier and faster. Method 2 is more precise; however, it takes significantly longer because you may have to scroll through thousands of frames. I generally use Method 2 because I like to be precise. You should shoot some junk movies and practice using both of these methods until you decide which you like best. It will take some practice to remember how the methods work because they are a bit complicated. Keep this book handy!

Save Selected Frame

You can save an individual low-resolution frame from anywhere in the movie. The still image frame size is based on the format of the movie (1080p or 720p), which is set in *Shooting Menu > Movie settings > Movie quality*:

- A still image created from a 1920×1080 movie is a little larger than 2 megapixels.
- A still image created from a 1280×720 movie is about 921 KB, or smaller than a 1-megapixel image.

Method 1 – Save Selected Frame by Using Movie Playback

Similar to the methods in the previous section about editing movies, there are multiple ways to cut a single frame out of the movie. Method 1 is the method shown in the User's Manual.

Figure 6.21C – Save an individual frame from a movie

Use these steps to save a single frame from the movie as a still image, using play-back (figure 6.21C):

1. Press the Playback button and scroll to the movie that contains the frame you want to save. Press the Multi selector center button to play the movie (figure 6.21C, screen 1).
2. Let the movie play until you reach the point where you want to grab the frame from the movie, and then press down on the Multi selector to pause the movie (figure 6.21C, screen 2).
3. The screen shown in figure 6.21C, screen 3, will now appear. You can scroll left or right with the Multi selector to move one frame at a time while the movie is paused. This allows you to find the exact frame that best suits your purposes. The red arrow points to an icon that appears to let you know you can access the Retouch Menu by pressing the OK button. Press the OK button now to open the Retouch Menu.
4. Figure 6.21C, screen 4, shows the Retouch Menu with the same two choices we discussed earlier. Select Save selected frame and press the OK button.
5. The movie will now appear again, still paused (figure 6.21C, screen 5), and the camera's Memory card access lamp will be shining brightly. Nothing will happen until you press up on the Multi selector (red arrow) or press the Playback button to cancel. (This was confusing to me until I did it several times!)
6. Press up on the Multi selector, and a message that says *Proceed?* will appear (figure 6.21C, screen 6). Highlight Yes on the menu and press the OK button again.
7. The camera will now cut out the frame you selected, a screen will show briefly saying *Done*, and the new, saved low-res image will appear on the Monitor (not shown).

Method 2 – Save Selected Frame by Using the Retouch Menu Directly

This method of saving a frame from somewhere in the movie is a bit more direct. You select your movie from a list of movies brought up directly by the Retouch Menu instead of choosing one from the playback screen on the Monitor. Let's see how.

Use these steps to save an individual frame from a movie by using the Retouch Menu directly (figure 6.21D):

1. Choose Edit movie from the Retouch Menu and scroll to the right (figure 6.21D, screen 1).
2. Select Save selected frame and scroll to the right (figure 6.21D, screen 2).
3. Choose one of the available movies and press the OK button. You can briefly zoom in on the movie to make sure it is the one that contains the frame you want to save by pressing and holding the Playback zoom in button (figure 6.21D, screen 3).

Figure 6.21D – Save an individual frame from a movie using the Retouch Menu

4. Press the Multi selector center button to start playing the movie (figure 6.21D, screen 4, red arrow). When you reach the point that contains the frame you want to save, press down on the Multi selector to pause the movie (figure 6.21D, screen 5, lower red arrow).
5. Scroll to the left or right with the Multi selector until the exact frame you want is showing on the screen. Press up on the Multi selector toward the little scissors icon (figure 6.21D, screen 5, upper red arrow).
6. A screen with a small box will appear that says *Proceed?* (figure 6.21D, screen 6). Choose Yes from the menu and the camera will make a copy of the frame as a separate image. While the selected frame is being extracted and saved, you will see an hourglass, then a screen that says *Done*, and a final screen showing the saved, low-res image with a new file name (not shown). The still frame will have the same 16:9 ratio of an HD movie and will generally be less than 1 megabyte in size.

Settings Recommendation: I like to use Method 2, even though the User's Manual recommends Method 1. Both get the job done, but I find Method 2 more satisfactory because I can select the movie from a list of several movies instead of scrolling through the playback. The camera displays movies only when you use Method 2, narrowing down your choices by hiding any image files.

Side-by-Side Comparison

(User's Manual – Page 264)

Side-by-side comparison allows you to compare an image you've retouched with its original source image. Interestingly, this function is not available from the main Retouch Menu. You'll find it on the Playback Retouch Menu only, which you access by pressing the OK button when a picture is displayed on the Monitor.

Here are the steps to compare an original and retouched image side by side on the camera's Monitor (figure 6.22):

1. Press the Playback button and find the image you want to compare (figure 6.22, screen 1).
2. Press the OK button to access the Playback Retouch Menu. Scroll all the way down to the bottom of the menu, select Side-by-side comparison, and scroll to the right (figure 6.22, screen 2). The original image will appear on the left, and one of the retouched versions will appear on the right (figure 6.22, image 3).

Figure 6.22 – Side-by-side comparison

3. If you retouched an original image more than once, a tiny yellow arrow will appear above and below the retouched image. This means that you can scroll up or down to see the other retouched images. The right-side pictures of the woman in figure 6.22, screens 4, 5, and 6, are three different retouched images; the left-side picture is the original image. Screen 4 shows a Resize operation, screen 5 shows the Color outline filter effect, and screen 6 shows the Color sketch filter effect.

Settings Recommendation: I often use this function when I want to see how images to which I've added a color cast compare to the original. It's very convenient because you can choose the original image or one of the retouched images, and the camera is smart enough to place them in the proper position in the Side-by-side comparison. You can tell an image has been retouched by looking for the retouch icon in the upper-left corner of the image when it's displayed on the Monitor.

Author's Conclusions

Nikon has given camera users who dislike computers many ways to work with their images in-camera. Although the Retouch Menu is not as fully featured as a computer graphics program, it does allow you to do quick one-off conversions for convenience.

I didn't think this group of Retouch Menu functions would be all that useful to me when I first read about them. However, in the field I find myself using them more than I expected. Whether you use them often or not, it's good to know you have them for emergency use.

Next, we'll move into the final menu system in the camera. It's called My Menu, and it may become very valuable to you as you learn how it works. It's a place to put your often-used, favorite settings so you can get to them very quickly. Let's see how My Menu and its cousin, Recent Settings, work in the next chapter.

My Menu and Recent Settings

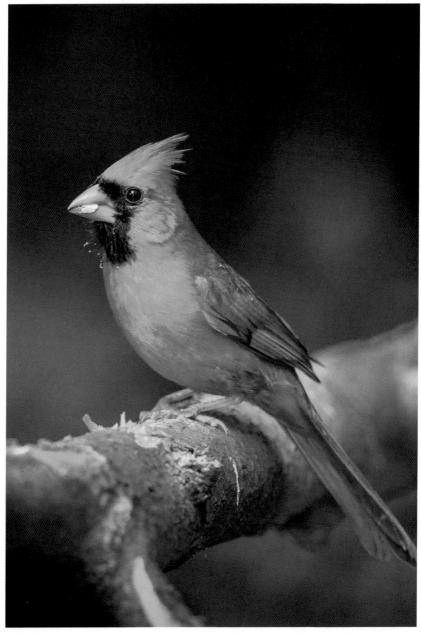

Red Bird Snacking – Courtesy of Dennis H. Miller (*dhmiller*)

As you have read through this book and experimented with your camera, you've surely noticed that the D800 has a large number of menus, screens, functions, and settings. When I took pictures of the camera's menus and screens for this book, I ended up with hundreds of images. That many screens can be somewhat complex to navigate. We need a shortcut menu for our most-used settings—a place to keep the functions we're constantly changing.

Nikon has given us two specialty menus in the D800: My Menu and Recent Settings. These are both designed to give us exactly what we need—a menu that can be customized with only the most-used functions, and a menu of recent changes to functions.

For instance, I often turn Exposure delay mode on and off. Instead of having to search through all the Custom settings, trying to remember exactly where Exposure delay mode lives, I simply added that Custom setting to My Menu. Now, whenever I want to add a 1- to 3-second exposure delay after pressing the Shutter-release button so that mirror vibrations can settle down, I can just go to My Menu and enable Exposure delay mode. I can do it quickly and without searching.

I rarely use Recent Settings. I prefer the control I get with my own personally customizable menu—My Menu. The Recent Settings menu has very little flexibility because it's an automatically updated, camera-controlled menu system. You really can't do much in the way of configuring it. You'll just select and use it. On the other hand, My Menu is a personal collection of links to my most-used settings. It is completely configurable.

We'll consider both menus in this chapter, with heavy emphasis on configuring My Menu.

What's the Difference between My Menu and Recent Settings?

You can add up to 20 settings from the Playback Menu, Shooting Menu, Custom Setting Menu, Setup Menu, and Retouch Menu to My Menu. Recent Settings will automatically show the last 20 settings you've modified in the other menus, but it's not configurable. The most important difference between the two menus is the level of control you have over what appears on them. My Menu is completely customizable and does not change unless you change it, and, as mentioned previously, Recent Settings simply shows the last 20 changes you've made to your camera's settings. Recent Settings will change every time you change a setting in your camera. However, because it shows the last 20 changes, you ought to be able to find the ones you change most often somewhere in the list. The two menus are mutually exclusive and cannot appear on the D800 at the same time. One takes the place of the other when you select the Choose tab setting at the end of each menu and choose your favorite.

My Menu

(User's Manual – Page 366)

My Menu is *my* menu! I can add or remove virtually any camera setting found on one of the primary menus. When I use My Menu, I don't have
to spend time looking for the function buried
in the main menus system. Because I often use
each function on My Menu, I'm glad to have it
immediately available.

My Menu is the last selection on the D800's
menu system (figure 7.1). Its icon looks like a file
folder tab turned sideways, with a check mark
on it.

Figure 7.1 – My Menu

When you first look at My Menu, you'll see nothing but the following menu
options:

- Add items
- Remove items
- Rank items
- Choose tab

Let's examine each of these menu choices in detail.

Add Items

To add an item to My Menu, you'll need to locate the item first. Search through the
menus until you find the setting you want to add, and then make note of where it's
located. You could do this from within the Add items menu, but I find that it's harder
to locate what I'm looking for if I haven't already confirmed where it lives. Is it under
the Custom Setting Menu or the Shooting Menu or maybe the Setup Menu? Make
a note of where items you want to add to My Menu are located before you start
adding them, or it may take longer than necessary.

Figure 7.2 – Adding items to My Menu

After you've found the item you want to add and made note of its location, use the following steps (figures 7.2, 7.3, and 7.4):

1. Select Add items from My Menu. Notice that I already have Set Picture Control and Active D-Lighting added to My Menu (figure 7.2, screen 1). I want to add something else.

2. Use the Multi selector to scroll right, and you'll find a list of menus to choose from. The Add items screen shows all the menus available in the D800 except My Menu and Recent Settings (figure 7.2, screen 2). Let's add one of my favorites, Exposure delay mode (figure 7.3).

Figure 7.3 – Adding Exposure delay mode to My Menu

3. Figure 7.3 picks up where figure 7.2 left off. We already know that Exposure delay mode is under the Custom setting menu, so let's scroll down to it and scroll to the right (figure 7.3, screen 1).

4. We now see the Custom setting menu and Custom settings banks a through f (figure 7.3, screen 2). Scroll down to Custom Setting > d Shooting/display and then scroll to the right so we can select d4 Exposure delay mode.

5. Figure 7.3, screen 3, shows the d4 Exposure delay mode function that we want to add. All we have to do is highlight it and press the OK button. Once that is done, the D800 switches to the Choose position screen (figure 7.3, screen 4).

6. Figure 7.4 begins where figure 7.3 ends. Since I've already added a couple of other items to My Menu, I now have to decide the order in which I want them to be presented. The new d4 Exposure delay mode setting is on top because it is the newest entry (figure 7.4, screen 1). I think I'll move it down two rows and put Set Picture Control in the top position.

Figure 7.4 – Choosing a position for Custom setting d4 Exposure delay mode on My Menu

7. To move the position of the selected item, simply scroll down. The d4 Exposure delay mode setting has a yellow box around it (figure 7.4, screen 2). As you scroll down, a yellow underline moves down the list (figure 7.4, screen 2, red arrow). This yellow underline represents the place to which I want to move d4 Exposure delay mode. When I've decided on the position and have the yellow underline in place, I just press the OK button. The screen pops back to the first My Menu screen, with everything arranged the way I want it (figure 7.4, screen 3). Notice that d4 Exposure delay mode is now at the bottom of the list.

Remove Items

Now that I've shown you how to Add items, let's examine how to Remove items. The D800 allows me to open the Set Picture Control menu by pressing the Protect/Picture Control/Help button when nothing is showing on the Monitor. I think I'd rather just press the Picture Control button than use My Menu, so I'll remove it from My Menu and save one of the 20 slots for something else.

Figure 7.5 – Removing an item from My Menu

Use the following steps to Remove items from My Menu (figure 7.5):

1. Select Remove items from My Menu and scroll to the right (figure 7.5, screen 1).
2. The Remove items screen presents a series of selections with check boxes. Whichever boxes I check will be deleted when I select Done (figure 7.5, screen 2). You can check the boxes by highlighting the line item you want to delete and scrolling right. You can also simply press the OK button to place a check mark in a setting's box. I like to use the OK button because scrolling left does not work; it takes you back to the My Menu screen. Pressing the OK button acts like a toggle and will check or uncheck a line item.
3. When you've checked the settings you want to remove, simply scroll back up to Done and press the OK button (figure 7.5, screen 3). A small white box pops up and asks, *Delete selected item?*
4. Pressing the OK button signifies Yes and removes the Set Picture Control setting from My Menu. A screen displaying *Done* shows briefly, and then the D800 switches back to the My Menu screen. You can press the MENU button to cancel if you decide you don't want to remove an item.

Rank Items

Ranking items is similar to positioning new additions in My Menu. All the Rank items selection does is move an item up or down in My Menu. You can switch your most-used My Menu items to the top of the list.

Figure 7.6 – Ranking items in My Menu

Use the following steps to Rank items (figures 7.6 and 7.7):

1. Select Rank items from My Menu and scroll to the right (figure 7.6, screen 1).
2. Now you'll see the Rank items screen and all the current My Menu items (figure 7.6, screen 2). I've decided that I use d4 Exposure delay mode more than Active D-Lighting, so I'll move it to the top.
3. Highlight d4 Exposure delay mode and press the OK button. A yellow box will appear around that item. Move appears at the bottom of the screen (figure 7.7, screen 1).

Figure 7.7 – Ranking items in My Menu (continued)

4. Next, scroll up with the Multi selector (figure 7.7, screen 2). This action moves the yellow positioning underline to the top of the list (figure 7.7, screen 2, red arrow).
5. Press the OK button to select the new position and d4 Exposure delay mode will move to the top of the list (figure 7.7, screen 3).

Choose Tab

Choose tab allows you to switch between My Menu and Recent Settings. Both menus have the Choose tab selection as their last menu choice.

Figure 7.8 – Selecting My Menu or Recent Settings (Choose tab)

Use the following steps to switch between My Menu and Recent Settings (figure 7.8):

1. At the bottom of My Menu, select Choose tab and scroll to the right (figure 7.8, screen 1).
2. You'll now have a choice between My Menu and Recent Settings. Choose Recent Settings and press the OK button (figure 7.8, screen 2).
3. The Recent Settings screen will now appear, completely replacing My Menu on the main menu screen (figure 7.8, screen 3). Notice that it has a Choose tab selection at the bottom, just as My Menu does.
4. Select Choose tab and press the OK button to return to My Menu (figure 7.8, screen 3).

Clearly, this is a circular reference. You can use the Choose tab selection as a toggle between the two menus. When you do, one menu replaces the other as the last selection on the camera's main menu screen.

Settings Recommendation: You can see how My Menu gives you nice control over a customized menu that is entirely yours. Configure it however you want by choosing from selections in the primary menus. My Menu will save you significant time when you look for your 20 most-used selections.

If you're inclined to use Recent Settings, just remember that after you pass 20 camera setting adjustments, the next setting you use will jump to the top of the list, moving everything down by one position. The last item on the list will simply disappear.

Now, let's take a look at Recent Settings in a little more detail.

Recent Settings

(User's Manual – Page 268)

Recent Settings is very simple. This menu re-members the last 20 changes you've made to your D800 camera. Each menu selection that was modified is stored in a temporary place called Recent Settings.

If you change something in your camera that's not already on the Recent Settings menu, it will be added to the menu, replacing the old-

Figure 7.1 – My Menu

est change with your new one—at the top of the list—if there is no room left at the bottom (i.e., you've exceeded 20 items).

This can be a convenient way to find something you've changed recently but whose location you have trouble remembering on the main menu systems.

Settings Recommendation: If you want a more permanent menu for your favor-ite changes to the D800, you'll need to enable the My Menu system instead of the Recent Settings Menu. The Recent Settings Menu is fine, but I want to directly con-trol what settings I have quick access to without searching. My Menu is my choice!

Author's Conclusions

This is the last of the text-based menus we'll cover in the D800. We've been through all the menu screens in the last several chapters!

Now it's time to see how to use the controls we've carefully configured. Our next chapter takes up the subjects of exposure metering, exposure modes, and the histogram. Please pay extra attention to the section on the histogram if you want excellent exposures every time.

Metering, Exposure Modes, and Histogram

A Long Way Up – Courtesy of Alexandre Rosen (*klrbee25*)

I've been using Nikon cameras since 1980. It seems that with each new camera, there have been improvements in metering and exposure modes. The Nikon D800 is no exception. Within this camera, Nikon has designed metering and exposure to work not only with still images, but also with broadcast-quality video (D-Movies).

In this chapter, you'll learn how the exposure metering system and modes work. We'll look at how each of three different light meter types is best used. We'll examine the various modes you can use when taking pictures, and finally, we'll look in detail at how the histogram works on the Nikon D800. This little readout gives you great control over metering and will help you make the most accurate exposures you've ever made. It is very important that you understand the histogram, so we'll look at it in detail. This chapter is divided into three parts:

- **Section 1 – Metering** – The Nikon D800 provides three major light metering systems: 3D Color Matrix Metering III, Center-weighted, and Spot.
- **Section 2 – Exposure Modes** – The camera's MODE button allows access to various shooting or exposure modes, such as Programmed auto (P), Shutter-priority auto (S), Aperture-priority auto (A), and Manual (M).
- **Section 3 – Histogram** – The histogram is a digital bell-curve readout that shows how well an image is exposed. It's an important tool for advanced photographers. This chapter discusses how to read the histogram and better control your exposures.

Let's get started by looking more deeply into the three exposure metering systems.

Section 1 – Metering

(User's Manual – Page 115)

The basis for the Nikon D800's exposure meter is a 91,000-pixel RGB sensor that meters a wide area of the frame. Figure 8.1 shows a closeup of that sensor, which is used to meter the light and provide a correct exposure.

When used with a Nikkor G or D lens that contains a CPU, the camera can set the exposure based on the distribution of brightness, color, distance, and composition. Most people leave their light meter set to Matrix metering and enjoy excellent results.

Figure 8.1 – D800's 91,000-pixel RGB sensor (light meter)

The Nikon D800 uses a newly developed Advanced Scene Recognition System that includes the 91,000-pixel RGB sensor that measures each scene's light properties, color spectrum, and brightness levels. It then compares your subject against the camera's built-in image database to provide even more accurate autoexposure. With a metering sensor this sensitive, the D800 can do things with ease that other cameras struggle to accomplish.

Figure 8.2 shows the Metering selector set to Spot metering, Matrix metering, and Center-weighted metering. The Metering selector surrounds the AE-L/AF-L button.

Figure 8.2 – Three meter types (in order): Spot, Matrix, and Center-weighted

To switch among the three exposure meter types, simply rotate the Metering selector so that its white indicator dot lines up with the exposure meter type you want to use, as shown in figure 8.2 (red arrows).

Figure 8.3 shows the Information display screen with the three metering symbols and all the other icons you'll normally see. These same symbols, shown at the point of the red arrows, can be seen at the bottom-left corner when you look through the Viewfinder. On the left you will first see the Focus indicator, then the Metering symbol. Learn to recognize what each Metering symbol means.

Figure 8.3 – Metering mode symbols on the Information display

Now, let's examine the three meter types to see which you will use most often.

3D Color Matrix III Metering

The Nikon D800 contains the 3D Color Matrix III metering system, one of the most powerful and accurate automatic exposure meters in any camera today.

In figure 8.4, you can see a closeup of the Metering selector dial set to Matrix metering. This is the factory default meter.

How does Matrix metering work? There are character-istics for many thousands of images stored in the cam-era. These characteristics are used along with proprietary Nikon software and complex evaluative computations to analyze the image that appears in your Viewfinder or in

Figure 8.4 – Matrix metering mode symbol

Live view. The meter is then set to provide accurate exposures for the greatest majority of your images.

Whether you are taking a scenic picture with the bright sky above and the darker earth below, or a group shot with one or several human faces, the metering system evaluates the image and compares it to hundreds of similar images in the camera's database; then it automatically selects and inputs a meter setting for you.

The meter examines four critical areas of each picture. It compares the levels of *brightness* in various parts of the scene to determine the total range of EV values. It then notices the *color* of the subject and surroundings. If you are using a G or D lens with a CPU chip, it also determines how far away your lens is focused so it can determine the *distance* to your subject. Finally, it looks at the *compositional* ele-ments of the subject.

When it has all that information, it compares your image to tens of thousands of image characteristics in its image database, makes complex evaluations, and comes up with an exposure value that is usually right on target, even in complex lighting situations.

Center-Weighted Metering

If you're a bit old-fashioned, raised on a classic cen-ter-weighted meter and still preferring that type, the D800's exposure meter can be transformed into a flexible center-weighted meter with variable-sized weighting that you can control.

In figure 8.5, you can see a closeup of the Metering selector dial set to Center-weighted metering. The Cen-ter-weighted meter in the D800 meters the entire frame but concentrates 75 percent of the metering into an adjustable circle in the middle. The 25 percent of the frame outside the circle provides the rest of the metering. If you'd

Figure 8.5 – Center-weighted metering mode symbol

like, you can make the circle as small as 8 mm or as large as 20 mm. You can even completely eliminate the circle and use the entire Viewfinder frame as a basic averaging meter.

Let's examine the Center-weighted meter more closely. Using *Custom Setting Menu > b Metering/exposure > b5 Center-weighted area*, you can change the size of the circle where the camera concentrates the meter reading. (See **Custom Setting b5 – Center-weighted Area** in the chapter **Custom Setting Menu**.)

The default circle is 12 mm in the center of your camera's Viewfinder (figure 8.6). However, by changing Custom setting b5 Center-weighted area, you can adjust this size to one of the following:

- 8 mm (0.31 inch)
- 12 mm (0.47 inch) (default)
- 15 mm (0.59 inch)
- 20 mm (0.79 inch)
- Average (full frame)

Figure 8.6 – Center-weighted metering

Again, the Center-weighted meter is a pretty simple concept. The part of your subject that's in the center of your D800's Viewfinder influences the meter more than the edges of the frame, on a 75/25 basis. The circle gets 75 percent importance. The red circles shown in figure 8.6 are just rough approximations. Simply meter the subject with the center of the Viewfinder, and you should have good results.

Note: If you are using a non-CPU lens, the Center-weighted meter defaults to 12 mm and cannot be changed. Adjustments to Custom setting b5 Center-weighted area have no effect.

Where's the Circle?

You can't actually see any indication of circles in the Viewfinder, so you'll have to imagine them, as I did in figure 8.6.

Locate your current autofocus (AF) sensor in the middle of your Viewfinder. Now imagine the smallest circle, 8 mm, which is about one-third of an inch. The largest circle is 20 mm, which is a little bigger than three-quarters of an inch. This unseen circle in the center area of the Viewfinder provides the most important 75 percent metering area.

Settings Recommendation: If I used the Center-weighted meter often, I would stay with the 8 mm setting. That's a pretty small circle—almost a spot meter—so it should give you good readings. I would point the circle at the most important part of my subject, get a meter reading, use the AE-Lock button to lock the exposure, recompose the picture, and then release the shutter.

The most sensitive area is large enough at 8 mm to see more than a pure spot meter, though, so you have the best of both worlds. There is so little difference between 8 mm and 15 mm that it probably makes little difference which one you use. If you are concerned, then experiment with the settings and see which one works best for you.

Using the Average Setting

If you set your meter to Average (Avg) in Custom setting b5 Center-weighted area, the light values of the entire Viewfinder are averaged to arrive at an exposure value. No particular area of the frame is assigned any greater importance (figure 8.6).

This is a little bit like Matrix metering but without the extra smarts. In fact, on several test subjects, I got similar meter readings from the Average and Matrix meters. However, Matrix metering should do better in difficult lighting situations because it has a database of image characteristics to compare with your current image—including color, distance, and where your subject is located in the frame.

Spot Metering

Often only a spot meter will do. In situations where you must get an accurate exposure for a very small section of the frame, or if you must get several meter readings from various small areas, the D800 can, once again, be adjusted to fit your needs. The Spot meter evaluates only 1.5 percent of the frame, so it is indeed a *spot* meter.

In figure 8.7, you can see a closeup of the Metering selector dial set to Spot metering. The D800's Spot meter consists of a 4 mm circle (0.16 inch) surrounding the currently active AF point in both Single and Continuous AF modes (AF-S and AF-C).

Figure 8.7 – Spot metering mode symbol

How big is the 4 mm spot? The Spot meter barely surrounds the AF point square in your viewfinder (figure 8.8). It is a little larger than the brackets that appear around the active AF sensor when you slightly press the Shutter-release button. In fact, the Spot meter follows the currently active AF point around the Viewfinder, so you can move the Spot meter around the frame with the Multi selector.

When your D800 is in Spot meter mode and you move the AF point to some small section of your subject, you can rest assured that you're getting a true spot reading. In fact, you can use your Spot meter to determine an approximate EV range of light values in the entire image by taking multiple manual spot readings from different parts of the subject and comparing the values. If the values exceed 8 or 9 EV steps, you have to decide which part of your subject is most important and meter for it.

Figure 8.8 – Spot metering size

On an overcast day, you can usually get by with no worries since the range of light values is often within the recording capability of the sensor. On a bright, sunny day, the range of light can be more than a single image can record, and you might have to use a graduated neutral-density filter or HDR imaging to rein in the excessive light range.

Just remember that spot metering is often a trade-off. Either you have the highly specific ability to ensure that a certain portion of an image is exposed with spot-on accuracy (Spot meter) or you can use the camera's multiple averaging skills (Matrix meter), to generally get the correct exposure throughout the frame. The choice is yours, depending on the shooting situation.

If you spot meter the face of someone who is standing in the sun, the shadows around the person may contain little or no data. They will usually be underexposed and have little or no detail. If you spot meter the areas in the shadows instead, the person's face is likely to blow out and lose detail. We'll discuss this in more detail in section 3 of this chapter, which explores the histogram.

Settings Recommendation: Use your Spot meter to get specific meter readings of small areas on and around your subject; then make some exposure decisions yourself and your subject should be well exposed. Just remember that the Spot meter evaluates only for the small area that it sees, so it cannot adjust the camera for anything except that one tiny area. Spot metering requires some practice, but it is a very professional way to expose images.

On cameras previous to the D800, I often used the Spot meter on a person's face when I was taking pictures in darker surroundings so that the person's face was not blown out (due to the meter being influenced by the dark surroundings). However, the D800 is much better at locating and exposing for faces accurately, even when using the Viewfinder instead of Live view. I now use the Spot meter much less than I did before.

Section 2 – Exposure Modes

(User's Manual – Page 117)

My first Nikon was an FM, which I remember with fondness because that was when I first got serious about photography. It's hard for me to imagine that it has already been 32 years since I last used my FM. Things were simpler back then. When I say simple, I mean that the FM had a basic center-weighted light meter, a manual exposure dial, and manual aperture settings. I had to decide how to create the image in all aspects. It was a camera with only one mode—M, or manual.

Later on, I bought a Nikon FE and was amazed to use its A mode, or Aperture-priority auto. I could set the aperture manually and the camera would adjust the shutter speed for me. The FE had two modes, M-manual and A-Aperture-priority.

A few more years went by and I bought a Nikon F4 that was loaded with features and was much more complex. It had four modes, including the two I was used to (M and A) and two new ones, Shutter-priority auto (S) and Programmed auto (P). I had to learn even more stuff! The F4 was my first P, S, A, M camera.

Does this sound anything like your progression? If you're older than 40 years, maybe so; if not, I ought to stop reminiscing and get to the point.

Today's cameras are amazingly complex compared to cameras only a few years ago. Let's examine how we can use that flexibility for our benefit. The D800 is also a P, S, A, M camera. That's the abbreviated progression of primary shooting modes that allow you to control the camera's shutter speed and aperture yourself.

To select the P, S, A, or M mode, simply hold down the MODE button (found to the left and rear of the Shutter-release button) and turn the rear Main command dial in either direction. The mode changes will be displayed in the upper-left corner of the Control panel and Information display screen. You will also see a tiny P, S, A, or M at the bottom middle of the Viewfinder. Let's examine each exposure mode in detail.

Programmed Auto Mode (P)

Programmed auto mode (P) is designed for those times when you just want to shoot pictures and not think much about camera settings but still want emergency control when needed. The camera takes care of the shutter speed and aperture for you and uses your selected exposure meter type to create the best pictures it can without human intervention. You can override the aperture by turning the rear Main command dial.

The big *P* in the upper-left corner of the Control panel in Figure 8.9 shows that the camera is set to Programmed auto mode (P). This mode is called Programmed auto because it uses a software program built into the camera. It tries its best to create optimal images in most situations.

However, even the User's Manual calls this a "snapshot" mode. P mode can handle a wide variety of situations well, but I wouldn't depend on it for my important shooting. It can be great at a party, for example, when I want some nice snapshots. I don't have to think about the camera then, and I can just enjoy the party. P mode to me is "P for Party."

Figure 8.9 –Programmed auto (P) mode on the Control panel

It's a good mode to use when you want to let the camera control the aperture and shutter while you control the flash. In a sense, it's like auto mode on lesser cameras, except that you decide when to use the pop-up Speedlight instead of letting the camera decide.

Programmed auto mode also lets you override the camera's aperture in an emergency. You may need more depth of field and decide to use a smaller aperture. The camera allows you to do that by turning the rear Main command dial. When you do, the aperture is under your control, and the camera controls the shutter.

P mode actually comes in two parts: Programmed auto and Flexible program. Flexible program is similar to Aperture-priority auto (A) mode. Why do I say that? Let me explain with an example.

Get Down, Uncle Ben!

You're shooting at a family reunion and suddenly you see a perfect shot of a somewhat tipsy Uncle Ben dancing on the dinner table and Aunt Myrtle standing on the floor behind him with her hand over her mouth. You (being a well-trained photographer) glance down at your camera and realize that the f/4 aperture showing on the Control panel won't give you enough depth of field to focus on Uncle Ben and still have a sharp image of Aunt Myrtle, who by this time is tugging at his pants leg. With only seconds to spare, you turn your rear Main command dial to the left. The D800 realizes that it is being called upon to leave snapshot mode and give you some control. It displays a small P* (P with an asterisk, as seen in figure 8.10) on the Control panel to let you know it realizes you are taking over control of the aperture. Since you are turning the dial to the left, it obligingly starts cranking down the aperture. A few clicks to the left and your aperture is now at f/8. As soon as the D800 detected you were turning the Main command dial, it started adjusting the shutter speed to match the new aperture. With only seconds before Aunt Myrtle starts dragging Uncle Ben off the dinner table, you get the camera to your eye, compose the shot, press the Shutter-release button, and the D800 starts grabbing frames. You get several frames off in the few seconds it takes Aunt Myrtle to get Uncle Ben down from the table. A "priceless" family memory, captured!

What you did in this imaginary scenario was invoke the Flexible program mode (P*) in your D800. How? As soon as you turned the rear Main command dial, the D800 left normal P mode and switched to Flexible program. Before you turned the Main command dial, the D800 was happily controlling both shutter speed and aperture for you. When you turned the dial, the D800 immediately switched to Flexible program mode and let

Figure 8.10 –Flexible program (P*) mode on the Control panel

you have control of the aperture. It then controlled only the shutter speed. In effect, the D800 allowed you to exercise your knowledge of photography very quickly and only assisted you from that point.

When you enter Flexible program (P*) and turn the rear Main command dial to the left, the aperture gets smaller. Turn it to the right and the aperture gets larger. Nothing happens if you turn the front Sub-command dial. Nikon gives you control of the aperture only in Flexible program mode. Can you see why I say Flexible program mode acts like Aperture-priority auto mode (A)?

Beware the Extra Clicks

If you turn the rear Main command dial to the right until the aperture reaches its maximum size, the camera starts counting clicks but does nothing else. The same thing happens if you try to go smaller than the minimum aperture. In order to start making the aperture change again, you have to turn back the same number of clicks (up to five). I have no idea why Nikon does it this way, but it has for many years. Other Nikons will remember up to fifteen clicks past the maximum and minimum aperture. The D800 seems to remember only about five extra clicks.

It's confusing to have the camera stop letting you control the aperture just because you turned the Main command dial past wide open by several clicks and then give you control again when you turn it back the same number of clicks. It's no big deal, really; just be aware that this will happen so you won't think the camera is not working correctly.

Shutter-Priority Auto Mode (S)

Shutter-priority auto is for those who need to control their camera's shutter speed while allowing the camera to maintain the correct aperture for the available light. You'll turn the rear Main command dial to adjust the shutter speed, while the camera controls the aperture.

In Figure 8.11, the Control panel shows that Shutter-priority auto (S) mode is set. If you find yourself shooting action, you'll want to keep the shutter speed high enough to capture an image without excessive blurring.

Shooting sports, air shows, auto races, or any quickly moving subject requires careful control of the shutter. If you shoot a bird in flight, you may want to use a fast shutter speed that allows for just a tiny bit of motion blur in its wings, while completely stopping the body of the bird, or a faster shutter speed to eliminate all blur.

Figure 8.11 – Shutter-priority auto (S) mode on the Control panel

Sometimes you'll want to set your shutter speed to slow settings for special effects or time exposures, such as a small waterfall in a beautiful autumn stream. See figure 8.12 for both stop-motion and blurring effects.

Figure 8.12 – Fast shutter speed to stop bird and slow shutter speed to blur water

To change the shutter speed, simply rotate the rear Main command dial to any value between 30 seconds and 1/8000 of a second. Turn the dial to the left (counterclockwise) for faster shutter speeds and right (clockwise) for slower. The camera will adjust your aperture to maintain a correct exposure and will warn you when it can't.

Watch Out for Camera Shake!

Be careful when the shutter speed is set below 1/125 second. Camera shake becomes a problem for many people at 1/60 second and slower. If you are careful to stand still, brace your arms against your chest, and spread your feet apart with one in front of the other, you'll probably be able to make sharp images at 1/60 to 1/30 second (figure 8.13, image on the left).

Surprisingly, your heartbeat and breathing is reflected in your hands during slow shutter speed photography. At 1/15 second and slower, most people cannot take sharp pictures without having the camera on a tripod (figure 8.13, image on the right). If you are going to shoot at slow shutter speeds, buy yourself a solid tripod. You'll make much nicer pictures. You can also use a monopod for a very portable device to steady the camera, with results in between handholding and tripod use.

Bad Exposure Warning

If the light changes drastically and the camera cannot maintain a correct exposure due to your current settings, it will blink the offending setting in the Viewfinder, Control panel, and Information display. It will also display the -/+ Exposure indicator (as you use in Manual mode) with an approximate number of EV steps of over- or underexposure.

If you see the aperture or shutter-speed setting blinking in any of the displays along with the -/+ Exposure indicator displaying a -/+ EV value, please validate your exposure before taking the picture.

Figure 8.13 – Woman holding camera for steady shooting, and pro photographer using a tripod

The picture of the small waterfall in Great Smoky Mountains National Park in figure 8.12 was taken at a shutter speed of several seconds. It is virtually impossible to hold a camera perfectly still for several seconds, so a shot like that would be unachievable without a tripod.

Aperture-Priority Auto Mode (A)

Nature, macro, and portrait shooters, and anyone concerned with carefully controlling depth of field, will often leave their cameras set to Aperture-priority auto (A) mode. This mode allows you to control the aperture while the camera takes care of the shutter speed for optimal exposures. To select an aperture, you'll use the front Sub-command dial. Turn the dial to the right (clockwise) for smaller apertures and to the left (counterclockwise) for larger apertures.

Figure 8.14 – Aperture-priority auto (A) mode on Control panel

The Control panel in Figure 8.14 shows that Aperture-priority auto (A) mode is set. The minimum and maximum aperture settings are limited by the minimum and maximum aperture available on the lens you've mounted on the camera. Most consumer lenses run from f/3.5 to f/22. More expensive, pro-style lenses may have apertures as large as f/0.95 or f/1.4, but they generally start at f/2.8 and end at f/22–f/32.

For those new to digital photography, the aperture directly controls the depth of field (DOF)—or zone of sharpness—in an image. DOF is an extremely important concept for photographers to understand. Simply put, it allows you to control the range or depth of sharp focus in your images. In the bird image in figure 8.15, the DOF is very shallow, and in the scenic shot it is very deep.

Figure 8.15 – Large aperture to blur background (left) and small aperture for deep depth of field (right)

Manual Mode (M)

Manual mode takes a big step backward to days of old. It gives you complete control of your camera's shutter and aperture so that you can make all the exposure
decisions, with suggestions from the light meter.

The big *M* in the upper-left corner of the Control panel in figure 8.16, screen 1,
and the Information display in screen 3 shows that the camera is in Manual (M)
mode. You can't see it in the figure, but there is a tiny M showing in the Viewfinder
just above the Exposure indicator.

You should have no problem knowing when you have the camera in Manual
mode.

Figure 8.16 – Manual (M) showing along with the -/+ Exposure indicator on all display screens
(Control panel, Viewfinder, and Information display)

Also in figure 8.16, notice the analog Exposure indicator display (red arrows on the
Control panel, Viewfinder, and Information display). The Exposure indicator display
has a minus sign (-) on the left and a plus sign (+) on the right. Each tiny square on
the scale represents 1/3 EV step, and each slightly larger tiny rectangle represents 1
EV step. You can control how sensitive this scale is by changing Custom setting b2
EV steps for exposure cntrl. You can set Custom setting b2 to 1/3, 1/2, or 1 EV step.
The camera defaults to 1/3 step from the factory.

When you are metering your subject, a bar will appear underneath the analog
Exposure indicator and extend from the zero in the center toward the plus side to
indicate overexposure or toward the minus side to indicate underexposure.

You can gauge the amount of over- or underexposure by the number of dots
and lines the bar passes as it heads toward one side or the other. The goal in Manual mode is to make the bar disappear. In figure 8.16, screens 1 and 3, the Exposure
indicator shows that the scene is underexposed by 1 EV step (1 stop). The Viewfinder is showing the same thing, except you can't see it in the tiny graphic. Check
your camera's Viewfinder in Manual mode to see how it looks. You should zero the
Exposure indicator for a good exposure.

You can adjust the aperture with the front Sub-command dial, and you can
adjust the shutter speed with the rear Main command dial. When you put the camera in Manual mode (M), you have control over the aperture for depth of field and

Figure 8.17 – A cascading waterfall at Tremont in Great Smoky Mountains National Park, Tennessee, United States in springtime. Nikon D800, AI Nikkor 35mm f/2 non-CPU, manual focus lens with aperture of f/11, shutter speed of 5 seconds, Manual (M) mode, SD picture control, circular polarizer to remove reflections, on a tripod with Exposure delay of 3 seconds (d4).

the shutter speed for motion control. If your subject needs a little more depth of field, just make the aperture smaller, but be sure to slow down the shutter speed as well (or your image may be underexposed). If you need a faster shutter speed, then set it faster, but be sure to open the aperture to compensate.

The point is, you are in complete control of the camera and must make decisions for both the shutter speed and aperture. The camera makes suggestions with its meter, but you make the final decision about how the exposure will look. Manual mode is for taking your time and enjoying your photography. It gives you the most control over how the image looks but also expects you to have a higher level of knowledge to get correct exposures.

Most people who use the D800 are advanced photographers, reflecting the purpose of this feature-laden camera, and they fully understand things like depth of field, shutter speed, and aperture. If you're new to the world of DSLRs, you can find in-depth coverage of these important concepts in my book *Beyond Point-and-Shoot*.

Settings Recommendation: As a nature photographer, I am mostly concerned with getting a nice sharp image with deep depth of field. About 90 percent of the time, my camera is set to Aperture-priority auto (A) and f/8. I control the aperture opening, and the camera controls the shutter speed. I started using this mode in about 1986 when I bought my Nikon FE, and I've used it ever since.

However, if I were shooting sports or action, I would set my camera to Shutter-priority auto (S) most often, which would allow me to control the speed of the shutter and capture those fast-moving subjects without a lot of blur. The camera controls the aperture so that I only have to concentrate on which shutter speed best fits my subject's movement.

I use the other two modes, Programmed auto (P) and Manual (M), only for special occasions.

Manual mode is for when I have time to just enjoy my photography. When I want to control the camera absolutely, I go to Manual. I've even been known to carry a small blanket with me so that when I'm shooting in Manual mode I can toss it over the back of the camera and my head. That way I can feel like Ansel Adams or another view camera artist. I do admit that people (especially kids) seem to find that hilarious. Well, I bet they don't know how to use Manual mode!

I probably use Programmed auto (P) mode least of all. I might use it when I am at a party and just want to take nice pictures for my own use. I'll let the camera make most of the decisions by using P mode and still have the ability to quickly jump into Flexible program (P*) mode when events call for a little more aperture control.

Section 3 – Histogram

Back in the good old film days, we didn't have a histogram, so we had to depend on our experience and light meter to get a good exposure. Because we couldn't see the exposure until after we had left the scene, we measured our success by the number of correctly exposed images we were able to create. With the exposure meter/histogram combination found in the D800, and the ability to zoom in to our images with the high-resolution Monitor on the back, our success rate is much higher than ever before.

The histogram can be as important, or even more so, than the exposure meter. The meter sets up the camera for the exposure, and the histogram verifies that the exposure is a good one.

If your exposure meter stopped working, you could still get perfect exposures using only the histogram. In fact, I gauge my efforts more by how the histogram looks than anything else. The exposure meter and histogram work together to make sure you get excellent results from your photographic efforts.

Figure 8.18 shows the D800's three histogram screens.

Figure 8.18 – The D800's three histogram screens

RGB Histogram, Screen 1 – Figure 8.18, screen 1, is the RGB histogram screen, and it shows an individual histogram for each color channel. On the top is a luminance histogram followed by the red, green, and blue (RGB) channels.

If your camera does not display the RGB histogram screen shown in figure 8.41, screen 1, you'll need to select the check box found at *Playback Menu > Playback display options > RGB histogram.* This setting enables or disables the RGB histogram screen, which you can then find by displaying an image on the Monitor and then scrolling up or down with the Multi selector.

One important reason to examine the RGB histogram is to see if any one color channel has lost all detail in the dark or light areas. Later in this chapter, we will examine how you can determine when detail has been lost.

Luminance Histogram, Screen 2 – Figure 8.18, screen 2, shows a slightly larger luminance histogram along with image information. This luminance histogram screen is one of the camera's main screens and can always be called into use, regardless of what is selected in *Playback Menu > Playback display options > RGB histogram.*

This is a basic luminance histogram, which is a weighted view of the brightness and color in a scene based on how the human eye perceives light. How does the luminance histogram differ from the RGB histograms? The luminance histogram is a representation of the perceived brightness (luminosity) from a combination of the red, green, and blue channels.

In other words, the luminance histogram tries to accurately reflect the light you see by weighting its color values in a particular way. Since the human eye sees green most easily, the luminance histogram is heavily weighted toward green. Notice in figure 8.18, screen 1, how the luminance histogram at the top (the white one) looks very similar to the green channel histogram below it.

Red and blue are also represented in the luminance histogram but in lesser quantities (59 percent green + 30 percent red + 11 percent blue = luminance). The luminance histogram measures the perceived brightness in 256 levels (0–255).

The luminance histogram is an accurate way of looking at the combined color levels in real images. Because it more accurately reflects the way our eyes actually see color brightness, it may be the best histogram for you to use, most of the time.

Luminance Histogram, Screen 3 – The yellow histogram shown in figure 8.18, screen 3, is exactly the same as the white luminance histogram seen in screen 2 and the top white histogram in screen 1.

This particular histogram (figure 8.18, screen 3) is available only by assigning one of the camera's buttons to open it. In *Custom Setting Menu > f Controls > f2 Multi selector center button > Playback mode*, I assigned View histograms to the Multi selector center button.

Now, whenever I am viewing an image on the camera's Monitor, I can press the Multi selector center button and the camera will display the histogram seen in figure 8.18, screen 3, as long as I hold down the button. This works only when you're using Playback mode (viewing images). It is a fast and convenient way to get a histogram open without scrolling through a bunch of image data screens.

Now, that we have discussed how to open the various histograms screens in the D800, let's discuss how a histogram works.

Understanding the Histogram

Using your D800's histogram screens will guarantee you a much higher percentage of well-exposed images. It is well worth spending time to understand the histogram. It's not as complicated as it looks.

I'll cover this feature with enough detail to give you a working knowledge of how to use the histogram to make better pictures. If you are deeply interested in the histogram, there is a lot of research material available on the Internet. Although this overview is brief, it will present enough knowledge to improve your technique immediately.

Best Dynamic Range Ever

The D800's sensor can record a certain range of light values—which according to DxO Labs is about 14.4 EV steps, an amazing amount of dynamic range. In fact, the D800 has the most dynamic range of any digital camera ever tested by DxO Labs, period.

Unfortunately, many of the higher-contrast subjects we shoot can contain more light range than any camera can capture in one exposure. It is important to understand how your camera records light so you can better control how the image is captured. Even though the dynamic range of the D800 is excellent, it still can't handle the range of light captured by the human eye.

Let's look into the histogram so you can determine how well you have captured the light in the scene before your lens. The gray rectangular area in figure 8.19 represents an in-camera histogram. Examine it carefully! Think about it for a minute before reading on.

Figure 8.19 – A basic histogram

The histogram is basically a graph of 256 steps that represents the maximum range of light values your camera can capture (0 = pure black and 255 = pure white). In the middle of the histogram are the midrange values that represent middle colors like grays, light browns, and greens. The values from just above zero and just below 255 contain detail.

The actual histogram looks like a mountain peak, or a series of peaks, and the more there is of a particular color, the taller the peak that represents that color. In some cases the graph will be rounder on top, and in other cases it will be flattened or have several peaks.

The left side of the histogram represents the maximum dark values that your camera can record. The right side represents the maximum light values your camera can capture. On either end of the histogram (0 or 255), the light values contain no detail. They are either completely black (0) or completely white (255).

The height of the histogram (top of mountain peaks) represents the amount of individual colors. You cannot easily control this value in-camera, other than changing to a Picture Control with more or less saturated color, so it is for your information only.

We are mostly concerned with the left- and right-side values of the histogram because we do have much greater control over those (dark versus light). In figure 8.20, we see a basic histogram tutorial with three separate histograms that have different exposures. Refer to figure 8.20 as we discuss the histogram further.

Simply put, the histogram's horizontal scale is related to the darkness and lightness of the image, and the vertical scale of the histogram (valleys and peaks of the mountains) have to do with the amount of color information.

The left (dark) and right (light) directions of the horizontal scale are very important for your picture taking. If the image is too dark, the light values will be clipped off on the left side; if it's too light, the light values will be clipped off on the right side. This will become easier to understand as we look at well-exposed and poorly exposed images.

Figure 8.20 – Three histograms: underexposed, well exposed, and overexposed

When you see the three histograms next to each other (figure 8.20), does it make more sense? See how the underexposed histogram is all the way to the left of the histogram window and is clipped midpeak? Note how both edges of the well-exposed histogram just touch the horizontal edges of the histogram window. Finally, notice how the overexposed histogram is crammed toward the right and clipped. Now, let's look at some histogram details.

Histogram Shape
The image in figure 8.21 is well exposed with no serious problems. The entire light range of this particular image fits within the histogram window, which means that it's not too light or too dark and will need very little or no adjustment to view or print. This image is similar to the well-exposed image in figure 8.20. It contains no more than 6 or 7 stops (EV steps) of light. To finalize the image, I might increase the brightness in the trees a little, but otherwise it's a sound image with potential for immediate usage.

Compare the histogram in figure 8.21 to the histogram in figure 8.22. Notice that the histogram in figure 8.21 is not crammed against the dark value side (left side) like the histogram in figure 8.22. In other words, the dark values in figure 8.21 are not clipped on the left. This means that the camera recorded all the dark values in this image with no loss of shadow detail.

Now look at the right side of the histogram in figure 8.21 and note that it is not completely against the light value side (right side), although it is quite close. The image contains all the available light values. Everything between the right and left sides is exposed quite well, with full detail. A histogram does not have to cover the entire window for the exposure to be correct. When there is a very limited range of light, the histogram may be rather narrow.

Figure 8.21 – Good image with normal histogram shape, no clipping

The image in figure 8.21 is a relatively bland image with smooth gradations of tone, so it makes a smooth mountain-shaped histogram. This will not occur every time because most images contain quite a bit more color information. Each prominent color will be represented with its own peak on the histogram. The most prominent colors will have higher peaks, and the less prominent colors will have lower or no peaks.

As we progress into images with more color or light information, we'll see that the corresponding histograms look quite different.

Look at the image in figure 8.22. This image exceeds the range of the camera's digital sensor.

Figure 8.22 – Histogram showing underexposure (dark side)

Notice that, overall, this image is dark and looks underexposed. The histogram is crammed to the left and is clipped. There are no gradual climbs as on a mountain range, from valley to peak and back to valley. Instead, the image shows up on the left side in midpeak.

The most important thing to understand when you see a histogram like the one in figure 8.22, with part of the peak clipped off on the left, is that some or all of the image is significantly underexposed.

Figure 8.23 – Histogram showing overexposure (light side)

In figure 8.23 a larger aperture was used and more light was allowed in. We can now see much more detail. But once again, the range of light is too great for the sensor, so it is clipped on the highlight side (right). The dark values (left side) are not clipped; instead, the graph extends to the left edge and stops before it is clipped.

The image in figure 8.23 shows more detail but is not professional looking and will win no awards. The range of light is simply too great to be recorded fully. Many of the details are overly light, and that can be seen by the clipping of the histogram on the right side. The most important thing to remember is that when you see a histogram that is crammed all the way to the right and clipped, some or all of the image is significantly too light. A portion of the image in figure 8.23 is recorded as pure white and is permanently gone, or blown out.

From the clipping on the left, you can see that some dark detail has been lost in the image, too. Looking at the base of the closest trees in the picture, you can clearly see dark shadows with little or no detail. This image simply has too much light range for the camera to record it all. We will discuss what to do about this later in the chapter.

It is important that you try to center the histogram without clipping either edge. This is not always possible, as shown in figure 8.23, because the light range is often too great and the sensor or histogram window can't contain it. If you center the histogram, your images will be better exposed. If you take a picture and the histogram is shifted toward the left or right, you can retake the photograph and adjust the exposure.

If there is too much light to allow the histogram to be centered, you must decide which part of the image is more important—the light or dark values—and expose for those values.

How Does the Eye React to Light Values?

With its imaging sensor and glass lenses, the D800 is only a weak imitation of our marvelously designed eye and brain combination. There are very few situations in which our eyes cannot adjust to the available light range. So, as photographers, we are always seeking ways to record a portion of what our eyes and mind can see.

Since our eyes tend to know that shadows are black, and we expect that, it is usually better to expose for the highlights. If you see dark shadows, that seems normal. We're simply not used to seeing light so bright that all detail is lost. An image exposed for the dark values will look weird because most highlight detail will be burned out.

Your eyes can see a huge range of light in comparison to your digital sensor. The only time you will ever see light values that are so bright that detail is lost is when you are looking directly at an overwhelmingly bright light, like the sun. In a worst-case scenario, if you expose the image so the right side of the histogram just touches the right side of the histogram window, and the image will look more normal.

Since photography's beginning, we have always fought with being able to record only a limited range of light. But with the digital camera and its histogram, we can now see a visual representation of the light values. We can immediately review the image, reshoot it emphasizing lighter or darker values, or use a graduated neutral-density filter to hold back part of the light in the scene.

Many of today's digital photographers prefer to use high dynamic range (HDR) imaging, where multiple images are exposed with different values to capture a much broader range light. The images are then combined into one image with a much greater range of light displayed.

Computer Adjustment of Images

Looking at the image in figure 8.24, taken in midday with overhead sunshine, we see an example of a range of light too great to be captured by a digital sensor but exposed in such a way that we can get a usable photo later.

Notice how the dark values are clipped and the dark detail is lost. But look to the right side of the histogram and notice how the light values are not clipped. The camera recorded all of the light values but lost some dark values.

Figure 8.24 – Cabin picture and histogram with correct exposure but dark shadows

Since our eyes see this as normal, this image looks okay. If we were standing there looking at the cabin ourselves, our eyes would be able to see much more detail in the front porch area. But the camera just can't record that much light range. If we want to get a bit more detail in the shadows than this image seems to contain, we can do it. Normally, a camera does not give us enough control to add light values on the fly, so we use the histogram to get the best possible exposure and then adjust the image later in the computer. Some cameras can be profiled to capture light ranges more effectively in one direction or the other, but when you push one area, the opposite area must give. So we need a way to take all this light and compress it into a more usable range.

We are now entering the realm of post-processing, or in-computer image manipulation. Look at the image in figure 8.25. This is the same image as figure 8.24, but it has been adjusted in Photoshop to cram more image detail into the histogram by compressing the midrange values. Notice that the mountain peak of the histogram is farther right, toward the light side, than the histogram for figure 8.24, and that the whole histogram fits within the histogram window without any clipping. We removed a good bit of the midrange, but since there was already a lot of midrange there, our image did not suffer greatly.

How this computer post-processing was done is outside the scope of this book, but it is not very difficult. Buy a program like Nikon Capture NX 2, Photoshop, Photoshop Elements, Lightroom, Aperture, or another fine graphics program designed for photographers. Your digital camera and your computer are a powerful imaging combination—a digital darkroom, where you are in control from start to finish, from releasing the shutter to printing the image. Retreating from philosophy, let's continue with our histogram exploration.

Figure 8.25 – Post-processed cabin picture and its histogram

Notice in figure 8.25 that the histogram edge is just touching the highlight side of the histogram window. If it had gone a tiny bit past the right edge and clipped a small amount, the image would not have been damaged too badly or at all, for a reason we will discuss in a moment. Sometimes a very small amount of clipping does not seriously harm the image, especially when you are shooting in RAW mode.

The photographer must be the judge. The greater apparent detail in the image in figure 8.25 is the result of compressing the midrange of the light values a bit in the computer. If you compress or make the midrange light values smaller, that will tend to pull the dark values toward the light side and the light values toward the dark side. It's like cutting a section out of the middle of a garden hose. If you pull both of the cut ends together, the other two ends of the hose will move toward the middle, and the hose will be shorter overall. If you compress or remove the midrange of the histogram, both ends of the graph will move toward the middle. If one end of the graph is beyond the edge of the histogram window (clipped), it will be less so when the midrange is compressed.

We are simply trying to make the histogram fit into the frame of its window. We can cut out some of the middle to bring both ends into the window because there is usually plenty in the middle to cut out, so the image rarely suffers. Remember, this is done outside of the camera in a computer. You can't really control the in-camera histogram to compress values, but you need to be aware that it can be done in a computer so that you can expose accordingly with your camera's histogram. Then you will be prepared for later post-processing of the image. Now that we have compressed the midrange values, figure 8.25 more closely resembles what our eye normally sees, so it looks more normal to us.

Shooting in RAW Can Benefit Your Images

In many cases, your progression from the shooting site to your digital darkroom can benefit if you shoot NEF (RAW) images. A RAW digital image contains an adjustable range of light, in a sense. With a RAW image, you can use controls in Capture NX 2, Photoshop, or even the basic Nikon ViewNX 2 software included with the D800 to select from the range of light within the big RAW image file. It's like moving the histogram window to the left or right over all that wide range of RAW image data. You select a final resting place for the histogram window, capture the underlying RAW data, and your image is ready for use.

This is a serious oversimplification of the process, but I hope it is more understandable. In reality, the digital sensor records a wider range of light than you can use in one image. You always have that extra information available to you in a RAW image, but it is thrown away when you shoot or convert to JPEG.

Although you can't get all of that range into the final image without special processing, it is there in the RAW file as a selectable range. I prefer to think of it as a built-in bracket because it works in a similar way.

In reality—and this is an important point—the histogram we use in our D800 cameras (and other Nikons) is based on a camera-processed JPEG file. Therefore, when you are shooting in RAW mode, there is a little more headroom for clipping on the dark and light sides of the histogram than what the histogram window shows. You can over- and underexpose by a slight amount when shooting in RAW mode and still pull out good detail, where the detail would be gone had you been shooting in JPEG mode.

In my experience with the D800, the dark detail contains an amazing amount of information that can be recovered, with a little added noise as a penalty. The bright values do not have quite the same amount of headroom, so be careful not to seriously overexpose your images or nothing will recover the light detail.

Using Active D-Lighting for Expanded Dynamic Range

Interestingly, the Active D-Lighting function on the D800 is a good example of what I mean by there being extra detail available in a RAW file. Where do you suppose Active D-Lighting gets its detail? From the extra headroom in the RAW sensor data, of course. A JPEG file especially benefits from Active D-Lighting in many cases.

When you have Active D-Lighting turned on, the JPEG is created from RAW sensor data, with expanded dynamic range from Active D-Lighting applied as the JPEG file is created and saved to the memory card. The D800 is especially powerful when it comes to using Active D-Lighting. It is the first digital camera I have ever used where I will leave this function turned on most of the time. It does a simply marvelous job at extending the range of light your images can contain.

Settings Recommendation: As you know by now, the Nikon D800 has a Multi selector that can be pressed right or left to scroll through the images you have already taken. You can also press the Multi selector up or down to scroll through the various informational screens, such as the histogram display. When you take a picture of an important subject, find the histogram view of your image.

If you can't find the screen with multiple histograms, as shown in figure 8.18, screen 1, see the *Playback Menu > Playback display options*, and select (check) RGB histogram. You can also assign the Multi selector center button to show you a histogram when you are playing back images (see Custom setting f2 Multi selector center button). Very convenient!

Your camera meter should be used to get the initial exposure only. Then you can look at the histogram to see if the image's light range is contained within the limited range of the sensor. If it is clipped to the right or the left, you may want to add or subtract light with your +/- Exposure compensation button or use Manual mode. Expose for the light range with your histogram. Let your light meter get you close, then fine-tune with the histogram.

There are also other Monitor viewing modes that you can use along with the histogram, such as the Highlights (blink) mode for blown-out highlights (see the *Playback Menu > Playback display options* and select Highlights). This mode will cause your image to blink from light to dark in the blown-out highlight areas. This is a rough representation of a histogram in which the highlight value is clipped, and it is quite useful for quick shooting. Using your camera's light meter, histogram, and Highlights (blink) mode together is a very powerful way to control your exposures. If you master using the histogram, you will have a fine degree of control over where you place the light range of your images. This is sort of like using the famous Ansel Adams black-and-white Zone System, but it is represented visually on the Monitor of your D800.

The manipulation of histogram levels in-computer is a detailed study in and of itself. It's part of having a digital darkroom. Learn to use your computer to tweak your images, and you'll be able to produce superior results most of the time. Even more important, learn to use your histogram to capture a nice image in the first place!

Your histogram is simply a graph that lets you see at a glance how well your image is contained by your camera. If it's too far left, the image is too dark; if it's too far right, the image is too light. If clipped on both ends, there is too much light for one image to contain. Learn to use the histogram well and your images are bound to improve!

Author's Conclusions

This camera certainly gives you a lot of choices for light meters and exposure modes. You can start using this camera at whatever level of photographic knowledge you have. If you are a beginner, use the P mode. If you want to progress into partial automation, use the S or A mode. And if you are a dyed-in-the-wool imaging fanatic, use the M mode for full manual control of the camera. You have a choice with the D800!

The next chapter is about a subject of great importance to digital photographers—white balance (WB). Understanding WB gives you an edge over other photographers. Learning about the histogram and white balance will place you in a spot occupied by relatively few people. When you have mastered those two subjects and learned about color spaces, you will indeed be an advanced digital photographer. Let's proceed!

White Balance

9

Rescue Me! – Courtesy of Eric Bowles (*ericbowles*)

Back in the good old days, photographers bought special rolls of film or filters to meet the challenges of color casts that come from indoor lighting, overcast days, or special situations.

The D800's method for balancing the camera to the available light comes with the White balance (WB) controls. Fortunately, the D800's two Auto White balance settings do a great job for general shooting. However, discerning photographers learn how to use the White balance controls so they can achieve color consistency in special situations.

How Does White Balance (WB) Work?

(User's Manual – Page 145)

Normally White balance is used to adjust the camera so that whites are truly white and other colors are accurate under whatever light source you are shooting. You can also use the White balance controls to deliberately introduce color casts into your image for interesting special effects.

Camera WB color temperatures are exactly the opposite of the Kelvin scale we learned in school for star temperatures. Remember that a red giant star is cool, while a blue/white star is hot. The WB color temperatures are the opposite because the WB system adds color to make up for a deficit of color in the original light of the subject.

For instance, under a fluorescent light, there is a deficit of blue, which makes the subject appear greenish yellow. When blue is added, the image is balanced to a more normal appearance.

Another example might be shooting on a cloudy, overcast day. The cool, ambient light could cause the image to look bluish if it's left unadjusted. The White balance control in your camera sees the cool color temperature and adds some red to warm the colors a bit. Normal camera White balance on a cloudy, overcast day might be about 6000K.

Just remember that we use the real kelvin temperature range in reverse and that red colors are considered warm and blue colors are cool. Even though this is the opposite of what we were taught in school, it fits our situation better. To photographers, blue seems cool and red seems warm! Just don't let your astronomer friends convince you otherwise.

Understanding WB in a fundamental way is simply realizing that light has a range of colors that go from cool to warm. We can adjust our cameras to use the available light in an accurate and neutral, balanced way that compensates for the actual light source. Or we can allow a color cast to enter the image by unbalancing the settings. In this chapter, we will discuss this from the standpoint of the D800's camera controls and how they deal with WB.

Color Temperature

(User's Manual – Page 152)

The D800 WB range can vary from a very cool 2500K to a very warm 10,000K. Figure 9.1A shows the same picture adjusted in Photoshop, with the use of photo filters, to three WB settings. Notice how the image in the center is about right; the image on the left is cooler (bluish cast) and the image on the right is warmer (reddish cast).

Figure 9.1A – Same image with three different WB Color Temperature settings

The same adjustments we made with film and filters can now be achieved with the White balance settings built into the D800. To achieve the same effect as daylight film and a warming filter, simply select the Cloudy White balance setting while shooting in normal daylight. This sets the D800 to balance at about 6000K, which makes nice, warm-looking images. If you want to really warm up the image, choose the White balance setting called Shade, which sets the camera to 8000K. Or you could set the D800's White balance to AUTO2, which warms up the colors and automatically adjusts for current light sources.

On the other hand, if you want to make the image appear cool or bluish, try using the Fluorescent (4200K) or Incandescent (3000K) setting in normal daylight.

Remember, the color temperature shifts from cool values to warm values. The D800 can record your images with any color temperature from 2500K (very cool or bluish) to 10,000K (very warm or reddish) and any major value in between. There is no need to carry different film emulsions or filters to deal with light color range. The D800 has very easy-to-use color temperature controls and a full range of color temperatures available.

There are two separate methods for setting the White balance on the D800:

- Manual WB using the WB button and selecting options
- Manual WB using the Shooting Menu and selecting options

We'll consider each of these techniques because you may prefer to use different methods according to the amount of time you have to shoot and the color accuracy you want.

Camera Control Locations for WB Adjustment

In this chapter we will often use the WB button, Main and Sub-command dials, and Control panel when adjusting White balance (figure 9.1B). You may want to place a bookmark here for future reference if you are not sure where these controls are.

Figure 9.1B – Camera controls for White balance adjustment

Figure 9.1B provides a list of controls as follows:

1. WB button
2. Sub-command dial
3. Control panel
4. Main command dial

Remember these control names and locations for use in this chapter and later in the field.

9

> **What Is Mired?**
>
> Often in this chapter I will talk about adjusting White balance in mired incre-ments. *Mired* stands for *micro reciprocal degree*. It is a unit of measurement used to express color temperature value differences. It is based on a just-noticeable difference between two light sources and founded on the difference of the recip-rocal of their kelvin color temperatures (not the temperatures themselves). The use of mired values dates back to 1932 when Irwin G. Priest invented the method. It is based on a mathematical formula, as follows: **M = 1,000,000 / T**, where M is the desired mired value and T is the color temperature in units of kelvin. Most of us don't need to be concerned about understanding the term mired. Just realize that it means a visual difference between color values.

Manual White Balance Using the WB Button

(User's Manual – Page 146)

Sometimes you might want to control the WB in a totally manual way. This and the next section's methods accomplish the same thing, except this first method config-ures the WB using a button and dial and the next uses the camera's menu system.

Each of these methods will allow you to set a particular WB temperature. If you want your image to appear cool, medium, or warm, you can set the appropriate color temperature, take the picture, and then look at the image on the Monitor.

Here is how to manually choose a WB type using the WB button, Main command dial, and Control panel (figure 9.1B and figure 9.2):

1. Press and hold the WB button above the Release mode dial on top of your D800 (figure 9.1B).
2. Rotate the rear Main command dial (figure 9.1B).
3. The symbols in the following list will appear one at a time on the Control panel (figure 9.2, red arrow). Each click of the dial will change the display to the next WB setting. These symbols, options, and their kelvin values are as follows:

- A Auto White Balance – 3500K to 8000K
  (A on Control panel, Auto in camera menus, and AUTO1 or AUTO2 on Information display)
- ☀ Incandescent – 3000K
- ☀ Fluorescent – 2700K to 7200K
- ☀ Direct sunlight – 5200K
- ⚡ Flash – 5400K
- ☁ Cloudy – 6000K

Figure 9.2 – Manual White Balance with Control panel

- • ⚐ Shade – 8000K
- • ⓚ K – Choose a color temperature (2500K–10,000K)
- • ᴘʀᴇ PRE (Preset manual) – White balance measured from actual ambient light

Manual White Balance Using the Shooting Menu

(User's Manual – Page 146)

This method uses the Shooting Menu screens to select the appropriate White balance.

Figure 9.3A – Manual White balance with Shooting Menu screens

Here are the steps used to select a White balance setting (figure 9.3A):

1. Select White balance from the Shooting Menu and scroll to the right (figure 9.3A, screen 1).
2. Select one of the preset values, such as Flash, and scroll to the right (figure 9.3A, screen 2).
3. Press the OK button immediately, without moving the little square from its center position, unless you want to fine-tune the White balance setting (figure 9.3, screen 3). Fine-tuning is discussed in detail in the upcoming section **Fine-Tuning White Balance**.

Normally, you'll use only the first two screens in figure 9.3A to select one of the preset WB values, such as Cloudy, Shade, or Direct sunlight. Then you'll press the OK button on the final screen without changing anything. If you'd like, you can fine-tune the white balance with the third screen. As mentioned in step 3, we'll discuss how later in the chapter.

Additional Screen for Auto and Fluorescent WB

If you choose Auto or Fluorescent, you will find an additional screen before you get to the final fine-tuning screen.

Figure 9.3B – Extra Auto WB screen before fine-tuning screen

Figure 9.3C – Extra Fluorescent WB screen before fine-tuning screen

Auto White balance has two values from which to choose: AUTO1 Normal and AUTO2 Keep warm lighting colors (figure 9.3B). AUTO2 can make a somewhat warmer image than AUTO1.

Fluorescent includes seven types of Fluorescent lighting: Sodium-vapor lamps, Warm-white fluorescent, White fluorescent, Cool-white fluorescent, Day white fluorescent, Daylight fluorescent, and High temp. mercury-vapor (figure 9.3C).

Manual Color Temperature with the WB Button

(User's Manual – Page 153)

The K selection on the Control panel is flexible and allows you to manually select a WB value between 2500K and 10,000K.

Here are the steps to select a specific kelvin (K) White balance value using external camera controls (figure 9.1B and figure 9.4):

1. Select the K symbol on the Control panel by holding down the WB button and rotating the rear Main command dial (figure 9.1B and 9.4).
2. While still holding down the WB button, rotate the front Sub-command dial to select the actual WB kelvin temperature you desire, from 2500K to 10,000K. In figure 9.4, I used the front Sub-command dial to select 5000K.

Figure 9.4 – Manual Color temperature (K) with external camera controls

Manual Color Temperature with the Shooting Menu

(User's Manual – Page 152)

You can also manually select a color temperature using the Shooting Menu screens.

Figure 9.5 – Manual Color temperature (K) with Shooting Menu screens

Here are the steps to select a specific kelvin (K) White balance value using Shooting Menu screens (figure 9.5):

1. Choose White balance from the Shooting Menu and scroll to the right (figure 9.5, screen 1).
2. Select Choose color temp. from the White balance menu and scroll to the right (figure 9.5, screen 2).
3. Using the Multi selector to scroll up or down in the color temperature box, you can choose a number from 2500K to 10,000K. In figure 9.5, screen 3, you can see that I selected 5000K. Notice how a large yellow rectangle is surrounding the Choose color temp. area of the screen? This screen has two sides, one for color temperature selection and the other for fine-tuning. Scroll to the right to move the yellow triangle to the fine-tuning area.
4. Now you can fine-tune the color temperature to include more green or magenta in six steps, G1–G6 or M1–M6. You simply press up or down on the Multi selector to fine-tune. Up adds green (G) and down adds magenta (M).
5. Once you have fine-tuned the color temperature to your liking, press the OK button.

When you have selected an exact White balance temperature, all images you shoot from that point forward—until you change to another WB—will have that setting. You can have very consistent White balance from image to image by using this method. For in-studio product shoots, or in any circumstance where you need a constant White balance, this is a desirable function.

Measuring Ambient Light by Using PRE

(User's Manual – Page 154)

This method allows you to measure ambient light values and set the camera's WB. It's not hard to learn and is very accurate because it's an actual through-the-lens measurement of the source light's kelvin temperature.

You'll need a white or gray card to accomplish this measurement. Figure 9.6A shows the popular WhiBal white balance reference cards, which are available at **http://michaeltapesdesign.com/whibal.html**. The WhiBal card set is very convenient because it contains card versions that will easily fit in your pocket or camera bag.

Figure 9.6A – WhiBal cards

Here's how to select the PRE White balance measurement method (figures 9.1B, 9.6B, and 9.6C):

1. Press and hold the WB button (figure 9.1B).
2. Rotate the rear Main command dial until PRE shows at the lower-right of the Control panel (figure 9.6B). You'll also see d-1 at the top of the Control panel.
3. While still pressing the WB button, turn the front Sub-command dial and select one of the preset memory locations, d-1 to d-4. Your measured White balance reading will be stored in that location.
4. Release the WB button.
5. Press and hold the WB button again until PRE starts blinking* in the lower-right corner of the Control panel (figure 9.6C, red arrow). You will see the preset memory location number just above the flashing PRE (figure 9.6C shows that we are adjusting d-4).
6. Point the camera at a white or neutral gray card lit by the same light source you will be using to take pictures. The camera does not have to focus on the card, but the card should fill the frame, so try to get close without making a shadow.

Figure 9.6B – PRE White balance measurement method

Figure 9.6C – PRE White balance measurement method

7. Press the Shutter-release button fully, as if you were photographing the card. The shutter will fire, but nothing will appear on the Monitor.
8. Check the Control panel to see if *Good* is flashing and PrE (with lowercase r) appears on the lower-right portion of the Control panel (above the tiny PRE). If *Good* is flashing, you have successfully measured for a correct White balance under the light in which you are shooting. If you see *no Gd* flashing (instead of *Good*), the operation was not successful. Your available light may not be bright enough to take an accurate reading.

*Note: Once PRE starts blinking on the Control panel, you must take the new White balance measurement (step 6) within about six seconds, or you will have to repeat steps 4 and 5. If you have Custom Setting c2 Auto meter-off delay set to longer than six seconds, the PRE measurement time-out (how long PRE flashes) will match it. The PRE measurement time-out is tied directly to the Auto meter-off delay.

The PRE measurement is very sensitive because it uses the light coming through the lens to set the WB. Unless you are measuring in extremely low light it will virtually always be successful.

Fine-Tuning White Balance

(User's Manual – Page 148)
You can fine-tune White balance using the camera's external WB controls or the Shooting Menu. Fine-tuning with external controls allows for adjustment of only amber or blue. The Shooting Menu allows you to fine-tune not only amber and blue, but also green and magenta.

Fine-Tuning with External Controls
Only certain White balance values can be fine-tuned with external controls, including Auto, Incandescent, Fluorescent, Direct sunlight, Flash, Cloudy, and Shade. Basically, you select one of the White balance values provided by the camera and add amber or blue in 5-mired increments. You can add or subtract amber or blue in

up to six steps—A1 to A6 or b1 to b6. That means you can change the color from a minimum of 5 mired to a maximum of 30 mired. Remember, a 1-mired step is equivalent to a barely perceptible change in color.

Figure 9.7A – Fine-tuning White balance with external controls

Here is how to add or subtract amber or blue from a Nikon-provided White balance value, using external camera controls (figures 9.1B and 9.7A):

1. Press and hold the WB button and turn the rear Main command dial (figure 9.1B) until you select a White balance value you would like to fine-tune. In figure 9.7A, you can see the results of selecting a WB value; I selected auto (A) White balance.
2. While still holding down the WB button, turn the front Sub-command dial to the left (counterclockwise) for amber values (A1–A6) or to the right (clockwise) for blue values (b1–b6). Remember that each Sub-command dial click is a 5-mired value. In figure 9.7A, there are two Control panel screens showing the two color types that I selected (A1 and b1). Screen 1 is one 5-mired step of additional amber, and screen 2 is one 5-mired step of extra blue added to the current WB value.
3. Release the WB button, and you're ready to take pictures with your fine-tuned WB value. It stays fine-tuned until you change it back. You'll see a small asterisk next to the WB symbol on the Control panel when you are using a fine-tuned WB value. You can see the asterisk in both images in figure 9.7A between WB and A. If you select a different White balance that has not been fine-tuned, the asterisk goes away.

Unfortunately, external control fine-tuning is not a visual process. You'll need to examine the images taken with your new WB* value to determine if you like the results of your fine-tuning effort.

Fine-Tuning with the Shooting Menu

You can use the Shooting Menu to fine-tune even more effectively than you can with the camera's external controls. Instead of two colors (amber and blue), you can adjust four colors (amber, blue, green, and magenta).

If you want to fine-tune a previously saved White balance value, you can do it with the Shooting Menu screens, too. The value in any of the d-1 to d-4 memory locations can be manually fine-tuned. The color balance can be moved toward G (green), A (amber), M (magenta), or B (blue), or it can be moved toward intermediate combinations of those colors.

Figure 9.7B – Fine-tuning White balance with Shooting Menu screens

Here are the steps used to fine-tune a White balance setting using Shooting Menu screens (figure 9.7B):

1. Select White balance from the Shooting Menu and scroll to the right (figure 9.7B, screen 1).
2. Choose one of the White balance types. I chose Direct sunlight. Now scroll to the right or press the OK button (figure 9.7B, screen 2).
3. You will now see the fine-tuning screen with its color box. In the middle of the color box is a small black square (figure 9.7B, screen 3, red arrow). When this square is in the middle, as shown in screen 3, nothing has been changed. Each press of the Multi selector in a given direction is equal to one 5-mired step in that direction—up is green (G), down is magenta (M), left is blue (B), and right is amber (A). You can see in figure 9.7B, screen 4, that I have added both G and A by moving the little square to a position in between those two values (see red arrow in screen 4).
4. Press the OK button to save your change. An asterisk will appear after the name of the fine-tuned White balance selection on the Shooting Menu screen (figure 9.7C, screen 6, red arrow). To remove the fine-tuning adjustment, simply return to the screen with the color box and center the little square, as in figure 9.7B, screen 3.

Note: If you aren't familiar with adjusting the preset's default color temperature, or if you don't want to change it (most people don't), then simply press the OK button without moving the little square from the center (figure 9.7B, screen 3).

Fine-Tuning a PRE Measured White Balance

Previously we examined how to take a PRE measurement from a white or gray card to balance the camera to the available light. What if you want to fine-tune one of the d-1 to d-4 Preset values? Let's do it!

Figure 9.7C – Fine-tuning a Preset WB value

Use these steps to fine-tune a Preset White balance value (figure 9.7C):

1. Select White balance from the Shooting Menu and scroll to the right (figure 9.7C, screen 1).
2. Choose Preset manual from the menu and scroll to the right (figure 9.7C, screen 2).
3. Use the Multi selector to scroll to the memory location you want to fine-tune, d-1 to d-4 (figure 9.7C, screen 3). Press the Multi selector center button to select it.
4. Choose Fine-tune from the Preset manual menu and scroll to the right (figure 9.7C, screen 4).
5. Use the Multi selector to adjust the color balance in 5-mired increments (figure 9.7C, screen 5). Scroll around in the color box toward whatever color you want to add to the currently stored White balance (red arrow). You'll see the color-mired values change on the right side of the screen in the fields next to A–B and G–M. Each increment (click) of the Multi selector is equal to about 5 mired.
6. Press the OK button to save your adjustments to the stored White balance. The camera will return to the main Shooting Menu screen and PRE* will appear next to White balance (figure 9.7, screen 6). The asterisk shows that this particular Preset White balance has been fine-tuned.

Editing the PRE WB Comment Field

(User's Manual – Page 160)

You can edit (add text to) the comment field of the memory location (d-1 to d-4) in which you just stored a White balance setting. Change the comment to something that will remind you of this measured WB setting's purpose.

Figure 9.8 – Editing the comment field

Here are the steps to edit a WB setting's comment field (figure 9.8):

1. Select White balance from the Shooting Menu and scroll to the right (figure 9.8, screen 1).
2. Choose Preset manual from the menu and scroll to the right (figure 9.8, screen 2).
3. Select the memory location for which you want to edit the comment (d-1 to d-4) and press the Multi selector center button (figure 9.8, screen 3). This will open the Preset manual menu.
4. Choose Edit comment from the menu and scroll to the right (figure 9.8, screen 4).
5. The character-selection panel will now appear (figure 9.8, screen 5). Use the Multi selector to navigate among the letters and numbers. Press the Multi selector center button to add a character to the comment line at the bottom of the screen. To scroll through characters already added, hold down the Thumbnail/playback zoom out button while navigating to the left or right with the Multi selector. Press the Delete button to delete the current character. Press the OK button to save the memory location comment.
6. The White balance memory location screen will now appear with the new memory location comment displayed (figure 9.8, screen 6, red arrow). I changed the comment field for memory location d-1 to Halogen headlights for a really weird portrait session I was doing at the time.

Using the White Balance from a Previously Captured Image

(User's Manual – Page 158)

You can also select a White balance setting from an image you have already successfully taken. This value can be applied to the picture you are about to take, or it can be copied to memory locations d-1 to d-4 (using the function described previously) for later use.

Figure 9.9 – Using White balance from a previously taken image

Here are the steps to recover the White balance setting from an image stored on your camera's memory card (figure 9.9):

1. Select White balance from the Shooting Menu and scroll to the right (figure 9.9, screen 1).

2. Choose Preset manual from the menu and scroll to the right (figure 9.9, screen 2).

3. Choose a memory location to which you want to save the White balance setting from an existing picture. I chose d-2 (figure 9.9, screen 3). Press the Multi selector center button to select the Preset memory location. This opens the Preset manual menu.

4. Choose Select image from the Preset manual menu and scroll to the right (figure 9.9, screen 4). Select image will be grayed out if there are no images on your current memory card.

5. You will now see the Select image screen (figure 9.9, screen 5). Navigate through the available images until you find the one you want to use for white balance information. You can zoom in to look at a larger version of the image by pressing the Playback zoom in button. Press the OK button to select the image.

6. A small picture of the image will appear in your selected Preset White balance memory location and is saved there for future use (figure 9.9, screen 6). The White balance setting from that picture is now the White balance setting for the camera, until you change it.

Protecting a White Balance Preset

(User's Manual – Page 161)

You may have gone to great efforts to create a particular White balance Preset value that you will use frequently. Maybe you have a studio with a certain type of lighting that does not vary, and you want to have a dependable Preset value available for it. Let's see how to protect a Preset (d-1 to d4) value.

Figure 9.10 – Protecting a PRE White balance from deletion or change

Here are the steps to protect a White balance Preset value:

1. Select White balance from the Shooting Menu and scroll to the right (figure 9.10, screen 1).
2. Choose Preset manual from the menu and scroll to the right (figure 9.10, screen 2).
3. Choose the memory location you want to protect (d-1 to d-4). I chose d-3 (figure 9.10, screen 3). Press the Multi selector center button to select the Preset memory location. This opens the Preset manual menu.
4. Choose Protect from the Preset manual menu and scroll to the right (figure 9.10, screen 4).
5. Choose On to protect or Off to remove protection from a White balance memory location. I am protecting d-3, so I chose On (figure 9.10, screen 5).

9

6. The camera will now display the White balance screen with a protection symbol showing on the memory location you protected. The key symbol at the point of the red arrow in figure 9.10, screen 6, shows that memory location d-3 is locked from deletion and change. You cannot modify the protected value in any way, including fine-tuning or editing the comment field, until you remove the protection.

Auto White Balance

(User's Manual – Page 145)

Auto White balance works pretty well in the D800. As the camera's RGB meter senses colors, it does its best to balance to any white or midrange grays it can find in the image. However, the color will vary a little on each shot. If you shoot only in Auto WB mode, your camera considers each image a new WB problem and solves it without reference to the last image taken.

The Auto WB setting also has the White balance fine-tuning screen, as discussed in the section **Fine-Tuning White Balance** earlier in this chapter. I don't see how this is particularly useful because each image is likely to have slightly different color temperatures. That would mean the fine-tuning would have little value for more than an image or two. If you were shooting in the exact same light for a period of time, I suppose the fine-tuning would be useful; however, wouldn't it make more sense to do a PRE reading of the light for exact WB? This choice will depend on your shooting style and personal preferences.

Using Auto WB (AUTO1 and AUTO2)

Auto White balance comes in two flavors: AUTO1 and AUTO2. The difference is that AUTO2 uses warmer colors in comparison to AUTO1.

For general shooting, AUTO1—or AUTO2, if you prefer warm colors—is all that's needed.

Here are the steps to select one of the Auto White balance options (figure 9.11):

1. Choose White balance from the Shooting Menu and scroll to the right (figure 9.11, screen 1).
2. Select Auto from the menu and scroll to the right (figure 9.11, screen 2).
3. Choose AUTO1 Normal or AUTO2 Keep warm lighting colors (according to your color warmth preference) and scroll to the right (figure 9.11, screen 3).
4. Press the OK button to lock in the WB setting, or scroll to the right to fine-tune if you'd like (figure 9.11, screen 4). See the section Fine-Tuning White Balance earlier in this chapter.

Figure 9.11 – Auto White balance choices

Settings Recommendation: I often use AUTO1 White balance on my D800. The only time I use anything but AUTO1 is when I am shooting special types of images. For instance, if I am shooting an event with flash and I want consistent image color, I often choose the Flash White balance setting. Or, if I am shooting landscapes under direct sunlight, I often shoot with the Direct sunlight White balance setting. Other than special occasions, Auto White balance works very well for me. Give it a try, along with each of the others in their respective environments. This is all part of improving our digital photography. A few years back, we carried different film emulsions and colored filters to get these same effects. Now it's all built in!

Should I Worry about White Balance If I Shoot in RAW mode?

The quick answer is no, but that may not be the best answer. When you take a picture using NEF (RAW) mode, the sensor image data has no White balance, sharpening, or color saturation information applied. Instead, the information about your camera settings is stored as markers along with the RAW black-and-white sensor data. Color information, including White balance, is applied permanently to the image only when you post-process and save the image in another format, like JPEG, TIFF, or EPS.

When you open the image in Nikon Capture NX 2, or another RAW conversion program, the camera settings are applied to the sensor data in a temporary way so you can view the image on your computer screen. If you don't like the White balance or almost any other setting you used in-camera, you can simply change it in the conversion software, and the image will look as if you used the new setting when you took the picture.

Does that mean I am not concerned about my WB settings because I shoot RAW most of the time? No. The human brain can quickly adjust to an image's colors and perceive them as normal, even when they are not. This is one of the dangers of not using correct WB. Because an unbalanced image on your computer screen is not compared to another correctly balanced image side by side, there is some danger that your brain may accept the slightly incorrect camera settings as normal, and your image will be saved with a color cast.

As a rule of thumb, if you use your WB correctly at all times, you'll consistently produce better images. You'll do less post-processing if the WB is correct in the first place. As RAW shooters, we already have a lot of post-processing work to do. Why add WB corrections to the workflow? It's just more work, if you ask me!

Additionally, you might decide to switch to JPEG mode in the middle of a shoot, and if you are not accustomed to using your WB controls, you'll be in trouble. When you shoot JPEGs, your camera will apply the WB information directly to the image and save it on your memory card—permanently. Be safe; always use good WB technique!

White Balance Tips and Tricks

When measuring WB with a gray or white card, keep in mind that your camera does not need to focus on the card. In PRE mode, it will not focus anyway because it is only trying to read light values, not take a picture. The important thing is to put your lens close enough to the card to prevent it from seeing anything other than the card. Three or four inches (about 75 mm to 100 mm) away from the card is about right for most lenses.

Be careful that your lens does not cast a shadow onto the card in a way that lets your camera see some of the shadow. This will make the measurement less accurate. Also, be sure that your source light does not produce glare on the card. This problem is not common because most cards have a matte surface, but it can happen. You may want to hold the card at a slight angle to the source light if the light is particularly bright and might cause glare.

Finally, when the light is dim, use the white side of the card because it is more reflective. This may prevent a no Gd reading in low light. The gray card may be more accurate for color balancing, but it might be a little dark for a good measurement in dim light. If you are shooting in normal light, the gray card is best for balancing. You might want to experiment in normal light to see which you prefer.

Author's Conclusions

With these simple tips and some practice, you can become a D800 WB expert. Starting on page 145 of your D800 User's Manual, you'll find extensive WB information if you want another perspective on Nikon WB.

Learn to use the color temperature features of your camera to make superior images. You'll be able to capture very accurate colors or make pictures with color casts to reflect how you feel about the images. Practice a bit, and you'll find it easy to remember how to set your WB in the field.

Now, let's turn our attention to the autofocus (AF) system in the D800. Many people find the various modes hard to remember and even a bit confusing. In the upcoming chapter, we'll examine how the AF modes work and how they relate to other important camera functions, such as the AF-area and Release modes.

Autofocus, AF-Area, and Release Modes

10

Seagull in Flight – Courtesy of Christian Coombes (*Chiefmasterjedi*)

Autofocus (AF) and Release modes are active settings that you'll deal with each time you use your camera. Unlike adjusting settings in the menus, which you'll do from time to time, you'll use Autofocus and Release modes every time you make an image or movie. You will adjust AF-area modes less often; however, these critical functions affect how and where the camera focuses on your subject.

To take pictures and make movies, you need to be very familiar with these settings, so this is a very important chapter for your mastery of the Nikon D800. Grab your camera and let's get started!

This chapter is divided into three sections:

- Section 1 – Autofocus in Viewfinder Photography
- Section 2 – Autofocus in Live View Photography
- Section 3 – Release Modes

Section 1 – Autofocus in Viewfinder Photography

The Nikon D800 has two types of autofocus built in, with different parts of the camera controlling AF in different shooting modes (figure 10.1). When you take pictures through the Viewfinder, one type of autofocus is used, and when you shoot a picture or movie using Live view, a different type is used. They are as follows:

- ***TTL phase detection autofocus*** – The Multi-CAM 3500 FX autofocus module provides through-the-lens (TTL) phase detection autofocus, with 51 AF points in a grid-like array in the central area of the Viewfinder (figure 10.1, image 1). This type of AF is known simply as *phase detection AF*. It is a very fast type of autofocus and is used by the camera only when you are taking pictures through the Viewfinder.
- ***Focal plane contrast AF*** – The camera's imaging sensor provides focal plane contrast AF, which uses pixel-level contrast detection (figure 10.1, image 2). A simple name for this is *contrast-detect AF*. The entire surface of the imaging sensor can be used to detect contrast between light and dark boundaries to provide autofocus. This is a relatively slow form of autofocus, but it is extremely accurate because it is done at the pixel level. This form of autofocus is used only while you are shooting in Live view mode.

What Is the Multi-CAM 3500 FX Autofocus Module?

The Multi-CAM 3500 FX AF module is a very accurate autofocus system that controls where and how your camera's AF and AF-S lenses achieve the sharpest focus on your subject.

The Nikon D800 offers a significant boost in the number of Viewfinder AF points over lesser cameras, with a total of 51. What do we gain from all these extra AF points and more powerful modes? As we progress through this chapter, I'll discuss these things in detail, along with how your photography will benefit most from using all the features of the Multi-CAM 3500 FX AF system.

Figure 10.1 – (1) Multi-CAM 3500 FX AF module and (2) CMOS FX format imaging sensor

Three Mode Groups

There are three specific mode groups that you should fully understand: Autofocus modes, AF-area modes, and Release modes.

Many people get these modes confused and incorrectly apply functions from one mode to a completely different mode. It *is* a bit confusing at times, but if you read this carefully and try to wrap your brain around the different functionalities provided, you'll have much greater control of your camera later.

Note: The Nikon User's Manual page numbers are provided in case you want to see what the manual has to say. Using the manual is entirely optional because this book covers the information in more explicit detail.

First, let's consider how autofocus works when using the Viewfinder. The three mode groups for Viewfinder shooting are as follows:

Autofocus modes (User's Manual – Page 91):

- Single-servo (AF-S)
- Continuous-servo (AF-C)

AF-area modes (User's Manual – Page 93):

- Single-point AF
- Dynamic-area AF (9, 21, and 51 AF points)
- 3D-tracking AF
- Auto-area AF

> **Custom Settings for Viewfinder AF and Live view/Movie AF**
>
> The AF module has eight configurable Custom settings, a1–a8. We've examined each of those Custom settings in the chapter titled **Custom Setting Menu**. You may want to review each of them.

Release modes (User's Manual – Page 103):

- Single frame (S)
- Continuous low speed (CL)
- Continuous high speed (CH)
- Quiet shutter-release (Q)
- Self-timer
- Mirror up (MUP)

What is the difference between these modes? Think of them like this: The AF-area modes control *where* the AF module focuses, the Autofocus modes control *how* it focuses, and the Release modes control *when* focus happens, or how often a picture is taken.

While the Release modes are not technically Autofocus modes, it is a good idea to consider them at the same time because they control when Autofocus functions.

In upcoming sections, we'll look into all of these mode types and see how they work together to make the D800's autofocus and subject tracking system one of the world's best.

With the controls built into the D800 body, you'll be able to select whether the AF module uses 1 or many of its 51 AF points to find your subject. You'll also select whether the camera simply locks focus on a static subject or whether it continuously seeks a new focus if your subject is moving, and how fast (in frames per second) it captures the images.

Settings Recommedation: If you are having trouble remembering what all these modes do—join the club! I've written multiple books about Nikon cameras and I still get confused about what each mode does. I often refer back to my own books to remember all the details. I have both the print and e-book versions of my books so they are always nearby (I love my Kindle).

You'll become familiar with the modes you use most often, and that is usually sufficient. Try to associate the type of mode with its name, and that will make it easier. Learn the difference between an AF-area mode (focus *where*), an Autofocus mode (focus *how*), and a Release mode (focus *when*).

10

Using Autofocus and AF-Area Modes for Viewfinder Photography

(User's Manual – Pages 9, 94, 427)

The D800 has distinct modes for how and where to focus. We'll examine each of those modes as a starting point in our understanding of autofocus with the Multi-CAM 3500 FX AF module. We'll tie together information about the AF-area modes, Autofocus modes, and Release modes since they work together to acquire and maintain good focus on your subject. Release modes are covered in the last section of this chapter because both Viewfinder and Live view photography use the same Release modes.

Figure 10.2 shows the controls we'll use in combination to change how the camera focuses and captures images. The caption helps you identify each control.

Figure 10.2 – (1) AF-mode button, (2A) Front Sub-command dial, (2B) Rear Main command dial, (3) Release mode dial, and (4) Multi selector, with AF-lock switch below

Notice in figure 10.2, image 4, that the Multi selector has a lock switch below it. You can see a white dot and an L to the left side of the switch. Move the switch to the dot setting (as shown), which unlocks the internal AF point movement capability. Otherwise, you won't be able to move the AF point around the Viewfinder within the 51 available points.

Settings Recommendation: I leave my D800's AF-lock switch unlocked all the time, but I check as the camera is focusing to make sure I am using the AF point I want to use. I can use the Multi selector to move a single AF point around the array of 51 available points when using Single-point AF, or a group of points when using Dynamic-area AF. We'll discuss this in more detail later.

Cross-Type AF Sensors at Various Apertures

Cross-type AF sensors will initiate autofocus in either a horizontal or a vertical direction, unlike standard AF sensors, which work only in a horizontal direction. The ability of the AF system to function properly is dependent on the maximum aperture of the lens in use (or of the lens and teleconverter combination). Lenses normally autofocus at maximum aperture and only stop down to the aperture you have selected when you take a picture. Most cameras are designed to autofocus with lenses having a maximum aperture of f/5.6 or larger (e.g., f/1.4, f/2.8, f/4).

The Nikon D800 is in a special class of camera since its autofocus can work with lenses that have a maximum aperture smaller than f/5.6. The camera can autofocus using lenses or teleconverter/lens combos that have maximum apertures from f/5.6 to f/8.

Figure 10.3 shows the various arrangements of cross-type and extra-sensitive AF sensors the camera can use when you are working with small maximum apertures. You must be sure to select one of the AF sensors shown in figure 10.3 if you are using a lens or teleconverter/lens combo that has a maximum aperture smaller than f/5.6. The camera will not prevent or warn you if you try to use an AF sensor inappropriate to the small maximum aperture.

You cannot in some way select one of the overall patterns shown in figure 10.3. You simply move your active AF sensor into one of the locations in the patterns, according to how small the maximum aperture happens to be. Study this carefully if you regularly use teleconverters on telephoto lenses with autofocus.

Figure 10.3 – (1) 15 Cross-type AF sensors at f/5.6 or larger aperture in red; (2) 9 Cross-type AF sensors in red and 6 AF sensors that work between f/5.6 and f/8 in blue; (3) 1 Cross-type AF sensor in red and 12 AF sensors that work at f/8 in blue.

- *Figure 10.3, image 1*, shows the 15 AF points (in red) that are cross-type AF points. The center three columns of AF points are cross-type and work with lenses that have a maximum aperture of f/5.6 or larger.
- *Figure 10.3, image 2*, shows the arrangement of 9 cross-type AF sensors (in red), along with 6 extra-sensitive AF sensors (in blue) that are not cross-type, all of which work with lenses that have a maximum aperture between f/5.6 and f/8.

- *Figure 10.3, image 3*, shows the arrangement of 1 cross-type sensor (in red), along with 12 extra-sensitive AF sensors (in blue) that are not cross-type, all of which work with lenses that have a maximum aperture of f/8.

The remaining 51 AF sensors not marked in red or blue in figure 10.3 are standard AF sensors that work only at apertures between wide open and f/5.6. You may be able to get the standard-sensitivity AF sensors to respond at smaller apertures, but you shouldn't depend on consistency of autofocus when a standard AF sensor is in use at maximum apertures smaller than f/5.6.

Autofocus Modes in Detail

(User's Manual – Page 91)

The focus modes allow you to control how the autofocus works with static and moving subjects. They allow your camera to lock focus on a subject that is not moving or is moving very slowly. They also allow your camera to follow focus on an actively moving subject. Let's consider the two servo-based focus modes to see when and how you might use them best.

Figure 10.4 – Selecting an Autofocus mode

Here are the steps to select an Autofocus mode (figure 10.4):

1. Hold in the AF-mode button (figure 10.4, image 1).
2. Turn the rear Main command dial (figure 10.4, image 2).
3. The Control panel will show each of the two modes (AF-S and AF-C) as you turn the rear dial (figure 10.4, image 3, red arrow). Single-servo Autofocus mode (AF-S) is selected.
4. Let go of the AF-mode button when the mode you want to use is displayed on the Control panel.

Let's consider what each of the two modes does.

Single-Servo AF Mode (AF-S)

Single-servo AF (AF-S) works best when your subject is stationary—like a house or landscape. You can use AF-S on slowly moving subjects if you'd like, but you must be careful to keep autofocus adjusted as the subject moves. The two scenarios listed next may help you decide:

- **Subject is not moving** – When you press the Shutter-release button halfway down, the AF module quickly locks focus on your subject and waits for you to fire the shutter. If your subject starts moving and you don't release and reapply pressure on the Shutter-release button to refocus, the focus will be obsolete and useless. When you have focus lock, take the picture quickly. This mode is perfect for stationary subjects or, in some cases, very slowly moving subjects.

- **Subject is regularly moving** – This will require a little more work on your part. Since the AF system locks focus on your subject, if the subject moves even slightly, the focus may no longer be good. You'll have to lift your finger off the Shutter-release button and reapply pressure halfway down to refocus. If the subject continues moving, you'll need to continue releasing and pressing the Shutter-release button halfway down to keep the focus accurate. If your subject never stops moving, is moving erratically, or stops only briefly, AF-S is probably not the best mode to use. In this case, AF-C is better because it never locks focus and the camera is able to track your subject's movement, keeping it in constant focus.

Continuous-Servo AF Mode (AF-C)

Using Continuous-servo AF (AF-C) is slightly more complex because it is a focus-tracking function. The camera looks carefully at whether the subject is moving, and it even reacts differently if the subject is moving from left to right, up and down, or toward and away from you. Read these three scenarios carefully:

- **Subject is not moving** – When the subject is standing still, Continuous-servo AF acts a lot like Single-servo AF with the exception that the focus never locks. If your camera moves, you may hear your lens chattering a little as the autofocus motor makes small adjustments in the focus position. Because focus never locks in this mode, you'll need to be careful that you don't accidentally move the AF point off the subject because it may focus on something in the background instead.

- **Subject is moving across the Viewfinder** – If your subject moves from left to right, right to left, or up and down in the Viewfinder, you'll need to keep your AF point on the subject when you are using Single-point AF area mode. If you are using Dynamic-area AF or Auto-area AF mode, your camera can track the subject across a few or all of the 51 AF points. We'll cover this in more detail in the upcoming section called AF-Area Modes in Detail.

- **Subject is moving toward or away from the camera** – If your subject is coming toward you, another automatic function of the camera kicks in. It is called *predictive focus tracking*, and it figures out how far the subject will move before the

10

shutter fires. After you've pressed the Shutter-release button all the way down, predictive focus tracking moves the lens elements slightly to correspond to where the subject should be when the shutter fires a few milliseconds later. In other words, if the subject is moving toward you, the lens focuses slightly in front of your subject so that the camera has time to move the mirror up and get the shutter blades out of the way. It takes 42 milliseconds for the camera to respond to a press of the Shutter-release button.

Predictive Focus Tracking

Let's talk about the practical use of these Autofocus modes. If you are shooting an air show, for instance, a fast-moving airplane can move enough to slightly change the focus area by the time the shutter opens. If you press the Shutter-release button all the way down until the shutter releases, autofocus occurs first, and then the mirror moves up and the shutter starts opening. That takes about 42 milliseconds in the D800. In the time it takes for the camera to respond to your press of the Shutter-release button, the airplane has moved slightly, which just barely throws the autofocus off. With predictive focus tracking, the camera predicts where the airplane will be when the image is actually exposed, and it adjusts the focus accordingly.

Let's say you're playing a ball game and you throw the ball to a running player. You would have to throw the ball slightly in front of the receiving player so that the player and the ball arrive in the same place at the same time. Predictive focus tracking does something similar for you. It saves you from trying to focus your camera in front of your subject and waiting 42 milliseconds for it to arrive. The timing would be a bit difficult!

Effect of Lens Movement

Lens movement (especially with long lenses) can be misinterpreted by the camera as subject movement. In that case, predictive focus tracking follows your camera movement while simultaneously trying to track your subject.

Attempting to handhold a long lens will drive your camera crazy. Use a vibration reduction (VR) lens or a tripod for best results. Nikon says that there are special algorithms in predictive focus tracking that allow it to notice sideways or up-and-down movement, and the camera shuts down the predictive focus tracking. That is, predictive focus tracking is not activated by the D800 for sideways or up-and-down subject movement or panning.

10

Settings Recommendation: I leave my camera's Autofocus mode set to AF-S most of the time because I shoot a lot of static nature images and portraits. If I am shooting sports, though, I switch to AF-C mode so that the camera will keep updating its autofocus as the subject moves very quickly. Wildlife photography is another type of imaging that begs for AF-C and its continuously updating autofocus.

AF-Area Modes in Detail

(User's Manual – Page 93)

The AF-area modes are designed to let you control how many Viewfinder AF points or sensors—the area of focus attention—are in use at any one time. Three of the four modes will track subject movement.

You can use 1 AF point in Single-point AF mode; you can use 9, 21, or 51 AF points in Dynamic-area AF mode. You can even use 3D-tracking mode (51 AF points), which uses the color of the subject to help track it, keeping it in focus while it moves around.

If you don't want to think about the autofocus area, you can let the camera automatically control the AF-area mode by selecting the Auto AF-area mode setting.

Figure 10.5 – Controls to set AF-area mode

Here are the steps to choose an AF-area mode:

1. Hold in the AF-mode button (figure 10.5, image 1).
2. Turn the front Sub-command dial (figure 10.5, image 2) as you watch the four available modes scroll by on the Control panel (figure 10.5, screen 3), which shows the camera set to 21-point Dynamic-area AF mode (red arrow).
3. Release the AF-mode button when the mode you want to use is displayed on the Control panel.

Note: Some of the AF-area modes will not show up if you have your camera set to Single-servo AF mode (AF-S), which allows only these AF-area modes: Single-point AF and Auto-area AF. You cannot use the following AF-area modes unless you switch the Autofocus mode to Continuous-servo AF mode (AF-C): 9-point Dynamic-area AF, 21-point Dynamic-area AF, 51-point Dynamic-area AF, and 3D-Tracking.

In other words, to use most of the AF-area modes, you must make sure your camera's Autofocus mode is set to AF-C.

Remember, you adjust the Autofocus mode with the rear Main command dial and the AF-area mode with the front Sub-command dial, while holding in the AF-mode button. Let's discuss each AF-area mode.

Single-Point AF

Single-point AF uses 1 AF point out of the array of 51 points to acquire good focus. As mentioned earlier, you can control which AF point is used by selecting it with the Multi selector. In figure 10.6, notice that the center AF point (of the 51 sensor points) is the one that provides focus information.

Figure 10.6 – Single-point AF mode

If two people are standing next to each other, with a gap in the middle, the single center AF point will examine the space between the two subjects. You can do one of two things to overcome this problem:

- You can get the focus first by pointing the center AF point at the face of one of the subjects, pressing the Shutter-release button halfway to focus, and then holding it down while recomposing the image. When you have recomposed the shot—without releasing the button—press the Shutter-release button the rest of the way down and take the picture.
- You can compose the picture first by centering it however you'd like, then use the Multi selector to move the single AF point until it rests on the face of one of the subjects. With the AF point repositioned, press the Shutter-release button halfway down to get good focus and the rest of the way down to take the picture.

Either of these methods will solve the age-old autofocus problem of having a perfectly focused background with out-of-focus subjects, caused by the center AF point concentrating on the background between the subjects.

Single-Point AF Example

If a subject is not moving—like a tree or a standing person—then Single-point AF and Single frame (S) Release mode will allow you to acquire focus. When the focus is acquired, the AF module will lock focus on the subject and the focus will not change. If the subject moves, your focus may no longer be perfect and you'll need to recompose while releasing and then pressing the Shutter-release button halfway down.

Release Priority Settings
When you switch your D800 out of Single frame (S) Release mode, you must be aware of how Custom settings a1 and a2 are configured. These two Custom settings allow you to choose focus or release priority when shooting in AF-S and AF-C Autofocus modes. It's important that you understand these two priorities before you start using your camera on critical shoots, or some of your images may not be in focus at all. I won't cover that information in this chapter, but we've looked at Custom settings a1 and a2 in detail in the chapter titled **Custom Setting Menu**. Please be very sure that you understand what they do! (Hint: Use Focus priority.)

Often, if the subject is moving very slowly or sporadically, I don't use Continuous low speed (CL) Release mode. Instead I leave the camera in Single frame (S) Release mode. I tap the Shutter-release button halfway to acquire focus when the subject moves and tap it again as needed. When I'm ready, I simply press the Shutter-release button the rest of the way down, and I've got the shot!

Dynamic-Area AF

This mode is best used when your subject is moving. Instead of using a single AF point for autofocus, several sensors surrounding the one you have selected with are also active. The top row of figure 10.7 shows the Control panel with *Dynamic-area AF* selected in 9, 21, and 51 point modes. You must select one of the three AF point patterns using the controls shown in figure 10.5.

Figure 10.7 – Dynamic-area AF mode

The bottom row of figure 10.7 shows the three AF point patterns (9, 21, and 51) in the Viewfinder. While taking pictures, you will not actually see all these extra AF points light up, only when you first select a pattern (see the upcoming subsection, **Viewing Autofocus Patterns**). Instead you will see only the AF point in the center of the pattern. You will have to imagine the other points surrounding the single point you can see. You can move the 9- and 21-point patterns around the Viewfinder with your camera's Multi selector.

The AF point you can see in the Viewfinder provides the primary autofocus; however, the surrounding points in the pattern you've selected are also active. If the subject moves and the primary AF point loses its focus, one of the surrounding points will quickly grab the focus.

If the subject is moving slowly or predictably, you can use a smaller pattern, such as the 9-point selection. If the subject's movement is more erratic or unpredictable, you might want to increase the number of AF points involved. If 9 won't do it, try 21, or even 51, for subjects that are very unpredictable and move quickly.

One caution is that the more AF points you use, the slower the initial autofocus may be, especially in low light. However, when the initial focus is acquired, the camera can track the subject quite well with all three patterns.

Can you see how flexible Dynamic-area AF could be for you, especially when you adjust the patterns? If your subject will move only a short distance—or is moving slowly—you can simply select a pattern of 9 points. Maybe you're doing some macro shots of a bee on a flower and the bee is moving around the blossom. Or you might be photographing a tennis game, in which case you could use 21 or 51 points to allow for more rapid side-to-side movement without losing focus. You'll have to decide which pattern best fits your needs for the current shooting situation.

Using Dynamic-area AF, you can more accurately track and photograph all sorts, sizes, and speeds of moving subjects. The initial focus reaction speed of the AF system is somewhat slower when you use 51 points because the camera needs to process a lot more information. Take that into consideration when you are shooting events. However, I have used 51-point Dynamic-area AF at both weddings and graduation ceremonies with great success. The D800 is faster than my previous Nikons at acquiring the initial focus.

Viewing Autofocus Patterns

You can actually see the autofocus patterns if you use the camera's Viewfinder or Information display (info button) while choosing the setting. Unlike previous Nikons, the pattern display on the top Control panel is not very detailed.

In the Viewfinder and on the Information display, the 9-, 21-, and 51-point patterns are shown accurately. However, when seen in the Viewfinder, the patterns for Auto-area AF and 3D-tracking do not actually reflect the pattern the camera uses. Instead, the camera shows an outline surrounding all 51 AF points when displaying the Auto-area AF mode in the Viewfinder. In reality, when in Auto-area, the camera chooses any combination of the 51 AF points it deems necessary to use. The camera spells out "3 D," using the AF points, when you select 3D-tracking, which, like Auto-area, uses whatever AF point it needs to track the moving subject.

You may notice that the 9-, 21-, and 51-point AF-area patterns shown on the Information display have tiny + signs on each active AF point in the pattern. The little + signs represent the fact that each AF point in the pattern can actively seek focus on your subject, and you can select which AF point(s) to use. On the other hand, when showing Auto AF-area on the Information display, the tiny + signs are missing. This simply means the camera will choose which AF point(s) it likes best.

3D-Tracking AF

The mode called *3D-tracking* (shown as 3D on the Control panel, Information display, and in the Viewfinder) adds color-detection capability to the tracking system (figure 10.8). The camera not only tracks by subject area, but also remembers the color of the subject and uses it to track even more accurately.

Figure 10.8 – 3D-tracking AF mode

3D-tracking works like the 51-point pattern except that it is more intelligent. Often your subject will be a different color from the background, and the D800's color-based system will provide more accuracy in difficult conditions. Be careful if the subject is a similar color to the background because this may reduce the autofocus tracking accuracy.

3D-tracking is a good mode for things like action sports, air shows, races, and so on. It allows the camera to become a color-sensitive, subject-tracking machine.

Note: As mentioned in an earlier section, you will see "3 D" in the Viewfinder only when you first select 3D-tracking AF. After that, you will just see the AF point move around the Viewfinder as it tracks your subject.

Auto-Area AF

Auto-area AF turns the D800 into an expensive point-and-shoot camera. Use this mode when you simply have no time to think and would still like to get great images. The AF module decides what the subject is and selects the AF points it thinks will work best.

Figure 10.9 – Auto-area AF mode

If you are using a D or G lens, there is "human recognition technology" built into this mode. Using Auto-area AF, your D800 can usually detect a human face and help you avoid shots with perfectly focused backgrounds and blurry human subjects. Additionally, the D800 specifically tries to expose for faces when it can find them. This is great for when you are using flash with people against dark backgrounds. The camera tries its best to keep the exposure accurate for the faces.

Previous to the D800, I rarely used Auto-area AF for anything except snapshots. However, I have been trying it when shooting quickly at events such as weddings and graduations, and am finding the camera quite accurate at finding and exposing for people. This is a great people mode. Give it a try!

Now, let's talk about how the camera uses the mode groups in unison. See the sidebar **Capturing a Bird in Flight** for an example of how the camera uses the three mode groups—AF-area, Autofocus, and Release modes—to track a flying bird.

Settings Recommedation: Many people use Single-point AF-area mode quite often. It works particularly well for static or slowly moving subjects. When I'm out shooting beautiful nature images, I use Single-point AF-area mode along with Single frame (S) Release mode almost exclusively.

If I'm shooting a wedding where the bride and groom are walking slowly up the aisle, Single-servo Autofocus mode (AF-S), Single-point AF-area mode, and Continuous low speed (CL) Release mode seem to work well for me, although recently, I have been successfully experimenting with Continuous-servo Autofocus mode (AF-C), Auto-area AF mode, and Continuous-high (CH) Release mode. The D800 is uncannily accurate at finding and tracking human faces in Auto-area AF mode. You must use AF-C along with Auto-area to let the camera track a face. If you use AF-S and Auto-area, the camera will quickly find the face but not track it. That's okay

> **Capturing a Bird in Flight**
>
> Let's imagine that you are photographing a colorful bird perched in a tree but you want some shots of it in flight. You are patiently waiting for it to fly. Your camera is set to 3D-tracking (51-point) AF-area mode and Continuous high speed (CH) Release mode. You are using Continuous-servo (AF-C) Autofocus mode so that autofocus never locks and will track the bird instantly when it starts flying. You've already established focus with the AF point you selected with the Multi selector, and you are holding the Shutter-release button halfway down to maintain focus. Since you've set the Release mode to CH (Continuous high), you can fire off rapid bursts of images (up to four per second). Suddenly, and faster than you can react, the bird takes flight. By the time you can get the camera moving, the bird has moved to the left in the Viewfinder, and the focus tracking system has adjusted by instantly switching away from the primary AF point you used to establish focus. It is now using other AF points in the pattern of 51 points to maintain focus on the bird. You press the Shutter-release button all the way down, and the images start pouring into your memory card. You are panning with the bird, firing bursts until it moves out of range. You've got the shot! (See this chapter's opening image of the bird in flight.)

when you're taking a group shot, but it's not so good when you're tracking a moving face, such as a bride walking up the aisle.

I suggest experimentation with all these modes. You will need to use them all for different types of photography, so take the time necessary to learn how each mode functions for your styles of shooting.

Now, let's examine how the camera uses autofocus in Live view photography mode (non-Viewfinder).

Section 2 – Autofocus in Live View Photography

(User's Manual – Page 48)
Live view (LV) mode is one of the new features that many old-timers love to hate. New DSLR users generally like to use it because they are accustomed to composing on the LCD screen of a point-and-shoot camera.

Both types of users should reconsider Live view. An old-timer who is used to using only the Viewfinder to compose images might find that some types of shooting are easier with Live view. Point-and-shoot graduates may want to see if they can improve image sharpness by using the Viewfinder.

10

I've been using SLR, DSLR, rangefinder, and point-and-shoot cameras for more than 40 years, and with the D800 I'm now using my first HD-SLR. When LV mode first came out, my initial thought was "gimmick." However, since I've been shooting macro shots with LV mode, the ease of use has changed my thinking. When I need extreme, up-close focusing accuracy, LV mode can be superior to the Viewfinder. If you're an experienced DSLR photographer, try shooting some macros with LV mode. I think you'll find that your work improves, and your back feels much better, too.

If you've come over from the point-and-shoot world with your new D800, then use LV mode if it makes you comfortable—at first. However, please realize that it is difficult to make sharp images when you are waving a heavy HD-SLR around at arm's length while composing a picture on the Monitor, especially with the 36-megapixel D800 having such massive image resolution. Also, the extra weight of the DSLR will tire your arms needlessly. Learn to use the Viewfinder for most work and LV mode for specialized pictures. Both image composition tools are useful.

Using Autofocus and AF-Area Modes for Live View Photography

Live view mode is a little different than the Viewfinder when it comes to autofocus. In some ways it is simpler, and in other ways it is more complex. The Autofocus modes have only two settings, and the AF-area modes have four.

The Release modes that we will discuss in **Section 3 – Release Modes** are the same whether you're using LV mode or the Viewfinder.

The three mode groups available in Live view mode are as follows:

Autofocus modes (User's Manual – Page 48):

- Single-servo (AF-S)
- Full-time-servo AF (AF-F)

AF-area modes (User's Manual – Page 49):

- Face-priority AF
- Wide-area AF
- Normal-area AF
- Subject-tracking AF

Release modes (User's Manual – Page 103):

- Single frame (S)
- Continuous low speed (CL)
- Continuous high speed (CH)
- Quiet shutter-release (Q)
- Self-timer
- Mirror up (MUP)

Autofocus in Live View Mode

In some instances, a live view through the Monitor is quite useful. For instance, what if you want to take an image of a small flower growing very close to the ground? You can lie down on the ground and get your clothes dirty, or you can use LV mode instead. Live view photography mode allows you to see what your camera's lens sees without using the Viewfinder. Anytime you need to take pictures up high or down low, or

Figure 10.10A – Choosing Live view photography mode

even on a tripod, the D800 will happily give you that power with LV mode.

To set your camera to Live view photography mode, simply flip the little Live view selector switch on the back of the camera to the top position so that the white dot lines up with the small camera icon, as shown in figure 10.10A.

Most of the Autofocus mode, AF-area mode, and Release mode information discussed in this chapter for Live view photography mode also applies to Movie live view mode (bottom movie-camera-on-tripod position in figure 10.10A). We will discuss Movie live view mode in a later chapter.

Once you have chosen Live view photography mode, press the Lv button, and you are ready to start taking well-focused still pictures.

A Difference in Live View Mode Compared to Earlier Nikons

The Nikon D800 differs from previous Nikons when using Live view mode. Whereas previous semi-pro Nikons had Handheld and Tripod modes, the D800 combines the two modes, sort of. In previous Nikons, the reflex mirror would drop during an autofocus operation in Handheld mode so the camera could use standard phase-detection autofocus. The mirror stayed up in Tripod mode only with contrast-detection autofocus.

The D800 is different in that it raises the reflex mirror at the beginning of Live view mode and does not lower it for autofocus operations. Therefore, the Nikon D800 always uses mirror-up shooting when in Live view. That means the camera cannot use the fast phase-detection autofocus provided for shooting with the Viewfinder. The primary problem is that contrast-detection AF is usually slower than phase-detection AF. However, the contrast-detection AF in the Nikon D800 is vastly improved over previous Nikons.

Many photographers were initially confused by the sounds coming from the D800 when taking a picture in Live view. It sounds like the mirror is dropping when you take a picture, but it isn't. The Monitor blacks out briefly, as on previous Nikons, while the camera fires the physical shutter. However, the Monitor blackout happens only while the shutter is firing. It has nothing to do with movement of the reflex mirror.

10

What is so confusing about the sounds coming from the camera is that they sound very similar to what we heard with previous Nikons that did drop the mirror during Handheld mode AF. The shutter on the D800 is rather noisy and, in my opinion, is nearly as loud as the reflex mirror drop and shutter release cycle in previous Nikons.

Now, let's examine the two Autofocus modes. Remember, the Autofocus modes tell the camera *how* to focus.

Figure 10.10B – Choosing an Autofocus mode under Live view

Use the following steps to change the Autofocus mode (figure 10.10B):

1. Press and hold the AF-mode button (figure 10.10B, image 1).
2. Rotate the rear Main command dial (figure 10.10B, image 2).
3. AF-S and AF-F will appear on the Monitor as you turn the dial. Release the AF-Mode button when your chosen mode appears. Singe-servo AF (AF-S) is selected in figure 10.10B, image 3.

The two Autofocus mode selections are covered next. I photographed the screen with the lens cap on so you can clearly see the selections on a black background.

Single-Servo AF

Figure 10.11 has a red arrow pointing to the Single-servo AF (AF-S) mode symbol on the Live view screen. You control the focus by pressing the Shutter-release button halfway down or the AF-ON button all the way down. When focus is acquired, it locks and does not update unless you deliberately update it. You will have to refocus if you or your subject moves by releasing pressure on the button and then reapplying pressure to refocus.

Figure 10.11 – Single-servo AF (AF-S) mode

A single red or green AF point square (with a dot) will appear in the middle of the Monitor. It will be red when the scene is not in focus and green when the scene is in good focus. You can move the square around the screen to select the area of your subject on which the camera will focus. If your subject doesn't move or moves very slowly, use this AF mode.

Full-Time Servo AF

Figure 10.12 has a red arrow pointing to the Full-time servo AF (AF-F) mode symbol on the Live view screen. The red or green AF point square appears in the middle of the Monitor, as in Single-servo AF mode. It blinks on and off in red as the camera focuses, then turns green and stops blinking when good focus is acquired. As focus changes and is reacquired, you will see it blink green a few times. You can move the focus square around the Monitor to select a focus area.

Figure 10.12 – Full-time-servo AF (AF-F) mode

This mode provides constantly updating autofocus that is tempered by the AF-area mode (discussed next) you have selected. The size and shape of the focus square changes with the AF-area mode you have selected.

The focus doesn't lock on the subject initially, which simply means it updates continuously (like AF-C) until you press the Shutter-release button halfway down, at which time the camera locks focus. If you release pressure from the Shutter-release button, the camera unlocks the focus and resumes continuous autofocus. The camera acts as if it is in AF-S mode when you have pressure on the Shutter-release button and AF-C mode when you remove pressure.

In Movie live view mode, you won't press the Shutter-release button at all, except to force a refocus. The camera will maintain focus on your subject automatically.

Settings Recommedation: Unless I am going to do some very specialized macro shooting, I leave Live view mode's Autofocus mode set to AF-F, or Full-time servo AF. That way, the camera will automatically attempt to keep a good focus on my subject.

If I am shooting a macro shot, I want to control exactly where the focus falls for depth of field control, so I use AF-S, or Single-servo AF.

Professional video shooters will invariably focus manually to prevent the frequent and noisy refocus operations of the camera when it detects changes in subject distance or contrast.

AF-Area Modes

The AF-area mode lets you choose *where* the camera senses your subject. Autofocus works differently for each of the four AF-area modes. You can cause the camera to look for people's faces, track a moving subject, widen out for landscapes, or pinpoint the focus on a small area of the frame.

Let's look at how to select the four AF-area modes, then examine what each one does.

Figure 10.13 – Choosing an AF-area mode under Live view

Use the following steps to change the AF-area mode (figure 10.13):

1. Press and hold the AF-mode button (figure 10.13, image 1).
2. Rotate the front Sub-command dial (figure 10.13, image 2).
3. Various symbols will appear on the Monitor as you turn the dial. They represent four choices: Face-priority AF, Wide-area AF, Normal-area AF, and Subject-tracking AF. Release the AF-Mode button when your chosen mode appears. Face-priority AF is selected in figure 10.13, image 3.

Face-Priority AF

The red arrow in figure 10.14 points to the *Face-priority AF* symbol. When you are taking portraits in Live view mode or shooting movies with people in Movie mode, you may want to consider using Face-priority AF. The camera has the ability to track focus on the faces of several people at the same time. It is quite fun to watch as the little green and yellow AF point squares find faces and stay with them as they move—

Figure 10.14 – Face-priority AF

green squares are for focused faces and yellow squares are for unfocused faces.

Nikon claims the camera can detect up to 35 faces at the same time. That's a lot of people! According to Nikon, "When multiple faces are detected, the camera will focus on the subject recognized to be the closest. Alternatively, you can also choose a different subject with the Multi selector."

Wide-Area AF

The red arrow in figure 10.15 points to the *Wide-area AF* symbol. If you are a landscape shooter who likes to use Live view mode or shoot movies of beautiful scenic areas, this is your mode. The camera will display the AF point square on the Monitor, and it will be red when out of focus, green when in focus. You can move this AF point

Figure 10.15 – Wide-area AF

around until it rests exactly where you want the best focus to be. The camera will sense a wide area and determine the best focus, with priority on the area under the focus square.

Nikon says, "Suitable for hand-held shooting such as landscape."

Normal-Area AF

The red arrow in figure 10.16 points to the *Normal-area AF* symbol. This mode is primarily for shooters who need to get very accurate focus on a small area of the frame.

If you are shooting a butterfly up close and want to focus on one of the antennae, use Normal-area AF. This is a great mode to use with a macro lens because it gives you a much smaller AF point square that you can move around the

Figure 10.16 – Normal-area AF

frame. Compare it to the AF point in Wide-area AF mode and you'll see that it is about 25 percent of the size. You can pinpoint the exact area of the subject that you want to have the sharpest focus.

Nikon says, "Suitable for tripod shooting with pinpoint focus such as close up."

Subject-Tracking AF

The red arrow in figure 10.17 points to the *Subject-tracking AF* symbol. When autofocus is locked in—either by using the Shutter-release button in AF-S mode or automatically in AF-F mode (discussed previously)—this mode lets you start subject tracking with the Multi selector center button. When the subject is selected (after you press the Multi selector center button), the camera locks its attention on the sub-

Figure 10.17 – Subject-track-ing AF

ject and tracks it whether the subject or the camera moves.

If you are making a movie of a black bear in the Great Smoky Mountains, you just move the focus point to the bear, focus, and press the Multi selector center button, and focus will stay with the bear. It is amazing to watch the camera do this.

I suggest that you try AF-F, or Full-time servo AF, with this mode. Full-time autofocus allows your camera to fully track the subject without you worrying about keeping it in focus yourself.

Nikon says, "Suitable for a moving subject."

Using Focus Lock

Focus lock is a tool for those times when you need to lock the focus on a certain area of the subject and recompose for a different composition. If the AE-L/AF-L button is configured correctly, you can lock the focus on your subject whenever you want to. The Custom setting that controls the AE-L/AF-L button is Custom setting f6: *Custom Setting Menu > f Controls > f6 Assign AE-L/AF-L button > AE-L/AF-L button press*. It defaults from the factory to AE/AF lock. You can leave the setting at the default, which locks both the exposure and autofocus, or choose AF lock only so you can lock just the autofocus at any time. This is convenient when you are using the AF-C Autofocus mode, which never locks focus on the subject but keeps updating. For a picture or two, you may want to lock the focus and recompose without the focus changing. Assign AE/AF lock or AF lock only to the AE-L/AF-L button so that whenever you press the button, the focus is locked until you release it.

Settings Recommendation: Why not leave the AF-area mode set to Face-priority AF if you photograph people a lot? If you are using Live view for macro shooting, Normal-area AF gives you the smallest, most accurate mode for detailed, up-close focusing. Landscape shooters should use Wide-area AF, and wildlife or sports shooters should use Subject-tracking AF.

Now, let's carefully examine the Release modes, which affect the camera for Viewfinder and Live view shooting.

Section 3 – Release Modes

(User's Manual – Page 103)

The D800 has several *Release modes*, which apply to both Viewfinder and Live view photography.

Release modes involve *when* images will be taken and how fast you can take them. In figure 10.18, we see the Release mode dial with its lock release button. Press the lock release button (left red arrow) and turn the Release mode dial (right red arrow) to select a mode. CH is selected in figure 10.18.

Now, let's look at each of the six release modes in more detail.

- S – Single frame
- CL – Continuous low speed
- CH – Continuous high speed
- Q – Quiet shutter-release
- Self-timer
- MUP – Mirror up

In the "good-old" film days, the first three release modes would have been called motor-drive settings because they are concerned with how fast the camera is allowed to take pictures.

We've already talked about these modes to some degree in the sections on the AF-area modes.

Single Frame (S) Release Mode

Single-frame Release mode is the simplest frame rate because it takes a single picture each time you press the Shutter-release button fully. There is no speed here. This is for photographers shooting a few frames at a time. Nature shooters often use this mode because they are more concerned with correct depth of field and excellent composition than blazing speed (which the D800 is incapable of anyway at only 4 fps without a battery pack).

Figure 10.19 – Single frame (S) Release mode

Continuous Low Speed (CL) Release Mode

Continuous low speed Release mode allows you to select a frame rate between one and five frames per second (fps). When you hold down the Shutter-release button, the camera will fire at the chosen frame rate continuously until you let up on the button or the internal memory buffer gets full. Choose CL on the Release mode dial to select this mode (figure 10.20).

The default CL frame rate from the factory is 2 fps. If you want more or less speed, simply open *Custom Setting Menu > d Shooting/display > d2 CL mode shooting speed* and select your favorite frame rate (figure 10.21). Your camera cannot exceed 4 fps, even if you select 5 fps, unless you have an MB-D12 battery pack installed on your camera.

Figure 10.20 – Continuous low speed (CL) Release mode

Figure 10.21 – Choosing a Continuous low speed Release mode frame rate

Continuous High Speed (CH) Release Mode

Continuous high speed Release mode is designed for when you want to shoot at the highest frame rate the camera can manage (figure 10.22). The D800 will attempt to capture 4 fps every time you hold down the Shutter-release button or 5 fps when you mount the MB-D12 battery pack on the camera. If you switch the camera out of FX mode (36.2 MP) and into DX mode (15.4 MP), the camera can manage up to 6 fps with the battery pack or 5 fps without.

Figure 10.22 – Continuous high speed (CH) Release mode

Internal Memory Buffer

The camera's internal memory buffer limits how many frames you can take. When shooting in JPEG mode, you may be able to shoot as many as 100 frames in one burst. You can control this maximum by adjusting *Custom Setting Menu > d Shooting/Display > d3 Max. continuous release*.

In lossless compressed NEF (RAW) mode, you can shoot only 17 images at 14 bits or 21 pictures at 12 bits before the memory buffer is full. You'll have to wait for the camera to offload some buffered images to the memory card before you can shoot another long burst.

See the "Buffer capacity" column in the chart on page 436 of your Nikon User's Manual for a list of Image quality/Image size modes and buffer capacity.

Requirements for Fast Frame Rates
All of the settings for fast frame rates (high fps) are based on the assumption that you are shooting with at least a 1/250s shutter speed, have a fully charged battery, and have some buffer space left in your camera's memory.

Quiet Shutter-Release (Q) Release Mode

When not in Live view mode, *Quiet shutter-release* (Q) Release mode is designed to help the camera make as little noise as possible when you fire the shutter (figure 10.23). Instead of raising the reflex mirror, taking the picture, then lowering the mirror in one smooth step, the D800 ties the raising and lowering of the mirror to the position of the Shutter-release button.

Figure 10.23 – Quiet shutter-release (Q) Release mode

When you press the Shutter-release button down and take a picture in Q mode, the mirror raises and the shutter fires. However, the mirror does not lower until you fully release the Shutter-release button.

If you want to reduce noise, you can hold the Shutter-release button down longer than normal and separate the raising and lowering of the mirror into two steps. This tends to draw out the length of the mirror/shutter action and reduces the perception of noise volume. In reality, the noise is not much quieter, but since it is broken into two parts, it sounds quieter.

In Live view mode the mirror is always raised; therefore, Q mode does nothing special for the mirror when using Live view. However, in Live view mode, the camera's focal-plane shutter is always open for viewing (obviously) and closes only long enough to time the image exposure. When you press the Shutter-release button in Q mode, the camera's shutter closes, reopens for the exact length of the selected shutter speed, then closes again. It does not reopen for viewing until you release pressure from the Shutter-release button. That breaks the shutter action into four parts when you fully press the Shutter-release button: shutter closes > shutter opens for shutter speed time length > shutter closes at the end of shutter speed time > shutter reopens for Live view. The final step, shutter reopens for Live view, happens only after finger pressure is released from the Shutter-release button. This quiets the shutter a tiny bit.

What makes this a little confusing is that the camera seems to act in a similar manner even when you are not using Q mode. In non-Q mode, the Monitor does not come back on when you are taking a Live view picture until you release pressure from the Shutter-release button, even though the shutter has already reopened. The only real difference between Q and non-Q mode is the fact that the final click of the shutter reopening is delayed until you let go of the Shutter-release button. You'll have to take a few pictures in Q and non-Q modes while counting the clicks to see what I mean.

10

Self-Timer Release Mode

Use the *Self-timer* Release mode to cause your camera to take pictures a few seconds after you press the Shutter-release button (figure 10.24). The camera will autofocus when you press the Shutter-release button halfway down and start the Self-timer when you press it all the way down.

Figure 10.24 – Self-timer Release mode

The factory default time-out for the Self-timer is 10 seconds. You can use *Custom Setting Menu > d Shooting/display > c3 Self-timer* to set the time-out to 2, 5, 10, or 20 seconds.

If you like to hear that little *beep beep beep* when the Self-timer is counting down the seconds before firing the shutter, you can control that sound with *Custom Setting Menu > d Shooting/display > d1 Beep*.

After you press the Shutter-release button in Self-timer mode, the AF-assist illuminator will blink about twice per second and the beeping will start. When the last two seconds arrive, the AF-assist illuminator will shine continuously and the beeping will double in speed. You are out of time when the beeping speeds up! The image is taken at about the time the beeping stops.

If you want to stop the self-timer, all you have to do is press the MENU or Playback button.

Mirror Up (MUP) Release Mode

Use *Mirror up* Release mode to raise the camera's mirror, allowing vibrations to die down before releasing the shutter (figure 10.25). The camera will first autofocus when you press the Shutter-release button halfway down and then raise the mirror when you press it all the way down.

Figure 10.25 – Mirror up (MUP) Release mode

You can then use a remote release to fire the shutter, or even press the Shutter-release button again (not recommended because it cancels out the benefit of using MUP mode by introducing new vibrations). If you do nothing after raising the mirror, the camera will fire by itself after about 30 seconds.

In Live view mode, the mirror is already raised. Therefore, the primary benefit from MUP mode is the fact that the camera delays firing the shutter until you press the Shutter-release button a second time. That means you can allow camera vibrations to die down before the final shutter release happens, even when shooting in Live view mode.

This mode is very simple and very effective. I use this constantly when I am doing nature photography.

Don't Touch That Shutter Release!

Please buy an electronic shutter release (Nikon MC-30 or MC-DC2) so you don't have to use your finger to press the Shutter-release button when the camera is on a tripod and in MUP mode. Touching the camera seems a bit silly after going to all that trouble to stabilize the camera and raise the mirror. A finger press could shake the entire tripod! If you do not have a wireless or cabled shutter release, simply wait 30 seconds after pressing the Shutter-release button in MUP mode, and the camera will fire on its own. This could be used as a slow but high-quality self-timer.

Custom Settings for Autofocus (a1–a8)

For a complete discussion of the autofocus-related Custom settings a1 through a8, please see the chapter titled **Custom Setting Menu**. When considering autofocus issues, it is very important that you read the information in that chapter concerning Custom settings a1 and a2. If you don't read and understand that section, you may get quite a few out-of-focus images as a result.

Also, please consider using Focus tracking with lock-on when you are using any mode that does focus tracking (9 point, 21 point, 51 point, or 3D-tracking). This will prevent your camera from losing focus on the subject if something comes between the camera and the subject while the subject is moving. Otherwise, the camera may switch the focus to the intruding object and lose the tracked subject. To enable Focus tracking with lock-on, go to *Custom Setting Menu > a Autofocus > a3 Focus tracking with lock-on* and choose a tracking delay time-out.

With lock-on enabled, the camera remembers the subject you are tracking for up to a couple of seconds after it loses contact with it. If the subject reappears, the camera will continue tracking it.

Author's Conclusions

I've followed the development of Nikon autofocus systems since the late 1980s. Autofocus with the Nikon D800 is a real pleasure. It has a more powerful AF system than many cameras before it, and yet it is somewhat simplified in its operation by comparison. The system can still seem complex, but if you spend some time with this chapter, you should come away with a much greater understanding of the D800's AF module. You'll better understand how you can adapt your camera to work best for your style of photography. Enjoy your D800's excellent Multi-CAM 3500 FX autofocus system!

Live View Photography

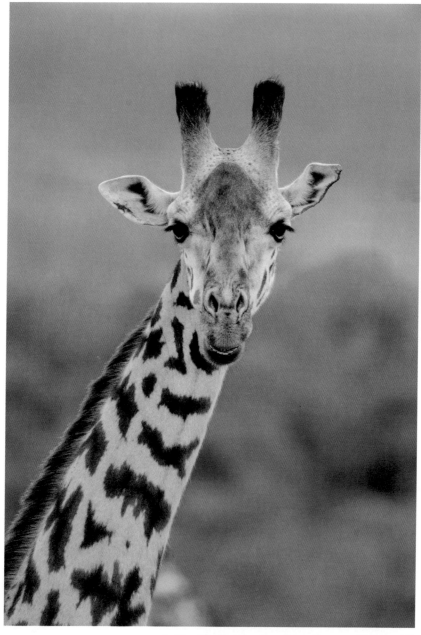

Smiling Giraffe – Courtesy of Joan Hammond (*Silversmith*)

Live view photography mode in the Nikon D800 is a mature still-imaging system that's easy to use and full featured. It allows you to take your eye away from the camera and use the Monitor on the back as your viewfinder. If you need to shoot with your camera at arm's length, such as in a crowd while taking pictures over the top of people's heads, the big 3.2-inch (8.13 cm) Monitor makes it easy to see your subject. If you need to take pictures that require you to bend over, such as when shooting closeups (macros) of plants or insects, the Live view mode will save your back a lot of pain.

The contrast-detection autofocus used by Live view photography mode detects contrast at the pixel level, providing literally microscopic focus accuracy. Additionally, you can move the focus square to any point on the Monitor that will give you the most accurate autofocus.

Live view is divided into two parts in the Nikon D800, Live view photography mode and Movie Live view mode. In this chapter, we will examine Live view photography mode, which is used exclusively for shooting still images. You cannot shoot video in Live view photography mode; the Movie-record button will not respond.

In the next chapter, we'll investigate Movie live view mode for special format (16:9) still images and broadcast-quality HD movies.

Live View Mode

(User's Manual – Page 45)

To enter *Live view photography* mode you'll flip the Live view selector lever to its top position (figure 11.1A, image 1) and press the Lv button. To exit Live view photography mode, simply press the LV button again. Figure 11.1A, screen 2, shows the Live view screen you'll see first. Normally, this screen would show the subject you are about to photograph, but I left the lens cap on to provide maximum contrast for all the controls we will discuss.

Figure 11.1A – Entering and exiting Live view mode

Opening Notes on Using Live View Photography Mode

As discussed in the previous chapter, Live view photography mode uses contrast-detection autofocus, which is activated by the Shutter-release or AF-ON button if you are using Single-servo AF (AF-S) mode, or automatically if you selected Full-time servo AF (AF-F) mode.

You can move the red focus square to any location on the screen to select off-center subjects. When you have good focus, the red square turns green. You are not limited to the central 51-point AF area as you are when you're looking through the Viewfinder.

Screen Blackout During Exposure

The screen doesn't black out while autofocus is active because the camera focuses by detecting contrast changes on the imaging sensor. When you fire the shutter, the Monitor will black out briefly while the picture is taken. The blackout is necessary to allow the camera to fire the shutter, which blocks light to the imaging sensor briefly. The reflex mirror does not drop when you are taking a picture in Live view photography mode, therefore the blackout period is brief.

Extreme Focusing Accuracy

Use Live view photography mode when you need extreme autofocus accuracy. Contrast-detection AF is slower than phase-detection AF but very accurate. You can zoom in to pixel-peeping levels with the Playback zoom in button before starting autofocus. This is great for macro shooting because you can select very specific sections of the subject for focusing (figure 11.1B).

Taking Pictures in Live View Photography Mode

Hold the Shutter-release button down all the way and wait a moment for the camera to take the picture. It's usually slower than taking a picture with the Viewfinder because autofocus takes more time. When you take a picture in Live view photography mode, it appears on the Monitor. To return to Live view photography to take more pictures, just press the Shutter-release button halfway down.

According to Nikon, one important consideration in Live view photography mode is to close the Eyepiece shutter when using Live view. Very bright external light coming in the eyepiece of the Viewfinder may influence the exposure detrimentally.

However, I experimented with this by shining an *extremely* bright LED flashlight directly into the Viewfinder eyepiece while I was metering the subject with Live view and saw absolutely no change in exposure. I then switched to standard Viewfinder-based photography mode and found that shining the flashlight in the Viewfinder eyepiece had an immediate and large effect on exposure.

You may want to test this for yourself and see if your D800 reacts to light through the Viewfinder during Live view photography. Or, you can play it safe and close the Eyepiece shutter.

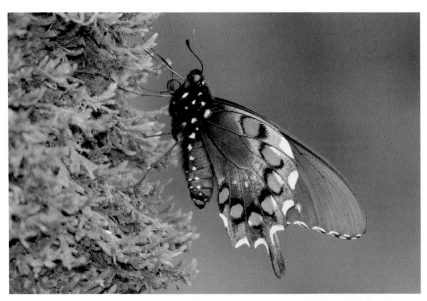

Figure 11.1B – Pipevine Swallowtail (*Battus philenor*) captured in Great Smoky Mountains National Park with a mid-70s AI Nikkor 200 mm f/4 on a bellows for macro, from about six feet (two meters) away.

Settings Recommendation: You can use Live view photography mode on or off your tripod. I normally use Live view for macro images (figure 11.1B), for which I especially need the extra accuracy and focus positioning capability. With older Nikons, I was not all that interested in Live view photography because it didn't feel mature or complete. However, the Nikon D800 has a very refined Live view photography mode. It can be used in almost any situation where standard Viewfinder-based photography will work.

One exception is action shooting. Live view photography is not as good for many types of action shots because the autofocus method is slower and the shutter lag seems longer. If you are prefocused in Live view, maybe you could capture some action, but I wouldn't try it for action shots that require rapid autofocus.

Live view photography mode is for when you have the time and inclination to stand back from your camera and take excellent photos in a more contemplative manner. To my way of thinking, it is like using a small view camera instead of an HD-SLR. If you've not been in the habit of using Live view, I would suggest you give it a try. The D800 makes it a lot easier and more effective to use.

Live View Photography Mode Screens

(User's Manual – Pages 51–54)

There are five screens available in Live view photography mode. You move between these screens by pressing the info button repeatedly.

Note: One of the screens will not be visible unless you have selected Exposure preview mode with the OK button. We will discuss how when examining screen 4.

Live View Photography – Screen 1

Figure 11.2 shows numerous symbols that allow you to see how various features are configured. To help examine the small symbols shown, I have numbered them and provided an explanation.

Figure 11.2 – Live view photography screen 1

1. **Autofocus mode** – Set with AF-mode button and rear Main command dial. Available settings are AF-S and AF-F.
2. **AF-area mode** – Set with AF-mode button and front Sub-command dial. Available settings are Face-priority AF, Wide-area AF, Normal-area AF, and Subject-tracking AF (uses graphical symbols).
3. **Active D-Lighting** – Controlled by *Shooting Menu > Active D-Lighting*, with settings Low to Extra High and Auto or Off (L = Low, N = Normal, H = High, H* = Extra high, A = Auto, Off).
4. **Picture Control** – Controlled by *Shooting Menu > Set Picture Control*. You can also control this setting by pressing the Protect/Picture Control/Help button and selecting a Picture Control from the Monitor with the Multi selector. See the upcoming subsection **Selecting a Picture Control in Live View** for more detail.

5. **White balance** – Set the camera's White balance by holding down the WB button and rotating the rear Main command dial. Select from nine white balance settings, including Auto, Incandescent, Fluorescent, Direct sunlight, Flash, Cloudy, Shade, Choose color temp., and Preset manual (uses graphical symbols).

6. **Image size** – Controlled by Shooting Menu > Image size with settings Large (L), Medium (M), and Small (S). You can also hold down the QUAL button on top of the camera and rotate the front Sub-command dial to select this value.

7. **Image quality** – Controlled by Shooting Menu > Image quality, with settings NEF (RAW) + JPEG, NEF (RAW), JPEG, and TIFF. You can also hold down the QUAL button on top of the camera and rotate the rear Main command dial to select this value. The abbreviations you'll see on the Monitor for these settings are FINE, NORM, BASIC, RAW+F, RAW+N, RAW+B, RAW, and TIFF.

8. **Image area** – Controlled by the Shooting Menu > Image area setting. You can select any of the available image areas, including: FX, 1.2x, DX, and 5:4. The Monitor will display an image cropped to the various sizes selected in Image area. This value must be selected before you enter Live view photography mode. It cannot be changed during an active Live view photography session.

9. **AF point (focus)** – Can be moved around the screen with the Multi selector to select the subject for autofocus. This focus rectangle will vary in size and color according to the AF-area mode selected (#2) and whether the subject is in focus.

10. **Guide** – This control informs you of available Live view photography mode options. It shows that you can use the Thumbnail/Playback zoom out button and the Multi selector to change between the screen hue (LvWB) and brightness (sun symbol). See the upcoming subsection **Changing the Monitor's Brightness and Hue**.

11. **Metering mode** – Set by turning the Metering selector dial, with the following choices: Matrix, Center-weighted, and Spot (graphical symbols on body above Metering selector dial).

12. **Shooting mode** – Selected by holding down the MODE button on top of the camera while turning the rear Main command dial. The available selections you will see on the Monitor are P, S, A, and M.

13. **Shutter speed** – Set with the front Sub-command dial, with settings from 30 seconds to 1/8000 second (8000). Manual change is available only in Shutter-priority auto (S) and Manual (M) modes. Camera controls this value in Aperture-priority auto (A) and Programmed auto (P) modes.

14. **Aperture** – Set by turning the rear Main command dial, with aperture minimum and maximums that vary according to the mounted lens. Manual change is available only in Aperture-priority auto (S), Flexible Program (P*), and Manual (M) modes. Camera controls this value in Shutter-priority auto (A) and Programmed auto (P) modes.

15. ***Exposure compensation*** – This symbol will appear only when +/- exposure compensation has been dialed into the camera. Adjust this value with the +/- Exposure compensation button near the Shutter-release button.

16. ***ISO mode*** – Controlled by *Shooting Menu > ISO sensitivity settings > Auto ISO sensitivity control*, with the choice of On or Off. You can also control this value by holding down the ISO button and turning the front Sub-command dial to select from ISO or ISO AUTO on the Monitor.

17. ***ISO sensitivity*** – Controlled by *Shooting Menu > ISO sensitivity settings*, with choices of ISO values from Lo 1 (ISO 50) to Hi 2 (ISO 25,600). You can also control this value by holding down the ISO button and turning the rear Main command dial. The ISO values will change on the Monitor.

18. ***Frame count (remaining pictures)*** – Approximately how many more pictures can be taken and stored on the currently selected memory card.

Live View Photography – Screen 2

Figure 11.3 shows a much cleaner screen with an almost blank area at the top and a single line of information along the bottom, which matches the descriptions #9 through #18 for figure 11.2. This is for users who prefer an uncluttered screen while shooting still pictures.

Figure 11.3 – Live view photography, screen 2

Live View Photography – Screen 3

Figure 11.4 shows a screen that is similar to the previous screen except that gridlines are added. Use these gridlines to level your subject in the Viewfinder, as is necessary when photographing things like a horizon in scenic photography or buildings, doors, and walls in architectural photography.

Figure 11.4– Live view photography, screen 3

Live View Photography – Screen 4

Figure 11.5 shows a live histogram and Exposure preview screen that you will not see unless you have pressed the OK button and turned on the Exposure preview indicator before you start scrolling through the overlay screens with the info button.

When you press the OK button, a small exposure indicator will appear on the right side of the Monitor allowing you to manually adjust

Figure 11.5 – Live view photography, screen 4

exposure compensation with the Exposure compensation button until the exposure looks good to you on the Monitor.

Figure 11.5 shows a Monitor view of my Smoky Mountains relief map and Nikon calendar with one stop of underexposure dialed into the Exposure preview indicator.

Once you have enabled the Exposure preview, the +/- indicator will stay on the right side of each screen in the entire series of overlay screens. In order to see and use the live histogram, the Exposure preview must be active. Otherwise, the camera will skip the Histogram screen shown in figure 11.5 and go directly to the Virtual horizon screen (next section).

Having a live histogram is a powerful tool in Live view photography. Use it for very accurate live exposures.

How to Use the Exposure Preview
To adjust the exposure, hold down the Exposure compensation button and turn the rear Main command dial. You will see the small exposure indicator displaying your exposure compensation changes, up to three stops plus or minus. You can actually adjust exposure up to five stops +/- but the little indicator shows only an arrow point when you have exceeded three stops in either direction.

Note: Exposure in Live view may differ from exposure in Viewfinder-based photography. The exposures in Live view are automatically adjusted to better work with the Live view display. What you see in the Live view display will closely match the final exposure.

Live View Photography – Screen 5
The final screen, shown in figure 11.6, displays a Virtual horizon that allows you to level the camera in a dual-axis horizontal and vertical direction. If you are an aviation pilot, you'll feel right at home with this new tool because it resembles the artificial horizon used to keep an airplane's wings and nose level.

Figure 11.6 – Live view photography, screen 5

Selecting a Picture Control in Live View
Picture Controls are easy to change in Live view photography mode. Interestingly, you can see their effects on the subject actually displayed on the Monitor as you select each Picture Control. You can see some samples in figure 11.7A applied to my Jeep hat.

Figure 11.7A – Samples of Vivid, Neutral, and Monochrome Picture Controls

To choose a Picture Control in Live view photography mode, you can press the MENU button and select *Shooting Menu > Set Picture Control* while a Live view session is active, or you can use external camera controls as described in the following steps.

The camera displays a special screen when you press the Protect/Picture Control/Help button, as seen in figure 11.7B, screen 2.

Figure 11.7B – Selecting a Picture Control while in Live view photography mode

Use these steps to select a Picture Control while in a Live view photography session (figure 11.7B):

1. With the camera already in Live view photography mode, press the Protect/ Picture Control/Help button (figure 11.7B, image 1, red arrow).
2. The Picture Control screen will appear while the camera is still in Live view photography mode (figure 11.7B, screen 2). The current Picture Control in use will be highlighted in yellow. Select a different Picture Control by highlighting one of the others with the Multi selector; then press the Multi selector center button (or OK button). Notice how the sharpness, contrast, brightness, saturation, and hue of the subject being viewed changes when you select different Picture Controls.
3. The camera will switch back to the Live view photography screen with the new Picture Control now providing services. It will be listed at the top of the screen (figure 11.7B, screen 3, red arrow).

Changing the Monitor's Brightness and Hue

You can change the brightness and hue (White balance) of the Monitor while you are in Live view photography mode. These changes do nothing to the pictures you are taking and are only for your comfort while taking pictures.

If you are shooting in a very bright or dark area, you may need to quickly adjust the Monitor brightness. Also, the D800 allows you to set a different White balance for the Monitor than the camera itself is using, in case you want to view the subject on the Monitor with a different hue than the actual picture will have. Let's see how to accomplish both.

Changing Monitor Brightness

Figure 11.8A shows examples of the maximum, middle, and minimum screen brightness settings. In my opinion, there is not a large difference between the maximum and middle screen brightness settings shown in screens 1 and 2. However, the difference in brightness between the middle and minimum brightness settings shown in screens 2 and 3 is striking.

Figure 11.8A – Samples of Monitor brightness changes while in Live view photography mode

Following are the screens and steps used to adjust Monitor brightness while in Live view photography mode (figure 11.8B). Remember, these adjustments in no way affect the image itself, just the view of the subject on the Monitor.

1. With the camera already in Live view photography mode, press and hold the Thumbnail/Playback zoom out button (figure 11.8B, image 1, red arrow).
2. The camera will display both the hue and brightness controls on the Monitor. Scroll to the right with the Multi selector to select the brightness control slider if the hue control (LvWB) on the left is currently selected. Figure 11.8B, screen 2, shows the brightness control at the point of the red arrow.
3. Once you have selected the brightness control, press up on the Multi selector to brighten the screen and down to dim it (figure 11.8B, image 3).
4. Release the Thumbnail/Playback zoom out button to set the brightness level for use. Figure 11.8B, screen 4, shows the brightness set to maximum on the brightness control.

Figure 11.8B – Changing Monitor brightness while in Live view photography mode

You can use these steps and screens to quickly adjust monitor brightness any time you are using the Live view photography system. Now let's see how to adjust the Monitor's hue while in Live view.

Changing Monitor Hue

When you make a Monitor hue adjustment, the camera's exposure system and the Monitor use different White balance settings. I admit this is an unusual idea, and I've been trying to think of situations in which it might be useful. One situation I can think of is when I am shooting in JPEG mode. I might want the Monitor to display the subject on screen with a neutral look, so I select the Direct sunlight setting for the Monitor. However, I want the image itself to be warm, so I select the Shady setting for the camera.

Figure 11.9A – Samples of Incandescent, Direct sunlight, and Shady White balance applied to the Monitor only

Maybe you can think of some clever ways to adjust the hue of the Monitor. It could be you just don't like the color of the Monitor and want to make it less green, more blue, or a warmer red. You can see some samples in figure 11.9A with different White balance settings applied to the Monitor only.

Following are the screens and steps used to adjust Monitor hue while in Live view photography mode (figure 11.9B). Again, remember that this does not affect the actual image in any way, just the coloration of the subject when viewed on the camera's Monitor.

Figure 11.9B – Changing Monitor hue (Picture Control) while in Live view photography mode

1. With the camera already in Live view photography mode, press and hold the Thumbnail/Playback zoom out button (figure 11.9B, image 1, red arrow).
2. The camera will display both the hue and brightness controls on the Monitor. Scroll to the left with the Multi selector to select the hue control (LvWB) if the brightness control on the right is currently selected. Figure 11.9B, screen 2, shows the hue control at the point of the red arrow, with Direct sunlight LvWB selected.
3. Once you have selected the hue control, turn the rear Main command dial to change to a different White balance, or hue (figure 11.8B, image 3).
4. Release the Thumbnail/Playback zoom out button to set the hue for use. Figure 11.8B, screen 4, shows the White balance set to a very warm Shady setting.

You can use these steps and screens to quickly adjust the Monitor's hue anytime you are using the Live view photography system. Some have complained that the Monitor on a D800 has a greenish tint—well, not if you don't want it to have a greenish tint. Now you know how to change it to whatever tint you prefer.

Note: To restore the most recently used hue when reentering Live view, hold down the WB button and press the Lv button.

Closing Notes on Live View Photography Mode

Movie Live View Still Images

An important fact to note is that when you first place your camera in Movie live view mode, before you press the Movie-record button, it can take 25.4 megapixel still pictures in a 16:9 format (6720×3776 pixels). The Movie live view still image size matches most HD devices, so if you are shooting stills for display on HD devices closely matching the 16:9 format, use Movie live view to take some pictures.

Nearly all the information we have considered in this chapter applies to Movie live view still images, too. Just flip the Live view selector switch to the bottom position (figure 11.10), press the Lv button, and start taking excellent 25.4 MP still images for HD devices (e.g., tablets, HDTVs, and newer computer monitors). We will consider more about Movie live view in the next chapter.

Using Autofocus in Live View

Nikon strongly recommends using an AF-S lens when you are shooting in Live view modes. According to Nikon, "The desired results may not be achieved with other lenses or teleconverters."

You may see darkening or brightening in the Monitor as autofocus takes place, and autofocus will be slower than it is with Viewfinder-based photography. From time to time, the focus indicator square may remain green (instead of red) when the camera is not actually in focus. Simply refocus when that occurs.

Figure 11.10 – Selecting Movie live view mode

There are several issues that may cause the camera to have difficulty focusing in Live view, as follows (according to Nikon):

- The subject contains lines parallel to the long edge of the frame.
- The subject lacks contrast.
- The subject under the focus point contains areas of sharply contrasting brightness or includes spotlights, a neon sign, or another light source that changes in brightness.
- There is flickering or banding under fluorescent, mercury-vapor, sodium-vapor, or similar lighting.
- A cross-screen (star) filter or other special filter is used.
- The subject appears smaller than the focus point.
- The subject is dominated by regular geometric patterns (e.g., window blinds or a row of windows in a skyscraper).
- The subject is moving.

There are several issues that may cause focus tracking to fail in Live view mode:

- The subject is moving too fast.
- Another object gets between the camera and the subject, obscuring it.
- The subject changes visibly in size.
- The subject's color changes.
- The subject gets brighter or dimmer.
- The subject gets too small, too close, or too light or dark.
- The subject is the same color as the background.

Live View Camera Protection System

If conditions may harm the camera when using Live view, such as using Live view for extended periods on a hot day, causing the camera to overheat, the D800 will protect itself by automatically shutting down Live view. A countdown will show on the Monitor 30 seconds before the Live view system shuts down. If conditions warrant, the countdown timer may appear immediately upon entering or reentering Live view. This countdown allows your expensive camera to protect its internal circuits from overheating and causing damage.

Author's Conclusions

Live view photography mode in the D800 is a mature and very usable way to shoot still images. Using the Monitor is not just for point-and-shoot photographers any more. There are several good reasons for using the Live view system, such as extreme focusing accuracy when shooting macro images and when composing the image on the Monitor gives you a better feel for the subject than the Viewfinder.

The next step in learning about the Nikon D800 is to examine Movie live view mode. This mode can be used for special HD-format still images, but it's primarily designed for shooting excellent, broadcast-quality HD movies. Let's examine the powerful video subsystem in your D800 and see how it works.

Movie Live View

Bride and Groom – Courtesy of Darrell Young (*DigitalDarrell*)

12

With each new DSLR camera released, Nikon has advanced the capability of the video recording system. The Nikon D800 is no exception. In fact, this camera has achieved a level of video capability that few other cameras can claim, even outside the 35 mm form factor. Due to the power and flexibility of its Movie live view video mode, it has led the way in establishing a new type of camera, the *hybrid digital single-lens reflex* camera, or HD-SLR. Where previous Nikon DSLR cameras were primarily still-image producers that happened to have video recording capability, the new HD-SLR D800 was constructed with a video system just as capable as the still-image system.

When you use the still-imaging side of the Nikon D800, you are taking extreme-resolution images that no other 35 mm form-factor DSLR can match (at the time of writing). When you create videos with the D800, again you can create video that no other 35 mm form-factor camera can match. The Nikon D800 has the ability to stream broadcast-quality, uncompressed, HD (720p) or Full HD (1080p) video with no camera control overlays—called clean video—from its HDMI port. At press time, no other 35 mm camera has that capability.

In a sense, the Nikon D800 has two video subsystems. One is for recording high-quality, compressed home videos in MOV format, up to 29 minutes and 59 seconds long each, to the camera's CF and SD memory cards. The second is for out-putting a clean, uncompressed 1080p video stream from the HDMI port with no time constraints. The second video type allows true commercial use of the Nikon D800 for shooting Full HD video.

This camera is so appealing and powerful in both its still-image and video modes that it is causing a large influx of other-brand users to come over to Nikon. And why not? The Nikon D800 has the most dynamic range of any production digital camera ever created (14.4 EV), the highest-quality medium-format imaging sensor ever seen in a 35 mm camera, and a video system that is more capable than any 35 mm camera before it. And the nice thing is—you own a Nikon D800!

High Definition vs. Hybrid Digital

You will find quite a bit of discussion on the Internet about what HD-SLR truly stands for. Some claim it stands for *High Definition Single Lens Reflex* and others claim *Hybrid Digital Single Lens Reflex*. In fact, the *HD* in HD-SLR stands for hybrid digital. The camera is a hybrid that shoots both stills and video.

Honestly, though, where do the acronyms stop? What new acronyms will the next generation of cameras bring? If you want to go all out on acronym usage, the Nikon D800 is a high-definition, video enabled, hybrid, digital single-lens reflex camera (HDVEHDSLR?). Now that's a satisfying acronym. ☺

No Tripod and Hand-held Modes

By separating the discussions of *Live view photography* mode and *Movie live view* mode into separate chapters, I hope to make the differences and similarities between the two modes clear. When I first got my D800, I was quite confused about how the two modes worked. I had gotten used to having a *Tripod* mode and a *Hand-held* mode in previous Nikons.

When I first started using the D800, I thought switching between the two modes was simply switching between tripod and hand-held modes, which were marked by similar-looking icons on previous Nikons. I was wrong and confused because the D800 works differently. In a sense, the tripod and hand-held modes have been combined in the D800, doing away with the ability to use phase-detection autofocus in a hand-held mode and contrast-detection autofocus in a tripod mode.

The D800 raises and doesn't lower its reflex mirror for pictures or video once you enter either of the new Live view modes. The shutter on the D800 is loud enough to make it sound like the mirror is being lowered, but it isn't. The Monitor blackout that occurs when a picture is taken seems to imply that the mirror is being lowered, but it isn't. The camera simply blacks out briefly while the shutter is fired.

There is no way to use phase-detection autofocus in Live view photography or Movie live view mode. Autofocus for both modes is now based entirely on contrast-detection autofocus at the pixel level on the imaging sensor. If you felt comfortable with tripod and hand-held modes, forget part of what you learned. The Nikon D800 works differently!

Selecting Movie Live View Mode

(User's Manual – Page 59)

Just in case you are a new HD-SLR user and have never used Nikon's Live view modes, let's see how to switch the camera into Movie live view mode. In figure 12.1, the camera is set to Movie live view mode, which is just below the setting for Live view photography mode on the Live view selector switch.

Figure 12.1 – Selecting Movie live view mode

Once you have entered Movie live view mode, you can take HD-ratio (16:9) still images and HD videos in the 16:9 aspect ratio only. No matter how you have the camera set in *Shooting Menu > Image area*, the still images and video are still in 16:9 ratio.

If you are shooting in DX mode or with a DX lens attached, the images and movies are still in the 16:9 aspect ratio; however, the camera creates a cropped, DX-sized 16:9 ratio image or video that gives the appearance of pulling the subject in closer. It isn't really magnifying the image, just using less of the imaging sensor to capture the subject, so it appears larger in the image or video when displayed.

It is apparent from experimentation that the 1.2x and 5:4 formats under *Shooting Menu > Image area* do not influence the image or video in Movie live view mode. When you are shooting in the 1.2x or 5:4 formats, the camera simply creates an FX-sized 16:9 ratio image or movie.

Movie Live View Still Images

As mentioned at the end of chapter 11, the Nikon D800 provides a still-image capability in Movie live view mode that is very similar to that of Live view photography mode. In fact, most of what is written in the chapter **Live View Photography** applies equally to Movie live view mode's 16:9 ratio still images.

For that reason, we will not discuss all the capability of the Movie live view still-imaging function because that would merely be a repeat of the previous chapter. When you decide to take a picture (instead of a movie) using Movie live view mode, let the information in chapter 11 govern how you shoot, tempered by the differences discussed in this chapter.

I know this seems a little odd, and I wish that Nikon had simply included a 16:9 aspect ratio format in the *Shooting Menu > Image area* menu. However, that is not the case and some may enjoy shooting in the 16:9 aspect ratio, so let's consider the available options and sizes listed in the following table.

Image Area	Image Size	Pixel Size	Print Size (in/cm)
FX	L	6720×3776	22.4×12.6 / 56.9×32.0
FX	M	5040×2832	16.8×9.4 / 42.7×24.0
FX	S	3360×1888	11.2×6.3 / 28.4×16.0
DX	L	4800×2704	16.0×9.0 / 40.6×22.9
DX	M	3600×2024	12.0×6.7 / 30.5×17.1
DX	S	2400×1352	8.0×4.5 / 20.3×11.4

Table 12.1 – Movie live view mode 16:9 still Image area and Image size with pixel and print dimensions

Figuring Print Sizes in Inches and Centimeters

The print sizes listed in table 12.1 are based on printing the image at 300 dpi. The print size will be different at different dots per inch (dpi) settings. The formula to figure print sizes at various dpi settings is as follows (1 inch = approximately 2.54 cm):

Print size (in) = Pixel size (one dimension) / dpi

Therefore, a pixel size of 6720 pixels / 300 dpi = 22.4 inches (56.9 cm), as shown in table 12.1. That means the same pixels at 240 dpi would provide a larger image, as the formula shows: 6720 pixels / 240 dpi = 28 inches (71.12 cm). For metric system users, the formula would have one more step:

Print size (cm) = (Pixel size / dpi) x 2.54

So, a pixel size of (6720 pixels / 300 dpi) × 2.54 = 55.89 cm. Remember this useful formula, whether in inches or centimeters, if you use dots per inch as the standard for printing. This formula works for any pixel-to-print size conversion (in dots per inch), not just in Movie live view mode. Use the pixel size for each dimension (height and width) of the image to determine an overall print size.

Image Area in table 12.1 represents the values found in *Shooting Menu > Image area > Choose image area* but includes only values from FX and DX because those are the only formats supported for the 16:9 aspect ratio of Movie live view mode. You must select the Image area before you enter Movie live view mode. The Image area choice is grayed out on the Shooting Menu when you are in Movie live view.

Image Size in table 12.1 represents the values found in *Shooting Menu > Image size.* The table reflects the Large (L), Medium (M), and Small (S) Image sizes available in Movie live view mode. You can select these values from the Shooting Menu by pressing the MENU button while in Movie live view mode.

A still image taken in Movie live view in FX mode is approximately 91 percent of the width of a normal FX image.

Movie Live View Screens

Let's start out by examining each of the five screen overlays you can use while taking stills or shooting movies in Movie live view mode. You can scroll through each of the five screens by pressing the info button repeatedly.

Movie Live View – Screen 1

The Nikon D800 has two screens for each overlay in Movie live view. The first screen is available when you are shooting still images and the second when you are recording video. I am using the first screen as a guide initially so that we can examine each of the controls on the screen. Once you start recording movies, some of the controls in the overlay disappear. Figure 12.2 shows the first screen you should see when you enter Movie live view. Let's examine each of the controls displayed in the overlay.

Figure 12.2 – Movie live view screen overlay 1

Here is a list of controls shown on the first screen. Each number in figure 12.2 has a corresponding entry in the list that follows:

1. ***Autofocus mode*** – Set with AF-mode button and rear Main command dial. Available settings are AF-S or AF-F.
2. ***AF-area mode*** – Set with AF-mode button and front Sub-command dial, with settings Face-priority AF, Wide-area AF, Normal-area AF, and Subject-tracking AF (uses graphical symbols).
3. ***Picture Control*** – Controlled by *Shooting Menu > Set Picture Control*. You can also control this setting by pressing the Protect/Picture Control/Help button and selecting a Picture Control from the Monitor with the Multi selector. See the upcoming subsection **Choosing a Picture Control** for more information.

12

4. ***White balance*** – Set the camera's White balance by holding down the WB button and rotating the rear Main command dial. Select from nine White balance settings: Auto, Incandescent, Fluorescent, Direct sunlight, Flash, Cloudy, Shade, Choose color temp., and Preset manual (uses graphical symbols).

5. ***Frame size/frame rate*** – This is controlled by *Shooting Menu > Movie settings > Frame size/frame rate* and shows the frame size and frame rate to which your Movie mode is currently set, with the choices of 1080p at 30, 25, or 24 fps or 720p at 60, 50, 30, or 25 fps.

6. ***Time remaining*** – When you are recording a movie, this shows how much time is left before the camera automatically stops recording. 720p30 and 720p25 have maximum recording times of 29 minutes and 59 seconds. 1080p30, 1080p25, 1080p24, 720p60, and 720p50 all have maximum recording times of 20 minutes. When you remove the camera's memory cards and stream video through the HDMI port to an external video recording device, there is no limit on the recording time.

7. ***Movie destination*** – This setting reflects the configuration stored in *Shooting Menu > Movie Settings > Destination*. You have a choice of the SD card slot or the CF card slot. Movies will be recorded only to the selected destination card unless it has been removed from the camera, at which time the D800 will record video to the only available card.

8. ***AF point (focus)*** – Can be moved around the screen with the Multi selector to select the subject for autofocus. This focus rectangle will vary in size and color according to the AF-area mode selected (#2) and whether the subject is in focus.

9. ***Guide*** – This control informs you of available Movie live view mode options. It shows that you can use the Thumbnail/Playback zoom out button and the Multi selector to change between the Headphone volume level (headphone symbol), Microphone sensitivity (mic symbol), and Monitor brightness adjustments (sun symbol). See the three subsections **Adjusting the Headphone Volume**, **Adjusting the Microphone Sensitivity**, and **Changing the Monitor Brightness** later in this chapter.

10. ***Headphone volume*** – This setting lets you adjust the volume output by the camera to a set of headphones. You can adjust the volume level anywhere between off (level 0) and level 30. You adjust the volume level by holding down the Thumbnail/Playback zoom out button and scrolling left or right with the Multi selector until you have selected Headphone volume. You then scroll up or down with the Multi selector until you have selected a comfortable volume level. You must adjust the volume before starting a movie recording session.

11. ***Sound level*** – This setting allows you to adjust the current Microphone sensitivity setting. This setting is controlled by *Shooting Menu > Movie settings > Microphone*, with the choice of Auto sensitivity, Manual sensitivity (in 20 steps),

and Microphone off. This value can be adjusted only before a recording session begins. The D800 does not allow adjustment of mic sensitivity during a video recording session.

12. ***Metering mode*** – Movie live view mode uses Matrix metering only. Unlike Live view photography mode, Spot and Center-weighted metering are not available. This icon is merely a label informing you that Matrix metering is active.

13. ***Exposure mode*** – Selected by holding down the MODE button on top of the camera while turning the rear Main command dial. The available selections you will see appear on the Monitor are P, S, A, and M.

14. ***Shutter speed*** – The shutter speed is limited to values from 1/30 to 1/8000 second while recording video. Set shutter speed with the front Sub-command dial, with settings from 30 seconds to 1/8000 second (8000). Manual change is available only in Shutter-priority auto (S) and Manual (M) modes. The camera controls this value in Aperture-priority auto (A) and Programmed auto (P) modes. Change Exposure modes as described in #13.

15. ***Aperture*** – Set by turning the rear Main command dial, with aperture minimums and maximums that vary according to the mounted lens. Manual change is available only in Aperture-priority auto (S), Flexible Program (P*), and Manual (M) modes. The camera controls this value in Shutter-priority auto (S) and Programmed auto (P) modes. Change Exposure modes as described in # 13.

16. ***Exposure compensation*** – This symbol will appear only when +/- exposure compensation has been dialed into the camera. Adjust this value with the +/- Exposure compensation button near the Shutter-release button.

17. ***ISO label*** – In Live view photography mode (previous chapter), this value could reflect whether the camera was set to use the Auto ISO sensitivity control (ISO AUTO) or manual ISO sensitivity (ISO). However, in Movie live view, ISO is merely a label showing that the number to the right is an ISO value.

18. ***ISO sensitivity*** – Controlled by the camera's Auto ISO sensitivity control in three of the four Exposure modes (P, S, and A). Movie live view uses the camera's Auto ISO sensitivity control in all Exposure modes except Manual (M), where the D800 relinquishes ISO control to the camera user for adjustment using the ISO button and rear Main command dial only. The ISO sensitivity settings menu selection is grayed out under the Shooting Menu.

19. ***Movie camera icon*** – This cool movie camera icon reflects the fact that the camera is in Movie live view mode.

When you press the Movie-record button, the screen removes several of the controls in the overlay along the top, as shown in figure 12.3. You can tell this is a screen from a video being recorded by the REC symbol in the top-left corner, next to the red dot. REC blinks the whole time you are recording.

12

Why do many of the controls disappear during a video recording? Basically, to clean up the screen a bit so the overlay is less distracting while you are concentrating on your subject. During the video recording, you can still change some of the control functions shown in figure 12.2, with the exception of the following functions (see numbers in previous list):

Figure 12.3 – Movie live view screen overlay 1, during a video recording

- Picture Control (#3)
- Frame size/frame rate (#5)
- Movie destination (#7)
- Headphone volume (#10)
- Sound level (#11)
- Metering mode (#12)
- Exposure mode (#13)

The MENU button has no effect during a video recording, so you are locked out of even attempting to make any serious camera adjustments that have no button/dial combinations on the camera. However, you can still adjust many of the control functions shown or not shown.

For instance, if you press the AF-mode button while recording a video, the Autofocus and AF-area mode symbols will reappear, allowing you to turn the rear Main command dial to change the Autofocus mode or the front Sub-command dial to change the AF-area mode. Try it.

Likewise, if you press the WB button during a recording, you can change White balance on the fly. According to which Exposure mode was previous selected (P, S, A, or M), you can adjust the aperture, shutter speed, and ISO sensitivity. Finally, you can always add or subtract Exposure compensation with the +/- Exposure compensation button.

Shooting in Manual (M) mode gives you the greatest control over the camera during a video recording. In Manual, you can adjust the following functions (see previous list again for numbers):

- Autofocus mode (#1)
- AF-area mode (#2)
- White balance (#4)
- AF point (focus) (#8)
- Guide - Monitor brightness (#9)
- Shutter speed (#14)
- Aperture (#15)
- Exposure compensation (#16)
- ISO sensitivity (#18)

Aperture-priority auto (A) and Shutter-priority auto (S) let you control many of the same functions as Manual (M) does. Programmed auto (P) gives you less control and could almost be considered a point-and-shoot mode when recording video.

Now, let's consider the other available screen overlays and their purposes. Press the info button when you see screen 1 (figure 12.2 or 12.3) and the camera will switch to screen 2 (figure 12.4).

Movie Live View – Screen 2

Screen 2 in the overlay series is a very bare screen for those times when you want very little distraction while making a still image or recording a video (figure 12.4). You can still see the most important controls at the bottom of the screen (aperture, shutter speed, and ISO sensitivity), but everything else is stripped out of the overlay.

Figure 12.4 – Movie live view screen overlay 2, for still images (1) and video recording (2)

Nikon calls the screen in figure 12.2 the *Information on* screen, while the screen in figure 12.4 is called the *Information off* screen.

Movie Live View – Screen 3

Most photographers have a tendency to tilt their cameras to the left or right slightly. The *Framing guides* screen is designed to help keep things level in the Viewfinder (figure 12.5). The grid lines are very useful for keeping horizons level and architecture straight.

Figure 12.5 – Movie live view screen overlay 3, for still images (1) and video recording (2)

I leave these grid lines turned on in my Viewfinder-based photography all the time and use them in Live view mode when I need to level things in comparison to a feature in my subject, such as the horizon.

12

Movie Live View – Screen 4

The *Histogram* screen gives you a live histogram to help you judge exposure during video recording (figure 12.6). In Manual (M) mode, you can adjust the aperture, shutter speed, or ISO sensitivity to correct for under- or overexposure. In other Exposure modes, you can use the +/- Exposure compensation button to push the exposure toward the dark or light sides, making the exposure better.

Figure 12.6 – Movie live view screen overlay 4, for still images (1) and video recording (2)

If you are a video perfectionist who wants to control all aspects of the video production, you will certainly enjoy having a live histogram to keep you informed immediately when light levels change in a way that will damage your video's quality. This is a truly professional tool and one all serious videographers should use regularly, especially in Manual (M) mode!

Movie Live View – Screen 5

The *Virtual horizon* screen displays roll and pitch from the camera's built-in tilt sensor (figure 12.7). If the lines are green, it means the camera is level. The tilt sensor senses left and right tilts and forward and backward tilts. When the camera is not level in one direction or the other, the line for that direction turns yellow and signifies the approximate degree of tilt.

Figure 12.7 – Movie live view screen overlay 5, for still images (1) and video recording (2)

This is very useful when setting up a camera on a tripod to shoot a video. You can start the video with the knowledge that the camera is level both left to right and front to back. While you're shooting a video handheld, this screen may be invaluable to prevent introducing tilt into an otherwise excellent video.

Preparing to Make Movies

(User's Manual – Page 59)
The Movie mode in the D800 is one of the best video recording systems Nikon has put in a DSLR. It has automatic or manual focus, 1080p HD recording, stereo sound, 20- or 29-minute and 59-second recording segments according to frame size and rate, a 4 GB movie length maximum, and excellent rolling shutter correction.

Another excellent improvement is the fact that you can control the D800 in a fully manual way while recording video, just as when taking still images. This is an important level of control for serious video mavens. If you want to buy all the cool attachments, like stabilization frames, bigger external video monitors, external streaming video recorders, a headphone set, and an external stereo mic, this camera has the ports and controls to support them.

Let's examine how to prepare for and record videos and then how to display them on various devices. Keep in mind that the D800 offers two levels of video recording; first, to the camera's memory card as a compressed (b-frame H.264/MPEG-4 AVC) QuickTime MOV file; and second, as an uncompressed, clean (overlay-free) 1080i60 HDMI standard video stream through the HDMI port to an external recording device.

Basic HD Video Information

Before shooting your first movie, you'll need to configure the camera for your favorite video frame size and rate. We'll look into the actual configuration in a later section. For now, let's briefly discuss some basics.

A video frame is much smaller, in terms of pixels, than a normal still-image frame. Although your D800 can create beautiful 36-megapixel still images, its best HD video image is just above 2 megapixels (2,073,600 pixels).

Whoa! How can 2 megapixels be considered high definition (HD)? Simply because it matches one of the high-definition television (HDTV) broadcast resolutions. In the good old days of standard-definition television (SDTV) that we all grew up watching, there was even less resolution. Would you believe that the old TV you have stored in the garage displays only 345,600 pixels, or 0.3 megapixels?

I've been talking about the number of megapixels, but that's not normally how HD devices are rated. Instead of the number of pixels, most HD information talks about the number of lines of resolution. There are several HD standards for lines of resolution. The most common standards are 720p, 1080i, and 1080p. The p and i after the numbers refer to *progressive* and *interlaced*. We'll talk about what that means in the next section.

The D800's best Movie mode captures video at 1080p, which is a display-quality HDTV standard. At the time of this writing, most over-the-air broadcast-quality HD is 720p. I'm sure that will change now that TVs have gone digital. The 1080p designation simply means that your camera captures and displays HD images with 1,080 lines of vertical resolution. Each of those lines is 1,920 pixels long, which allows the D800 to match the 16:9 aspect ratio expected in HDTV. An older SDTV usually has an aspect ratio of 4:3, which is taller and narrower than the HDTV 16:9 aspect ratio.

Progressive versus Interlaced

What's the difference between progressive and interlaced? Technically speaking, progressive video output displays the video frame starting with the top line and then draws the other lines until the entire frame is shown. The D800 displays 1,080 lines progressively from the top of what the imaging sensor captured to the bottom (lines 1, 2, 3, 4 . . . 1,080).

Interlaced video output displays every even line from top to bottom, then comes back to the top and displays every odd line (lines 2, 4, 6, 8 . . . 1,080, then 1, 3, 5, 7 . . . 1,079).

Progressive output provides a higher-quality image with less flicker and a more cinematic look. I'm sure that's why Nikon chose to make the D800 shoot progressive video. Now, let's set up our cameras and make some movies!

Camera Setup for Making Movies

The D800 is capable of creating movies at any time and with little thought, by simply using the following settings and actions:

- Select Autofocus mode AF-F (Full-time-servo AF).
- Set the Exposure mode to Programmed auto (P).
- Flip the Live view selector lever to Movie live view.
- Press the Lv button to enter Live view.
- Press the Movie-record button.

Setting up the camera in this way makes it act like a standard video camera, where you give little consideration to camera settings and simply shoot the video.

However, you have purchased an advanced-level camera, and you may want to do more than just take automatic movies. The D800 can do it either way. Let's discuss how to set up the camera for more professional movie creation. Before you make your first semipro movie, you'll need to configure several things on your D800:

- Choose a Picture Control with *Shooting Menu > Set Picture Control*.
- Select a White balance with *Shooting Menu > White balance*.
- Choose a Frame rate and size with *Shooting Menu > Movie settings > Frame size/ frame rate*.
- Select the Movie quality with *Shooting Menu > Movie settings > Movie quality*.

- Set a Microphone level with *Shooting Menu > Movie settings > Microphone sensitivity level*.
- Adjust the Headphone sound output level with the Thumbnail/Playback zoom out button and the Multi selector.
- Set the brightness of the Monitor with the Thumbnail/Playback zoom out button and the Multi selector.
- Choose which memory card will save the video with *Shooting Menu > Movie settings > Destination memory card*.
- Set Autofocus mode with the AF-mode button and rear Main command dial.
- Set AF-area mode with the AF-mode button and front Sub-command dial.
- Set Exposure mode (P, S ,A, M) with the MODE button and rear Main command dial.
- Adjust initial aperture and shutter speed settings (according to Exposure mode).
- Adjust ISO sensitivity (according to Exposure mode).
- Flip the Live view selector lever to Movie live view.
- Press the Lv button to enter Live view.
- If streaming through HDMI to an external device, use *Setup Menu > HDMI* to set Output resolution, range, and display size; and overlay status.
- Press the Movie-record button.

Let's examine each of these settings individually and prepare for recording premium-quality videos. Some of the settings are fully covered in previous chapters of this book, so we won't go into extreme detail about how to select the settings; only the screens are necessary. If you need more detail about a particular setting, refer to the chapter that covers it; for example, *Shooting Menu > Set Picture Control* is covered in the chapter **Shooting Menu**.

Choosing a Picture Control

Using different Picture Controls can give you powerful control over the look of your videos. Since videos are not still-image RAW files that can be adjusted after the fact for errors, it's a good idea to carefully choose a look based on a Picture Control that you are comfortable with and that matches the current situation.

For instance, let's say you are shooting a video on an overcast, low-contrast day and you want to add some snap to your movie. You can simply preselect the Vivid Picture Control, which will saturate the colors and darken the shadows.

Or you might be shooting on a very high-contrast, sunny day and want to tone down the contrast a bit. Simply preselect the Neutral Picture Control, which will open up the shadows and extend the dynamic range of the sensor for a lower-contrast look.

Just remember, you must select the Picture Control before you start recording the video. Here's how.

12

Figure 12.8 – Choosing a Picture Control for best movie look

1. Using figure 12.8 as a guide, while in Movie live view mode, press and release the Protect/Picture Control/Help button (figure 12.8, image 1)
2. Choose a Picture Control with the Multi selector (figure 12.8, screen 2).
3. Press the Multi selector center button or OK button to choose the control.

Fortunately, you can actually see the effect each Picture Control will have on your video. Use the Movie live view screen to select Picture Controls and see how they look by pointing the camera at your subject. When you have found a Picture Control that benefits the subject, use it for the video.

Settings Recommendation: I like to shoot with the Neutral Picture Control for most of my videos that involve people because I like the skin colors better with that control. However, when I am outdoors enjoying the beauty of nature, I will often select the Landscape (LS) Picture Control, or if I am feeling a bit frisky in the autumn colors, I might even use the Vivid (VI) Picture Control. The key is to use the Picture Controls enough to know what you'll get with each one. That way, you are in command of your camera.

Choosing a White Balance

White balance sets the color tint of the video. It is very important to use a White balance that matches where you will be shooting the video. Auto WB works most of the time but can sometimes have problems with mixed lighting. You should be aware of the White balance and even experiment with it for your videos. Maybe you should switch to Shade White balance when in the shade or Direct sunlight when in the sunlight. If you pay careful attention to your camera's White balance, your videos will have superior quality.

1. Using figure 12.9 as a guide, while in Movie live view mode, press and release the WB button (figure 12.9, image 1)
2. Choose a White balance by rotating the rear Main command dial (figure 12.9, image 2 and screen 3).
3. Release the WB button to choose the White balance.

Figure 12.9 – Choosing a White balance

Watch carefully as you select the different White balance settings. You will see the color tint of the current White balance on your camera's Monitor. You can change the White balance during the actual video recording. This shows how serious it is to use a correct White balance. Fortunately, the Nikon D800 makes it easy.

Settings Recommendation: I often use Auto WB unless I am in tricky lighting situations, such as inside under fluorescent lighting with some outside lighting coming in the windows. In situations like that, I try to match the camera to the most prevalent light source, in this case fluorescent.

The camera does well outside in natural light, although I have at times seen a little blueness in the shade. If the look seems a little blue in shade, I might use Shade WB. The critical thing is whether the color tint in the video you are seeing on the Monitor looks like the scene you see with your own eyes. If not, try to make the camera match what you see.

Selecting a Frame Size and Frame Rate

There are two *Frame size* settings available in *Shooting Menu > Movie settings > Frame size/frame rate*, and five *frame rate* settings. The frame sizes are both HD standards at 1920×1080 and 1280×720. The frame rates are 60, 50, 30, 25, and 24 fps.

The camera records video using the progressive (p) scanning method (sequential lines) and can output both progressive (p) and interlaced (i) standards through its HDMI port to external devices. Choose your favorite rate and size using the menu screens shown in figure 12.10. For more information on choosing a Frame size/frame rate, see the section **Movie Settings** in the chapter **Shooting Menu**.

Figure 12.10 – Choosing a Frame size/frame rate

> ### Why Different Frame Rates?
>
> The NTSC encoding format, established in the 1940s, originally used two frame rates: 30 and 60 fps. In the 1960s a new German standard was created called PAL, which used 25 and 50 fps. Today, frame rates of 24, 25, 30, 50, and 60 are common in DSLR cameras. These rates can also be expressed as a hertz (Hz) rate on progressive scan monitors. The primary frame rate used in the movie industry is 24p.
>
> A video is many still pictures joined together and moved past your eye at a very fast rate. The human eye maintains an image at about 10 to 16 fps (1/10 to 1/16 second), so frame rates faster than that do not flicker for many people. However, some people's eyes are more sensitive and can see flicker in slower frame rates. I am afraid to say much more about this issue because it can rapidly degrade into an almost religious discussion, with people having very strong opinions about their favorite frame rates.
>
> Let me just say that many people prefer 24 fps because that is normal for cinema movies. This rate is called a cinematic rate. Other people like the faster frame rate of 30 fps due to its lack of flicker. I suggest that you try all the frame rates and see which you like best. You might even want to shoot some 720p video at 60 fps and play it back at 30 fps for cool slow-motion effects.

1. Using figure 12.10 as a guide, select Movie settings from the Shooting Menu and scroll to the right (figure 12.10, screen 1).
2. Choose Frame size/frame rate from the menu and scroll to the right (figure 12.10, screen 2).
3. Select one of the frame sizes and rates (figure 12.10, screen 3).
4. Press the OK button to lock in the size and rate.

Obviously, you must set the Frame size/frame rate before you actually start recording video. The Frame size/frame rate setting changes how large the resulting movie will be when it's stored on your memory card and computer hard drive. The maximum the camera will allow is 4 GB in any single movie segment. All frame sizes and rates are limited in length to 20 minutes, except for 720p30 and 720p25 (the last two settings in figure 12.10, screen 3), which allow recording for up to 29 minutes and 59 seconds.

Video File Format

The file format used by the D800 is the popular Apple QuickTime MOV format. This format is handled by virtually all computer movie players. The video compression used inside the MOV file is H.264/MPEG-4 Advanced Video Coding.

A computer should display any of the Movie quality modes. Using a mini-HDMI (type c) to HDMI standard (type a) cable, you can play full HD videos on an HDTV. An HDMI cable is not included with the camera. They are easily available online and in many electronics stores. We'll talk more about how to display video in a later section, which includes pictures of the cables.

Settings Recommendation: There are three considerations when selecting a Movie quality setting: First, how much storage capacity do you have on your camera's memory cards? Second, what type of display device will you show the movies on? Third, are you a video fanatic?

If you are fanatical about video, you'll shoot only at the fastest rates and highest quality. Others may want to shoot a lot of family videos and hate storing the huge files that result from high frame sizes and rates. In that case, the normal quality setting and lower resolutions may be sufficient.

If you can't stand watching a non-HD video on YouTube, maybe you should stick to maximum quality. If standard YouTube videos are sufficient for your needs, nearly any quality setting from the D800 will look great on your computer.

This is a personal decision, and you'll need to experiment with video modes to find a balance between quality and file size.

Movie Quality

The Movie quality setting has to do with the Maximum bit rate (Mbps) that the camera can flow while making the movie. The higher the bit rate, the higher the quality. The bit rate can go as low as 8 Mbps in Normal quality mode and as high as 24 Mbps in High quality mode. Here is a table that shows the Mbps flow in High and Normal quality modes:

Frame size/frame rate	High Quality	Normal Quality
1920×1080/30 fps	24 Mbps	12 Mbps
1920×1080/25 fps	24 Mbps	12 Mbps
1920×1080/24 fps	24 Mbps	12 Mbps
1280×720/60 fps	24 Mbps	12 Mbps
1280×720/50 fps	24 Mbps	12 Mbps
1280×720/30 fps	12 Mbps	8 Mbps
1280×720/20 fps	12 Mbps	8 Mbps

Table 12.2 – Bit rates per Movie quality setting

Figure 12.11 – Choosing a Movie quality (bit rate)

1. Using figure 12.11 as your guide, choose Movie settings from the Shooting Menu and scroll to the right (figure 12.11, screen 1).
2. Select Movie quality from the menu and scroll to the right (figure 12.11, screen 2).
3. Choose High quality or Normal from the menu (figure 12.11, screen 3).
4. Press the OK button to lock in your choice.

Changing the bit rate is one way to control the amount of data the video contains. The higher the bit rate, the better the movie. The higher the bit rate, the larger the movie. You will need to decide which is more important, quality or size.

Settings Recommendation: Unless I am just shooting a video for the Internet only (Facebook or YouTube) and of a subject with no commercial value, I shoot with the camera set to Maximum frame rate, frame size, bit rate, and whatever other maximums I can find and max out. If a video has potential to make me some money or is of an interesting subject that others will enjoy watching, I want the best quality I can wring out of those little 2 MP frames. However, that comes with a trade-off of much larger file sizes, so I have committed to buying larger and larger hard drives each year or two. One thing about the D800, it will certainly increase the stock prices of the hard drive manufacturers. The quality from this camera is amazing, and so are the file sizes!

Adjusting the Microphone Sensitivity

(User's Manual – Page 70)

The Microphone sensitivity setting is designed to give you the ability to set how sensitive the Microphone is to surrounding sound. This setting affects the Built-in microphone until you plug in an external Microphone in the camera's Microphone jack under the rubber Connector cover. Let's look at the best way to set the Microphone level just before recording a video.

1. While in Movie live view, press and hold the Thumbnail/Playback zoom out button (figure 12.12A, image 1).
2. Press the Multi selector to the left or right to move the yellow highlight around and select the Microphone sensitivity icon (figure 12.12A, image 2 and screen 3).

3. Press up or down on the Multi selector to choose a sensitivity level. Your choices include Auto (A), Off, and 1 to 20.
4. Release the Thumbnail/Playback zoom out button to set the level.

Figure 12.12A – Manually setting the Microphone sensitivity with camera controls

The D800 offers the ability to plug in an optional stereo microphone. It disables the built-in mono mic and overcomes some of its limitations. There are several microphones available for the D800, including a few that mount onto the camera's Accessory shoe like a flash unit does. I like Nikon's ME-1 microphone (figure 12.12B).

The Microphone must be set before you start recording a video, so you may want to test the level to see if the sound gets into the yellow or red zones. The lower area of the mic indicator is white (figure 12.12A, screen 3). As the sound increases, the indicator hits a yellow zone and finally a red zone, where clipping may occur. Keep the indicator in the mid to upper white zone for normal sound, to give a little room for louder sounds.

Note: You can also set the Microphone sensitivity from the Shooting Menu. See the section **Movie Settings** in the chapter **Shooting Menu** for more information on adjusting the Microphone level with the camera's menus. Since using the camera controls instead of the menus is a very visual process, it may be better to adjust the mic with the previously mentioned steps (figure 12.12A).

In figure 12.12B you can see where an external Microphone plugs into the camera. The top plug is for a microphone and the bottom one is for a headphone. If you decide to simply use the Built-in microphone, just be sure you don't accidentally cover it with your finger while recording a video. The Built-in microphone is a series of three holes below the front Nikon D800 logo and near the Flash mode/Compensation button (figure 12.12C, red arrow).

Sound Output from Camera

The video's sound is output during camera playback through a small speaker on the back of the camera. You'll see three small holes between the Live view selector and Multi selector (figure 12.12D). This little speaker can put out an amazing amount of volume.

Figure 12.12C – Nikon D800
Built-in microphone

Figure 12.12B – Nikon D800 with Nikon ME-1 microphone in Accessory shoe (Photo © Nikon)

Figure 12.12D – Nikon D800
Speaker

You can control the volume output of the speaker with the Thumbnail/playback zoom out button (volume down) and Playback zoom in button (volume up). The setting range is 1 through 30 and off. I find that level 20 is about right to hear well in a normal environment.

You can use headphones to listen to the sound from the video, too (next section). I find that 12 or 13 is plenty loud for my headphones.

Settings Recommendation: First of all, I strongly suggest that you acquire the Nikon ME-1 external microphone. I bought mine at the same time as I got the camera and have really enjoyed using it. It vastly improves the quality of sound flowing into the camera during a video and isolates the camera's clicking and whirring noises more effectively. The ME-1 is relatively inexpensive—well, compared to a lens, anyway.

I leave the sound level set to Auto (A) most of the time. However, if I am in an especially loud environment, I will set the sound manually to about 15. When there are sudden loud sounds in Auto mode, the camera seems to struggle and often clips the sound as it overwhelms the camera's sound circuitry.

I suggest experimenting with this because normally it's not a problem. Where the problem occurs is at something like a ball game. You will be recording the game and someone scores, to the crowd's great yelling and stomping happiness. Auto may not be the best setting under those circumstances. I wish Nikon would just give us control of the sound *during* a video shooting session, not only before!

Adjusting the Headphone Volume

(User's Manual – Page 65)

The Headphone port under the rubber Connector cover is an excellent addition to the Nikon D800 (figure 12.13B). It allows you to plug in a headphone set to isolate yourself from surrounding sounds and focus on hearing what the camera is actually recording. This is important for those who are concerned about maximum sound quality.

Figure 12.13A – Manually setting the Headphone output level with camera controls

1. While in Movie live view, press and hold in the Thumbnail/Playback zoom out button (figure 12.13A, image 1).
2. Press the Multi selector to the left or right to move the yellow highlight around and select the Headphone sound level icon (figure 12.13A, image 2 and screen 3).
3. Press up or down on the Multi selector to choose a sensitivity level. Your choices include off and 1 to 30.
4. Release the Thumbnail/Playback zoom out button to set the level.

Figure 12.13B – Headphone port under rubber Connector cover

Settings Recommendation: The headphone you use doesn't have to be an expensive outfit to be effective. I often simply use a set of normal isolation ear buds, like the ones you would plug into your smartphone or iPod. Ear bud headsets can be stored in a small pocket in your camera bag, so they will always be with you. I like the type that have good bass response and can be inserted in your ear, instead of the type that kind of hang off of your ear (like the ones that come with an iPhone).

I have found that output level 15 is about right for my ears while recording and for playback. However, I'm a little hearing impaired these days from listening to my Walkman at high volume as a kid. Be careful not to go too loud because sudden sound increases might damage your hearing. You may be more comfortable with the volume around 10 or 12.

The really cool thing is how people react when you have a set of ear buds connected to your camera. Invariably someone with a cheap point-and-shoot camera will ask me why, and I tell them, of course, that my camera has a built-in iPod so I can listen to music as I take pictures. They are amazed and don't even realize I am recording video as we talk!

Changing the Monitor Brightness

(User's Manual – Page 65)

The Monitor brightness function is merely for your convenience when shooting in very light or dark environments. You can quickly turn the brightness up or down with camera controls. The brightness setting in no way affects the video recording itself. It is just for your comfort while recording video.

Figure 12.14 – Setting the Monitor brightness to a comfortable level for viewing

1. While in Movie live view, press and hold in the Thumbnail/Playback zoom out button (figure 12.14, image 1).
2. Press the Multi selector to the left or right to move the yellow highlight around and select the Monitor brightness indicator (figure 12.14, image 2 and screen 3).
3. Press up or down on the Multi selector to choose a brightness level. You can adjust it in 11 steps or simply select the tiny A (Auto) at the top of the indicator for automatic adjustment. If you select A, the camera will use its Ambient brightness sensor just above the Live view selector lever to sense the light level and adjust the Monitor accordingly.
4. Release the Thumbnail/Playback zoom out button to set the level.

Note: You can also adjust the Monitor brightness with *Setup Menu > Monitor brightness*. However, by using the preceding method (figure 12.14), you can adjust the brightness even while recording a video, which you cannot do from the camera's menus because they are disabled during recording. If you want more information on adjusting Monitor brightness with the camera's menus, see the section **Monitor Brightness** in the chapter **Setup Menu**.

Settings Recommendation: I like to manually control the Monitor brightness. I find that it stays too dim for my liking while in Auto (A) mode. However, you may enjoy the way it adjusts the brightness level like your smartphone does. Try it both ways and see which you prefer. I generally leave my camera set to the middle setting (0) unless I am out in sunshine, when I will crank it all the way up to the + sign on top of the indicator (maximum).

Choosing a Destination for Video Recordings
(User's Manual – Page 70)

The D800 allows you to choose which of your camera's two cards slots will receive the video. It also gives you an estimate of available video recording time available for each card, based on the current Frame size/frame rate and Movie quality settings.

Figure 12.15 – Choosing a Destination for your movies

1. Select Movie settings from the Shooting Menu and scroll to the right (figure 12.15, screen 1).
2. Select Destination and scroll to the right (figure 12.15, screen 2).
3. Select one of the two memory card slots, paying attention to how much recording time is available at the camera's current video frame size. The SD card slot on my camera has 2 hours, 48 minutes, and 56 seconds available (02h 48m 56s), and the CF card slot has only 1 hour, 54 minutes, and 31 seconds available (01h 54m 31s; figure 12.15, screen 3).
4. Press the OK button to lock in the slot selection.

Settings Recommendation: Deciding which card to use is based on the speed and quality of your current cards. CF cards often have better transfer rates, so you may want to default video output to your CF card. However, SD cards are cheap, plentiful, and fast enough that you may want to have several with you to swap out as you create video.

This boils down to personal preference. All I can advise is to have either big (16 or 32 GB minimum) cards or a bunch of smaller ones because the Nikon D800 can quickly fill up a memory card with its video files.

I generally relegate video to the secondary slot, which is my SD slot. I don't shoot as much video as I do still images, so it's SD for me. I just bought a handful of brand-name 16 GB SD cards (class 10) for about what a good hamburger costs each. Memory cards, especially SD, are getting cheaper every day. With a D800, that's a good thing!

Selecting an Autofocus Mode

(User's Manual – Page 48)

The Autofocus modes available in Movie live view are AF-S and AF-F. AF-S is single-point AF and you control it. AF-F is camera-controlled Autofocus. There are no other Autofocus modes available for Movie live view. You can move the focus square to any point on the Monitor to focus on the best area of your subject in either Autofocus mode. If you are using AF-S, you can focus with either the Shutter-release button or the AF-ON button. You can even change Autofocus modes while recording a video. Here's how to select the AF mode with external camera controls.

Figure 12.16 – Choosing an Autofocus mode

1. While in Movie live view, press and hold in the AF-mode button (figure 12.16, image 1).
2. Rotate the rear Main command dial to the left or right to select AF-S or AF-F (figure 12.16, image 2 and screen 3).
3. Release the AF-mode button to set the Autofocus mode.

Settings Recommendation: Many people use Full-time-servo AF (AF-F mode) for fun video shooting. However, for commercial purposes, AF-F mode is lacking. It struggles to remain in focus in low light, and even in the best light it tends to rack in and out on a frequent basis, which is very distracting to viewers. That's why many serious videographers use manual focus lenses, so they can control the focus with great smoothness—after much practice, of course.

I like videoing with my manual and autofocus prime lenses, such as my AI Nikkor 35 mm f/2 or AF-S Nikkor 50 mm f/1.4G in MF mode. I'm sure you already have, or will soon have, several favorite lenses that work well for video. Just be sure to try them in Manual mode for best focus results.

Choosing an AF-Area Mode

(User's Manual – Page 49)

The AF-area mode lets you choose *where* the camera will autofocus on your subject (see the chapter **Autofocus, AF-Area, and Release Modes**). The setting modifies the basic way autofocus decides what part of the subject is important. Let's examine each screen and AF-point style and then see how to select one of the four AF-area modes.

Figure 12.17A – The four AF-area modes

The following list explains the four available AF-area modes (figure 12.17A):

• **Face-priority AF** (figure 12.17A, image 1) – The camera has the ability to track focus on the faces of several people at the same time. It is quite fun to watch as the little green and yellow AF point squares find faces and stay with them as they move. Nikon claims it can detect up to 35 faces at the same time.

- **Wide-area AF** (figure 12.17A, image 2) – For the landscape shooters among us who like to use Live view mode or shoot movies of beautiful scenic areas, this is the mode to use. The camera will display a big red (out of focus) or green (in focus) AF point square on the Monitor. You can move this big AF point square around until it rests exactly where you want the best focus to be. The camera will sense a wide area and determine the best focus, with priority on the area under the green square.
- **Normal-area AF** (figure 12.17A, image 3) – This is a mode primarily for shooters who need to get very accurate focus on a small area of the frame. This is a great mode to use with a macro lens because it gives you a much smaller AF point square that you can move around the frame.
- **Subject-tracking AF** (figure 12.17A, image 4) – In this mode you have to autofocus first with the Shutter-release button or AF-ON button (AF-F mode does this automatically). Then you start subject tracking by pressing the Multi selector center button once. To stop subject tracking, press it again.

Now, let's see how to select one of the AF-area modes using external camera controls and the Monitor (figure 12.17B).

Figure 12.17B – Choosing an AF-area mode

1. While in Movie live view, press and hold in the AF-mode button (figure 12.17B, image 1).
2. Rotate the front Sub-command dial to the left or right to select one of the four AF-area modes (figure 12.17B, image 2 and screen 3).
3. Release the AF-mode button to set the AF-area mode.

Settings Recommendation: Why not leave the AF-area mode set to Face-priority AF if you photograph people a lot? If you are using Movie live view for macro shooting, Normal-area AF gives you the smallest, most accurate area mode for detailed, up-close focusing. Landscape shooters should use Wide-area AF, and wildlife or sports shooters should use Subject-tracking AF.

There is more detail available on this subject in the chapter titled **Autofocus, AF-Area, and Release Modes** in the subsection **AF-Area Mode**.

Selecting an Exposure Mode

(User's Manual – Page 117)

The Exposure, or Shooting, modes—Programmed auto (P), Shutter-priority auto (S), Aperture-priority auto (A), and Manual (M)—give you various levels of control over the D800.

When you control the aperture, you can also control depth of field for cinematic blurred backgrounds in videos containing people and deep focus in landscapes. When you can adjust the shutter speed during the video, you can capture a beautiful blur effect for a waterfall (slow shutter speed) and quickly switch to a fast shutter speed to get that deer leaping over a fence. With ISO sensitivity control, you can select the best ISO for the current video and vary it only when needed.

Or, you can relinquish part or all of the control to the camera. The Nikon D800 lets you decide. The following list provides information about using the aperture, shutter speed, and ISO sensitivity settings during a movie. Unlike previous Nikons, the D800 gives you full control of the camera in Manual mode, including all three corners of the exposure triangle: aperture, shutter speed, and ISO senstivity.

- *Aperture* – When using Aperture-priority mode (A), Flexible program mode (P*), and Manual mode (M), you have complete control over the aperture of the mounted lens. You can change the aperture anytime you want while shooting the movie when in those three modes, allowing you to change depth of field throughout the video. You simply turn the front Sub-command dial anytime you need to change the aperture. Be careful, though, because the camera makes an audible noise that will even be picked up by an Accessory-shoe mounted microphone for each aperture change. Unfortunately, you cannot use the new Power aperture setting provided in Custom settings g1 and g2 while recording a video. However, you can use the Power aperture to get set for a video recording session and manually change the aperture during the recording with the front Sub-command dial. See the sections **Custom Setting g1 – Assign Fn Button** and **Custom Setting g2 – Assign Preview Button** in the chapter **Custom Setting Menu** for more information on using the Power aperture setting.
- *Shutter speed* – When using Shutter-priority mode (S) and Manual mode (M), you have complete control of the shutter speed during the video recording session. This allows you to control the level of motion blur by simply rotating the rear Main command dial, thereby changing the shutter speed to any value between 1/30 and 1/8000 second. You cannot reduce the shutter speed to below 1/30 second when in Movie live view mode.
- *ISO sensitivity* – You have full control over the ISO sensitivity of the camera when using Manual mode (M). You control the ISO sensitivity by holding in the ISO button on top of the camera while rotating the rear Main command dial. Use this in conjunction with the shutter speed to make adjustments when conditions change. You can adjust ISO sensitivity to anywhere between ISO 100 and H2.0 (25,600).

12

Figure 12.18 – Selecting an Exposure mode (P, S, A, or M)

Here are the steps to select an Exposure mode (figure 12.18):

1. While in Movie live view, press and hold in the MODE button (figure 12.18, image 1).
2. Rotate the rear Main command dial to the left or right to select one of the four Exposure modes: P, S, A, or M (figure 12.18, image 2 and screen 3).
3. Release the MODE button to set the Exposure mode.

Note: If you use semi-automated Exposure modes (P, S, and A), the camera will change the ISO sensitivity to maintain a good exposure. The Nikon D800 uses the ISO sensitivity as a failsafe to make sure the video is usable. It will raise the ISO up to noisy levels pretty quickly when light starts falling, so be aware of that and use artificial light (e.g., LED) to prevent having noisy videos.

If you are shooting in Manual mode and change the aperture or shutter speed quickly, the camera cannot adjust the ISO to compensate, so your video will get dark or overbright until you change the ISO or opposite control to match the new settings. Video is a little harder to shoot in Manual compared to still images because it is live and everything you do to affect exposure is immediately apparent to all viewers. Practice, practice, practice!

Settings Recommendation: The Nikon D800 is a truly professional video camera. It can do things that even expensive pro video cameras cannot do because the large sensor makes such shallow depth of field and the lens selection is so great. However, that puts a burden on you when you use the camera manually. You now have the control you need for expert usage, so go practice and make the camera's controls second nature so that you can react well to changes.

I recommend shooting in a semi-automated mode most of the time until you are fully comfortable with operating the camera manually and understand what will happen. As a videographer, you now have complete control to make masterpiece video or really bad video. Get some books on the subject and learn your new skills well. We are no longer just still photographers!

A couple of books I highly recommend are *How to Shoot Videos That Don't Suck: Advice to Make Any Amateur Look Like a Pro* by Steve Stockman (Workman Publishing Company, 2011) and *Mastering HD Video with Your DSLR* by Helmut Krause and

Uwe Steinmueller (Rocky Nook, 2010). These books set me on the path to much better videos by not only discussing the formats and cameras involved but also offering great advice on video technique.

Recording a Video with Your D800

(User's Manual – Page 59)

Now let's look at the process of recording a video to the camera's memory card. There are several easy steps, as shown in the upcoming description. This is assuming you've gone through the configuration process discussed in the first part of this chapter that readies your camera to record video in the modes you prefer to use. Let's record a video!

Figure 12.19 – Recording a video

Here are the steps to start recording a movie (figure 12.19):

1. Flip the Live view selector on the back of the camera to the bottom position to enable Movie live view (figure 12.19, image 1).
2. Press the Live view button to enter Movie live view (figure 12.19, image 2).
3. Press the Movie-record button to start recording (figure 12.19, image 3).
4. The video will now start recording with the REC icon blinking in the upper-left corner, the time-left counter counting down in the upper-right corner, the Microphone sensitivity indicator moving as the camera records sound, and your new video recording being written to the camera's memory card (figure 12.19, image 4).
5. To end the movie recording, simply press the Movie-record button once again.

Amazingly, that's all there is to it. You have a powerful, professional video camera built into your still camera. It is available with the flip of a switch and the press of a button.

Settings Recommendation: In most cases, unless you really want to try to control the camera manually, just shoot your video in a semi-automated mode and enjoy what you have captured. The camera will make a good exposure in almost all circumstances. When you are ready to move into high-end video production, the Nikon D800 is ready to help you move up.

Recording Video from the HDMI Port

(User's Manual – Page 257)

The Nikon D800 has a unique ability in the 35 mm camera genre: streaming uncompressed, broadcast-quality video out of its HDMI port to an external recording device. Doing so is a fairly complex process, requiring knowledge of wrappers, containers, formats, and interfacing with expensive recording equipment. The process of creating commercial video is beyond the scope of this book.

For those of you who are interested in learning about the much more complex process of streaming uncompressed HDMI video, I have prepared a document that should get you started. It is called **Streaming Uncompressed HDMI Video from Your Nikon D800** and is available at the following websites:

http://www.nikonians.org/NikonD800
http://rockynook.com/NikonD800

Please download this document and consider it. I give you the basics on working with the HDMI port along with format information to make your learning process easier. I also list several websites and forums where you can gain very deep knowledge on using your D800 for high-end video creation.

Displaying Movies

(User's Manual – Page 72)

Now the fun begins! You have created a video on one of your memory cards. What next? You can always simply transfer the video to your computer with Nikon View NX 2's Transfer button and view it there or upload it to Facebook or YouTube directly, both of which know how to covert the QuickTime MOV file to display on their respective sites.

Let's also discuss how to enjoy one of your movies directly from the camera, either on the camera's LCD Monitor or on an HDTV.

Displaying a Movie on the Camera LCD Monitor

Viewing a movie on the D800 Monitor is simplicity itself, just like video capture. Videos are stored on the camera's memory card just like still pictures. All you have to do is select the video you want and press the Multi selector center button to play it.

Figure 12.20 – Playing a movie on the Monitor

Use the following steps to play a movie on the Monitor:

1. Press the Playback button to display images on the Monitor (figure 12.20, image 1, red arrow).
2. Locate the video you want to play by scrolling through your images and videos with the Multi selector.
3. When the video appears on the camera Monitor, you'll be able to identify it by three signs: a small movie camera icon in the top-left corner, a minutes and seconds (total time) counter at the top of the screen, and the word Play at the bottom of the screen. The image you see is the first frame of the video (figure 12.20, screen 2).
4. Press the Multi selector center button to start playing the video (figure 12.20, image 3).

Settings Recommendation: The Monitor on the D800 is big enough for several people to enjoy one of your videos. Don't be afraid to show off a bit because your camera creates excellent high-resolution videos. Set it up on the kitchen table, put a jar next to it for tips, and start a video. You'll find viewers!

Displaying a Movie on an HDTV

To display a video from your camera on an HDTV, you'll need an HDMI cable with a mini-HDMI (type C) end to insert into your D800; the other end will have to match your HDTV's HDMI port, which is usually HDMI standard (type A). We'll talk more about the cable specs in a moment, but first let's discuss your camera's HDMI output frequencies.

Before you attempt to connect your Nikon D800 to your HDTV, be sure that you've correctly configured your HDMI output to match what your HDTV needs or you won't get a picture. Use the *Setup Menu > HDMI* setting to select a specific Output resolution, or just select Auto so the camera and HDTV can figure it out for you. Here is a list of formats supported by your camera for video playback:

- Auto – Allows the camera to select the most appropriate format for displaying on the currently connected device
- 480p – 640×480 progressive format

- 576p – 720×576 progressive format
- 720p – 1280×720 progressive format
- 1080i – 1920×1080 interlaced format

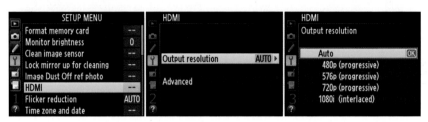

Figure 12.21 – Selecting an HDMI Output resolution

Here are the steps to select an Output resolution (figure 12.21):

1. Select HDMI from the Setup Menu and scroll to the right (figure 12.21, image 1).
2. Choose Output resolution from the menu and scroll to the right (figure 12.21, image 2).
3. Select one of the five output resolutions (figure 12.21, image 3). I suggest using Auto initially because it works well in most cases.
4. Press the OK button to lock in your selection.

Settings Recommendation: If you have any difficulty getting your camera to inter-face with your HDTV, please refer to the section **HDMI** in the chapter titled **Setup Menu**. In my experience with the camera, most of the time it just works when you plug it into the HDTV and video flows immediately. However, sometimes there are some configuration issues that involve using the Advanced setting on the HDMI menu. I won't go back over those here because most of the time the camera inter-faces well, and you can always refer back to the chapter on the Setup Menu if you have any problems.

One thing I will recommend is to make sure you have the correct HDMI port selected if your HDTV has more than one HDMI port. Often there is a control on the HDTV's remote that lets you select a particular HDMI port. Until that port is active, you will see nothing from the camera.

If the video appears too big to fit on the HDTV screen, you can reduce the size of the D800's video output by five percent with *Setup Menu > HDMI > Advanced > Output display size*. If the colors appear washed out in your video, you may have to try a different Output range (Full or Limited) with *Setup Menu > HDMI > Advanced >Output range*. Finally, if you don't want the camera to display its control overlays on the screen, just the pure video, you can turn off the overlays for the HDTV dis-play with *Setup Menu > HDMI > Advanced >Live view on-screen display* (set to Off).

Figure 12.22 – HDMI connectors, types A and C

Figure 12.23 – HDMI connector, type C (mini-HDMI)

Now your camera is ready to output video on a compatible HDTV. Figure 12.22 shows what compatible HDMI cable ends look like. Unfortunately, you'll have to purchase an HDMI cable because you don't receive one with your D800. You'll need to use a mini-HDMI (type C) to HDMI standard (type A) cable. And, of course, you'll need to plug your HDMI cable into the correct port on the D800.

In figure 12.23, you can see the port you'll need to use with your mini-HDMI (type C) connector. Before it is plugged in, here are the steps to display a video on your HDTV:

1. Turn your camera off. Why take a chance on blowing up your camera from a static spark?
2. Open the rubber flap on the left side of your D800 and insert the mini-HDMI (type C) cable end into the HDMI port (figure 12.23, red arrow).
3. Insert the HDMI standard (type A) cable into one of your HDTV's HDMI ports. (Both video and sound are carried on this one cable.)
4. Your HDTV may have multiple HDMI ports, and you may have other devices connected, like a cable box or satellite receiver. When you plug the D800's HDMI cable into your HDTV, be sure to select that HDMI input port on your HDTV or you won't see the D800's video output. You may have to select the input from your HDTV remote or use another method. If in doubt, check your HDTV manual. (If your HDTV only has one HDMI port, please ignore this step.)
5. Turn on the camera and press the Playback button; then locate the video you want to show off.
6. Press the OK button to play the video on your HDTV.

The Nikon D800 can display movies on both progressive and interlaced devices.

12

Settings Recommendation: Unless you are heavily into HDMI and understand the various formats, I would just leave the camera set to Auto. That allows the D800 to determine the proper format as soon as it's plugged into the display device and the HDMI input port is selected—if the HDTV has multiple ports.

Now, let's consider some information on rolling shutter effects. This is information that a newer videographer must know to keep from making wobbly videos. I suspect that there will be many new videographers now that such an incredibly powerful video maker has arrived (the D800).

Limitations in Movie Live View Video Capture

Let's look briefly at the limitations of the camera's implementation of video capture. No multiuse device can have all the features of a dedicated device. The D800 has some limitations on how it captures video.

The D800 uses a CMOS sensor to record video. This type of sensor uses a rolling shutter and has three potential issues that we need to discuss: skew, wobble, and partial exposure. We'll discuss each of these in some detail in the next section.

How the Rolling Shutter Works in Movie Mode

Because video is captured at 24 to 60 frames per second (fps), the D800 has an electronic shutter in addition to the normal mechanical shutter.

Have you ever used your D800 in Continuous-release mode where you are capturing up to four still images per second? The mechanical shutter activation combines with mirror movement to make the cool *chicka-chicka-chicka* sound that causes passersby—with their little point-and-shoot cameras—to look at you in awe.

However, you don't hear that sound when using the Movie mode, do you? That's because your D800 does not use the mechanical shutter when shooting movies. If it did, you would wear out the camera's shutter after only an hour or two of video capture. Remember, the camera captures video at a minimum of 24 fps. An hour of video requires 86,400 frames at that speed. You would quickly exceed the tested lifetime 200,000-image capacity of the mechanical shutter.

Instead, the camera uses its electronic shutter and turns the sensor's pixel rows on and off, as needed, in a scan from top to bottom. In other words, the camera records each video frame by scanning it—one line at a time—from top to bottom. This is called a rolling shutter. Not all parts of the image are recorded at exactly the same time! It can produce a skewed and/or wobbly video when you film rapidly moving subjects, like a race car or flying bird.

Rolling shutters are used by video cameras that have CMOS sensors, like the Nikon D800. Most dedicated video cameras have CCD sensors, with global shutters that do not scan the image. They are mostly immune to the effects we are about to discuss.

Here is a list of the effects that can be experienced in extreme circumstances when using a CMOS sensor's rolling shutter:

- **Skew** – The image leans in one direction as the camera or subject moves. This is often seen at the edges of buildings and other static objects.
- **Wobble** – This effect is harder to describe. The whole image wobbles in a strange way. It looks like the top of the image is out of sync with the middle and bottom of the image. Since video is a moving picture, the whole video can wobble back and forth in a very unnatural and dizzying way.
- **Partial exposure** – If another camera's flash goes off during the shot, the burst of light may be present for only some of the rows of pixels in a particular frame. The top part of the frame may be brightly lit by the flash, while the bottom part appears dark. The partial exposure appears as a bright band in one or a few frames, depending on how long the brighter light lasts. Some older forms of fluorescent light bulbs have slow ballasts and can cause the video to have a series of moving bands as the light flickers. Our eyes can't see it, but the fast video captures it well. If you are shooting images of an ambulance with its lights flashing, they can also cause banding. Anything that has intense bursts of light for short periods may cause partially exposed bands to appear in the video.

To understand skew and wobble better, let's compare our camera to a desktop scanner. It works in a similar way. If you place a paper document on a scanner and press the scan button, you'll see the little row of lights under the glass travel from the top of the document to the bottom as it records one line at a time. At the end of the scan, there is a copy of the document in your computer's memory that can be saved to the hard drive. You usually put the scanner's lid down on a paper document to hold it flat and keep it from moving.

Imagine that you're scanning a paper document on your desktop scanner and halfway through the scan you move the paper a little. The top part of the scan would look normal, since it was already captured by the scanner's sensor, but the bottom part of the scan would be at a different angle than the top part. You could say that it is skewed from the original angle. This is an example of the skew that can result with a rolling shutter.

Now, what if you grab the paper during a scan and rotate it back and forth all the way through the entire scan? The final scanned document would look like a series of zigzags, with some parts at one angle and other parts at a different angle. This is an example of the wobble that can result with a rolling shutter.

The D800 records video in a similar manner, except it is much faster than a scanner. It records a frame of video in 1/24 second, or 24 fps, and can go as high as 60 fps. Since the Nikon D800 scans the image at this speed, there's not a problem

12

in most cases. Most movement is too slow to be zigzagged (wobbled) or angled (skewed).

Skew and wobble become especially evident when a person is walking and recording a video at the same time. These combined movements can be enough to cause wobble in the video. I call this the "jellywobble effect." Like a bowl of Jell-O, your video looks like it is wobbling. What can you do to prevent it?

Avoiding the Jellywobble Effect

Primarily, you have to be careful not to allow too much camera movement. It truly is best to use the D800 on a nice fluid-head video tripod, or a stabilizing frame, if you want great results. I've found that Nikon's vibration reduction (VR) lenses help when you don't want to use a tripod because they stabilize the camera a little. VR won't help much if you're walking while recording a video because the camera movements are often too great for the VR system to overcome. If you're standing quietly and doing your best to hold the camera still, it will help overcome small movements caused by your heartbeat and breathing.

This is one of the main differences between a dedicated video camera and a hybrid like the D800. Most true video cameras use a CCD sensor instead of a CMOS sensor like the D800 has. A CCD sensor does not have a rolling shutter; it has a global shutter instead. A global shutter does not scan the image one line at a time. It uses the whole sensor at once to grab the image. There are some newer low-cost video cameras on the market that use a rolling shutter, but the better video cameras use a global shutter.

This is probably the worst problem with D800 video. True videophiles will turn up their noses at a rolling shutter. They'll buy a dedicated video camera with three separate CCD sensors—one for each RGB color—and nice global shutters to avoid jellywobbles. And they'll pay several thousand dollars for the privilege of owning that equipment.

You, however, realize that the D800 is primarily a very high-quality still camera with added video capabilities. Since video is combined with still-image capability, you'll have both with you when carrying your camera. You might be standing in a superstore parking lot one day when an alien spacecraft just happens to land. You'll get both still images and cool video from the same camera. So what if, in your excitement while running from the alien's heat ray, you get a few jellywobbles in your video? One of the rules for getting great video is having a video camera with you. With the D800, you have one at all times—with no extra effort. You do keep your camera with you just in case, right?

Settings Recommendation: Try to hold your camera still to greatly reduce any jellywobble effects. Use a tripod when you can, or even a VR lens. Anything that helps stabilize the camera will give you much higher-quality video.

Author's Conclusions

The video capability in the Nikon D800 is simply amazing. You will create some of the best videos of your life with this camera. When you are out shooting still images, why not grab some video, too? Years from now, actually hearing and seeing friends and family who are no longer with us will mean a lot.

Pictures are important, but so is video. Your camera does both, and either is available at a moment's notice. Carry your camera with you and record your life. Hard drives are cheap compared to the memories you will lose if you don't record them. Make good backups and give away family videos to your family. Share the good qualities of your powerful camera with others, and the goodwill will come back to you later.

Now, let's look into our last chapter in the book, **Speedlight Flash**. Pop up the built-in Speedlight on your D800, or plug in your favorite external Nikon Speedlight, and let's see how best to use a flash directly and to control banks of Speedlights with Nikon's Creative Lighting System (CLS).

Speedlight Flash

I See Mommy! – Courtesy of Daniel Diggelmann (*Aerobat*)

Light is the photographer's friend! Controlling light is the primary thing that separates excellent from not-so-excellent photographers. On beautiful, balmy summer evenings, the light wraps around the land and gives us that so-called golden hour that we crave. However, some days are rainy, and some are dark and gloomy.

As photographers, we want to take pictures. We don't want to stop just because the sun won't cooperate. We need light that we can take with us, and we want it to be available quickly. We need a Speedlight!

Fortunately, your D800 has a built-in Speedlight (figure 13.1). The little pop-up unit that's built in to your camera is a Nikon Speedlight flash. Speedlight is Nikon's name for its flash units, large and small.

Figure 13.1 – Nikon D800 with pop-up Speedlight flash open

You have several choices, from the tiny pop-up Speedlight flash on your camera to the flagship Nikon SB-910 Speedlight flash. You can even create a wireless flash array using your camera, a commander unit, and several Speedlight flash units. This type of setup is called the Nikon Creative Lighting System (CLS). We'll look at CLS later in the chapter. First, let's examine some general flash information and explore how the D800 uses flash. How can you determine which flash will work best for your style of shooting? Will the pop-up flash be enough with its limitations in range, or do you need more power to reach out and light up more distant subjects? How is the power output of a flash unit rated?

This chapter contains information that will help you make a good choice in flash units. First, we'll look at how to rate the power output of a flash by examining the guide number.

What Is a Guide Number?

The guide number (GN) for a flash unit measures how well it can light a subject at a specific ISO sensitivity and with a precise angle of view (wide angle versus tele-photo). To put it simply, a higher guide number means the flash is more powerful, all other things being equal.

Be careful when you are deciding on an external flash unit, whether it is a Nikon Speedlight or an aftermarket unit. Simply comparing the GN is not enough. You must understand the settings on which the GN is based. Many flash units have zoom capability and can light up subjects farther away when they are zoomed out. However, imagine buying a flash unit from a manufacturer who publishes the GN based on a longer zoom position, and then comparing it to a different flash unit based on a shorter nonzoom position. The GN rating on the flash that is zoomed out would seem to be higher than the same unit not zoomed out. Unless you are comparing flash unit GNs with exactly the same settings, it is truly like comparing apples to oranges. For instance, to get an exact comparison of GNs, you would have to know the following:

- Distance from flash head to the subject
- Aperture in use on your camera
- ISO sensitivity of your camera's image sensor
- Angle-of-view setting on the flash zoom head
- Actual angle of view your lens provides (must match flash head)
- Temperature of ambient air

In reality, the camera has little to do with figuring the GN other than providing an f-stop number and ISO sensitivity. So how can you decide what GN is best without whipping out a scientific calculator? Just look at the flash unit specifications to see what the GN is based on. Here are the most important figures:

- Flash zoom angle-of-view setting (e.g., 24 mm or 75 mm)
- ISO sensitivity

If you see a flash unit advertised as GN 98, realize that this is not enough informa-tion to make a decision. In this instance, 98 is the GN. It represents the number of feet from the flash head to the subject (98 feet). In countries that use the metric system, the equivalent GN is 30, which is the number of meters from the flash head to the subject. That number by itself is simply incomplete. Don't buy a flash unit based solely on a GN like 98 or 100 or 111.

Let's think about this for a second. Let's say I'm a manufacturer who is desperate to sell you a flash unit. I might stretch things a little bit. I might say my Super-Duper flash unit has a GN of 98 (feet) or 30 (meters) and hope you won't ask about the settings I used to arrive at that number. Here is a comparison of two flash units with a so-called comparable guide number:

Super-Duper flash unit GN information:

- GN 98 (30)
- 80 mm zoom-head setting
- ISO 200 sensitivity

Nikon SB-400 flash unit GN information (real values):

- GN 98 (30)
- 35 mm zoom-head setting
- ISO 100 sensitivity

Both of the flash units have the same GN, so which one is really more powerful? The Nikon SB-400 will literally blow away the Super-Duper unit. Yet the Super-Duper manufacturer lists the same GN! The Super-Duper unit must have its zoom head set to 80 mm, a much narrower beam, and have twice the camera ISO sensitivity to equal the Nikon SB-400 unit. Mr. Super-Duper is hoping you won't check the fine print at the bottom of the specifications so you'll think his much less powerful unit equals the Nikon SB-400. Surprisingly, there are flash unit manufacturers who do exactly this.

What can you learn from this example? The GN itself is not enough to make a decision on which flash unit to use. You must know what the GN is based on in order to make an informed decision. Take your time when buying a flash unit. You're safe in sticking with Nikon Speedlights, because the ratings are well known and they're designed to support all the features of your D800.

There are also excellent aftermarket flash units available from manufacturers like Vivitar, Sigma, Sunpak, Metz, Braun/Leitz, and others. Examine the underlying settings and not just the GN. What the GN is based on is as important as the actual number.

For comparison purposes, the GN of the D800's pop-up Speedlight is 39 (feet) or 12 (meters) at ISO 100. Nikon's flagship Speedlight, the SB-910, is 111.5 (feet) or 34 (meters) at ISO 100. Obviously, the larger external flash unit has a lot more power and can light up subjects that are farther away.

Now, let's examine the various flash modes found in the Nikon D800. Since I have no way of knowing which flash unit you'll be using, I'll write from the perspective of the built-in flash. Almost everything mentioned next applies to the built-in flash and most Accessory shoe–mounted Nikon-brand Speedlight units, plus many Nikon-specific aftermarket flash units.

Note: The built-in flash unit provides coverage for the angle of view of a 24 mm lens in FX mode and a 16 mm lens in DX mode.

> ### Technical GN Information
>
> The GN is based on a specific formula: GN = distance × f-stop. It is based on the inverse-square law, which states that doubling the GN requires four times more flash power. So, a flash with a GN of 100 is four times more powerful than a flash with a GN of 50. The guide number represents an exposure constant for a flash unit. For example, a GN of 80 feet at ISO 100 means that a subject 20 feet away can be completely illuminated with an aperture of f/4 (80 = 20 × 4) using a sensitivity of ISO 100. For the same guide number and an aperture of f/8, the light source should be 10 feet from the subject (80 = 10 × 8). Fortunately, your camera and flash combination is capable of figuring the correct values for you when you use TTL mode.

Flash Modes

(User's Manual – Page 183)

The built-in pop-up flash has two types of flash metering:

- *i-TTL balanced fill flash* – The flash fires in two stages. Nikon calls stage 1 *monitor preflash*. The built-in flash emits a series of almost invisible flashes before the main flash burst fires (stage 2). The preflashes allow the 1,005-pixel RGB flash sensor to examine all areas of the frame for reflectivity. The camera uses the Matrix meter and distance information from a D or G lens to calculate a flash output that is balanced between the main subject and the ambient lighting. You must use Matrix or Center-weighted metering to use this mode.
- *Standard i-TTL* – When the Spot meter is used, the camera automatically switches to standard i-TTL. This mode ignores the background and concentrates on whatever the camera's selected AF point is focused on. For the most accurate flash output for a specific subject, just set your camera to use its Spot meter, and the flash will meter for the subject only.

In addition to the types of flash metering, the camera has several Flash modes that affect how it controls light. We'll consider each of them shortly, but first let's talk about how the shutter blades work when the flash fires. This is basic information that will help you understand the Flash modes. To fully know what's happening when the flash fires, you must understand a little bit about the shutter curtains in your camera.

Figure 13.2 – Nikon D800 shutter assembly and front shutter curtain

13

Your D800 exposes the sensor to light for specific periods of time. This is controlled by the camera's shutter speed. The actual exposure is handled by two moving objects called curtains. The D800 has two shutter curtains. You can see the front curtain in figure 13.2 (red arrow). It's composed of several narrow blades and is in the closed position.

How do the curtains work? One curtain gets out of the way of the sensor to start the exposure, and the other curtain replaces it to stop the exposure. The first one is called the front curtain, and the second one is called the rear curtain. In this context, front and rear are not important as indicators of position but as indicators of which moves first and which moves second. The flash must fire when the first, or front, curtain is fully open and before the second, or rear, curtain starts closing. The time between the front curtain opening and the rear curtain closing is the actual shutter speed.

The whole sensor must be uncovered when the flash fires in normal Flash modes (non–Auto FP). If the shutter speed is too fast, the rear curtain will closely follow the front curtain and partially block the sensor when the flash fires. That's why the shutter speed is normally limited to a maximum of 1/250s on the D800 when a flash is used. With faster shutter speeds, the sensor is always partially covered by one of the shutter curtains. If the flash fires while one of the curtains covers part of the sensor, then that part of the sensor will not get a proper exposure from the flash and there will be an underexposed black band in your image.

The whole point of the Flash modes is to determine at what point during shutter curtain movement the flash fires and whether it's the main source of light or whether some ambient light is mixed in. Keep this information in mind as we discuss the Flash modes.

Be sure to read the upcoming sidebar called **Auto FP High-Speed Sync** because Auto FP affects the maximum shutter sync speed, allowing you to take it higher than 1/250s. Also, see the section **Custom Setting e1 – Flash Sync Speed** in the chapter titled **Custom Setting Menu**, where this mode is discussed in great detail.

Auto FP High-Speed Sync

The D800 has an additional mode that lets it exceed the normal flash sync speed of 1/250s. It is called Auto FP high-speed sync mode. Remember how normally both the front and rear shutter curtains must be out of the way before the flash fires? Auto FP high-speed sync mode lets you use shutter speeds all the way up to 1/8000s. At these speeds, the rear shutter curtain follows the front shutter curtain so closely that only a traveling narrow horizontal slit exposes the sensor at any given time.

When you select a sync speed faster than the normal 1/250s, the camera fires the flash in thousands of short pulses instead of one big flash. The pulses fire as the narrow shutter curtain slit moves across the face of the sensor. The faster the shutter speed, the less power the flash can manage. You must be able to depend on ambient light in addition to flash when using Auto FP high-speed sync mode, especially at higher shutter speeds. However, this lets you use your fast lenses (e.g., f/1.4, f/2.8) wide open while in direct sunlight, due to the very fast shutter speed.

You can expose properly with a very shallow depth of field due to a large aperture, even though the light is very bright. We covered this mode in detail in the chapter titled **Custom Setting Menu**, under the heading **Custom Setting e1 – Flash Sync Speed**.

To set your camera to Auto FP high-speed sync mode, choose *Custom Setting Menu > e Bracketing/flash > Flash sync speed*. Select 1/320 s (Auto FP) or 1/250 s (auto FP) from the menu. Afterward, use Shutter-priority auto (S) mode or Manual (M) and adjust your camera's shutter speed to any speed between 30 seconds and 1/8000 second. An external Speedlight will fire its pulses to match the shutter blade slit traveling across the imaging sensor. The maximum shutter speed the built-in flash will allow is the Auto FP mode you've selected (250 or 320). You must use an external Speedlight flash unit (such as the SB-910 or SB-700) to use Auto high-speed sync mode.

Figure 13.3 – Selecting a Flash mode

Here are the steps to select one of the Flash modes:

1. Hold down the Flash mode button on the front of your camera, just below the D800 logo (figure 13.3, image 1).
2. Turn the Main command dial while watching the various modes change on the Control panel (figure 13.3, image 2 and screen 3).
3. Release the Flash mode button to lock in the Flash mode.

The five basic Flash modes and how they work are described next. The camera will often combine these Flash modes as you use different shooting modes on the Mode dial.

Front-Curtain Sync

In *Front-curtain sync* mode, the camera tries its best to balance the light if you're using a lens that has a CPU in it (figure 13.4). Older non-CPU lenses cause the camera to ignore the ambient light completely and use only the flash to expose the subject. A CPU lens, like an AF-S Nikkor G or D lens, can balance ambient light and light from the flash equally and makes the lighting look very natural. If you use this correctly outdoors, it

Figure 13.4 – Front-curtain sync

will be hard to tell that you were using flash, except for the catch light in your subject's eyes and the lack of damaging shadows. The flash simply fills in some extra light without overpowering the ambient light. In a situation where there is very little ambient light, the camera will use only the flash to get a correct exposure. It balances with ambient light only if there is enough.

There is a side effect to using this mode with slow shutter speeds. Front-curtain sync causes the flash to fire as soon as the front shutter curtain is out of the way before the rear shutter curtain starts closing. If there is some ambient light, the shutter speed is long (like 1/2 second), and the subject is moving, you'll see a well-exposed subject with a blurry trail in front of it. The flash correctly exposes the subject as soon as the front curtain gets out of the way, but the ambient light continues exposing the subject before the rear curtain closes. Since the subject is moving, you may see a ghostlike blur before or in front of the well-exposed moving subject in the picture. This can be seen at shutter speeds as fast as 1/60s if the ambient light is strong enough and the subject is moving.

Red-Eye Reduction

Red-eye reduction is not really a flash mode, per se (figure 13.5). It simply means that the AF-assist illuminator on the front of the camera shines brightly in the face of your subject for one second before Front-curtain sync flash fires. The intention is that the bright AF-assist illuminator will cause your subject's pupils to close somewhat and reduce the red-eye effect. Otherwise it performs the same as Front-curtain sync.

Figure 13.5 – Red-eye reduction

Red-Eye Reduction with Slow Sync

Red-eye reduction with slow sync combines two modes, Red-eye reduction and Slow sync, so that you can take portraits at night while still recording some of the surroundings (figure 13.6). Slow sync flash allows the camera to leave its shutter open for a normal non-flash exposure time in low ambient light, thereby exposing the surroundings well, and just before the flash fires to light the subject, the AF-assist illuminator shines in your subject's face for one second to reduce pupil size.

Figure 13.6 – Red-eye reduction with slow sync

When you are shooting with a slow shutter speed in a dark environment, you should have your camera on a tripod to prevent blurry pictures. You should also ask your subject to stand perfectly still, or there is a chance of subject ghosting.

Slow Sync

Slow sync mode lets the camera use ambient light to make a good exposure and then fires the flash to add some extra light, rounding out the shadows or better exposing a foreground subject (figure 13.7). Use this mode in people shots outdoors or where you want ambient light to provide the primary exposure and the flash to add a sparkle to your subjects' eyes and remove dark shadows from their faces.

Figure 13.7 – Slow sync

This is closely related to Fill flash, except the ambient light is more important than the light from the flash. Be careful when using this mode indoors because it will expose for ambient light and only assist with some flash light. You can get some terrible ghosting and blurred handheld shots when using Slow sync indoors. Ambient light rules in this mode!

Rear-Curtain Sync

Rear-curtain sync (figure 13.8) is the opposite of Front-curtain sync. The flash waits to fire until just before the rear curtain starts to close. The entire shutter speed time is just ending when the flash fires. This causes a ghosting effect for moving subjects in higher ambient light with slow shutter speeds.

Figure 13.8 – Rear-curtain sync

When you press the Shutter-release button, the front curtain opens, ambient light starts hitting the sensor, and the sensor starts recording the subject. Just as the shutter's rear curtain is about to close, the flash fires, exposing the subject at its current position. The subject was fully exposed by the flash at the end of the shutter speed time, so the ambient light had time to register the subject before the flash fired. If the subject is moving, this can produce a blurred ghost behind or after the well-exposed subject.

Settings Recommendation: I use Front-curtain sync (Fill flash) for normal, everyday flash. It balances ambient light with flash light. I'll often switch to Spot metering mode when using Fill flash for extremely accurate exposures of a particular subject.

External Speedlight flash units offer modes like TTL BL, TTL BL FP, TTL FP, or just TTL. TTL stands for "through the lens" and represents an i-TTL mode (intelligent though the lens). BL stands for balanced. FP stands for Auto FP high-speed sync mode. Refer to the user's manual for your flash unit for exact details on how to switch between modes on the flash unit.

When I'm shooting outside (only) and want a great exposure of my subject's surroundings, along with the subject, I often use Slow sync mode. The only caveat is that you must be aware that slow shutter speeds will cause ghosting and blurring as the light falls.

I don't use the Red-eye reduction modes often because they seem to confuse people. They think the initial shine of the AF-assist illuminator is the flash firing and then look away just as the main flash fires. If you are going to use Red-eye reduction modes, you might want to tell your subject to wait for the main flash.

Rear-curtain sync creates a cool effect if you want to show a ghosted image stretching out behind your subject when you use slow shutter speeds. Rear-curtain sync is sometimes used by sports shooters in situations where there may be some blurring from fast movement in low light. It is much more acceptable to have a ghosted blur after the subject since it implies motion. Front-curtain sync makes the blur show up in front of the subject, which looks just plain weird.

I suggest experimenting with all of these modes. You'll want to use each of them at various times.

Flash Compensation

No metering system works well in all conditions. When you are having some mild subject overexposures due to shooting against a dark background, you may want to dial in -0.3 EV or more *Flash compensation*. The D800 makes adding or subtracting flash exposure very simple.

You can add up to one full stop of overexposure to your subject (1.0 EV) and up to three stops (3.0 EV) underexposure.

Figure 13.9 – Dialing in Flash compensation

Following are the steps to dial in Flash compensation with the Flash mode/compensation button and other camera controls (figure 13.9):

1. Press and hold down the Flash mode/compensation button (figure 13.9, image 1).
2. Turn the front Sub-command dial while examining the Control panel for changes in the flash compensation (figure 13.9, image 2 and screen 3). In figure 13.9, screen 3, I have + 1.0 EV compensation dialed in.
3. Release the Flash mode/compensation button and take your pictures. Be sure to set Flash compensation back to zero (0.0) when you are finished shooting.

Settings Recommendation: My particular Nikon D800 tends to shoot a bit hot (overly bright) when I am shooting a human subject against a dark background, so I often dial in -0.3 or -0.7 EV compensation, especially when shooting up close. It can be terribly hard to expose for a bride's white dress in a dark area, such as the romantic dance with the new husband. You will often have to use Flash compensation that varies with each shot. Learn to use this feature well, and your event images will be better for it.

Shooting flash with the subject over 10 feet away is not as critical for compensation with an external Speedlight. Most of my difficulties arise when up close. Your D800 may respond differently, so experiment before shooting a wedding or event.

Now let's look into the Nikon CLS, which allows your camera to control multiple flash units in a wireless array.

Nikon Creative Lighting System (CLS)

(User's Manual – Page 380)

CLS is an advanced wireless lighting technology that allows you to use your imagination in designing creative lighting arrangements. No wires are used because the CLS-compatible remote flash units are controlled by a commander device, or what Nikon refers to as a master flash unit. You can use the Commander mode built into the D800; an Accessory shoe–mounted commander, such as the SB-910, SB-900, SB-800, and SB-700 Speedlights; or the SU-800 Wireless Speedlight Commander unit. The SB-600 has only a remote mode, so it cannot be used as a commander unit.

We'll consider only the camera's built-in Commander mode in this chapter. I suggest buying a copy of *The Nikon Creative Lighting System, 2nd Edition*, by Mike Hagen (Rocky Nook and Nikonians Press, 2012). It goes into excellent detail on how to use CLS with multiple groups of external Nikon Speedlight flash units. I have read Hagan's book cover to cover and really enjoyed learning all about CLS. If you want to successfully control complex arrangements of Nikon Speedlights easily, you need this book. It's worth the price merely for the knowledge you gain on configuring your complex flash unit(s).

Using CLS, you can easily experiment with setups and flash output. You can obtain a visual preview of how things will look by pressing the Depth-of-field preview button, which will fire the pulsed modeling capability within Nikon Speedlights.

Figure 13.10 – The Nikon Creative Lighting System, 2nd Edition, by Mike Hagen, Rocky Nook and Nikonians Press

There is no need to calculate complex lighting ratios when you can control your flash banks right from the camera and see the results immediately. CLS simplifies the use of multiple flash-unit setups for portraiture, interiors, nature, or any situation in which several Speedlights need to work in unison.

You can simply position the flash units where you'd like them to be and let CLS automatically calculate the correct exposure, or you can change the lighting ratios directly from the *Custom Setting Menu > e3 Flash cntrl for built-in flash > Commander mode* menu of your D800.

Nikon's CLS is world class in power and not too difficult to use. The Nikon D800 contains everything you need to control a simple or complex CLS setup. Let's learn how to use it!

How Does the D800 Fit into the CLS Scheme?

In Commander mode, the camera functions as a controller for multiple Nikon Speedlight flash units. Although the professional-level Nikon D4/D3/D3S/D3X requires the separate purchase of an Accessory shoe–mounted commander device, the D800 body has full Nikon CLS technology built right in.

You can use normal i-TTL flash technology with the camera's built-in flash, or use Commander mode and the built-in flash to control up to two groups of an unlimited number of external Nikon Speedlight flash units. Nikon currently makes the powerful SB-910 flash unit, along with its slightly less powerful SB-700 brother, and other smaller Speedlight units such as the SB-400 and SB-R200. You can also still acquire older flash units such as the SB-900, SB-800, and SB-600. The small SB-400 is not CLS compatible, while the SB-R200 is designed especially for CLS.

Many people who use the D800 have an external flash unit or two—usually the SB-910, SB-900, SB-800, SB-700, or SB-600. The SB-R200 flash is designed to be used on various brackets available from Nikon and will work in conjunction with the bigger Speedlight flash units. The Nikon D800 is happy to let you arrange professional lighting setups using these relatively inexpensive and very portable Speedlights.

The cool thing about the D800 is that it can serve as a CLS flash commander device or use Nikon's other CLS flash commander devices at will. You have great control with this fine camera!

What Is Commander Mode and How Does It Work?

Commander mode is controlled through a menu on your D800. If you examine the Commander mode screen shown in figure 13.11, you'll note that you have controls for the built-in flash and two groups (A and B), or banks, of external flash units. You'll also see that you can set Exposure compensation for either of these groups (Comp.).

Figure 13.11 – Commander mode

If the main flash is too bright, you can either move it farther away or dial its power down by setting Exposure compensation (Comp.) to underexpose a little. You can set Comp. in 1/3-stop increments, so you have very fine control of each group's flash output. You can experiment until you get the image just the way you want it. Sure, you can do things the old way and use a flash meter, or get your calculator and figure out complex fill ratios. Or you can simply use CLS to vary your settings visually until the image is just right (figure 13.12).

Isn't it more fun to simply enter some initial settings into your Commander mode screen and then take a test shot? If it doesn't look right, change the settings and do it again. Within two or three tries you'll probably get it right, and you will have learned something about the performance of your CLS. In a short time, you'll have a feel for how to set the camera and flash units and will use your flash/camera combo with authority.

Figure 13.12 – J. Ramón Palacios (JRP) used a Commander device and two SB-800 Speedlights to take this CLS photo

Note: If you leave *Custom Setting Menu > e Bracketing/flash > e4 Modeling flash* set to On, you can test fire the built-in modeling light of your single Speedlight—or all Speedlights in Groups A and B—by pressing and holding the camera's Depth-of-field preview button.

Using Commander Mode

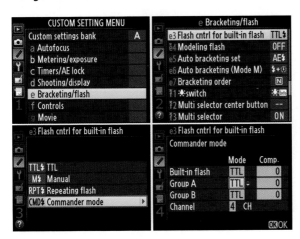

Figure 13.13 – Setting the camera to Commander mode

Let's start by putting your camera into Commander mode. We'll do that by changing *Custom Setting Menu > e Bracketing/flash > e3 Flash cntrl for built-in flash* to Commander mode (CMD). Look at figure 13.13 for the steps to set this option.

Since this section is about controlling multiple flash units, we'll have to change the settings in Commander mode, using the screen shown in figure 13.13, screen 4. We'll examine each of the settings available in Commander mode.

First, we'll consider TTL. It's the easiest to use because it allows you to set Exposure compensation for the built-in flash as well as each of your flash groups. Second, we'll briefly look at AA mode, which is an old-fashioned mode not often used by new photographers. Third, we'll look at M mode, because that gives you fine control of your flash from full power (1/1) to 1/128 power. Finally, we'll consider the – – (double-dash) mode, which prevents the camera's built-in flash from firing the main flash output but does not stop the necessary monitor preflashes or the firing of the external flash units. Double-dash mode turns off the main flash bursts for a group of Speedlights when it is selected; however, it does not turn off the monitor preflashes.

When your camera is controlling external Speedlights using its built-in Commander mode, you must raise the built-in flash on your D800. The camera communicates with the external flash units during the monitor preflash cycle.

Always position the small round sensor windows on the external Speedlights where they will pick up the monitor preflashes from the built-in flash. Take particular care when you are not using a tripod.

Commander Mode Settings

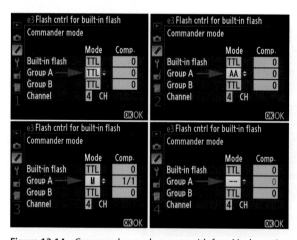

Figure 13.14 – Commander mode screen with four Mode settings

Basically, the Mode fields on the Commander mode screen will display the selections in the following list. Use the Multi selector to change the values, as shown in figure 13.14. Here are the four Commander mode settings:

- TTL, or i-TTL mode
- AA, or Auto Aperture mode
- M, or Manual mode
- – –, or double-dash mode (What else would one call it?)

You'll find each mode in the Mode box shown in yellow in figure 13.14. Use the Multi selector to scroll up or down and select a mode. AA mode is not available for the Built-in flash, so you will see AA only in the Mode boxes following Groups A and B. Now, let's examine each mode in more detail:

- **TTL mode** – The TTL setting allows you to use the full power of i-TTL technology. By leaving Mode set to TTL (as shown in figure 13.14, screen 1) for the Built-in flash, Group A, and Group B, you derive maximum flexibility and accuracy from all your flash units. In this mode, the Comp. setting will display exposure values from -3.0 EV to +3.0 EV, a full six-stop range of exposure compensation for each group of Speedlights. You can set the Comp. in 1/3 EV steps for very fine control.
- **AA mode** – The AA mode is an older non—i-TTL technology included for people who are accustomed to using it. It is not available for the built-in Speedlight on the D800 or for the SB-600. You can safely ignore the AA mode unless you want to experiment with it. It may not provide as accurate a flash exposure as TTL mode because it is not based on the amazing i-TTL technology. Otherwise, it works pretty much the same as TTL mode.
- **M mode** – This allows you to set different levels of flash output in 1/3 EV steps for the Built-in flash or the Speedlights in Group A or B. The settings you can put in the Comp. field are between 1/1 (full) and 1/128. The intermediate 1/3-stop settings are presented as decimals within the fractions. For example, 1/1.3 and 1/1.7 are 1/3 and 2/3 stops below 1/1 (full). Many people are used to working with flash units this way, so it seems more familiar to them. CLS is willing to oblige people who have experience with working manually.
- **- - mode (double-dash mode)** – The built-in Speedlight will not fire the main flash burst in this mode. It will fire the monitor preflashes because it uses them to determine exposure and communicate with the external flash groups. Be sure you always raise the camera's built-in flash in any of the Commander modes; otherwise, the external flash groups will not receive a signal and won't fire their flashes. When you set Mode for Group A or B to double-dash (– –) mode, that entire group of flashes will not fire any flash output. You can use this mode to temporarily turn off one of the flash groups for testing purposes.

> ## What Are Monitor Preflashes?
>
> When you press the Shutter-release button with the pop-up flash open, the camera's built-in Speedlight fires several brief preflashes and then fires the main flash burst. These preflashes fire whenever your camera is set to TTL mode, even if your D800 is controlling multiple flash units through CLS. The camera can determine a very accurate exposure by lighting your subject with a preflash, adjusting the exposure, and then firing the main flash burst.

Since the preflashes of the built-in flash always fire, be careful that they do not influence the lighting of your image. Use a smaller aperture, or move the camera farther away from your subject if the preflashes add unwanted light.

Setting the Channel (CH) for Communication

Look at figure 13.15, the camera's Commander mode screen, and you'll notice that just below Group B there is a Channel (CH) selection (red arrow). The number 1 that is selected in the yellow box is the communication channel my D800 will use to talk to the external flash groups (the factory default is 1).

Figure 13.15 – Commander mode channel selection

There are four channels available (1 through 4), just in case you happen to be working in the vicinity of another Nikon photographer who is also using Commander mode. By using separate channels, you won't interfere with each other.

Note: It is important to realize that all external flashes in all groups must be on the same channel. This involves setting up your individual flash units to respond on a particular channel. They might be in separate groups, but they must be on the same channel. Each external Speedlight flash will have its own method for selecting a group and channel.

Author's Conclusions

The Nikon D800 gives you control over the world-class Nikon Creative Lighting System. It is the envy of many other camera brand manufacturers and users.

I recommend that you buy a copy of Mike Hagen's book *The Nikon Creative Lighting System, 2nd Edition*, as an excellent way to increase your knowledge of the Nikon CLS. It goes into great detail on using Nikon cameras to control several of the major Nikon flash units. *Mastering the Nikon D800* covers CLS only in relation to the Nikon

D800 camera body. With these two books and some practice, you can become a Nikon CLS expert!

I also suggest that you find a good book on lighting techniques and study it well. You'll have to learn how to control shadows and reflections, plus you'll have to understand lighting ratios so you can recognize a good image when you see one.

Buy a couple of light stands and some cheap white flash umbrellas and set up some portrait sessions of your family, or even some product shots. With the Nikon D800 and just one extra Speedlight, you can create some very impressive images with much less work than ever before.

The really nice thing is that the Nikon CLS—executed by your camera's Commander mode and external Speedlight flashes—will allow you to shoot without worrying so much about detailed exposure issues. Instead, you can concentrate on creating a great-looking image.

Afterword

Check the book's downloadable resources section from time to time because I intend to keep on adding material to supplement *Mastering the Nikon D800*. The downloadable resources are found at these two web addresses:

http://www.nikonians.org/NikonD800
http://rockynook.com/NikonD800

Stay in touch with me by using the following points of contact:

- Website: **http://www.pictureandpen.com**
- Facebook: **http://www.facebook.com/DigitalDarrell**
- Twitter: **http://twitter.com/#!/DigitalDarrell**
- Google+: **http://bit.ly/IPK5Nc**

Thank You!

I'd like to express my personal appreciation to you for buying this book and for sticking with me all the way to the end of it. I sincerely hope that it has been useful to you and that you'll recommend my books to your Nikon-using friends.

Keep on capturing time . . .

Index

MIRROR UP (MUP) — 478

Credits for Chapter Opening Images

Chapters 1 and 13 – Daniel Diggelmann (*Aerobat*), *You Are Funny Dad!*, and *I See Mommy!*
Nikon D800 and AF-S Nikkor 85mm f/1.4 G lens, 1/800 sec at f/2.8, ISO 100
The portraits of my son and daughter were set up in our garden to illustrate the arrival of the long-awaited spring. The weather was slightly overcast, which produced a nice, diffuse light. The matrix metering of the D800 did a great job with the backlit situation. No compensation was dialed in.

Chapter 2 – Nigel Danson (*ndanson1*), *Delighted Emily*
Nikon D800 and AF-S Nikkor 70-200mm F2.8G IF-ED VR lens at 105mm, 1/320 sec at f/9, ISO 50
A studio shot of my daughter, Emily. It was a couple of days after the D800 was launched, and I involved most of my family in photos! It was taken with Bowen studio lights and a black backdrop.

Chapter 3 – David Jolley (*DAJolley*), *Sunrise on Clingman's Dome*
Nikon D800 and AF-S Nikkor 24-70mm f/2.8 AF-S G ED lens at 70mm, 1/2 sec at F/8, ISO 100
This image was taken at sunrise from the top of Clingman's Dome in Great Smoky Mountains National Park on my first outing with my new D800. The camera was mounted on a Gitzo tripod, and the image was taken using MLU with an MC-30 cable release.

Chapter 4 – Jaques Scheepers (*mrpenguin*), *Mohawk Bad Boy*
Nikon D800 and AF-S Nikkor 70-200mm f/2.8 VR lens at 200mm, 1/250 sec at f2.8, ISO 100
This photo of my son was taken in my office. I closed all the curtains and used a black backdrop with one off-camera flash in a soft box on his left-hand side and a reflector on his right-hand side. The camera was hand held from about 20 feet away.

Chapter 5 – Johnny Yun (yunjo), *Seattle Space Needle and Skyline*
Nikon D800E and AF-S Nikkor 70-200mm f/2.8G ED VR II lens at 195mm, 1.6 sec at f/4, ISO 100
This image was taken from Kerry Park in Seattle just around sunset. I was able to capture the Seattle Skyline with the glow of the Space Needle. The top of the Space Needle was painted the orange color for its 50th birthday earlier this year. This was the 21st picture out of my D800E as I had just received it the previous day.

Chapter 6 – David Hays (*Haysys*), *Two Leopards Descending*
Nikon D800 and AF-S Nikkor 200-400mm f/4 VR-I lens at 400mm, 1/200 sec at f/5, ISO 400
The image is an 18 percent crop of a capture taken from atop a safari vehicle, with the camera and lens resting on a beanbag. The male and female leopards were descending an acacia tree about 100 meters from the vehicle in Tarangire National Park, Tanzania. April, 2012.

Chapter 7 – Dennis H. Miller (*dhmiller*), *Red Bird Snacking*
Nikon D800E and Nikkor 600mm f/4 lens, 1/160 sec at f/5.6, ISO 400
I caught this little guy, a male Northern Cardinal "red bird" (*Cardinalis cardinalis*), with my 600mm as he was having a nice snack on a branch in my backyard.

Chapter 8 – Alexandre Rosen (*klrbee25*), *A Long Way Up*
Nikon D800 and Nikkor 24-70mm f/2.8G ED AF-S lens at 24mm, 1/25 sec at f/4, ISO 2000, EV –1.33
After stepping off the longest escalator I've ever experienced, I crouched down and waited for another person to include a sense of scale. The lighting was poor and harsh, so I underexposed to preserve more wall texture around the lights, knowing that the D800 captures an incredible amount of shadow detail. Shadows were lifted in Aperture and black-and-white processing performed in Silver Efex Pro 2.

Chapter 9 – Eric Bowles (*ericbowles*), *Rescue Me!*
Nikon D800E and AF-S Nikkor 70-200mm f/2.8G ED-IF VR lens at 116mm, 1/1600 sec at f/3.5, ISO 200
This puppy was photographed at a local pet rescue. A good photo goes a long way in finding a permanent home for rescued pets. With dog photography, it helps to be near the eye level of the animal with a clean, attractive background. A few colorful props or toys add interest, and in this case the pink plastic bucket helped slow down the active puppy. I try to photograph dogs using a 70-200mm lens with camera settings for a shallow depth of field and a fast shutter speed.

Chapter 10 – Christian Coombes (*Chiefmasterjedi*), *Seagull in Flight*
Nikon D800 and AF-S Nikkor 24-120mm f/4 VR lens at 58mm, 1/400 sec at f/5.6, ISO 100
This image was captured in my hometown of Burnham-on-sea while I was on vacation, visiting my family in England. I had always viewed the seagulls as pests; however, the D800 shows their true beauty and grace. I used 21-point AF-C autofocus to track the bird in flight, and center-weighted metering.

Chapter 11 – Joan Hammond (*Silversmith*), *Smiling Giraffe*
Nikon D800 and AF-S Nikkor 500mm f/4G ED VR lens, 1/800 sec at f/6.3, ISO 640
I captured this giraffe as he was grazing near the road in Arusha National Park, Tanzania. I stabilized my camera with a bean bag on the edge of an open-topped safari vehicle.

Chapter 12 – Darrell Young (*DigitalDarrell*), *Bride and Groom*
Nikon D800 and AF-S Nikkor 24-120mm f/3.5–5.6G ED VR lens at 120mm, 1/160 sec at f/5.6, ISO 400
I took this picture after the reception of the first wedding I shot with my new D800. The sun had already set, and we decided to use up what was left of the card space by shooting a few final shots. We walked over to a field next to the reception hall for some fill-flash shots with my Nikon SB-900 in TTL BL mode. The camera and flash performed flawlessly. Even the old second-generation Nikkor 24-120 lens surprised me by performing well on the D800. This is truly one amazing and versatile camera!

Chapter 13 – See first credit on page 558.